Political Economy and Religion

Ever since Antiquity, reflections about economic problems have always been intertwined with questions relating to politics, ethics and religion. From the 18th century onwards, economic thought seemed to have been gradually disentangled from any other field, and to have gained the status of an autonomous scientific discipline, especially with the later use of mathematics. In fact, the growth of economic knowledge never broke off any ties with these other fields, and, especially with religion and ethics, even though the links with them became less obvious, they only changed shape. This is what this book illustrates, each chapter dealing with different periods and authors from the Middle Ages to the present times. Focusing in turn on the thought of the Scholastics, Ibn Rushd (Averroes), John Calvin, the French liberal Jansenists, Dugald Stewart, David Ricardo, Henri de Saint-Simon, Charles de Coux and French Christian Political Economy, Auguste Comte and Émile Durkheim, Henry Sidgwick, Arthur Cecil Pigou and finally John Maynard Keynes, the studies collected here show how religious themes played an important role in the development of economic thought.

This book was originally published as a special issue of *The European Journal of the History of Economic Thought.*

Gilbert Faccarello is Emeritus Professor at Panthéon-Assas University, Paris, France. He is a co-founder of *The European Journal of the History of Economic Thought*, and acted as a Chairman of the Council of the European Society for the History of Economic Thought. His publications include books and articles in HET. Recently, he also edited *The Reception of David Ricardo in Continental Europe and Japan* (Routledge, 2014, with Masashi Izumo), and *Handbook on the History of Economic Analysis* (Edward Elgar, 2016, 3 volumes, with Heinz D. Kurz). He is also, with H.D. Kurz, the co-editor of the Routledge Historical Resources site devoted to the History of Economic Thought.

Political Economy and Religion

Essays in the History of Economic Thought

Edited by
Gilbert Faccarello

Routledge
Taylor & Francis Group
LONDON AND NEW YORK

First published 2019
by Routledge
2 Park Square, Milton Park, Abingdon, Oxon, OX14 4RN, UK

and by Routledge
52 Vanderbilt Avenue, New York, NY 10017, USA

First issued in paperback 2020

Routledge is an imprint of the Taylor & Francis Group, an informa business

British Library Cataloguing in Publication Data
A catalogue record for this book is available from the British Library

ISBN 13: 978-0-367-58590-7 (pbk)
ISBN 13: 978-1-138-33205-8 (hbk)

Typeset in New Baskerville
by RefineCatch Limited, Bungay, Suffolk

Publisher's Note
The publisher accepts responsibility for any inconsistencies that may have arisen during the conversion of this book from journal articles to book chapters, namely the possible inclusion of journal terminology.

Contents

Citation Information vii
Notes on Contributors xi

Introduction – Sæculum 1
Gilbert Faccarello

1. Agency, exchange, and power in scholastic thought 16
Richard Sturn

2. The concept of "lawfulness" in economic matters. Reading Ibn Rushd (Averroes) 46
Ragip Ege

3. The necessity to work, according to John Calvin's duty of stewardship 65
Caroline Bauer

4. Liberal Jansenists and interest-bearing loans in eighteenth-century France: a reappraisal 84
Arnaud Orain and Maxime Menuet

5. Defending free trade after physiocracy: On Dugald Stewart's architectonic of passions, reason and Providence 118
Thomas Ruellou

6. Theological themes in Ricardo's papers and correspondence 160
Sergio Cremaschi

7. Religion and political economy in Saint-Simon 185
Pierre Musso

8. A dance teacher for paralysed people? Charles de Coux and the dream of a Christian political economy 204
Gilbert Faccarello

9. Religion and the sociological critique of political economy: Altruism and gift 252
Philippe Steiner

10. Henry Sidgwick, moral order, and utilitarianism 283
Keith Tribe

11. Pigou on philosophy and religion 307
Daniela Donnini Macciò

12. Keynes and Christian socialism: Religion and the economic problem 334
David Andrews

Index 355

Citation Information

The chapters in this book were originally published in *The European Journal of the History of Economic Thought*, volume 24, issue 4 (August 2017). When citing this material, please use the original page numbering for each article, as follows:

Introduction
Sæculum
Gilbert Faccarello
The European Journal of the History of Economic Thought, volume 24, issue 4 (August 2017), pp. 625–639

Chapter 1
Agency, exchange, and power in scholastic thought
Richard Sturn
The European Journal of the History of Economic Thought, volume 24, issue 4 (August 2017), pp. 640–669

Chapter 2
The concept of "lawfulness" in economic matters. Reading Ibn Rushd (Averroes)
Ragip Ege
The European Journal of the History of Economic Thought, volume 24, issue 4 (August 2017), pp. 670–688

Chapter 3
The necessity to work, according to John Calvin's duty of stewardship
Caroline Bauer
The European Journal of the History of Economic Thought, volume 24, issue 4 (August 2017), pp. 689–707

Chapter 4

Liberal Jansenists and interest-bearing loans in eighteenth-century France: a reappraisal
Arnaud Orain and Maxime Menuet
The European Journal of the History of Economic Thought, volume 24, issue 4 (August 2017), pp. 708–741

Chapter 5

Defending free trade after physiocracy: On Dugald Stewart's architectonic of passions, reason and Providence
Thomas Ruellou
The European Journal of the History of Economic Thought, volume 24, issue 4 (August 2017), pp. 742–783

Chapter 6

Theological themes in Ricardo's papers and correspondence
Sergio Cremaschi
The European Journal of the History of Economic Thought, volume 24, issue 4 (August 2017), pp. 784–808

Chapter 7

Religion and political economy in Saint-Simon
Pierre Musso
The European Journal of the History of Economic Thought, volume 24, issue 4 (August 2017), pp. 809–827

Chapter 8

A dance teacher for paralysed people? Charles de Coux and the dream of a Christian political economy
Gilbert Faccarello
The European Journal of the History of Economic Thought, volume 24, issue 4 (August 2017), pp. 828–875

Chapter 9

Religion and the sociological critique of political economy: Altruism and gift
Philippe Steiner
The European Journal of the History of Economic Thought, volume 24, issue 4 (August 2017), pp. 876–906

Chapter 10

Henry Sidgwick, moral order, and utilitarianism
Keith Tribe
The European Journal of the History of Economic Thought, volume 24, issue 4 (August 2017), pp. 907–930

Chapter 11

Pigou on philosophy and religion
Daniela Donnini Macciò
The European Journal of the History of Economic Thought, volume 24, issue 4 (August 2017), pp. 931–957

Chapter 12

Keynes and Christian socialism: Religion and the economic problem
David Andrews
The European Journal of the History of Economic Thought, volume 24, issue 4 (August 2017), pp. 958–977

Notes on Contributors

David Andrews is Professor and Chair of the Economics Department at the State University of New York at Oswego, USA. He serves as an Associate Editor at *History of Economic Issues.* His research has been focused on the writings of J.M. Keynes, Piero Sraffa, Adam Smith, and classical political economy. His publications include *Keynes and the British Humanist Tradition: the moral purpose of the market* (Routledge 2010) and papers in the *Cambridge Journal of Economics, Economic Thought, History of Political Economy,* and *The European Journal of the History of Economic Thought.*

Caroline Bauer is lecturer at Université Catholique de Lyon, France. She obtained a PhD in economics at the University of Strasbourg, France, and in Protestant theology at the University of Geneva, Switzerland. Her research interests include Christian ethics and theological justifications of economics.

Sergio Cremaschi is a former Professor of Moral Philosophy at Amedeo Avogadro University, Vercelli, Italy. His research focuses on ethics, religion, and the history of political economy. His recent publications include *Utilitarianism and Malthus's Virtue Ethics. Respectable, Virtuous and Happy* (Routledge, 2014), 2015 Best Book Award of the European Society of the History of Economic Thought, and *Tradizioni morali. Greci, ebrei, cristiani, islamici* (Storia e Letteratura, 2015).

Daniela Donnini Macciò, PhD (1991; 2013) is an independent researcher in the history of economic thought and a high school teacher. She is based in Italy. Her research interests include the relationships between Cambridge economics and ethical philosophy. Her essays have appeared in *The European Journal of the History of Economic Thought, European Journal of International Relations, History of European Ideas,* and *Cambridge Journal of Economics.*

Ragip Ege is Emeritus Professor of Economics at the University of Strasbourg, France, and a member of the Bureau d'Économie Théorique et Appliquée (BETA). His recent research activities focus on the history of economic thought (especially on 18th- and 19th-century authors) and the relations between economics and ethics. He is particularly interested in Hegelian economic and political philosophy.

Gilbert Faccarello is Emeritus Professor at Panthéon-Assas University, Paris, France. He is a co-founder of *The European Journal of the History of Economic Thought*, and acted as a Chairman of the Council of the European Society for the History of Economic Thought. His publications include books and articles in HET. Recently, he also edited *The Reception of David Ricardo in Continental Europe and Japan* (Routledge, 2014, with Masashi Izumo), and *Handbook on the History of Economic Analysis* (Edward Elgar, 2016, 3 volumes, with Heinz D. Kurz). He is also, with H.D. Kurz, the co-editor of the Routledge Historical Resources site devoted to the History of Economic Thought.

Maxime Menuet is a postdoctoral research fellow, Aix-Marseille School of Economics, France. His areas of research include macroeconomic theory, political economy, and history of economic thought during the Enlightenment.

Pierre Musso, philosopher, is Emeritus Professor of Information Science and Communication at the University of Rennes 2 and at Telecom Paris Tech School, France. He is presently associated fellow of the IAS-Nantes. His research partly focuses on Henri Saint-Simon and Saint-Simonianism. His recent publications include *La religion du monde industriel. Analyse de la pensée de Saint-Simon* (L'Aube, 2006), *Saint-Simon, l'industrialisme contre l'Etat* (L'Aube, 2010), and *La religion industrielle. Monastère, Manufacture, Usine. Une généalogie de l'entreprise* (Fayard, 2017). He is also a co-editor of the *Œuvres complètes* of Saint-Simon (Presses Universitaires de France, 2013).

Arnaud Orain is Professor of Economics at the University of Paris 8, France, and was David Fellow of the History Department of Princeton University in 2015–2016. His research focuses on the history of economic thought during the French Enlightenment, with a particular emphasis on anti-Physiocracy, and the links between religion, literature and economics. His recent publications include *La politique du merveilleux. Une autre histoire du Système de Law (1695–1795)*, Paris: Fayard, 2018.

Thomas Ruellou is an independent scholar in economics. He has defended his PhD in Economics, *De la théorie des prix à la science du législateur: le moment Adam Smith*, at the Université Paris 1 Panthéon–Sorbonne, France, in 2017. His research in the history of economic thought focuses on classical political economy and aims at questioning the place of Adam Smith therein, regarding the theory of value as well as the political philosophy backdrop.

Philippe Steiner trained both in economics and sociology, is Professor of Sociology at Sorbonne University (Paris, France) and former fellow of the Institut Universitaire de France. He published extensively in the history of economic thought and in sociology. His recent research is devoted to 'economic sociology' and the history of social sciences. His recent publications include *Durkheim and the Birth of Economic Sociology* (Princeton University Press, 2011), *Donner... Une histoire de l'altruisme* (Paris, Presses Universitaires de France, 2016, 2017 Best Book Award of the European Society of the History of Economic Thought), and *Calculation and Morality in the Abolition of Slavery in France* (with C. Oudin-Bastide, Oxford University Press, 2019).

Richard Sturn is professor at the University of Graz, Austria, and Director of the Institute of Public Economics and of the Graz Schumpeter Centre. He is also a co-editor of *The European Journal of the History of Economic Thought* and of the *Jahrbuch für normative Grundfragen der Ökonomik*, and Chairman of the Standing Committee on Ethics and Economics of the German Economic Association (Verein für Socialpolitik). He published widely on topics such as the Scottish Enlightenment, the political economy of the public sector and social policy, Schumpeterian economics and institutional change, and normative political economy.

Keith Tribe is an independent scholar and translator. Recent publications include (edited with Pat Hudson) *The Contradictions of Capital in the Twenty-First Century* (2016); (edited with Marten Seppel) *Cameralism in Practice* (2017); (with Roger E. Backhouse) *The History of Economics* (2017). Recent translations include Friedrich Schiller, *On the Aesthetic Education of Man* (2016) and Max Weber, *Economy and Society: A New Translation* (2019).

Sæculum

Gilbert Faccarello

> The war against religious beliefs, in the last century was carried on principally on the ground of common sense or of logic; in the present age, on the ground of science ... Religions tend to be discussed ... less as intrinsically true or false than as products thrown up by certain states of civilization, and which, like the animal and vegetable productions of a geological period perish in those which succeed it from the cessation of the conditions necessary to their continued existence. (Mill [1874] 1969, pp. 429–30)

The development of political economy has long been depicted as the progressive emergence of a new science which, during the Enlightenment, and especially with Quesnay, Turgot and Smith, broke loose from religion, morals, and politics — all fields in which its roots and first blossoms had until then been embedded. Reaching a state of autonomy as a new discipline, the story goes, it was able to develop quickly during the nineteenth century and acquire an indisputable status of rigour and scientificity, increasingly supported by the use of mathematics. A celebrated restatement of this old thesis was made some decades ago by Louis Dumont in his *Homo Æqualis* (Dumont 1977), and the idea still survives today as an obvious fact in the mind of most economists. But is this story so simple and straightforward? There is obviously room for doubt. From its inception, the connections that economic thought has established with religion, morals, and politics are complex, changeable, and often contentious. Despite affirmations of the rigour and independence of its scientific approach, the development of economic concepts and theories was – and still is – often dependent on these connections and conflicts, and sometimes in a rather surprising way. During the last few decades, many studies in the history of economic thought eloquently illustrated this point. The research programme directed to "The conflict-ridden development of modernity: theology and political economy"[1] sought to go further and contribute to this reappraisal, focusing on the links between political economy and religion from a historical perspective.

Secularisation

This field of research is related to the old and still lively debate over "secularisation",[2] which raises important questions. These questions permit a better understanding of what is here at stake. The chief problem is to state the characteristics presented by modern Western societies with respect to their previous historical situation – in which religion pervaded individual, social and political life, including the organisation of knowledge – and to explain the transition. The main features defining modernity are the following: (a) a marked differentiation, within societies, between secular and religious spheres of action: religion has lost its power over secular activities and is now only one limited sphere among others; (b) with this withdrawal from its former eminent place in the public sphere, hitherto dominant religious belief becomes a matter of private individual choice and, no longer able to impose its rules, must face the competition of other forms of belief and non-belief: a situation susceptible to induce changes in religion itself; (c) within the secular sphere of society, collective action is supposed to be rational, independent of religious considerations: a process of "scientification" occurs, in which "science",[3] the new Weltanschauung, replaces religion and provides new and rational ways of organising society. There are of course many complementary ways

1 This programme is part of a wider project entitled "Constitution de la modernité: raison, politique, religion" — The constitution of modernity: reason, politics, religion — launched a few years ago by the LabEx COMOD (University of Lyon, France). A series of workshops on the theme of "Political economy and religion" have been organised since 2013, of which this special issue of EJHET is the outcome.

2 The literature is vast and reaches back over two centuries, even if the term "secularisation" is quite recent. It includes most of the great names in sociology — Auguste Comte, Ferdinand Tönnies, Herbert Spencer, Ernst Troeltsch, Max Weber, to mention only a few — and also philosophy: from G.F.W. Hegel to Carl Schmitt, Karl Löwith, Hans Blumenberg and Charles Taylor. For an initial survey of the use of the term, see Marramao (1994), and also Hunter (2015). For a detailed history of the sociological paradigm of secularisation, see Tschannen (1992) and, for the philosophical debates, Monod ([2002] 2012).

3 Among scientists, and also in books for a wider public, and in the press, the word "science" replaces "the sciences" during the nineteenth century. The idea became widespread that "science" provides an answer to everything.

of explaining the passage to modernity: it can simply be noted that the process of secularisation can originate in theology itself – for example with the sharp Augustinian distinction between the Earthly City and the City of God advanced by many authors, or the role of the Gnosis or of Nominalism and its theology of "potentia absoluta", both stressed by Blumenberg.[4] The questions raised are obviously not specific to the social sciences or political economy, but also of great relevance to the history of science. Discussion over the so-called "Merton thesis", for example, is well known (Merton [1938] 1970; Cohen ed. 1990), as are the recent writings of Peter Harrison, especially on the role of the Augustinian doctrine of Original Sin in the scientific revolution (1998, 2007, 2015).[5]

The place of religion in modern western societies is thus redefined and marginalised. But this does not mean that religion is doomed to a relentless decline. More modernity does not mean less religion. The old view, reflected by John Stuart Mill in the epigraph to this introduction, predicting that rationality and science necessarily lead to the retreat, or even the demise, of religion is now widely recognised as over-simplistic and contradicted by the facts – there are simply new conditions of beliefs and faith in a secular age, and this aspect of the secularisation process lies precisely at the core of Charles Taylor's reflection (Taylor 2007). Moreover, some basic religious attitudes can also be found transplanted into secular fields, into politics for instance (see for example Voegelin ([1938] 2000) or Gentile ([2001] 2007) and their analyses of "political religions"). Finally, and this is an important aspect of the secularisation approach, many symbols, values, or concepts that originated in religious thought tend to play a role in the secular sphere, either with new secularised names, or as an incentive for the production of new concepts.

Hence, a fundamental question: if religion itself played a role in the process of secularisation, are the main concepts of modernity no more than

4 "Secularisation" must not be confused with Weber's use of "disenchantement" ("Entzauberung") — he very seldom uses the term "Säkularisation". According to Weber, the process of disenchantment started very early in Judaism, and reached a climax with the Reformation. A better translation of the word "Entzauberung" would be "demagification".

5 See also Harrison (2010). A striking example of religious motivation in scientific research is that of Louis Pasteur, one of the foremost scientists in the nineteenth century. One of the stakes of his research against the theory of the "spontaneous generation" is the fight between materialism and spiritualism. "What a victory ... for materialism if it could rely on the proved fact of a self-organising matter, coming to life by itself ... What good having recourse to the idea of a primordial creation ...? Why then the idea of a Creator God?" (Pasteur 1864, p. 259).

theological notions with new names; or are they radically different in nature, in spite of their possible theological origin? The first option is, for example, that of Carl Schmitt who claimed in his first *Political Theology* that "All significant concepts of the modern theory of the state are secularised theological concepts" – sovereign and sovereignty for example, the "omnipotent god" becoming the omnipotent legislator – "not only because of their historical development ... but also because of their systematic structure" (Schmitt [1922] 1985, p. 36). Karl Löwith's approach is similar when analysing philosophies of history and the idea of progress as secularised forms of the Christian theology of history — Marx's approach, in this perspective, being only Messianism in the language of political economy: the proletariat is the new Chosen People and *The Communist Manifesto* is "eschatological in its framework, and prophetic in its attitude" (Löwith 1949, p. 36; see also pp. 44–5)

The second option is best exemplified in terms of Hans Blumenberg's *Die Legitimität der Neuzeit* (Blumenberg [1966] 1988). Schmitt's extreme statement – ironically called by Blumenberg "the secularisation theorem", meaning that "Y is nothing else than a secularised X" – is subjected to heavy criticism because it conveys the idea that history is only the deployment of a single "substance", and that the modern age is "illegitimate": if, in this age, institutions and leading concepts are still substantively theological despite their new appellation, this means that religion is still active in a concealed way and the novelty of modernity can be questioned. Blumenberg argues that the possibly theological origin of ideas and concepts is only part of the story – moreover, many Christian concepts have themselves been adopted from other systems of belief or civilisations. There is no inherent content that is necessarily transmitted from one age to another: functions change with contexts, and the new meanings of concepts and terminology are irreducible to and discontinuous with previous meanings. We might note that Marx, in his critique of Hegel's philosophy and also in his mature writings, already and repeatedly warned his readers not to make the mistake of believing in the persistence of hypothetical "natures" of things because of the existence of superficial similarities: what is important is not what they apparently share in common, but the "differentia specifica" they present. "The materials and means of labour ... play their part in every labour process in every age ... If, therefore, I label them 'capital' ... then I have *proved* that the existence of capital is an eternal law of nature of human production ... I could prove with equal facility that the Greeks and Romans celebrated Communion because they drank wine and ate bread, or that the Turks sprinkle themselves daily with holy water like Catholics because they wash themselves daily" (Marx [1863–66] 1976, p. 999, italics in the original).

Political economy and religion

How does this perspective bear upon the history of political economy, and, in particular, what do the essays included here offer? According to the above-mentioned criteria, (liberal) political economy is certainly considered to be a kind of flagship for modernity. Is not William Petty's celebrated statement, in the preface of his *Political Arithmetick*, that he sought to express himself solely in terms of "number, weight and measure",[6] usually seen as one of the very first symbols of the "scientific" foundation of economic thought? Similarly, William Culpeper wrote in his *Tract against the high rate of usury* that the problem of the legitimacy of lending at interest was something to be left to theologians, and that the only question he wanted to address was the magnitude of the rate of interest and its principal consequences for the economy.[7]

Thus, having no apparent or relevant reference to religion, political economy subsequently developed its own doctrines on the basis of the rational behaviour of agents in a competitive environment. Its role is twofold, positive and normative: it claims to explain the condition of societies, their levels of wealth and prosperity, the origin of dysfunctionality and crises; but it also imposes on agents a strict model of behaviour, a new personal and public form of "life conduct" (to borrow Weber's concept of "Lebensführung"). In this context, the anonymous working of economic forces in markets supposedly leads to an equilibrium and realises a kind of secular justice. It is in itself a new political philosophy (Faccarello and Steiner 2008a), and it can sometimes also generate a religious attitude: worshippers of a free market ideology exist everywhere – it can be a variety of "political religions", just like its opposite, the blind faith in the communist idea.[8] However, setting to one side these aspects, more interesting observations can be made if we turn to the core of economic theories. Let us take some examples.

---

6 Petty's phrase comes from the Bible (Wisdom of Solomon (Apocrypha) XI, 20), but at that time it was used by scientists to characterise the new scientific ethos.

7 This does not prevent Culpeper writing that a high rate of interest, which harms the economy, is a sin.

8 Keynes analysed Leninism in terms of a new religion. "Leninism is a combination of two things which Europeans have kept for some centuries in different compartments of the soul — religion and business. We are shocked because the religion is new, and contemptuous because the business, being subordinated to the religion instead the other way round, is highly inefficient" (Keynes 1925, p. 256). "But to say that Leninism is the faith of a persecuting and propagating minority of fanatics led by hypocrites is, after all, to say no more no less than that it *is* a religion and not merely a party, and Lenin a Mahomet, not a Bismarck" (1925, p. 257, italics in the original).

A first observation is that, as in other fields of knowledge, some religious beliefs played a decisive part in the development of basic economic doctrines. The very emergence of liberal political economy with Pierre de Boisguilbert stemmed directly from the Jansenist controversies of seventeenth-century France, involving questions of religious, moral, and political philosophy (Faccarello [1986] 1999). On the one hand, the strong Augustinian theological hypothesis of the Fall of Man, of Original Sin, was supposed to explain the systematically selfish and maximising behaviour of agents in every aspect of life. But, on the other hand, despite the war of all against all that was likely to result, Providence was supposed to provide for general equilibrium in markets — and Boisguilbert gave a name to this Providence: it was free competition, the coercive force that constrains people to be reasonable and generates a system of relative prices that could satisfy each agent. A further step was later taken by Turgot when, to explain the selfish and maximising attitude of agents, he no longer referred to Original Sin but instead to sensationist philosophy. The process of secularisation was completed at this point. The theological foundation was removed and replaced with a more neutral explanation. But the edifice remained intact, and could be developed on this new basis.

Other examples of the creations of new concepts, on similar bases, can be given. In nineteenth century, for example, Hermann Heinrich Gossen proposed what are now known as Gossen's laws in consumer theory, with the conviction that in this way people realise the plan that God designed for the benefit of all (Steiner 2011). "Mankind, once you have recognised completely and entirely the beauty of this plan of the Creation, steep yourself in adoration of the Being, which in its incomprehensible wisdom … has been able, by means apparently so insignificant, to bring about on your behalf something so enormously and incalculably beneficial" (Gossen [1854] 1995, p. 299). In the same way, it was also an explicit theological motivation and reference to Pope Leo XIII's 1891 encyclical *Rerum Novarum* that in the early twentieth century drove the Jesuit and mathematician Maurice Potron to develop a linear system of production and to identify, *inter alia*, long before later controversies, the conditions of existence of an equilibrium system of production prices (Bidard et al. 2009). Finally, a recently-published youthful work by John Rawls, *A Brief Inquiry into the Meaning of Sin and Faith* (Rawls 2009), shows how his former religious convictions were later translated into his mature developments, especially concerning the theory of justice (Cohen and Nagel 2009) – we have here another clear example of the secularisation of ideas and concepts.

But prior to the emergence of political economy proper, religious thought also paved the way, directly or indirectly, for the specification of some central economic concepts or ways or reasoning. Recent research by historians brought to light the discursive affinities between Medieval moral theology and the language of merchants, between the ethics of charity and the logic of commercial exchanges, or the role of a religious order like the Franciscans in the justification and development of economic activities and the idea of a virtuous circle of wealth (Todeschini 2002, 2004). Other research, by political philosophers, stressed that the word "interest", for example, in its modern sense of self-interest, while admittedly appearing in political writings in sixteenth-century Italy and seventeenth-century France, with Francesco Guicciardini and Henri de Rohan, also originate in sixteenth-century Spain in the writings of the Spanish mystics Teresa of Avila and John of the Cross (Taranto 1992, chap. 6).

There is an immense literature on Scholastic controversy over usury, money, and the just price. But we are rightly and repeatedly reminded to be cautious in the interpretation of writings that were embedded in pre-secularised societies governed by religion and its related ethics and morals. Even if the problems addressed by the schoolmen could seem familiar to modern readers, retrospective illusory interpretations must be avoided if we are to understand properly the meaning of the texts: here also the "differentia specifica" is fundamental. This is not to say that, much later, some writers could not draw inspiration from Scholastic discussion, nor that concepts and problems dealt with in these debates could not reappear in economic thought in new guises and with changed meanings: but all this must be carefully distinguished. From this perspective, and confronted with a multitude of interpretations of the schoolmen's opinions on the just price, Richard Sturn, in "Agency, exchange and power in Scholastic thought", carefully classifies these different interpretations using two criteria: agency, which brings into the picture the role of knowledge, information and ethics, and indeterminacy: when several solutions exist in exchange, morals and fairness come to the fore. Despite the modern vocabulary, this approach allows a critical evaluation of the interpretations along more accurate historical lines.

The same cautious perspective is of course appropriate for the problem of the legitimacy of usury. Long debated among Christian schoolmen, it was also addressed in Muslim thought. Ragip Ege, in his paper on "The concept of 'lawfulness' in economic matters" carefully presents Ibn Rushd's arguments on this topic,[9] and shows the structural similarities in the mode of reasoning of Christians and Muslims – the question of usury was a problem of "lawfulness" and justice. As centuries went by, of course, the perspective changed progressively and, in the eighteenth century, in a

9 Ibn Rushd, that is, Averroes, a prominent figure of the so-called Medieval Enlightenment and a major champion of the "freedom to philosophise".

more secularised society where market activities were beginning to be recognised as a basic structural element in the social and political order, there was finally a convergence between the analyses of members of the clergy and economists – and here we once more discover the presence of Jansenism. Maxime Menuet and Arnaud Orain's paper on "Liberal Jansenism and interest-bearing loans in eighteenth-century France" shows how the debate on the prohibition of usury could evolve during the French Enlightenment, thanks in particular to the liberal strand of Jansenism,[10] and lead, against traditional Catholic thought, to the recognition of the legitimacy of interest-bearing loans – thus opening the way to the first economic theory of the rate of interest presented by Turgot at the end of the 1760s.

Finally, any inquiry into the relation between religion and the economy cannot avoid the fundamental theme of the Reformation, which played an important role in the demagification and secularisation processes, and on which so much has been written since the celebrated publications of Ernst Troeltsch and Max Weber – and even before: the contrast between Protestant and Catholic nations had long been a theme in French political and social thought. But there have been some misunderstandings, especially regarding Jean Calvin's views. Weber in particular emphasised that he was studying Protestant, mainly Calvinist, sects, and not the writings of Calvin himself, even if he sometimes alluded to them. Caroline Bauer, in her study of "The necessity to work, according to Jean Calvin's duty of stewardship", questions the commonly accepted interpretations of Calvin and shows that his conception of the economy, based on the "duty of stewardship" for all human beings, and the subsequent necessity of work, is more positive and optimistic than the later view of Calvinists who laid emphasis upon an earthly engagement in economic activities as an anxious or desperate quest for a sign of salvation.

From the end of the eighteenth century onwards, when the legitimacy of political economy became largely undisputed, religious themes appeared to fade from economic thought. But this might be an illusion, as more recent research has shown. There are now several works that draw attention to the role of religion, morality, and ethics in Adam Smith (see, *inter alia,* Griswold 1999, Hill 2001, Oslington 2011, or, for a critical view, Cremaschi 2017), Malthus (Winch 1996, Cremaschi 2014), John Stuart Mill (Lipkes 1999), or in nineteenth-century political economy in general (Hilton 1988, Waterman 1991).[11] In the present issue, the opinions of

10 See also Orain (2014) for a broad description of the context.

11 For a broader coverage, see Waterman (1987, 2004) and Bateman and Banzhaf (2008).

Dugald Stewart and David Ricardo are more specifically addressed: they are two examples of the changing place of religious concerns in the works of economists at the turn of the nineteenth century. Thomas Ruellou, in "Defending free trade after Physiocracy" deals with Stewart's "architectonic of passions, reason and Providence" and shows how his acceptance of free trade is justified by reasons different from those advanced by Adam Smith and, in a different way, by François Quesnay, and how the resulting "natural identity of interests" involves the reference to a theodicy. The acquisition of abstract reasoning, thanks to which agents overcome their passions, their prejudices, and, ultimately, know their enlightened interest, is inseparable from religious education. Such a perfectibility of the human mind enables to reach an individual and social state of happiness, according to the plan of Providence. Stewart would thus be one of the "Christian moralists" of the first half of the century. Likewise, Ricardo is depicted by Sergio Cremaschi, in his paper on "Theological themes in Ricardo's papers and correspondence", as a "rational Christian". From a very detailed scrutiny of his writing, and especially the hitherto mostly neglected *Commonplace Book*, it is shown that, while Ricardo rejected any theodicy and considered theology to be a vain pursuit because it reaches beyond human knowledge, there is evidence that he was neither an atheist nor an agnostic. Contrary to James Mill, whose opinions have often been (wrongly) attributed to him, he did not dismiss faith, nor his Unitarian convictions: morality is the essence of religion, not speculative truth – and his attitude is reflected in his conception of political economy.

To many economists later in the nineteenth century and at the beginning of the twentieth concerns with morals and ethics were important issues, as was the part played by religion in connection with these topics and with science. Unfortunately, as regards Henry Sidgwick and Alfred Marshall – that is, an important turning point in the history of economic thought – commentary has been somewhat superficial and often mistaken, neglecting the religious, institutional and philosophical debates of the time. In the case of Sidgwick, this is particularly striking, with the often quoted sentence, taken from a letter – in which Donald Moggridge sees the influence of Lytton Strachey – of John Maynard Keynes to Bernard Winthrop Swithinbank: "He [Sidgwick] never did anything but wonder whether Christianity was true and prove it wasn't and hope that it was" (Keynes, 27 March 1906, in Moggridge 1992, p. 102). In "Henry Sidgwick, moral order and utilitarianism", Keith Tribe points out the misunderstandings of Sidgwick's works and shows that his case was not a struggle between faith and science, that a critique of Anglicanism is not a critique of religion as such but of just one form of it, and that Sidgwick's religious and ethical convictions, and not only his critical relation to utilitarianism, inform his writings, *The Principles of Economics* as well as *The Methods of Ethics* – with a more or less silent influence until the 1930s.

In this context, the two other papers dealing with this period are particularly welcome. Daniela Donnini Macciò, in "Pigou on philosophy and religion", studies Pigou's youthful writings on philosophy, morals, and religion published prior to the First World War, which are, she states, as much inspired by G.E. Moore as by Sidgwick.[12] She shows that Pigou was in search of a moral philosophy, which, discarding religion as logically and philosophically untenable, would nevertheless keep its ethical plea and commitment to good, and that there is a correspondence between his developments in ethics and the main concepts of his welfare economics. For its part, "Keynes and Christian socialism. Religion and the economic problem", by David Andrews, states that, while Keynes rejected established confessions like Anglicanism, he was not hostile to some other forms of religious attitude. Andrews examines the two broad definitions of religion that Keynes outlined in short essays like "A short view of Russia", "The economic possibilities for our grandchildren" or "My early beliefs", and shows how and why Keynes, drawing on the ideas of the early generation of the Apostles[13] – Frederick Denison Maurice in particular – successively adopted these two views, with obvious consequences for his fight against Benthamism and in favour of social change and progress.

So far we have referred, broadly speaking, to what is usually but loosely termed liberal political economy. But there are also other conceptions of modernity and rationality in economics than the market-based model. Some other modern approaches have emerged, contesting and entering into debates with the dominant view. In this perspective, religious elements have in many cases been one of the driving forces behind a social critique, either progressive or conservative; they have also enriched reflection on social and economic progress. More generally, religion has been one of the weapons that can be used to maintain economics as a moral and political science and not simply as a technology in the hands of experts – it has supplied arms to opponents of the positivist and naturalist tendencies of the discipline.

First of all, liberal economic theory, in part born, ironically, out of religious controversies, found itself challenged from the beginning of the nineteenth century by religion itself. This opposition involved the rejection of sensationism and utilitarianism as the be-all and end-all for explaining human behaviour, and was also motivated by the damage wrought by

12 For a useful complement to the ethical and social concerns of the members of the Cambridge Apostles, see Donnini Macciò (2015, 2016).

13 On this point, see also Andrews (2010).

the industrial revolution, by economic crises, and their consequence: pauperism. Various denominations and confessions criticised liberal political economy and often proposed alternative theories, developing different models of social organisation. The irruption of religion into debates over political economy and economic policy has been well documented, in the case of Great Britain for example (see, e.g. Hilton 1988, Waterman 1991). In France, the Protestant critique was formulated very early in the century, in the writings of Germaine de Staël and Benjamin Constant, and then taken up by Catholic writers such as Jean-Paul Alban de Villeneuve-Bargemont, leading however to two alternative models of society: Social Catholicism and Social Christianity (Faccarello and Steiner 2008b, Faccarello 2014). In this issue, Gilbert Faccarello, in "A dance teacher for paralysed people? Charles de Coux and the dream of a Christian political economy", shows how, in this case, at the beginning of the nineteenth century, Catholic reaction against the negative social and economic consequences of liberal political economy was both relevant in its critique of the functioning of a free market economy, but theoretically ambiguous and unable to propose an alternative theoretical framework for political economy.[14]

A last, important point is worth noting. In the face of the dominant model, established religions can also be deemed inadequate or outmoded – as, again, John Stuart Mill reports in the epigraph to this introduction. A modern society could in this case be based on new religions, corresponding to the needs of a modernity that would not be that of the free market. The "New Christianity" of Saint-Simon, the "Saint-Simonian religion" that followed, Auguste Comte's "Religion of Humanity", or even the communist society that constitutes the utopia of Constantin Pecqueur are all illustrations of this perspective with its multiple ramifications. In "Religion and political economy in Saint-Simon", Pierre Musso, on the basis of the new outstanding (and finally complete) edition of the works of Claude Henri de Saint-Simon[15] (of which he is one of the editors), presents us with a detailed restatement of how the new industrial society should be organised, why it

14 Note that this critical use of religion or religious concepts also concerned criticism of liberal political economy by associationist, socialist, or communist authors who recycled old religious arguments to underpin their new points of view, and proposed alternative views of modernity and of the rational organisation of societies. One illustrative example concerns the controversy over usury: at a time when the Catholic Church was *de facto* relaxing its position, some traditional arguments against usury were borrowed and transformed in a socialist direction by Constantin Pecqueur. Another example is provided by the writings of Marx in which, independently of his critique of religion, the author makes religious references while discussing value, money and capital – references that are far from accidental and which allow him to consider the logic of capitalism.

15 Or Henri Saint-Simon, as he called himself at the end of his life.

needs a New Christianity and what precisely the "Industrial religion" is.[16] Finally, the links between religion and (the critique of) political economy are also a central aspect of the movement which led to the emergence of sociology. Criticism of the dominant model of rationality and modernity, a plea for another modernity, approaches in which economics, religion, and politics are very present, are also important themes in Auguste Comte – a former secretary of Saint-Simon – and Émile Durkheim, not to speak of the Durkheim school (Steiner [2005] 2010). In this issue, Philippe Steiner, in "Religion and the sociological critique of political economy: altruism and gift", shows how political economy, with its stress on the selfish behaviour of agents, was considered by Comte as a danger for the coherence of an industrial society, and how Comte's critique led, by contrast, to the concept of altruism and his Religion of Humanity. Reacting to Herbert Spencer's interpretation, Durkheim and his nephew, Marcel Mauss, subsequently developed Comte's approach, its religious dimension included, which culminated in Mauss's theory of gift-giving – also used to criticise political economy in the 1920s.

As can be seen from the papers presented in this issue, from a historical perspective the relationships between political economy and religion are multifaceted and show how the process of secularisation, in which the emergence and development of economic thought is a prominent aspect, is much more complex than often thought. Of course, religion lost its dominant role in society, but this does not mean that it disappeared, or became strictly confined to the private sphere of individuals. In many respects, whether redefined or not, it played a role in the shaping of key economic concepts or approaches, either directly as in the case of Boisguilbert, or indirectly through the close relationship it maintained with morals and ethics – thus contributing to the development of political economy, or alternatively to its critique.

Disclosure statement

No potential conflict of interest was reported by the author.

References

Andrews, D.R., 2010. *Keynes and the British humanist tradition. The moral purpose of the market.* Abingdon: Routledge.

Bateman, B. and Banzhaf, H.S., ed., 2008. *Keeping faith, losing fait: religious belief and political economy.* Annual supplement of *History of political economy*, 40.

16 See also Musso (2006, 2010).

Bidard, C., Erreygers, G. and Parys, W., 2009. 'Our daily bread'. Maurice Potron, from Catholicism to mathematical economics. *The European journal of the history of economic thought*, 16 (1), 123–54.
Blumenberg, H., ([1966]1988). *Die Legitimität der Neuzeit.* Frankfurt am Main: Suhrkamp.
Cohen, I. ed., 1990. *Puritanism and the rise of modern science. The Merton thesis.* New Brunswick: Rutgers University Press.
Cohen, J. and Nagel, T., 2009. Introduction. *In:* J. Rawls, *A brief inquiry into the meaning of sin and faith.* Harvard: Harvard University Press, 1–23.
Cremaschi, S., 2014. Utilitarianism and Malthus's virtue ethics. Abingdon: Routledge.
Cremaschi, S., 2017. Invisible beings. Adam Smith's lectures on natural religion. *The Adam Smith review*, 10, forthcoming.
Donnini Macciò, D., 2015. G.E. Moore's philosophy and Cambridge economics: Ralph Hawtrey on ethics and methodology. *The European journal of the history of economic thought*, 22 (2), 163–97.
Donnini Macciò, D., 2016. The Apostles' justice: Cambridge reflections on economic inequality from Moore's *Principia Ethica* to Keynes's *General Theory* (1903–36). *Cambridge journal of economics*, 40 (3), pp. 701–26.
Dumont, L., 1977. *Homo Aequalis. Genèse et épanouissement de l'idéologie économique.* Paris: Gallimard.
Faccarello, G., [1986]1999. *Aux origines de l'économie politique libérale: Pierre de Boisguilbert.* Paris: Anthropos. Revised edition: *The foundations of Laissez-faire. The economics of Pierre de Boisguilbert.* London: Routledge.
Faccarello, G., 2014. From the foundation of liberal political economy to its critique: theology and economics in France in the 18th and 19th centuries. *In:* P. Oslington, ed. *The Oxford handbook of Christianity and economics.* Oxford: Oxford University Press, 73–93.
Faccarello, G. and Steiner, P., 2008a. Interest, sensationism and the science of the legislator. French 'Philosophie économique', 1695–1830. *The European journal of the history of economic thought*, 15 (1), 1–23.
Faccarello, G. and Steiner, P., 2008b. Political economy and religion in early nineteenth century France. *In:* B.W. Bateman and H. Banzhaf, ed. *Keeping faith, losing faith: religious belief and political economy.* Annual supplement of *History of political economy*, 40, 26–61.
Gentile, E., [2001]2007. *Le religioni della politica. Fra democrazie e totalitarismi.* Roma: Laterza.
Gossen, H.H., [1854]1983. *Entwickelung der Gesetze des menschlichen Verkehrs und der daraus fliessenden Regeln für menschliches Handeln.* Brunswick: F. Vieweg. English translation. *The laws of human relations and the rules of human action derived therefrom*, Cambridge: MIT Press.
Griswold, C.L., 1999. *Adam Smith and the virtues of the Enlightenment.* Cambridge: Cambridge University Press.
Harrison, P., 1998. *The Bible, Protestantism and the rise of natural science.* Cambridge: Cambridge University Press.
Harrison, P., 2007. *The Fall of Man and the foundations of science.* Cambridge: Cambridge University Press.
Harrison, P., 2015. *The territories of science and religion.* Chicago, IL: The University of Chicago Press.
Harrison, P., ed., 2010. *The Cambridge companion to science and religion.* Cambridge: Cambridge University Press.

Hill, L., 2001. The hidden theology of Adam Smith. *The European journal of the history of economic thought*, 8 (1), 1–29.

Hilton, B., 1988. *The age of atonement. The influence of Evangelicalism on social and economic thought*, 1785–1865. Oxford: Clarendon Press.

Hunter, I., 2015. Secularization: the birth of a modern combat concept. *Modern intellectual history*, 12 (1), 1–32.

Keynes, J.M., 1925. A short view of Russia. *Nation and Athenaeum*, 10, 17 and 25 October. As in J.M. Keynes, ed. *Essays in persuasion*, new edition, vol. IX of *The collected writings of John Maynard Keynes*. London and Cambridge: Macmillan and Cambridge University Press, 1972, 253–71.

Lipkes, J., 1999. *Politics, religion and classical political economy in Britain: John Stuart Mill and his followers*. London: Palgrave Macmillan.

Löwith, K., 1949. *Meaning in history. The theological implications of the philosophy of history*. Chicago, IL: The University of Chicago Press (The original text, *Weltgeschichte und Heilsgeschehen. Die theologischen Voraussetzungen der Geschichtsphilosophie*, was published later, in 1953).

Marramao, G., 1994. *Cielo e terra. Genealogia della secolarizzazione*. Rome: Laterza.

Marx, K., [1863–66] 1976. Das Kapital. Erstes Buch, Der Produktionsprozeß des Kapitals. Sechstes Kapitel. Resultate des unmittelbaren Produktionsprozesses. *Arkhiv Marksa i Engelsa*, 2 (7), Moscow, 1933, 4–266. English translation 1976 by B. Fowkes in *Capital*, London: Penguin Books and New Left Review, vol. 1, 948–1084.

Merton, R.K., [1938]1970. *Science, technology and society in seventeenth century England*. New York, NY: Howard Fertig.

Mill, J.S., [1874]1969. *Three essays on religion*. London: Longmans, Green, Reader, and Dyer. As in *Collected works of John Stuart Mill*, vol. X: *Essays on ethics, religion and society*. Toronto: The University of Toronto Press, 369–489.

Moggridge, D.E., 1992. *Maynard Keynes: an economist's biography*. London: Routledge.

Monod, J.-C., [2002]2012. *La querelle de la sécularisation, de Hegel à Blumenberg*. Paris: Vrin.

Musso, P., 2006. *La religion du monde industriel. Analyse de la pensée de Saint-Simon*. La Tour d'Aigues: Éditions de l'Aube.

Musso, P., 2010. *Saint-Simon, l'industrialisme contre l'État*. La Tour d'Aigues: Éditions de l'Aube.

Orain, A., 2014. The second Jansenism and the rise of French eighteenth-century political economy. *History of political economy*, 46 (3), 463–90.

Oslington, P., ed., 2011. *Adam Smith as theologian*. New York, NY: Routledge.

Pasteur, L., 1864. Des générations spontanées. *Revue des cours scientifiques de la France et de l'étranger*, 1, 23 April, 257–65.

Rawls, J., 2009. *A brief inquiry into the meaning of sin and faith*. Harvard, MA: Harvard University Press.

Schmitt, C., [1922]1985. *Politische Theologie. Vier Kapital zur Lehre von der Souveränität*. English translation, *Political theology. Four chapters on the concept of sovereignty*. Cambridge: MIT Press.

Steiner, P., [2005]2010. *L'École durkheimienne et l'économie: sociologie, religion et connaissance*. Geneva: Droz. Revised edition: *Durkheim and the birth of economic sociology*. Princeton: Princeton University Press.

Steiner, P., 2011. The creator, human conduct and the maximisation of utility in Gossen's economic theory. *The European journal of the history of economic thought*, 18 (3), 353–79.

Taranto, D., 1992. *Studi sulla protostoria del concetto di interesse. Da Commynes a Nicole (1524–1675)*. Naples: Liguori.

Taylor, C., 2007. *A secular age.* Cambridge, MA: The Belknap Press of Harvard University Press.

Todeschini, G., 2002. *I mercanti e il tempio. La società cristiana e il circolo virtuoso della richezza fra Medioevo ed età moderna.* Bologna: Il Mulino.

Todeschini, G., 2004. *Richezza francescana. Dalla povertà volontaria alla società di mercato.* Bologna: Il Mulino.

Tschannen, O., 1992. *Les théories de la sécularisation.* Geneva and Paris: Droz.

Voegelin, E., [1938]2000. *Die politischen Religionen.* English translation, *Political religions. In:* E. Sandoz, ed. *The collected works of Eric Voegelin,* vol. 5: *Modernity without restraint.* Columbia: The University of Missouri Press, 19–73.

Waterman, A., 1987. Economists on the relation between political economy and Christian theology: a preliminary survey. *International journal of social economics,* 14 (6), 46–68.

Waterman, A., 1991. *Revolution, economics and religion. Christian political economy, 1798–1833.* Cambridge: Cambridge University Press.

Waterman, A., 2004. *Political economy and Christian theology since the Enlightenment. Essays in intellectual history.* London: Palgrave Macmillan.

Winch, D., 1996. *Riches and poverty. An intellectual history of political economy in Britain, 1750–1834.* Cambridge: Cambridge University Press.

Agency, exchange, and power in scholastic thought

Richard Sturn

> Later on from the mother science of theological philosophy an independent ethics detached itself which stood in close relation to political economy.
>
> Joseph A. Schumpeter (1954a, p. 19)

1. Theology and political economy

Discussing the role of scholastic theology in the development of Political Economy faces specific challenges. *First,* it implies dealing with a great transformation within the systems of human knowledge. The point of departure is a world where discussions of ethics and socio-economic affairs are located within theological frameworks. This reflects a hierarchical order: the theoretical mapping of the social world is not composed of co-evolving subsystems, each with its own functional logic. It is even less conceivable that the logic of an autonomous economic sphere is considered the core of socio-economic theory. *Second,* while one may expect certain parallels between the way in which theological thought influenced modern science on the one hand and politico-economic thought on the other, the scope of those parallels may be limited, as the issue is more complex in the latter case: take for instance Langholm's (1998, p. 175) cautious remark that "it is not at all unreasonable" to view the role of scholastic economic thought in intellectual history "as having been primarily normative." The cautious phrasing indicates that some ambiguities may be lurking in the background. What about the status of explanatory passages in scholastic writings? And shouldn't we take into account that the normative-positive distinction is itself a product of more recent thinking? *Third,* we are dealing with a heterogeneous range of influences, including

Aristotelian philosophy, Roman law thinking and Christian Patristic traditions, as well as controversial issues developing in the scholastic period. Those issues are part of the intellectual evolution taking place from the thirteenth to the sixteenth centuries and include the divides between voluntarism vs. intellectualism, and nominalism vs. essentialism. Some of those developments are of enduring relevance for different strands of thought in emerging modernity. *Fourth*, given what has been said so far, it may not come as a surprise that we are discussing a heterogeneous group of thinkers, a common religious horizon notwithstanding. Heterogeneity is associated with the changing historical contexts over roughly three centuries as well as the specificities of Dominican and Franciscan traditions, or of the late scholastic Salamanca School. *Fifth*, considering the secondary literature on the subject, we are still confronted with a puzzling diversity of interpretations. This seems to be partly related to the complex intellectual background indicated above, and partly to retrospective biases operating at various levels, including the tendency to draft authors of the past in defence of more recent currents of thought. Just to give an illustration of those enduring differences: while some scholars are promoting what Langholm (1998, p. 61) calls an amazing 'Austrian' (i.e. subjectivist) reinterpretation of scholastic economics, the legal historian Wolfgang Ernst (2014, p. 62) emphasises scholastic price determination relying on "inherent qualities of commodities" irrespective of market interdependencies: "Just as other qualities could be attributed to commodities, so every commodity carries with it its 'true' price."

To be sure, problematic interpretations were and are subject to circumspect criticism, showing that some claims are either untenable or at least need to be put into a more encompassing perspective. Chaplygina and Lapidus (2016) stress the duality of (1) normative considerations (How is the just price determined?) and (2) analysis of economic behaviour which may result in actual transactions violating the norm (see also Lapidus 1994). Ignoring the "scholastic duality" (e.g. assuming that scholastic economic reasoning is exclusively normative) is misleading. However, dealing with the duality in a retrospective manner is not without problems either, as it may be associated with retrospective biases (see Lapidus 1992; 1996): for instance, "scholastic duality" may be retrospectively taken to just foreshadow the duality between natural price and market price. Such a story would provide an illustration for Whig history of linear progress. It would imply the irrelevance of the epistemological and contextual specificities of the superseded ancestors. In contrast, discussing the role of seemingly analogous forms of "duality" in the context of two starkly different knowledge systems may give more accurate and interesting insights, as it sheds light on the evolution of knowledge by new combinations, including the possibility that certain questions are no longer part of the dominant mental models, even if they keep their relevance for the real world. What may be considered as progress in one respect may coincide with knowledge falling into undue oblivion, as stressed by Schumpeter (1954b, p. 6).

Odd Langholm's work is another example for circumspect criticism of one-sided interpretations of scholastic writings on economic issues. However, for the present paper another aspect of Langholm's work is still more important. I refer to his discussion of power and mixed will in "voluntary exchange", which may be taken as showcase example for the non-coincidence of obsolescence and oblivion in the evolution of political economy. Langholm's pertinent discussion is related to co-ordinates made explicit in the present paper. Those co-ordinates (called "agency" and "indeterminacy") avoid taking ideas and concepts as the starting point elaborated much later, such as the labour theory of value, or the autonomy of the market sphere, or the spontaneous order based on self-interest. Working with "agency" and "indeterminacy" as co-ordinates should allow for a reasonably critical account of some continuity with regard to foundational problems, while at the same time taking seriously profound transformations of knowledge systems. Addressing perennial issues in socio-economic thought, they allow for considering the evolution and recombination of concepts in historical comparison, while at the same time recognising fundamental shifts of perspective ("ruptures"). The *first* coordinate introduces "agency", or more precisely, the distinction between *agency-sensitive exchange* vs. agency-neutral transactions. Important dimensions of agency-sensitive exchange in scholastic thought have been discussed by Kaye (1998, 2014),[1] Lapidus (1994) and Langholm (1998). In the present paper, I expand on the role of agency with regard to "regulation." In the present paper, "regulation" is defined as non-spontaneous (agency-driven) adjustment of the terms and conditions of exchange by way of bargaining, arguing, norm-setting and norm-enforcement. (In contrast, self-regulation includes the spontaneous adjustment of relative prices and conditions of exchange). The *second* co-ordinate refers to *indeterminacy*. The strategic importance of indeterminacy for social

1 For instance, Kaye explains the concerns articulated by Henry of Gent in the second half of the thirteenth century in a way such that they can be understood in terms of agency-sensitive exchange. Henry used the metaphor of scales to support the idea of the just price system as a unique equilibrium accessible to human knowledge, insisting "on the place of subjective judgment and ordering (*justitia animata*) in establishing a true equality just price" (Kaye 1998, p. 106). Henry of Gent thus stresses ideas which are at odds with concepts entailing that prices are determined by blind system-wide forces, accidental circumstances, and incomprehensible interdependences.

theory comes to the fore in foundational writings by modern authors such as Binmore (2005, p. 66ff) and is summarised in Hardin's (2005) "Indeterminacy and Society." In the present paper, the conceptualisation of indeterminacy is related to the distinction between intellectualism and voluntarism. This distinction plays a prominent role in the historiography of natural sciences. Moreover, it is considered in the theory of international politics (see Pabst 2017) and is the central coordinate in Schneewind's (1998) history of modern moral philosophy, which was one of the main influences in the pre-history of economics, as stressed by Schumpeter (1954a, p. 19). In politico-legal theory, voluntarism is considered an ingredient of Carl Schmitt's "decisionism" (see Emon 2016). Schmitt's (1922, p. 5) *Political theology* claims that "all significant concepts of the modern theory of the state are secularised theological concepts not only because of their historical development – in which they were transferred from theology to the theory of the state ... – but also because of their systematic structure, the recognition of which is necessary for a sociological consideration of these concepts."[2]

In the history of economic thought, voluntarism is not referred to with comparable intensity. While some authors such as Fanfani (2011), Weber (1959) and Kaufer (1998) explicitly refer to the role of voluntarism, little convergence of understanding becomes visible. This lack of convergence includes the issue of regulation. The doctrine of the just price was often read as a doctrine of *thick regulation* of markets. As is well known, this view is not uncontested. Hoeffner, Kaufer and many others seek to demonstrate the extent to which selected authors anticipated the logic of price formation as a self-regulating mechanism. Kaufer (1998) stresses that *voluntarist* scholastic writers endorsed *thin*, quasi-liberalistic modes of regulation. In contrast, catholic authors such as Fanfani and Hoeffner emphasise links between voluntarism and interventionism. Apart from dealing with interpretive ambiguities concerning the questions

2 According to Schmitt, legal thinking on political sovereignty is anticipated by the theological emphasis of discretionary agency which (one may add along the lines suggested by Emon 2016) gets specific leverage in a voluntarist worldview. According to Schmitt, this kind of thinking is in tension with modern rationalism, including modern political economy. We cannot discuss here the theoretical, meta-theoretical and historiographic problems with Schmitt's view, including the problem that theological voluntarism influenced the natural sciences in a way which seems incongruent with the anti-rationalistic stance of his political theology. Irrespective of his eminent status as an influential and contested politico-legal theorist, Schmitt provides interesting speculations on combinatorial aspects in the history of ideas.

(1) Whether regulatory frameworks envisaged by scholastics are *thick or thin.*
(2) To which extent scholastic thought on prices is some kind of proto-economics and to which extent is it an ethical theory (see Hamouda and Price 1997).
(3) Whether certain authors anticipated a demand-and-supply model or rather a labour/cost theory of the just price or both.

shifting interpretive perspectives helps avoiding other retrospective biases. Moreover, it supports a richer discussion of the *status* and *mode* of regulation, including *extra-legal modes* of regulation guided by just prices in the context of contested, agency-sensitive exchange.

The rest of the paper is organised as follows. In Section 2, agency-sensitive exchange is introduced and used to shed some light on the diversity of interpretations in the literature. Section 3 expands on scholastic conceptualisations related to agency and discusses the background of coercion and mixed will in the context of the "principle of mutual benefit." Section 4 briefly summarises voluntarism and intellectualism as theological paradigms related to the issue of indeterminacy. In the final section, I discuss the enduring relevance of this for different perspectives of socio-economic regulation.

2. Agency and exchange

> Of the tendencies that are harmful to sound economics, the most seductive, and in my opinion the most poisonous, is to focus on questions of distribution.
>
> Robert Lucas (2004, p. 13)

In this section, divergent interpretations of scholastic economic thought are confronted with a discussion of agency. The main currents of scholastic economic thought promoted a regulatory agenda stressing some dimensions of ("moral") agency in exchange relations. They differ with regard to the foundations of regulation: the foundations of regulation may be more or less "economic." Referring to diverging interpretations, most of them may be taken to stress different (and in some sense plausible) stances regarding those foundations, at least on a charitable reading. Stressing the theological background of agency, mixed will, and the voluntarism-intellectualism distinction provides an interpretive framework for making explicit pertinent differences.

By contrast, agency-neutrality plays a key role in an influential conception of the core of economic analysis, a crucial implication of which is epitomised by the introductory quote from Lucas (2004). The key assumption is exogenous enforcement of contract-related rights, providing the basis for spontaneous adjustment of the terms of free exchange. The sphere of free exchange is free from agency-sensitive issues which create room for regulation by ethical guidance, normative discourse, political bargaining, or arbitrary power. Less than perfectly well-defined legal norms (which would leave room for strategic manoeuvring) are an anathema. In particular, it is assumed that the *distributive properties of contract terms do not influence the way in which exchange partners perform their contractually stipulated obligations.* The scope of implications is vividly expressed in Lerner's (1972, p. 259) AEA Presidential Address: "An economic transaction is a solved political problem. [...] economics has gained the title Queen of the Social Sciences by choosing solved political problems as its domain." Lerner's considerations highlight the analytical status of a stable and enduring sphere of autonomous market transactions for economic theory. This is a sphere of human interaction based on voluntary exchange according to the principle of mutual benefit. On this basis, a sphere of social interdependences mediated by prices comes into existence. It is determined by anonymous, depersonalised forces conditioned by the objective data of the environment. Insofar the micro-foundations of pertinent theories invoke human agency, it is some abstract logic of consistent, instrumentally rational choice which is considered neutral with respect to substantive dimensions of human agency. The goals, needs and motives of choosing and transacting agents need not be taken into consideration. As famously stressed by Robbins (1932, p. 25f), the economic problem is the same for a society of sybarites and a society of ascetics: only relative prices may be expected to differ.

In recent decades, economic frameworks abstracting from agency and agency problems were complemented by theories of incomplete contracts, efficiency wages, credit rationing and behavioural economics. While those developments re-introduced dimensions of agency-sensitive exchange (called "contested exchange" by Samuel Bowles and Herbert Gintis), foundational implications have mostly been explored by authors somehow attached to non-mainstream currents, such as Bowles and Gintis (1993a and b; see also Bowles 1985) and Samuels 2005 (see also Sturn 2004). By contrast, mainstream currents tend to "solve" pertinent "agency problems" by getting rid of contested exchange and incomplete contracts, designing ever more perfect mechanisms. I will come back to that.

Taking agency and contested exchange into explicit consideration allows for a better understanding of the regulatory horizons of scholastic economic thought as well as of the scope of the intellectual transformation culminating in (what Langholm 1998 calls) Hobbes's anti-thesis. This does not hinge upon particular views or interpretations underpinning the concept of the just price.

One of those interpretations holds that norms of the just price *facilitate* voluntary exchange. Another interpretation emphasises the extra-economic character of such norms. From an economic point of view, such heteronomous norms basically operate as *constraints* on voluntary exchange. I start with currents of thought endorsing the second interpretation. According to one prominent view, the scholastic concept of just price is closely connected to a theory of "fair income" which, in turn, depends on certain ideas of political community entailing a specific pattern of income distribution. The underlying structure of social stratification is associated with an institutional pattern supporting some kind of static division of labour and is complemented by oligopolistic markets with a low degree of competition. Moreover, this view is the basis of a "social policy which [is] [...] necessarily conservative" (Johnson 1938, p. 171). The *justum pretium* is conditioned by these social structures and institutional patterns and "could be applied if one accepted the *status quo* as functionally satisfactory."

Johnson's conception envisages the just price in its functional relation to a certain given social order whose stability depends on a system of "just" prices as regulatory framework for market exchange. Such models of statically embedded markets are useful as point of departure for further reflection. They correspond to Aristotle's view of ethical guidance and institutional anchors necessary for preventing the destabilisation of ethical-political institutions. Such models appear as a version of what Joel Kaye (1998, p. 88) summarises as prevailing doctrine in the history of ideas until the middle of the twentieth century: "[...] it was generally assumed that all aspects of medieval economic thought were similarly characterized by the determination to maintain ideal definitions, whether in opposition to or in ignorance of, actual economic practice. [...] Seen in this way, just price theory was a sister to usury theory, another manifestation of the medieval desire to control economic activity in the name of religious ideals and social equilibrium."

In Johnson's interpretation, "ideal definitions" are not corresponding to intrinsic values which have nothing to do with the working of human society (a view alluded to in the above quote from Kaye and recently stressed again by Ernst 2014), but are derived from a framework of norms and virtues imposing their requirements on economic exchange relations and prices. In his classical work on the pre-capitalist economy, Sombart (1916, pp. 180–7) envisages a similar corporatist-communitarian model of the medieval town, drawing on concepts such as Tönnies's Gemeinschaft (community) and the Aristotelian *polis*. In particular, Sombart (1916, pp. 272–315) takes pains to provide historic evidence for the view that medieval merchants were subordinate to the corporatist community of the town: medieval commerce is *just another handicraft*[3].

The corporatist model suggested by Sombart as well as the institutionally less specific reasoning by Johnson imply that scholastic authors were basically unaware of the main agenda of modern economics: dealing with the logic of the market sphere. Rather, the "laws" regulating prices are derived from the requirements imposed by spheres outside the market, for instance by the need to stabilise the non-market framework of institutions and social classes. Economic categories such as costs and needs reflect the "equilibrium" conditions established in spheres outside the market.

Irrespective of whether the extra-economic "equilibrium" imposing its requirements upon the economic sphere is anchored at a functional level or somewhere else, it is not assumed to be accompanied by a sufficiently strong mechanism ("gravitational forces") which would spontaneously establish the conditions of that "equilibrium" in the economic sphere. Put another way, the conditions of the "equilibrium" are not immediately translated into internalised norms. It seems that the just price is providing a learning heuristic (developing the cognitive potentials allowing for the distinction of contingencies which should or should not influence just exchange ratios), including an institutionalised religious learning mechanism (the confession). This presupposes some space for agency in the economic sphere which is not fully determined by the gravitational forces of some "equilibrium": agents neither are price-takers, nor are the conditions of the envisaged extra-economic "social equilibrium" internalised as behavioural norms in the economic sphere. The specific weight of such agency problems may depend on theological views such as voluntarism and intellectualism, or assumptions on behavioural dispositions and cognitive limitations of humans after the fall (see Section 4). In any case, regulation invokes some dimension of agency.

In interpretations à la Johnson, agency is not (or not primarily) related to dealing with endogenous problems of the contract sphere. But what

3 Sombart's favourite source for this account is Henry von Langenstein. Views à la Sombart and Johnson have been criticised from different perspectives. Joseph Höffner who emphasises the extent to which the Aquinian high scholastic mainstream prepared the ground for a modern understanding of markets and prices, puts Henry von Langenstein (along with John Gerson and Gabriel Biel) into a category of more *interventionist and voluntarist* late scholastic thinkers off the Aquinian mainstream (e.g. Höffner 1955). More recently, Trusen (1997, pp. 536–7) presented textual evidence and context-based interpretations suggesting that even in the cases of these three thinkers the alleged *corporatism* is to a large extent an ideal retrospectively imposed.

about authors holding that various scholastic thinkers developed a kind of proto-economics, liberating the categories of costs, needs, and wants from extra-economic conditions. According to those interpretations, the just price cannot be reduced to an adaption of exchange conditions to extra-economic "equilibria". Various texts by Joseph Höffner (e.g. 1941 and 1955), De Roover (1958, 1971, 1974) and Hayek (1973) put forward this view. According to Höffner (e.g. 1941, p. 164), the idea of the market as a relatively autonomous sphere is *explicitly* foreshadowed in the writings of the more important scholastic thinkers. Referring to *lawyers* and theologians of the scholastic period, the German legal historian Winfried Trusen (e.g. 1997) provides furthermore detailed textual and historical evidence (notably regarding the scope of trade and the socio-economic status of merchants) pointing into the same direction, while being critical of Sombart's view. Schumpeter's (1954b) claims concerning the precursory status of scholastic economic reasoning with regard to analytical concepts of price theory should also be mentioned.

With reference to the writings of De Roover and others it has become common to say that for scholastic proto-economics the *justum pretium* "is simply the current market price" (as put by De Roover, 1958, p. 421; see also Hayek 1973; Kaufer 1998) and "viewed as anathema any interference ... with the workings of the free market in establishing the just price" (Blomquist 1975, p. 829). From the perspective suggested in the present article, this way of putting things is certainly interesting. However, upon closer reflection it raises more questions than it provides answers, as summarised by the title of Monsalve (2014): what does the assertion "the just price is the market price" mean? For instance: does it mean that we can say nothing about prices beyond collecting observations of their development over time? Or is this view based on the presumption that price theory makes sense at an abstract level as the pivotal element of our understanding of the autonomy of markets, but is neither useful for predicting prices nor for setting normative standards for prices? Obviously, the assimilation of *pretium justum* and market price has implications for the question of how the market is related to conceptions of justice: does it constitute a morally free zone where the agency-dimension of justice is substituted by a functionally equivalent mechanism? Such assumptions are implied when Blomquist (1975, p. 829) suggests (with reference to De Roover's work on the Florentine labour market around 1400, stressing in particular passages suggesting the conceptualisation of labour as a commodity) that scholastic economic doctrines were an active element in unleashing market forces.

De Roover, Kaufer and others emphasise that in the writings of early thinkers from Petrus Olivi to Bernardino of Siena, surprisingly far-reaching anticipations of stances very much resembling those of economic liberalism are to be found, particularly with regard to justice in exchange relations. As put forward in some detail by Kaufer (1998, p. 99), Franciscan thinkers such as Petrus Olivi and Duns Scotus are amongst those who are most advanced in their economic reasoning. Petrus Olivi is said to be close to a proto-liberal position[4] as far as the legitimacy-conferring effect of voluntary consent in exchange is concerned.

While such findings may shed doubt on retrospective views à la Sombart, the textual material referred to does not imply the anticipation of market autonomy. As will be explained in a moment, this is systematically related to the role of agency. However, it is also worth keeping in mind two caveats referring to historical context and to retrospective biases. Here is the first caveat: considering *Volenti non fit injuria* in the scholastic context, one should keep in mind the context of a social order that is not yet a market society including a fully-fledged labour market. In the medieval period, wage labour for the most part was under the regulatory framework of guilds (see Epstein 1991). Insofar market relations are rather at the fringe than in the core of socio-economic arrangements, the broader socio-economic problems associated with principles such as *Volenti non fit injuria* are unlikely to be in the focus of attention. Under such historical conditions, free labour markets will affect the livelihood of many people only in a limited way. However, the situation may have changed in the early Renaissance era. Late scholastic authors such as Francisco de Vitoria (1483–1546) perceived pertinent problems posed by labour markets more clearly (see Langholm 1998, pp. 118–36), as will be discussed in the next section.

Second, a comparison of retrospective approaches discussed so far gives the impression that scholastic authors to some extent are drafted in defence of stances in modern theoretical and political controversies. While De Roover criticises authors of the German Historical School for drafting the schoolmen in defence of corporatist ideals of the state, his criticism is not free of the retrospective biases implied by his own background assumptions. While interpretations à la Tawney of the just price as a forerunner of Marxian labour theory certainly begs problems (see Brentano 2003, p. 285, for an early attempt to resolve them by proper contextualisation), De Roover's (e.g. 1958, p. 422) dismissive remarks regarding the labour theory of value associated with Marxian "dialectics" do not much to clarify things.

Let us put aside those two caveats vis-à-vis what Langholm calls a "liberalistic" interpretation. Even if we put them aside, a reconstruction along the lines suggested by De Roover et al. does not seem fully satisfactory: If the link between *pretium justum* and market prices is as close as

4 See also Sturn (2009, 2007a and b).

suggested by the liberalistic interpretation, which kind of "justice" and which conception of justice-guided regulation is implied? On the basis of such questions, the approach suggested by Friedman (1987) offers a suitable perspective. Friedman's problem can be summarised as follows: suppose we accept De Roover's view that the just price essentially coincides with the market price[5]. However, the practical relevance of this concept is unclear. It requires additional explanations paralleling the above-mentioned question of why the gravitational forces of an extra-economic "equilibrium" fail to translate to the level of market agency: "To a modern economist, the idea of requiring people to buy and sell at the market price seems rather like the idea of compelling stones to fall when you drop them." (1987, p. 1043) Friedman (1987, p. 1044) finds a solution for this apparent paradox, making use of agency problems raised by economics of imperfect competition, asymmetric information and transaction costs. As emphasised by Friedman, the medieval era was characterised by high transportation costs, thin markets, bilateral monopolies, and so forth. One could add that rationality and foresight of the relevant agents cannot be always relied upon. As Aquinas emphasises, merchants in particular are often subject to incentives and temptations attracting them to a deceptive and sinful course of action. Under these circumstances the just price was "a device to promote economic efficiency ... It provided [...] an arbitrated solution to what would otherwise be costly bilateral monopoly bargaining." According to Friedman, framing justum pretium as a moral doctrine was functionally superior. *Pretium justum* "as a legal doctrine" would have been confronted with a host of problems, notably non-verifiability vis-à-vis third parties. ("How can the court determine whether the potential seller's claim that the good is especially valuable to him is true?") It works better as a moralised, agency-encompassing mechanism: "Both the seller and God know whether the seller is telling the truth."

According to Friedman's view, the doctrine of the just price is not considered as a program for stabilising a social state which itself is regarded as just or natural. Nonetheless, Friedman's approach entails the reconstruction of a functional role and a corresponding regulatory dimension beyond self-regulation. The functionality is clearly different as compared to earlier interpretations. The rules of *justum pretium* are no longer seen as constraints to transactions, but as the basis of a framework facilitating socially efficient transactions ("a device to promote efficiency"). The specific aspects of Friedman's interpretation can be expressed as follows: (1) Agency problems occur as a result of economically relevant contingencies which are not (yet) addressed by suitable institutional mechanisms.

5 See also Monsalve (2014).

(2) Justice is subordinated to (and explained in terms of) the *efficiency of allocation*, basically implying commutative justice. In contrast, the first interpretation suggests that (1) the roots of agency problems cannot be understood without considering a world beyond the economic sphere, and (2) regulatory norms are based on distributive justice conditioning commutative justice on the basis of extra-economic requirements of social live.

One class of functional interpretations restrict the economic logic of price determination to structures of costs and/or needs, both of which hinge upon socio-political properties of the community including their distributive patterns. In contrast, interpretations à la Friedman (1987) tend to assume the economic logic of price determination in an unrestricted way, assimilating justice to normative requirements of the principle of mutual benefit. The basic condition for justice in exchange is, then, the elimination of distortions occasioned by accidental asymmetries (e.g. imposed by specific circumstances of bilateral exchange in absence of competition) that are not sustainable in an encompassing equilibrium of exchange relations[6]: force, fraud, strategic deception, and exploitive behaviour which may be compatible with non-violation of legal rules of *laesio enormis* ("enormous injury", i.e. less than half of the proper price), but not with the just price.

Probably one can argue that both the "communitarian" (Johnson, Sombart et al.) and the "liberalistic" interpretations (De Roover, Kaufer et al.) lead to one-sided accounts of scholastic economics. Be that as it may, it is worth noting that the "communitarian" and the "libertarian" interpretation are based on specific assumptions with regard to justice in the economy and in economic theorising: in one case, knowledge about justice comes from a system of social interaction outside "the economy", while some knowledge of the working of the market may be required for its implementation. According to the other view, relevant knowledge is primarily based on market interactions: the just price either amounts to a conceptual anticipation of self-regulation or to an instrument for facilitating exchange.

The version of this view articulated by Friedman (1987) is an interesting reference point in two further respects. First, unlike more "traditional"

6 Those developments referring to the insight that one has to consider conditions beyond the ones immediately determining some exchange situation taken in isolation (such as the concept of *communal* valuation in markets) seem to have been in part adopted by some lawyers. Kaye (1998, pp. 93–4) quotes from writings of the lawyer Accursius (1263) according to whom *the value of a thing is determined by the price by which it can be commonly sold*: "res tantum valet, quantum vendi potest, scilicet communiter" (see also Gordon 1975, p. 133).

interpretations and unlike agency-related concepts of contested exchange with endogenous enforcement to be discussed below, Friedman stresses *efficiency*, while *distribution* hardly plays a role in his discussion. Second, Friedman envisages not only the nature and purpose of regulation, but (albeit in a nutshell) also the mode of regulation: he is trying to make sense of a particular mode of regulation in a framework of institutional economics. While he does not go into the details of the mode of regulation by just prices, he puts forward judicial enforcement as the relevant contrast: just price regulation implies a kind of ongoing moral examination: self-examination supported by mechanisms of moral disapproval provided by Christian religion, including the institution of confession.

To sum up: the degree of awareness of the logic of market transactions and prices (as documented by authors from Höffner 1941 to Trusen 1997) casts doubts on the Sombart–Johnson views of ethical regulations and their retrospective biases. In a pre-capitalist world of thin and distorted markets sketched by Friedman, the motivational power of suitable ethical concepts of justice supported by religious practices may indeed facilitate exchange by lowering transaction costs. Agency problems à la Friedman are consistent with a mode of regulation making some sense in a scholastic context. Nonetheless, it remains questionable whether the normative reasoning of scholastic thinkers can be captured by an efficiency-promoting model of the just price.

To discuss this in a broader perspective, consider the innovative anti-thesis to scholastic regulatory thought for which Langholm (1998) credits Hobbes (1651/1985). As indicated above, Lerner (1972) envisages an updated scheme of regulation along the lines of the Hobbesian anti-thesis. It entails a clear-cut division of labour between the self-regulating economic system (where the price system peacefully and smoothly mediates economic interdependences) and the politico-legal system where rules (including distributive rules) are deliberately created in a possibly more conflictual process. The clear-cut division of labour is accompanied by a specific mode of socio-economic regulation: "political problems" are "solved" once-and-for-all, thereby *creating* a self-regulating sphere determined by the spontaneous order of the market, free of ongoing deliberate regulation of social processes either at the micro or the macro level. While this sphere is regarded as basically stable and enduring, there may be changes over time. Whenever new scarcities emerge or new resources are discovered, a new political problem must be solved: pertinent interdependences henceforth are included in the sphere mediated by prices and economic transactions, contributing to the expansion of the economy.

Depending on the frame of reference, the basic architecture put forward by Lerner is either attractive, indispensable, problematically ambiguous, or misleading. *First*, it may be transformed into a political program of governance based on abstract rules, which exhibits *attractive* features when considering challenges of modern societies related to their dynamism and pluralism. *Second*, it is *indispensable* as an *analytical* starting point for pure economics as a science dealing with the autonomous workings of the market. *Third*, it is ambiguous regarding the extent to which it reflects the reality of modern governance: while for good reasons we observe a modern trend towards rule-guided governance congruent with a foundational vision à la Lerner, this has not led to governance by perfect depersonalised mechanisms, or an elimination of agency problems and power asymmetries. *Finally*, the kind of autonomy envisaged is misleading as an interpretive framework for discussing scholastic ideas with regard to the workings of the market, unless it is understood as an anti-thesis.

Borrowing Lerner's (1972) terminology, agency-sensitive exchange is exchange permanently contaminated by "unsolved political problems." Friedman (1987) refers to a limited class of such problems. Referring to scholastic authors, Friedman's interpretive framework does not invoke anachronistic views of self-regulation. However, it seems questionable whether the scholastics indeed anticipated regulation with an exclusive focus on commutative justice or efficiency. Hence it is worthwhile to consider more encompassing agency problems including the distributive dimension.

3. Economic coercion and the principle of mutual benefit

Friedman's reasoning referring to agency-sensitive exchange may be supplemented by an additional, more robust and more fundamental issue that is not captured by the idea of "saving transaction costs." Moreover, it happens to converge with a view which is closer to scholastic philosophical-theological backgrounds.

According to Friedman, ongoing "moralized" regulation by the just price is advantageous under contingent (in principle eliminable) circumstances, such as thin markets or monopolies. In contrast, Langholm (1998) discusses power-related aspects of agency-sensitive exchange in the scholastic literature. Langholm's pertinent account covers its development from the thirteenth to the sixteenth centuries including its application to the labour market by thinkers such as Gabriel Biel in the fifteenth century and Francisco de Vitoria in the sixteenth century, but also its long-lasting marginalisation commencing with other authors of the Salamanca School and Thomas Hobbes. Power-related aspects of agency-sensitive exchange cannot be assumed to become obsolete in the further development of the market system. However, they may get out of sight for some time.

The point of reference for this discussion is what Langholm (1998) refers to as the *principle of mutual benefit.* Kaushik Basu (2007) calls it the *principle of free contract* and lucidly discusses its pivotal importance for economic reasoning and its limits. The historical dimension of this principle is in itself an important illustration for combinatorial developments in socio-economic thought, as it highlights the role of Roman legal thought. According to Kuttner (1982, p. 299), "it is unthinkable that a science of law could have taken shape in the medieval West without the rediscovery of the Justinian Digest, about 1070 A.D. The central monument of ancient Roman jurisprudence presented a model and a challenge to the medieval mind for which it was ill prepared." *In Book 47, title 10,* section 1 § *5, the Digest quotes Ulpian (On the Edict, Bk. 56): "No injury is committed against one who consents." (*... nulla iniuria est, quae in volentem fiat). In the scholastic era, this Roman Law tradition was eventually confronted and combined with philosophical and theological ideas which allowed for a more thorough analysis of the sphere of exchange, including the role of power and coercion in this sphere. This led to a thorough discussion of the question, Which kinds of power asymmetries or information asymmetries shed doubt on the principle of mutual benefit?[7]

The Aristotelian model of an *encompassing embedment of exchange* in the context of the polis provided another point of reference. However, after the challenge of Roman law, medieval socio-economic thought is not a mere rejuvenation of Aristotelian ethics under Christian auspices, even though Aristotelian philosophy supplied important concepts. The development of economic concepts in the scholastic era can be understood as a process of integration of doctrines of "exchange regulation" in the Roman law tradition (see e.g. Trusen 1997) in a broader complex of socio-economic ideas and concepts. While some developments in the scholastic era may be seen as antagonistic to Roman law traditions (notably those captured by interpretations à la Johnson 1938), the just mentioned combinatorial process also brought about *more specific* discussions about limits of "volenti non fit iniuria."

In keeping with the main thrust of Langholm's (1998) arguments, those *more specific* discussions are the background of the following argument, focusing *agency problems cum distribution.* Langholm's chapter on labour and wages (1998, p. 135ff) summarises some of the most relevant developments related to agency-sensitive exchange throughout the scholastic period up to the School of Salamanca. They include concepts such as the "secret wage": suppose that the employer violates justice in a labour

7 See for instance Langholm's (1998: pp. 105–9) discussion of Summenhart and others on need as compulsion. See also Vaarkemaa (2011) and Decock (2012).

contract, benefitting from power asymmetries. In this case, the labourer may legitimately reciprocate by "secretly" appropriating some amount of goods compensating the violation.

Considering their conceptual basis in positive economics, discussions in the context of the secret wage (which was contested among scholastic authors) anticipated reciprocal moral hazard problems including "shirking" as well as the ideas of incomplete contracts and gift exchange. The key concept for discussing pertinent issues was the exchange-related interpretation of Aristotelian "mixed will", which allows for addressing power asymmetries and coerced exchange. As explained in some detail by Langholm (1998), scholastic theorists addressed limits of the principle of mutual benefit employing the Aristotelian concept of mixed will. In Aristotle's classical example illustrating mixed will, the ship crew jettisons the cargo in a heavy storm to save the ship. In the envisaged choice situation, elements of compulsion and free will are somehow mixed. In Scholastic discussions, the notion of compulsion is extended, including in particular economic coercion. Here is an example illustrating "mixed will" in an economic context: workers facing harsh economic conditions such as starvation may say yes to terms which they normally would decline. In such cases, the will is neither entirely free nor unfree, but "mixed." Authors such as Francisco de Vitoria used the concept of mixed will to discuss problems of economic coercion, notably in labour market contexts (see Sturn 2009).

Analyses of transactions based on "mixed will" converge with diagnoses of contested exchange. In order to grasp the far-reaching implications for the conceptualisation of economic exchange, notice that conceptions of wage justice taking on board mixed will combine two aspects of market interactions which are of more general relevance: first, they are invoking the existence of interdependences and circumstances putting the terms of a *particular* transaction into a *more encompassing* view: this is implied by the diagnosis that some actually observed contract terms are accepted only under certain sets of background conditions of exchange, which may impose a certain degree of economic coercion on one party. The contract terms would not be accepted by that party under different sets of background conditions. Second, the implied distributive aspect invites the thought that even though market interaction is governed by economic laws, these laws do not determine everything. If we additionally invoke some notion of indeterminacy ("multiple equilibria"), we may support the view that there are sustainable alternatives to the status-quo background conditions. Referring to the case of workers facing harsh economic conditions who say yes to terms which they normally would decline, invoking multiple equilibria may shed light on an important aspect which is missing in Aristotle's example invoking threats imposed by nature. No individual or collective agent can be held accountable for a heavy storm. Suppose, however, that a situation bringing about harsh economic conditions for some class of people is explainable as a bad equilibrium, while a better equilibrium would exist. This does not immediately imply that somebody can be held accountable, but treating the background conditions of exchange (implying "political" problems of distribution) on a par with heavy storms will not be acceptable. Unlike storms, general economic conditions as well as more specific circumstances of exchange may connote asymmetries of power, of knowledge, and of strategic options, and perhaps they may be subject to purposive public policies aiming at socio-political embedment of exchange, with the perspective of approaching a better equilibrium. In contrast, if we assumed uniqueness of the market equilibrium including wage rates, market outcomes appear natural and are not amenable to deliberate (sustainable) change.

This has important implications for the mode of regulation. Pertinent distributive aspects of agency-sensitive exchange *cannot* be solved once and for all by perfect mechanisms. Ongoing forms of regulation are needed for reasons beyond reducing transaction costs: they are related to permanently re-appearing distributive issues combined with the limits as well as the potentials of human agency in exchange relationships. It is both unlikely and undesirable that progress brings about norms and institutions which would lead to an *elimination of the agency-sensitive character* of exchange: given multiple equilibria and social processes reproducing asymmetries, perfect and permanent elimination of issues related to power and coercion is unlikely.

By contrast, consider the theoretical architecture introduced by the Hobbesian anti-thesis, which is influential in modern mainstream economics. Its theoretical and regulatory ideal is the elimination of agency problems by perfect mechanisms. In keeping with this tradition, the recent re-introduction of elements of agency-sensitive/contested exchange by way of concepts such as incomplete contracts was countered by models addressing contract incompleteness and non-verifiable information by way of clever mechanisms (see e.g. the literature on subgame-perfect implementation)[8]. Interestingly, recent work of experimental economists sheds light on a specific aspect of the reason why this may not be possible: *reciprocity and gift exchange behaviour preclude the solution of problems of incomplete contracts by "perfect" mechanisms* (see Fehr, Michael, and Tom 2015 for a

8 Conditions responsible for contract incompleteness are related to relevant circumstances which are observable, but non-verifiable to third parties. However, more perfect mechanisms may make everything verifiable which is observable.

succinct summary of pertinent arguments and experimental results). Experimental findings thus reveal a double role of aspects of agency summarised by the notion of "reciprocity", irrespective of whether "agency" is considered as shorthand for behavioural traits or for moral faculties: (1) reciprocity often factually functions as a contract enforcement device helping to solve problems of contract incompleteness. (2) At the same time, reciprocity undermines the solution of those problems by way of perfect mechanisms. This indicates a more profound role of exchange-related agency problems as compared to Friedman (1987). This more profound role reflects intricate interdependencies between contractual efficiency and distribution.

Agency-sensitive "contested" exchange is related to the non-separability of distribution and exchange (or of commutative and distributive justice, as stressed by Chaplygina and Lapidus 2016, p. 24). Friedman's (1987) question may thus be reformulated: Is *distributive* regulation always an obstacle for exchange imposing "excess burdens", or is it rather a facilitating condition? With agency-sensitive exchange, a view of certain distributive norms facilitating exchange becomes available, as those norms are associated with agency-related traits such as reciprocity as part of a contract enforcement mechanism. The practical importance of such insights depends to a considerable extent on the role of indeterminacy or multiple equilibria. In Section 4, we deal with some Scholastic roots of indeterminacy in politico-economic thought.

4. Voluntarism, intellectualism, and indeterminacy

In scholastic socio-economic thought, certain issues of enduring relevance play a role, even though the context of those discussions may have become "obsolete." The previous section brought to the fore issues related to the limitation of the principle of mutual benefit invoking will, power and agency. Agency implies the dimension of knowledge problems: what is known by whom, and what can be known by whom? Modern theories of incomplete contracts and contested exchange stress the difference between observable and verifiable information: incompleteness and the contested character of exchange is associated with observable information which is not verifiable vis-à-vis third parties.

As already indicated, the status and relevance of agency problems is associated with the issue of indeterminacy. For the sake of simplicity, the basis and scope of indeterminacy in intellectualism and voluntarism will first be discussed independently of economic agency problems. However, in Section 5 it will be argued that foundational perspectives related to different views of indeterminacy may have implications for the envisaged mode of regulation, if combined with certain assumptions on agency. Here is a brief summary of the theological differences between intellectualist and voluntarist scholastic thinkers. The intellectualists (the most prominent among them is Aquinas) emphasised the role of laws by which God governs the universe. Those laws are not subject to change: God and humans are bound by them. They are not to be altered even by God's will. Human intellect is, in principle, capable of knowing those laws, even though this knowledge is imperfect here and now. Hence intellectualists often emphasise the role of theoretical knowledge as a tool for discovering those unique laws. In contrast, the voluntarists (amongst them Duns Scotus[9] and Ockham) stressed the sovereignty of God's *will.* As it is sometimes put, they believed the will to be nobler than the intellect. There is some discussion regarding the precise meaning of God's sovereignty in that context and the potential "arbitrariness" of His decisions. We need not go into those issues here. Anyway, voluntarists were able to accommodate (a) notions of indeterminacy and (b) the role of empirical contingencies and empirical knowledge (given the limits of human reason assumed by such views) in a more straightforward and systematic way.

The voluntarism-intellectualism divide and its possible influence on developments in science, political theory and economics are referred to in various contexts, including

(1) Occasional references to voluntarism in the history of economic thought literature (e.g. Wilhelm Weber 1959 with reference to Molina; Fanfani 2011; Kaufer 1998). All in all, those references raise further questions, as they do not converge to a common view (see also Langholm 1998, p. 176 with reference to Fanfani).
(2) In his history of the development of modern moral and political theory, J.B. Schneewind (1998) attributes a prominent role to the theological outlooks of intellectualism and voluntarism. In that context, thinkers who are crucially important for the mental models of modern economics such as Hobbes, Pufendorf, Nicole, Locke, Newton, Hume, Smith and Bentham are discussed. Considering Langholm's (1998) discussion of Hobbes as "the antithesis" (opposing representative scholastic currents) in combination with Schneewind's (1998) emphasis of Hobbes's voluntarist roots is particularly instructive. Schneewind

9 For analyses of Duns Scotus's voluntarism, see e.g. Prentice (1968), Schneewind (1998) and Williams (1997), who contextualises his views on the role of reason within morality with regard to his voluntarism, and Ward (2017), who argues that his conceptions of merit and satisfaction are conditioned by two foundational commitments, voluntarism and his "Franciscan thesis" with regard to the problem of sin.

also discusses the application of "experimental philosophy to moral subjects" (suggested by Hume 1739/40) as the culmination of a quasi-voluntarist tradition expanding its scope beyond theology.

(3) In the history of science literature, scholars such as John Henry (2008) put forward a voluntarism-and-science thesis stressing the role of voluntarism in the development of modern science and empirical methods, while earlier writers such as Lovejoy (1936) had defended an intellectualism-and-science thesis. Harrison (2002) stresses the Augustinian tradition emphasising the epistemic imperfection of humankind after the Fall: after the Fall, humankind must rely on the cumbersome collection of empirical knowledge. Notice that the Augustinian heritage (via Jansenism) plays also a role regarding some roots of economic thought (see Faccarello 2014; Schneewind 1998 on Jansenism and its influence on social theory, including Nicole, Boisguilbert, and Mandeville). Some thinkers (including the protagonists of the reformation) seem to have been influenced both by voluntarist *and* Augustinian thought. As stressed by Henry (2009), the influences of Franciscan voluntarism and the Augustinian tradition may be seen as complementary.

(4) Some authors argue that modernity as a broader phenomenon rests on theological rather than secular foundations, invoking in particular voluntarism and nominalism. According to Gillespie (2009), William of Ockham and John Duns Scotus are main influences. Charles Taylor's *A Secular Age* (2007) and Milbank's (2005) *Theology and Social Theory* make similar points, emphasising the role of Franciscan thought with regard to the context of the roots of individualism and anthropocentrism. Classics of this kind of literature include Schmitt (1922) and Richard Weaver's (1948) *Ideas Have Consequences* with their markedly critical outlook on modernity and its tensions.

(5) Nominalism is looming large in Karl Popper's and Karl Pribram's writings as important co-ordinate for modern scientific thinking. Pabst (2017) invokes the combination of nominalism and voluntarism as the pivot for modern thinking with respect to contract, the economy and the international order. While nominalism is sometimes taken to be associated with voluntarism, the case of Duns Scotus (who was a voluntarist of sorts, but endorsed "Scotistic realism" with regard to universals) suggests caution. The dichotomy nominalism vs. essentialism is used by Popperian historians of thought for systematising economic thought up to the twentieth century. Along similar lines, Pribram's (1949, 1983) *History of Economic Reasoning* is mainly organised along the nominalism-universalism divide.

The voluntarism-and-science thesis invites the question of the plausibility of a parallel thesis related to economic analysis. However, a specific difficulty must be taken into account here: influences may occur at multiple levels and hence in the end may be more ambiguous. At a first level, when considering economics as a science paralleling the natural sciences, voluntarism may be associated with the role of empirics. However, the role of empirics in the history of economics is itself a difficult issue, given the disputes about universally valid theoretical knowledge, and at which levels it may or may not be challenged by empirics. At a different level, voluntarism is intricately associated with "political interventionism" (see Fanfani 2011 and 1935, p. 90ff). At a third level (which is most important in the present context), voluntarism may be associated with the role and degree of indeterminacy in economic theories. Aquinas, the most important thinker in the intellectualist tradition, accommodates some degree of indeterminacy (*latitudo).* Regarding exchange, the Divine law imposes tighter constraints than positive law, which is just ruling out *laesio enormis.* However, even in his theory of commutative justice subject to the Divine law, the just price may only be estimated with some latitude[10]. While accommodating the role of estimation instead of perfect knowledge, Thomas' intellectualism is nevertheless associated with theoretical concepts supporting the notion of unique socio-economic "equilibrium" conditions, determining some institutional structures and the basic patterns of exchange relations. However, this has to be reconciled with the observable variability of positive law, institutions, and of market prices. In intellectualist frameworks this variability can be made sense of by invoking lack of epistemic perfection and changing circumstances. But some degree of tension remains. As summarised by Weber (1959, p. 83), Aquinas's passages referring to the variability of social and economic institutions stand unconnected ("unüberbrückt") to passages in which the

10 "... the Divine law leaves nothing unpunished that is contrary to virtue. Hence, according to the Divine law, it is reckoned unlawful if the equality of justice be not observed in buying and selling: and he who has received more than he ought must make compensation to him that has suffered loss, if the loss be considerable. I add this condition, because the just price of things is not fixed with mathematical precision, but depends on a kind of estimate (non est punctualiter determinatum, sed majus in quadam aestimatione consistit), so that a slight addition or subtraction would not seem to destroy the equality of justice" (Summa Theologiae, 2, 2, 77, 1 ad 2; cf. Kaye 1998, p. 99 and Kaye 2014, ch. 2). For the thinkers under consideration, the concept of latitude plays a role beyond the economic context – *latitudo entium* and *qualitatum*; cf. Kaye 1998, pp. 183–90): perfect determination is more generally substituted by estimation – *quadam aestimatione.*

derivation of *jus gentium* on the basis of eternal principles of natural law by means of reason and logic is emphasised[11].

Weber (1959) compares those views on indeterminacy with voluntarist views put forward by Spanish authors such as Molina. Molina wrote three centuries after Aquinas, but Weber's comparison is nonetheless instructive: Molina develops a framework where it becomes understandable why voluntarism matters for social theory: it leaves more room for empirical contingencies influencing institutional patterns under specific historical circumstances as well as for contingencies influencing prices and outcomes of market exchange. Weber's interpretation seems to be in line with more recent work on Molina and his counterfactual reasoning, his conceptualisation of possible worlds and his idea of middle knowledge or "scientia media" (see Alonso-Lasheras 2011).

To sum up: Theorists with intellectualist mental models tend to think of latitude as a problem of knowledge subject to improvement, whereas for voluntarists the core of latitude is related to properties of the world[12]. Those foundational views have practical implications. Consistent with a more radical view of indeterminacy, Molina for instance explicitly rejects the family subsistence wage (which requires knowledge of an encompassing socio-economic equilibrium including the reproductive properties of the system!) as anchor of wage justice[13]. However, he thinks that *asymmetri-*

11 An interesting intermediate position was developed by some of the Spanish Jesuits. Schneewind (1998, p. 59) and Weber (1959, p. 83) summarize the way in which Suarez reflects upon the premises and the implications of the specifically contingent characters of jus gentium and of positive law. In this context, Suarez develops an approach for a systematic justification of quasi-natural law vis-à-vis contingent and variable normative institutions.

12 Weber (1959, p. 114) refers to a kind of epistemological indeterminacy concerning pretium justum – in a passage quoted by von Hayek (1973, p. 21). "Only de Lugo holds that there is a pretium justum mathematicum, licet soli Deo notum". In contrast, the voluntarist Molina conceives of latitude as a property of the real world and not merely as a result of epistemological imperfection. Interestingly, Hayek (1973, p. 21) emphatically refers to Lugo in his attempt to recruit the Salamanca School for an intellectual family tree of theories of spontaneous order favoured by himself. Notice however that the thinkers related to the Salamanca School are not homogenous (see, for instance, Azpilcueta 2004). Lugo holds that unique just prices exist – but knowledge of the unique equilibrium price system is not accessible to men. Weber (1959, p. 114) emphasizes that Molina's reference to the multiple contingencies of the real world implies a much more encompassing set of "natural" reasons conditioning indeterminacy.

13 As repeatedly stressed by Molina, there are circumstances in which workers accept wages insufficient for their families' and even for their own individual reproduction, without implying injustice. "Molina wiederholt [...] dreimal, dass es viele Arbeiter gebe, die sich gern für einen Lohn verdingen, der nicht zu

cal starting positions of exchange (extreme inequities including monopolies, information asymmetries) may limit to the legitimacy-conferring effect of consent in contractual exchange. Information about such asymmetries does not presuppose such far-reaching knowledge of an encompassing equilibrium.

Differences in the determination of the just price between different strands of scholastic thought thus include different views:

(1) Concerning existence and degree of indeterminacy.
(2) The role of human reason and knowledge in equilibrating processes.

All this is related to a different way of conceptualising the relations between natural law, *jus gentium*, Christian morality and the prevailing politico-economic state of affairs. The different views prepare the ground for different theoretical approaches with respect to the role of just regulation in socio-economic systems remaining important throughout the modern era.

5. Regulatory perspectives

Fanfani (2011) associates voluntarism with currents of thought emphasising deliberate regulation aiming at economic progress. Lacking the perspective of a rational natural economic order, they are protagonists of a civilisation deriving its guiding principles from modernist rationalism[14]. In Fanfani's reading, this tendency includes post-scholastic currents of economic thought before Adam Smith such as mercantilism as well as interventionist currents of twentieth century institutionalism. In contrast, Erich Kaufer, Wilhelm Weber and others stress liberalistic tendencies of thinkers endorsing a voluntarist view. Considering the arguments of the previous sections, it is problematic to straightforwardly associate certain principles of regulation (for instance, a libertarian stance emphasising self-regulating mechanisms of the market) with one of those theological doctrines. With the background of both co-ordinates introduced in this essay, we may suggest an interpretive scheme with four possible combinations: (1) the absence of specifically exchange-related problems of economic agency combined with intellectualism is compatible with a view of the economic domain as a sub-ordinate sphere. Its relevant ends and virtues are *not* associated to its own logic, but are derived from some extra-economic social

ihrem Lebensunterhalt und noch weniger zum Lebensunterhalt ihrer Familie ausreicht. Dennoch ist dieser Lohn nicht ungerecht" (Weber 1959, p. 139).

14 See footnote 4. Cardinal Joseph Höffner (1955) is another prominent catholic intellectual emphasising early cases of the association of voluntarism and interventionism.

"equilibrium." This may support the conservative and static social policy described by Johnson (1938) as the outcome of the scholastic doctrine of just price. Notice that Aristotelian and scholastic versions of such views include human virtues as a part of economic practice: economic practices are subsumed under a virtue-ethical perspective including standards of craftsmanship as well as distributive standards guiding transactions. This contradicts a purely instrumental view of the economic sphere: a morally embedded market is not a mere instrument, but an integrative part of a unique social "equilibrium" realising the good live not only by way of decent outcomes for all, but also of decent procedures. Hence concerns with regard to the proper scope and limits of markets ("Not everything ought to be for sale!") are also most naturally expressed in such a framework. (2) The combination of agency-sensitive exchange with intellectualism is exemplified by the idea of exchange-enhancing reduction of the costs of private transactions as spelt out by Friedman (1987). In the background of such reasoning, a unique all-encompassing socio-economic "equilibrium" is assumed, excluding distribution as a genuine problem. To be sure, local bargaining indeterminacies are crucial for Friedman's scenario. However, those indeterminacies are caused by contingent imperfections and not by more fundamental problems. Anyway, the realisation of the equilibrium needs continuous "help" by agents guided by exchange-supporting "bourgeois" virtues, as long as economic interactions are complicated by specific market imperfections associated with agency-problems. Along such lines, a market-oriented version of virtue-ethics may be "reclaimed for economics" (see Bruni and Sugden 2013) (3) When voluntarism is combined with the *rejection* of agency-sensitive exchange, we are confronted with what Langholm (1998) described as Hobbes's antithesis to scholastic thought on agency-sensitive regulation. Hobbes recognises the analogy between coercion by (i) physical force/threats and (ii) asymmetric socio-economic conditions of exchange (as is aptly pointed out by Langholm 1998, p. 152), but deals with it in a radical way: unless some form of coercion is ruled out as "unjust" by positive law, (i) is (or ought to be) as irrelevant as (ii)! Put another way, modern societies need a clear-cut system of enforceable rules, eliminating the need for appeals to moral agency in whatever form: perfect markets may be envisaged as "morally free zones" (Gauthier 1986, ch. 4). Along those lines, Hobbesian reasoning leads to the ideal of a once-and-for-all model of regulation, similar to theoretical models assuming "solved political problems", as summarised by Lerner (1972). Deliberate regulation may take a minimalist form (as expressed by Hobbes's thoughts on "Distributive Justice, the Justice of an Arbitrator" [Leviathan I, 15], which is confined to preserving peace). However, this model also offers the perspective of some normatively guided "choice of distribution" and a purely instrumental view of the market as a mechanism for implementing more far-reaching political or ethical goals[15]. (4) The combination of *voluntarist emphasis on indeterminacy* and agency-sensitive exchange leads to the most interesting architecture. To see why, we return for a moment to some premises and implications of Friedman's (1987) argument relating the just price as a device for "lowering transaction costs." It is assumed that *difficult conditions of exchange are exogenous, accidental and in principle eliminable distortions* – mostly obtaining in an early and rude state of the market economy. "Decentralized" regulation based on the just price helps under those circumstances. However, institutional development should make the *system of property rights and contract law ever more perfect, eliminating* difficult conditions of exchange and eventually *supporting a complete web of (quasi-)contractual relations.* Market failures may be addressed by creating additional property rights and additional markets. Progress is associated with the idea of transforming more and more unsolved political problems (which contaminate the sphere of exchange) into economic transactions.

As stressed above, an efficiency-oriented view à la Friedman is dubious as an interpretive framework for scholastic economic thought. However, taking on board the basic idea of contractual agency problems associated with the concept of transaction costs is useful: the ethical doctrine of the just price may indeed have had the function of facilitating exchange, even though it had been developed in a context which had no conceptual space for "a device to promote efficiency." Over and above that, we may try to develop Friedman's idea in the context of broader classes of perennial agency problems, thus establishing an interpretive framework for developments in economic thought for which combining issues of distributive and commutative justice is essential. This is provided by an agency-sensitive vision of regulation operating under conditions of latitude (indetermi-

15 Such an instrumental view of the market also plays a role in some "neo-liberal" approaches of governance *by* market mechanisms, or by mechanisms mimicking the market. The critics of "neo-liberal" governmentality emphasise that this may go along with transferring issues into the realm of the impersonal forces of markets that are inextricably intertwined with power: neo-liberal governmentality hence provides mechanisms for steering clear of political accountability. However, not all currents of thought in the wider family of "neo-liberalism" endorse such views. For instance, David Friedman's market anarchism indeed seems to be based on combination (2), while some forms of market fundamentalism imply (1), claiming that pure market interactions (and not something like the polis) are necessary and sufficient for realizing all important values in human life. This diversity (including three of the four foundational combinations sketched here) may be a source of the currently much-discussed resilience of "neo-liberalism" in the face of major crises (see e.g. Mirowski 2013).

nacy): the conditions responsible for contract incompleteness are not phenomena of the past vanishing with modern capitalism. They rather emerge endogenously and remain permanent challenges. Concomitant problems cannot be mitigated by institutional frameworks and mechanisms, but remain intertwined with "political" micro-processes of exchange. The combination of agency aspects and indeterminacy moreover provides the basis for thinking about equilibrium selection problems. This offers the perspective of "choice" with regard to regulatory frameworks. This "choice" is likely to be related to issues of power and distribution. If this is the case, it will be no longer plausible to steer clear of distributive justice.

Pertinent insights were put forward in traditions in economics which for a long time were strangely marginalised – even though that tradition includes some of the classics up to John Stuart Mill. More recent articulations of the points important for those traditions are provided by Bowles's and Gintis's "contested exchange" (e.g. 1993b; see also Sturn 2009), along with important strands of modern behavioural economics and the institutionalists discussed by Langholm (1998, p. 178ff). A specifically important class of arguments related to complexities of market regulations are concerned with the market-mediated utilisation of labour power. As indicated above, some of the ingredients needed for discussion of those issues had a place in the writings of scholastic authors, culminating in the oeuvre of writers such as Francisco de Vitoria (see Langholm 1998, pp. 118–36 and Sturn 2009). Corresponding concepts of regulation (including labour legislation and social policy) can neither be based on the idea that the market is regulated in the name of extra-economic ideals nor on the idea that the *only* goal of regulation is economic efficiency. Moreover, as regulation includes dealing with distributive background conditions of exchange beyond mere market imperfections, it cannot be reduced to rules and mechanisms creating a sphere of "solved political problems" where agency problems are neutralised.

By way of conclusion, here is a caveat. As argued above, some elements of contested exchange played a role in scholastic regulatory thought. However, it is not useful to talk of this thought as having anticipated modern currents emphasising contested exchange, such as institutionalist economics. In terms of a framework for understanding the scholastic literature, Hobbesian thought may function as an antithetical point of reference, as stressed by Langholm (1998). With regard to seemingly congruent strands of thought, one ought to be more cautious. Instead of talking of "anticipation", decomposing doctrines and comparing crucial ingredients makes more sense, at least if we wish to distinguish between perennial problems and context-specific theorisations, and to avoid overhomogenisation while at the same time being aware of the common perspectives of the era under consideration.

Acknowledgements

A first version of this paper was presented at a Workshop Theology and Political Economy at Triangle, Lyon. I thank Gilbert Faccarello, Ragip Ege; Peter Koller, Lara Pittrich, two referees for EJHET and the participants of the seminar for critical remarks and Ernst Fehr for directing my attention to experimental work on subgame-perfect implementation.

Disclosure statement

No potential conflict of interest was reported by the author.

References

Alonso-Lasheras, D., 2011. *Luis de Molina's De iustitia et iure: justice as virtue in an economic context.* Leiden: Brill.

Azpilcueta, M. de, 2004. Commentary on the resolution of money. *Journal of markets and morality*, 7, 171–312.

Basu, K., 2007. Coercion, contract, and the limits of the market. *Social choice and welfare*, 29, 559–79.

Binmore, K., 2005. *Natural justice.* Oxford: Oxford University Press.

Blomquist, T., 1975. De Roover on business, banking, and economic thought. *Journal of economic history*, 35, 821–30.

Bowles, S., 1985. The production process in a competitive economy: Walrasian, neo-Hobbesian, and Marxian models. *American economic review*, 75 (1), 16–36.

Bowles, S. and Gintis, H., 1993a. A political and economic case for economic democracy. *Economics and philosophy*, 9 (1), 75–100.

Bowles, S. and Gintis, H., 1993b. The revenge of homo oeconomicus: contested exchange and the revival of political economy. *Journal of economic perspectives*, 7 (1), 83–102.

Brentano, L., 2003. *Konkrete Bedingungen der Volkswirtschaft.* Ed. by H.G. Nutzinger. Marburg: Metropolis. [Original: Leipzig, Felix Meiner 1924].

Bruni, L. and Sugden, R., 2013. Reclaiming virtue ethics for economics. *Journal of economic perspectives*, 27 (4), 141–64.

Chaplygina, I. and Lapidus, A., 2016. Economic thought in scholasticism. *In*: Gilbert Faccarello and Heinz D. Kurz, eds. *Handbook of the history of economic analysis*, vol. 2: Schools of thought in economics. Cheltenham: Edward Elgar, 20–42.

De Roover, R., 1958. The concept of just price: theory and economic policy. *Journal of economic history*, 18 (2), 418–34.

De Roover, R., 1971. *La pensée economique des scolastiques: Doctrines et méthodes.* Paris: Librairie Vrin.

De Roover, R., 1974. *Business, banking, and economic thought in late medieval and early modern Europe. Selected studies of Raymond de Roover.* Chicago, IL: University of Chicago Press.

Decock, W., 2012. *Theologians and contract law.* Leiden: Brill.

Emon, A., 2016. Beyond the protestantism of political theology: thinking the politics of theological voluntarism. *Studies in Christian ethics*, 29 (2), 190–201.

Epstein, S.A., 1991. *Wage labour and guilds in medieval Europe.* Chapel Hill: University of North Carolina Press.

Ernst, W., 2014. Mensura et mensuratum. *In*: Hagen Jürgen von and Welker Michael, eds. *Money as God? The monetization of the market and its impact on religion, politics, law, and ethics.* Cambridge: Cambridge University Press, 60–79.

Faccarello, G., 2014. Economics and theology in France in the 18th and 19th centuries. *In*: Oslington Paul, ed. *The Oxford handbook of Christianity and economics.* Oxford: Oxford University Press, 73–93.

Fanfani, A., 1935. *Catholicism, protestantism, and capitalism.* London: Sheed and Ward.

Fanfani, A., 2011. *Storia delle dottrine economiche.* Firenze: Le Monnier.

Fehr, E., Michael, P., and Tom, W., 2015. *Behavioral limitations of subgame-perfect implementation.* https://www.rse.anu.edu.au/media/850901/Wilkening-Paper.pdf Accessed 2 Dec 2016.

Friedman, D., 1987. Just price. *In*: John Eatwell, et al. eds. *The new Palgrave: A dictionary of economics*, vol. 2: *E-J.* London: Macmillan, 1043–44.

Gautier, D., 1986. *Morals by agreement.* Oxford: Oxford University Press.

Gillespie, M.A., 2009. *The theological origins of modernity.* Chicago, IL: The University of Chicago Press.

Gordon, B., 1975. *Economic analysis before Adam Smith.* London: Macmillan.

Hamouda, O.F. and Price, B.B. 1997. The justice of the just price. *European journal of the history of economic thought*, 4, 101–218.

Hardin, R., 2005. *Indeterminacy and society.* New Haven, CT: Princeton.

Harrison, P., 2002. Voluntarism and early modern science. *History of science*, 40, 63–89.

Hayek, F.A., 1973. *Law, legislation and liberty.* vol. I. London: Routledge.

Henry, J., 2008. *The scientific revolution and the origin of modern science.* Basingstoke: Palgrave Macmillan.

Henry, J., 2009. Voluntarist theology and the origin of modern science: a response to Peter Harrison. *History of science*, 47, 79–113.

Hobbes, T., 1651/1985. *Leviathan.* With an introduction by C. B. Macpherson. Harmondsworth: Penguin Classics.

Höffner, J., 1941. *Wirtschaftsethik und Monopole im 15. und 16. Jahrhundert.* Jena: Gustav Fischer.

Höffner, J., 1955. *Statik und Dynamik in der scholastischen Wirtschaftsethik.* Cologne/Opladen: Westdeutscher Verlag.

Hume, D., 1739/40. *Treatise of human nature.* London: John Noon.

Johnson, E.A.J., 1938. Just price in an unjust world. *Ethics*, 48 (2), 165–81.

Kaufer, E., 1998. *Spiegelungen wirtschaftlichen Denkens im Mittelalter.* Innsbruck: Studienverlag.

Kaye, J., 1998. *Economy and nature in the fourteenth century.* Cambridge: Cambridge University Press.

Kaye, J., 2014. *A history of balance 1250-1375: the emergence of a new model of equilibrium and its impact on thought.* Cambridge: Cambridge University Press.

Kuttner, S., 1982. The revival of jurisprudence. *In*: Robert L. Benson and Giles Constable, eds. *Renaissance and renewal in the twelfth century.* Cambridge, MA: Medieval Academy of America, 299–323.

Langholm, O., 1998. *The legacy of scholasticism in economic thought*. Cambridge: Cambridge University Press.

Lapidus, A., 1992. The limits and extent of a retrospective approach in the history of economics: the case of the middle-ages. *In*: S. Todd Lowry, ed. *Perspectives on the history of economic thought*, vol. 8: *Contributions to the history of economics*. Cheltenham: Edward Elgar. 1–18.

Lapidus, A., 1994. Norm, virtue, and information: the just price and individual behavior in Thomas Aquinas' Summa theologiae. *The European journal of the history of economic thought*, 1, 435–73.

Lapidus, A., 1996. Introduction à une "Histoire de la pensée economique" qui ne verra jamais le jour. *Revue èconomique*, 47 (4), 867–92.

Lerner, A., 1972. The economics and politics of consumer sovereignty. *American economic review*, 62 (2), 258–66.

Lovejoy, A.O., 1936. *The great chain of being*. Cambridge, MA: Harvard University Press.

Lucas, R., 2004. *The industrial revolution: past and future*. 2003 Annual Report Essay. Minneapolis, MN: Federal Reserve Bank of Minneapolis.

Milbank, J., 2005. *Theology and social theory: beyond secular reason*. Oxford: Basil Blackwell.

Mirowski, P., 2013. *Never let a serious crisis go to waste*. London/New York: Verso.

Monsalve, F., 2014. Scholastic just price vs. current market price: is it merely a matter of labeling? *The European journal of the history of economic thought*, 21, 4–20.

Pabst, A., 2017. International relations and the 'modern' middle ages: rival theological theorizations of internal order. *In*: William Bain, ed. *Medieval foundations of international relations*. London: Routledge, 166–85.

Prentice, R., 1968. The voluntarism of Duns Scotus, as seen in his comparison of the intellect and the will. *Franciscan studies*, 28, 63–103.

Pribram, K., 1949. *Conflicting patterns of thought*. Washington, DC: Public Affairs Press.

Pribram, K., 1983. *A history of economic reasoning*. 2 Vols. Baltimore, MD: John Hopkins University Press.

Robbins, L., 1932. *The nature and significance of economic science*. London: Macmillan.

Samuels, W., 2005. How I taught law and economics. *Australasian journal of economic education*, 2, 1–54.

Schmitt, C., 1922. *Politische Theologie*. Berlin: Duncker & Humblot. English trans. George Schwab. Chicago, IL: University of Chicago Press 1985.

Schneewind, J.B., 1998. *The invention of autonomy*. Cambridge: Cambridge University Press.

Schumpeter, J.A., 1954a. *Economic doctrine and method*. Oxford: Oxford University Press.

Schumpeter, J.A., 1954b. *History of economic analysis*. London: Allen and Unwin.

Sombart, W., 1916. *Die vorkapitalistische Wirtschaft*. Munich–Leipzig: Duncker & Humblot.

Sturn, R., 2004. Review: Economic governance and law. *European journal of the history of economic thought*, 11 (2), 328–30.

Sturn, R., 2007a. Theologische Konzepte und ihr Einfluss auf die ökonomische Doktrinenbildung. *In*: Harald Hagemann, ed. *Schriften des Vereins für Socialpolitik: Studien zur Entwicklung der ökonomischen Theorie XXIV*. Berlin: Duncker & Humblot, 93–119.

Sturn, R., 2007b. Gerechter Preis und Marktpreis. Zur Interdependenz von Religion, Ökonomie und Sozialtheorie. *In*: *Jahrbuch für normative und institutionelle Grundlagen der Ökonomik* 6: *Ökonomie und Religion*, 89–112.

Sturn, R., 2009. Volenti non fit Iniuria? Contract freedom and labor market institutions. *Analyse und kritik*, 31, 81–99.

Taylor, C., 2007. *A secular age*. Cambridge, MA: Harvard University Press.

Trusen, W., 1997. *Gelehrtes Recht im Mittelalter und in der frühen Neuzeit.* Bibliotheca Eruditorum 23. Goldbach: Keip Verlag.
Vaarkemaa, J., 2011. *Conrad Summenhart's theory of individual rights.* Leiden: Brill.
Ward, T., 2017. Voluntarism, atonement, and Duns Scotus. *The Heythrop journal*, 58, 37–43.
Weaver, R., 1948. *Ideas have consequences.* Chicago, IL: University of Chicago Press.
Weber, W., 1959. *Wirtschaftsethik am Vorabend des Liberalismus.* Münster: Aschendorffsche Verlagsbuchhandlung.
Williams, T., 1997. Reason, morality, and voluntarism in Duns Scotus. *Modern schoolman*, 74, 73–94.

Abstract

The socio-economic reasoning of the schoolmen originated from heterogeneous roots and influences and developed over centuries. This is reflected in divergent interpretations of scholastic economic thought. Two conceptual coordinates are used to put those discussions into a common perspective: (1) the distinction between agency-sensitive vs. agency-neutral exchange; (2) the divide between intellectualism and voluntarism. While focussing important theological influences on key issues of economic thought, this allows for a critical account of continuity of problems, while at the same time taking seriously the profound transformation of knowledge systems since the scholastic era.

The concept of "lawfulness" in economic matters. Reading Ibn Rushd (Averroes)

Ragip Ege

When reading the writings of medieval theologians on economic matters one striking point is how they systematically refer to the conceptual opposition between "licit" and "illicit" or "lawful" and "unlawful." The doctors' reasoning and argumentation, as a whole, are conducted in order to identify whether a given economic phenomenon meets the required standards. Is the studied economic topic, namely sale, purchase, loan, profit, interest, enterprise, partnership, association, agreement, contract, etc., allowed, authorised or is it not? Any economic act must be evaluated as being allowed/forbidden, authorised/prohibited, licit/illicit, legal/illegal, valid/invalid, acceptable/unacceptable, good/bad. The ideas of twelfth century Muslim theologian Ibn Rushd (1126–1198),[1] with regard to economic matters, respect the same

1 Ibn Rushd (ابن رشد; known as Averroes in Latin world) was Aristotle's great Commentator in twelfth century Andalusia. He was the Cadi (قاضي *qâḍî*: judge or magistrate) of Seville and Cordoba. He experienced the serious ups and downs during his public career (see Renan 1852, p. 44 and following). In European universities, his name is associated to his reading and rational exegesis of Aristotelian philosophy. In the thirteenth century his commentary of Aristotle is known as "Averroism". Ernest Renan notes that Ibn Rush had a boundless, quasi "superstitious" admiration for Aristotle: "Aristotle's doctrine, says Ibn Rushd, is the sovereign truth; because his intelligence was the limit of human intelligence (…) Before he (Aristotle) was born, nature was not yet accomplished" (quoted by Renan 1852, pp. 78–9). It is highly significant that Ibn Rushd did not know Greek; he read Aristotle in Arabic translations performed essentially from Syriac. This shows that at his time a great part of Aristotle's work was available in Arabic which allowed him to become the most famous specialist of Aristotle without knowing the language of the philosopher. Ibn Rushd is a typical representative of the universal spirit of the Middle Ages. His work is extremely rich

rationale. The major concept of his full argument on economic facts is the concept of جائز *jâ'iz*,[2] admissible, authorised, licit, allowed, lawful, possible, derived from the linguistic root جاز *jâza,* meaning "to traverse, to pass through." Ibn Rushd's questioning is pursued in order to examine whether a given economic act is conform to the standards of what is considered as *jâ'iz*, as lawful.[3] As De Roover points out, the question is "to determine the standards of justice which are supposed to govern economic relations" (De Roover 1971, p. 43). The point is that any economic act be addressed in the frame of ethics.

This paper is a reflection inspired by De Roover's thesis related to medieval economic thinking.[4] De Roover is known to be firmly opposed to the condescending and paternalistic vision of the Middle Ages. He insists on displaying the complexity and rigor of Scholastic Doctors' economic analyses. But we cannot satisfactorily appreciate the Doctors' analytical content without taking into account that their reasoning is driven by the leading concepts of "lawful" and "lawfulness." This statement also goes for Muslim theologians, and particularly for Ibn Rushd. De Roover emphasises especially on the importance that represents the lawfulness of the contract for how medieval thinkers consider lawfulness as being critical in a contract:

> What the Doctors in the Middle Ages were really interested in was to determine the rules of justice governing social relations. (...) The medieval mind was legalistic, and under the influence of Roman law, a great deal of importance was attached to the forms of contracts. The principal problem was always to determine whether a contract was licit or illicit. The emphasis tended to narrow the scope of economics to the

covering various areas as jurisprudence, logic, psychology, medicine, astronomy, geography, mathematics, physics, and obviously economics. There is an immense bibliography devoted to Ibn Rushd and to Averroism; on an indicative basis we may mention: Renan (1852), Gauthier (1909), Leaman (1988), Libera (1991, 2000), Urvoy (1998), Bazzana, Bériou, and Guichard (Ed.) (2005), Benmakhlouf (2007), Tamer (2011), Taylor and Omar (Ed.) (2012), Belo (2013) and a large list of publications on Islamic philosophy in Daiber (1999).

2 For the definitions of Arabic words we refer essentially to Reig (2006), and in some cases to Kazimirski (1860) and to Devellioğlu (1970).

3 The concept of *jâ'iz* is essentially a polysemous concept. But in order to avoid confusion, in the rest of our study, we translate it by the term "lawful".

4 The great place our study makes to De Roover's arguments doesn't mean that the thesis according to which a lawful contract yields a lawful income would be exclusively specific to this author. Such an observation is common to several other specialists of medieval economic life, as Noonan (1957) or Langholm (1992). In the present study we aim to demonstrate that the logic which governs the analysis of lawful transaction or contract conducted by a *Muslim* Doctor as Ibn Rushd is closely the same of a *Christian* Doctor's one at the same time. We estimate that De Roover's quotations we include in our text compared with Ibn Rushd's economic analyses emphasize particularly this proximity.

> study of the legal nature of contracts and their ethical implications, a tendency which reflects itself even in the title and the arrangement of scholastic treatises. (De Roover 1955, pp. 162–3)

De Roover concludes that

> the great difference between scholastic and contemporary economics is one of scope and methodology: the Doctors approached economics from a legal point of view. They attached an excessive importance to formalism, so that the study of economics nearly reduced itself to an investigation into the form and nature of contracts. Because of their preoccupation with ethics the Doctors were also more interested in what ought to be than what actually was. (De Roover, 1971, p. 185)

"What ought to be [rather] than what actually was" is a concern which perfectly characterises Ibn Rushd's thought. In his vision of the world the "what ought to be" also outweighs the "what is." The question is to know what are the criteria on the basis of which this "what ought to be" is established. In other words what are the criteria for what is *jâ'iz* and what is مكروه *makruh* (abhorrent, nasty, detested, hated, hateful, odious, abominable). In the present paper, we endeavour to know the precise content of these criteria. The two following concepts deserve special attention:

- *majhala* مخهلة; uncertainty, from the root جهل *jahala*: to ignore, to be ignorant, to be unaware of, and
- *gharar* غرر, from the root غرّ *gharra*, to abuse, to lose, to amaze, to dazzle, to dupe, to trick, to charm, to mislead, hence "chance"; "luck"; "risk".[5]

When an economic act is stained by these elements or by one of them its legality is partly or totally compromised.

The work which holds particularly our attention here is *Bidâyat al-mujtahid wa nihâyat al-muqtaṣid*, [بداية المجتهد و نهاية المقتصد "*The Beginning for the Exegete (commentator, interpret, analyst) and the Result for the Pragmatic (saver, moderate, average, manager*[6])"], translated into English as *The Distinguished Jurist's Primer* (1994–96).[7] It is generally considered as a treatise of law and

5 "بيع الغرر *bay*ᶜ *algharar* : random, illusory contract or sale; ex. of what is not within our power (as a fish in water or a bird flying)" (Kazimirski 1860, T. 2, p. 446).

6 In Arabic *muqtaṣid* (we translate by "pragmatic") is a derivative of the root قصد *qaṣada*, which means to aspire to, to envisage doing, to intend to do sth, to want, to will, to aim. The concept of "economics", اقتصاد *iqtiṣâd*, is also a derivative of the same root.

7 In the document references to Ibn Rushd's work are indicated as following: (Ibn Rushd, p. X; orig. p.Y), the first number refers to the English translation, the second to the original text. Ibn Rushd's book is also translated in Turkish (Ibn

jurisprudence. This definition however disregards the importance of voluminous parts of the work (entitled "books": كتاب *kitâb* -sing.; كتب *kutub* -pl.), devoted to the analyses of economic problems. Many "books" entirely focus on economic topics such as "The Book of *Buyû*ᶜ (بيوع sales)"; "The Book of *Ṣarf* (صرف exchange)"; "The Book of *Salam* (سلم advance payment)"; "The Book of *Khiyâr* (خيار sale with an option)"; "The Book of *Murâbaḥa* (مرابحة sale at stated cost price)"; "The Book of the ᶜ*ariyya* (عرية advance sale); "The Book of *Ijârâ* (إجارة hire)" ; "The Book of *Ju*ᶜ*l* (جعل wages)"; "The Book of *Qirâḍ* (قراض speculative partnership)"; "The Book of *Musâqâ* (مساقاة crop sharing)"; "The Book of *Sharika* (شركة partnership)".

The major references for Ibn Rushd's analyses are the Quran and the sayings of the Prophet (حديث *ḥadith* -sing.; احاديث *aḥâdith* -pl.). It must be recognised that these references are extremely limited since the considerations of the Prophet Muhammad are based on the modest experience of a small agrarian economy composed of small landowners. We are dealing here with too narrow a framework to nourish and inspire the analyses of an economy far more developed and complex in twelfth century Andalus. The selected examples or evoked standards are frequently incongruous. Therefore, in the present contribution we will keep our investigation at a quite general level, that of reasoning, addressing the logic which governs Ibn Rushd's argumentation.

In our reading we will focus on two issues: the sale and the partnership.

The sale issue

In his work Ibn Rushd devotes the major part of his economic considerations to the question of the lawfulness of the sale. This particular interest of Muslim theologians in the sale could be explained on the one hand by the fact that the Prophet was also a tradesman, and on the other hand by

Rushd, 1991) which added greatly to our understanding of Ibn Rushd's analyses. Our study focuses exclusively on the mentioned Ibn Rushd's text. Our ambition is to *understand*, as far as possible, the content and the criteria of what the author calls *jâ'iz*. In other terms, the field covered by our investigation is rigorously delimited by the Ibn Rushd's argumentation. We aim at an analytical investigation. We don't have any ambition to achieve immediately a synthetic study on the Islamic economic thought in general. The present study is the first step of a research program we would continue widening the scope of the interrogation to the philosophical texts of Ibn Rushd and to the important secondary literature on Islamic economic thought. As regards the very large literature in this area we may mention for information purposes: Essid (1987, 1995), Akalay (1998), Ghazanfar (Ed.) (2003), Thomas (Ed.) (2006), Hassan and Mervyn (Ed.) (2007), Baloglou (2012), and Islahi (2014).

the express warning formulated in the second sura of the Quran (*On the Heifer* البقرة *Al-Baqara*) concerning the prohibition of the interest:

"Those who swallow usury (ربا *ribâ*[8]) will not rise (on the Day of Resurrection) except as someone driven mad by Satan's (شيطان *Shaitân*) touch. That is because they say: 'Sale (بيع *bay*ᶜ) is like usury', but Allah has permitted (أحل *aḥalla*) sale and has forbidden (حرم *ḥarrama*) usury" (The Quran, 2, 275; cf. Ege 2014).

As Noonan rightly said: "it must be clearly understood that there is no scholastic opposition to profit as such. It is only profit on a loan that is condemned" (Noonan 1957, p. 32).[9] As with the other two monotheisms, profit (ربح *ribḥ*) is not prohibited by Islam, quite the contrary. But profit must be licit or lawful. *Ribâ* is prohibited because it constitutes an unlawful gain. The whole question is to know what constitutes the lawfulness of a sale. As noted above, all of Ibn Rushd's analyses on the sale and on other economic topics are conducted on the base of the fundamental difference between lawful and unlawful.

Indeed, from the beginning of his enquiry, in the introduction of his *Book on Sales,* Ibn Rushd formulates the question of sales in terms of lawfulness:

> The discussion of sales is covered in five parts:
>
> (1) the identification of the kinds of sale;
> (2) the conditions of validity [صحيح *saḥîḥ*: authentic, correct, exact, just, valuable, true; hence, جائز *jâ'iz:* lawful] for each kind;

8 There is no explicit difference between interest and usury in the Koranic text. *Ribâ* is from the same Semitic root as Hebrew words *ribbit, ribis* or *ribith.* But the *Old Testament* makes use also of another word to designate interest, *neshekh,* which means also "itching", "bite" or "biting". Calvin, in a famous letter entitled *De usuris* (1545) falls on this term (as other theologians, see Kerridge 2002) and observes that the lender behaves toward his borrower as the snake biting its prey. The use of the word *neshekh* in the *Old Testament* explains doubtless the fact that *Ribâ* is sometimes translated by "bite" (see our analysis on this question in Ege 2014, pp. 410–1)

9 It is important to underline that the profit on loan, that is interest, is prohibited when the legitimacy of the latter depends exclusively on loan itself. As money does not breed (Aristotle), there is no intrinsic title to interest (profit) in a loan. But when legitimacy of the profit depends "on the harm generated by the loan (…) the operation is not usurious. Extrinsic titles aim precisely at identifying this harm" (Chaplygina and Lapidus 2016, p. 35). The invention of the concept of "extrinsic titles" in an operation of lending money is proof that profit is never prohibited by the monotheisms.

(3) the causes of vitiation [فساد *fasâd* : alteration, damage, corruption, confusion, default, depravation, poor condition, immorality, perversion];
(4) the *aḥkâm* [احكام modalities, plural of حكم *ḥukm*: authority, judgment, decision, precept] of valid sales; and
(5) the *aḥkâm* of vitiated sales. (Ibn Rushd, p. 153; orig. p. 536)

The enquiry focuses on the criteria of the sale considered *jâ'iz* or *saḥîḥ*.[10] These criteria must arise from the examination of other four concepts and of how they interweave in different types of sales: "corporeal property", "liability", "immediate" and "delayed".

(1) "Corporeal property" is the English translation for the word عينا *ᶜaynân*, which is a derivative of عين *ᶜayn*, meaning "*eye*"; we can also translate it by "in kind", i.e. what is visible, what is present in "flesh and blood."
(2) "Liability" is the translation of ذمة *dhimma*, meaning caution, conscience, moral sense, guarantee, responsibility, protection, alliance; hence, the idea of a transaction based on the agent's given word and on the liability and guarantee provided by the agent who makes use of this kind of exchange.
(3) "Immediate" translates the word ناجز *nâjiz*, meaning well executed, consumed, complete, whole, entire, perfect; hence, the idea of the "cash sale", a sale "delivered by hand."
(4) Finally the last term, "delayed", one of the fundamental concepts in Ibn Rushd's and generally Muslim theologians' analyses, translates

10 Our understanding of Ibn Rush's argumentation in the present text leads us to consider the concept of *saḥîḥ* (validity) as a synonym of the concept of *jâ'iz*. More precisely, Ibn Rushd's argumentation reveals that the conditions of a valid sale are the same of as those of *jâ'iz* sale: both of them are analyzed on the basis of *majhala* and *gharar*. One of our referees wonder whether we can't draw the concept of *saḥîḥ* - through the meanings "authentic", "exact", "just" its polysemy covers-, closer to reason, in the sense that what is *saḥîḥ* must be consistent with reason. If such a hypothesis is accepted, and in so far as Ibn Rushd is the great commentator of Aristotle at his time, it is possible to draw a parallel between the question of *jâ'iz* and the essentialist approach of Aristotle. "I cannot argue in favor of a transaction which wouldn't be *jâ'iz*, because it would mean that I am arguing against reason" says our referee. Such an interpretation would be in line with our thesis that scholastic Doctors privilege the "ought to be" rather than the "is actually". This observation is highly interesting and suggestive; it opens an exciting perspective of research on the specific signification of the concept of *saḥîḥ* in Ibn Rushd's philosophical texts. However as far as this text is concerned, Ibn Rushd doesn't establish any explicit link between the concept of *saḥîḥ* and the concept of reason or intellect (العقل *al ᶜaql*).

the word نسيئة *nasî'a*, derivative of نسا *nasa'a*, meaning to move aside, to take or to push away; hence, *nasî'a* means purchase credit or forward sale.

In a transaction, the physical lack of the exchanged object and/or the intervention of the temporal dimension as delay will critically affect the "health" i.e. the lawfulness of the operation. These two circumstances introduce an element of ignorance جاهلية *jâhiliyya* and an element of risk, غرر *gharar.* Ibn Rushd says that the legality or lawfulness of a transaction where a visible thing (object) is exchanged for an invisible object or when two invisible objects are exchanged with one another, triggered dissension (إختلاف *ikhtilâf*: divergence, opposition), among Doctors of the law (فقهاء *fuqahâ'*, jurisconsults, scholars, holders of فقه *fiqh:* doctrine, knowledge, jurisprudence) of different law schools. The word حاضر *ḥâḍir,* attending something, current, present, is often found in the texts of jurists as opposed to the word غائب *ghâ'ib,* absent, in absentia, missing:

> The things sold are of two kinds: things present [*ḥāḏir*] and visible [مرئي *mar'iyy:* apparent, viewed, visible, observed], there being no dispute about (the validity *jâ'iz-*of) their sales; and things absent (*ghâ'ib*) or impossible [متعذر *muta^cadhdhir*: unattainable, difficult, impractical, unworkable, infeasible] to see (or examine), in these there is disagreement among the *fuqahâ'*. (Ibn Rushd, p. 187; orig. p. 562)

The discord has occurred on the question of description, وصف *wasf.* If the description of the lacking thing is precise and exhaustive, some Doctors estimate that the exchange could be considered as *sahîḥ* (valid), while others reject the validity of the exchange when it includes things which do not exist but only in the word, whatever the precision of its description (Ibn Rushd, pp. 187–8; orig. pp. 531–2). We observe that the description issue is directly related to that of the information issue. In earlier thinkers' writings, we always find this constant concern to ensure the quality and the wholeness of the information in a transaction, to prevent one or both parties from suffering a prejudice.

> The doubt arises, for those who prohibit hiring, (by looking at) the contracts of exchange (commutative) in which the delivery of the price becomes necessary through the delivery of the subject matter (*^cayn*), as in corporeal things, while the benefits of hiring are non-existent at the time of the contract. This amounts to *gharar* (uncertainty) and the sale of uncreated things. (p. 265, orig. p. 616)

The entirely legal exchange is an exchange which rigorously preserves the interest of both parties. This is why both parties should be provided with all the available information. We must keep in mind that what is at stake here is not the *perfect* information, but the *available* information. There should be no discrepancy between two parties as to the size of the information each one should get. Obviously the question of the information is not limited to the nature and the characteristics of exchanged things; it primarily concerns the quality of the knowledge related to prices. The following passage gives us an idea about the attention jurists pay to motive the question of prices insufficiently known or unknown:

> When one says to the other 'I will sell you this house for so much on the condition that you sell me this slave-boy for so much', al-Shâfi^c^î [one of the great doctors of law, funder of a law school, مذهب *madhhab* : religious denomination, belief, doctrine] stipulates that it is not permitted, because the price (ثمن *thaman*) in both cases is unkwon [(مجهول *majhûl*), from the same root جهل *jahala:* to ignore, to be ignorant, to misjudge, to underestimate]. Indeed if the two things were sold in separated sales, the parties would not agree on the price on which they will agree in a single contract (Ibn Rushd, p. 185, orig. p. 561).

As we can see here, Ibn Rushd's economic reflections, as the ones of other Doctors, *fuqahâ'*, focus on particular cases. In this sense his work is an example of "casuistry." In its common acceptation, the word "casuistry" bears a pejorative connotation; the casuistic thought is supposed to get lost into details, into insignificant peculiarities. But the Doctors were attentive to specific cases because all they cared about in the social activity, and more generally in the social fact, was the abidance to justice and legality. And the just, in ancient Greeks terms, is "what is good for the other." Casuistry is the theoretical genre which is concerned with the defence, the preservation of what is good for the other.

Concerning the non-cash transactions, i.e. the transactions which are not "immediate", *nâjiz*, the Doctors unanimously [إجماع *ijmâ^c^* : agreement, unanimity, consensus] prohibit exchanges for which there is a delay on both sides; in other words, when the payment and the property transfer are both forward contracts. The delay in transactions, *nasî'a,* is an element, which arises great suspicion and questioning among the Doctors. One of the most commented *ḥadith* of the Prophet focuses on this point: "There is no *ribâ* except in delay (*nasî'a*)" (Ibn Rushd, p. 58, orig. p. 539). The delay necessarily introduces uncertainty in the exchange and uncertainty generates risk. Pointing out the Doctors' quasi anxious, i.e. extremely careful and scrupulous questioning, Ibn Rushd shows that they seek to avoid any situation where a transaction is exclusively or to a very large extent based on the sole factor of confidence, often by declaring it non *jâ'iz.* One of the Doctors' main concerns was undeniably the fact that confidence can hardly suffice to prevent the abuse of promises. Therefore a contract based on the sole factor of confidence cannot enjoy of a real stability; at any time there is an unexpected risk of one of the contracting parties breaking his promise and rescinding the contract. A contract to be achieved in the future risks to run an inflation or a trivialisation. However, Doctors' suspicion concerning the time dimension in a transaction, does not exclusively stem from man's versatility, instability or inconsistency. Time per se makes them doubt that anything solid and stable may be built on future promises and conjectures. Hence, their preference for the "present", *hāḏir,* not so much in the modern economic meaning of the word but considering that only "being present" provides a solid base and guarantee for the health of a transaction or a contract. Ibn Rushd writes: "The contract [عقد *ᶜaqd* , de *ᶜaqada* : to attach, to tie a knot, to link] is not valid (*saḥîḥ*) except by the use of the words "sale" (*bayᶜ*) and "purchase" (شراء *shirâ'*), used in the past tense (ماضية *mâḍiya*). The seller says, "I have sold to you" and the buyer says, "I have bought from you" (Ibn Rushd, p. 204; orig. p. 574). One observes that the contractors' physical presence, their explicit recognising of the act of purchase and sale, by explicitly wording it to one another, makes the transaction *saḥîḥ* or *jâ'iz,* transforming it into an act passed and thus achieved. A legal transaction is an operation the accomplishment of which, as an act already achieved, is recognised by the protagonists and attested by their physical presence and by their words. The Doctors "disputed whether sale becomes binding until he (the buyer) says "I have bought them from you" (...) There is no dispute, as far as I know, that offer and acceptance effective for a binding sale are not to be delayed till after the parting from the session" (Ibn Rushd, p. 204, orig. p. 574).

All jurists unanimously agree that a sale, which does not include any delay, becomes a firm agreement. As soon as a delay breaks into an act of sale, i.e. if the word of one of the exchangers or of both of them is only enforceable in the future, the jurists become more and more meticulous and suspicious. This is because a contract, which is not already a concluded and accepted agreement, is exposed to the arbitrariness of contracting parties prone to changing preferences, since they can any moment wish to revise the clauses of the contract. In other words the delay is considered as the intrusion of arbitrariness in economic transactions. The jurists' principal concern is to build and safeguard justice, عدالة *adâlat* (from the root عدل adala, which means to straighten, to make something straight, to treat someone as equal) in exchanges. And justice in exchanges is the exchange between two equal values. Neither of the two partners shall suffer a prejudice. There is justice when the two partners freely agree on the value of exchanged things. Ibn Rushd quotes the 29th verse of forth sura of the Quran (النساء an-Nisâ' *Women*): "Do not consume each other wealth needlessly (بالبطل *bi'lbatili*) but trade by *mutual consent* (عن تراض *an tarâḍin*)" (my italics, p. 208; orig. p. 577). And when this agreement is reached it is highly preferable that the exchange be carried out immediately, without delay. If the completion of the operation is delayed to a future date, the exchange loses its stability. Therefore, each particular case involving a delay must be meticulously examined in order to prevent, at least to minimise the prejudice the contractors could risk as a result of the arbitrariness -which is the other name of uncertainty-, necessarily and logically implied in any further operation.[11]

This is obviously only a wish, the wish for a transaction or a sale perfectly transparent judged as legal by all Doctors. Yet forward sales, credit, transactions delayed to a future date, all are a logical necessity of any common economic activity. No Doctor declares illegal the totality of forward sales. However, they all estimate that each case asks for a detailed examination to identify the quite avoidable though imperceptible intrusion of any degree of uncertainty or ignorance into the contract.

Whatever the situation, as noted before, the Quran says that God has permitted, i.e. has made the sale حلال *ḥalâl*, lawful, legal, honest as opposed to the *ribâ* which is declared حرام *ḥarâm*, unlawful, illegal, and prohibited. The understanding of why the Quran and other monotheisms prohibit interest is complex and asks for multiple, i.e. juridical, economic, as well as institutional and ethical, and simultaneous approaches (cf. Ege 2014). Yet as to why the Doctors show such distrust of the delay, *nasî'a*, it is quite understandable that they judged it naturally reprehensible, condemnable and unlawful. There should be no possibility of gain or profit through the exploitation of the sole temporal factor. Time alone, i.e. the delay, should not generate a gain without making any effort, producing any labour in return. But as God has permitted the sale, the transformation of a loan situation into a sale situation could permit to circumvent the prohibition and to avoid the sin of *ribâ*. Such an operation can only be achieved through the substitution of a forward sale or purchase to a simple money loan. On the base of this stratagem an ingenious form of contract was invented, called *mukhâṭara* (مخاطرة) from the root خطر *khaṭara:* to shake, to

11 One of our referees notes: "Following the author, risk and ignorance are by themselves a cause of invisibility, whereas time generates invisibility only through risk and ignorance". We agree with this interpretation. Time (زمن *zaman* in Arabic, but here نسيئة *nasî'a* -delay), in itself, is not the *cause* of invisibility, hence the possibility of unlawfulness. The latter is the fact of risk and ignorance. The Doctors' mistrust concerns essentially the consequences of possibly risk and ignorance cases, and not the time itself. If risk and ignorance are not involved in the process of transaction (or contract), time shall not prevent the visibility.

sale through a random contract; for instance, a bird flying or a thing which is not owned; to risk; to bet; to pledge): the borrower sells a commodity (for instance a slave) to the lender for cash and he purchases it forward immediately at a higher price; the difference between prices constitute the disguised interests of the transaction. There should be no confusion between such an operation of double sale and the operation of borrowing money to a pawnbroker because in the case of *mukhâṭara* the borrower buys again effectively the object of the exchange and becomes again the owner of it. At the maturity date of the contract he must reimburse the lender in money; the contract doesn't include that in case of a breakdown of the payment the lender will become the owner of the object. This double sale contract was also adopted in the Christian world during the fourteenth century and abundantly put into practice under the name of *mohatara* (in Italia the same type of contract was called *scrocco, barocco, retrangolo, ciavanza* or *rompicollo* – cf. Le Bras 1947, p. 2358). Another form of circumvention of the prohibition of *ribâ* is إقالة *iqâla:* abolition, abrogation, rescission. Anyone having sold an object (for instance a slave) for a certain price, then regretting his act, would purchase it again for a higher price than the sale price. Muslim theologians do not see any reason to doubt the legality or lawfulness of such a practice. These two operations are actually two distinct sales, which explains the concept of "abolition." The restitution of an object at a different price than the one it was previously sold for is considered as a new transaction, which abolishes or repeals the former one (Ibn Rushd, p. 171; orig. pp. 548–9).

The partnership issue

The partnership or association is an issue where the concept of lawfulness is also extremely important. We are expressly dealing here with the question of contract (*ᶜakd*). Any economic act could be reduced to a kind of contractual act; but the contractual nature of an act is much more evident in the case of partnership. This question of contract refers to the fact that the scholastic Doctors in general and Ibn Rushd in particular are attentive to the symmetry of the conditions in which both partners exercise their will. An important distinction is established between "absolute voluntary agreement" and "conditioned voluntary agreement" (Lapidus 1992, p. 44; Chaplygina and Lapidus 2016, p. 31). Concerning the prohibition of interest Thomas Aquinas makes the same distinction in the following terms: "He who gives usury does not simply give it voluntarily, but under a certain necessity, in so far as he needs to borrow money which the owner is unwilling to lend without usury" (*Summa Theologica,* II-IIae, q.78, a.1, ad 7). Here Thomas Aquinas draws attention towards the inequality concerning the conditions in which will is exercised, and thus the conditions of liberty between contractors. The lender is free since his survival is not threatened in the operation. As for the borrower, he is in a position of forced dependence from the lender, in so far as he urgently needs the lent money for survival reasons. It is also this disparity in bargaining powers which seems to justify the prohibition of *ribâ* in the Islamic tradition. With regard to partnership the lawfulness of the contract is also evaluated on the basis of two criteria: *majhala* or *jâhiliyya* and *gharar*. We will examine two major concepts of Ibn Rushd's reflections on this question: قراض *qirâḍ* and شركة *sharika*.

The Book of *qirâḍ* (قراض) defines this partnership as follows: q*irâḍ* "is the giving of wealth (مال mâl) by one person to another saying that he may trade with it (in return) for a defined ratio of the profit (*ribḥ*) that the worker *(ᶜâmil)* earns, that is, a part that is agreed upon by both as a third, fourth, or half" (Ibn Rushd, p. 284, orig. p. 631). The concern is a partnership between capital and labour. It is established that "on the whole, conditions that are not permitted according to all (jurists) are those that lead to *gharar* or to greater uncertainty (مجهلة *majhala*)" (Ibn Rushd, p. 286, orig. p. 632). We are dealing here with two resources of different kinds:

- capital, رأس المال *râ's al-mâl*, this term, literally "head of the good", seems to be the translation of the Greek word κεφαλαιον which means the principal, or capital (from the Latin *caput/capitis*, "head") as opposed to the interests, in a lending operation; and
- labour عمل *ᶜamal*, from the root *ᶜamila* meaning to act, to do, to achieve, to make, to operate. Therefore, one should be careful not to increase the part of ignorance and risk in a contract relating to two different kinds of resources and thus to increase the asymmetry between the contractors' bargaining power: "They (the jurists) agreed generally about not stipulating conditions that may add to the uncertainty of the profit [مجهلة الربح *majhalat al-ribḥ*] or to the risk (*gharar*) that is found in it" (Ibn Rushd, p. 286, orig. p. 632). The question is to know if *qirâd* is *jâ'iz* when the capital does not consist of money but of goods;

> The argument of the majority is that when it is composed of goods it involves *gharar*, as the person takes over the goods when they have a certain value and returns them when they may have another. Thus, capital and profit may be rendered uncertain. (Ibn Rushd, p. 286, orig. p. 632).

In any case one should be careful to preserve the interests of both partners:

> Delayed *qirâḍ* is not permitted according to the majority (...). Those who did not permit it were of the view that such delay is a restriction on the worker, which leads to

additional *gharar*, as the goods may accumulate with him and he may be constrained to sell close to the end of the period, thus exposing himself to harm. (Ibn Rushd, p. 287, orig. p. 633)

The second kind of partnership, شركة sharika, is divided in four different forms:

- شركة العنان (*sharikat al-ᶜinân*) عنان *ᶜinân*, to be associated with someone, to become his partner, for only a part of his good or his gain, jointly buy something;
- شركة الأبدان, (*sharikat al-abdân*), أبدان *abdân,* pl. of بدن *badana,* human body;
- شركة المفاوضة (*sharikat al-mufâwaḍa*), du verbe فوض *fawwaḍa,* to autorize, to empower someone, to delegate, to mandate someone;
- شركة الوجوه (*sharikat al-wujûh*), وجوه *wujûh,* pl. of وجه *wujh:* appearance, aspect, goal, side, direction.

Sharikat al-ᶜinân is the partnership strictly speaking: the two parties bring a capital. The share of profits does not create any problem when each partner brings the same amount of capital to the enterprise. But "the jurists disagreed over whether it was permitted to share the profits equally when the capital contributed was unequal" (Ibn Rushd, p. 303, orig. p. 644). Some Doctors consider such a disposition as *jâ'iz,* some others do not. The question becomes more complex when, apart capital labour also is involved in *sharikat,* in that the partners would bring at the same time capital and labour. Some jurists as al-Mâlik estimate that labour "is to be in proportion to capital, and is not to be taken into account independently" (Ibn Rushd, p. 303, orig. p. 644). This refers to the proportion of capital brought into the enterprise, which will determine the profit part. But others estimate that in the case of *qirâd,* the partner who manages the capital does not contribute to the production other than with his labour, and as such he claims for a part of profit evaluated through a bargaining between two partners. If such an operation is *jâ'iz* in the case of *qirâd,* why not in the case of *sharikat*?

Sharikat al-abdân: association of bodies, in other words of "labor." In general, the jurists (*Mâlikits* and *Hanafits*) recognise the lawfulness of this kind of partnership, but the *Shafiᶜits* are opposed to it. Their argument "is that partnership is specific to wealth and not to work as it is variable, which amounts to *gharar* (…) because the work of each is unknown [مجهول *majhûl*] to his partner [صاحبه *sâḥiba* : companion, fellow, friend]" (Ibn Rushd, p. 305, orig. p. 645).

Sharikat al-mufâwaḍa: association by delegation. In this form of partnership "each partner delegates the undertaking of transactions to the other in his wealth, both in their presence and absence, and this takes place, according to them [Mâlik and Abû Hanîfa], in all their possessions" (Ibn Rushd, p. 304, orig. p. 645). For these jurists, this association is entirely *jâ'iz*. But for al-Shâfi^cî "the term *sharikat* is applied to the mixing of wealth, while the profits are an outcome, and it is not permitted that the outcome be common except by the joining of the sources. If each one of them stipulates, out of his own wealth, a share of the profits for the other, it amounts to *gharar*, which is not permitted" (Ibn Rushd, p. 304, orig. p. 645).

Sharikat al-wujûh: partnership of credit: "This is a partnership based on joining of liabilities (credit) without contributing work or wealth. The argument of Mâlik and al-Shâfi^cî is that partnership is related to wealth or work, and both are lacking in this issue besides the presence of *gharar* because each has delegated (authority) to his partner without qualification of a particular skill or work." However according to Abū Hanīfa, the credit is "a kind of work and, therefore, it is valid to contract partnership with it" (Ibn Rushd, p. 305, orig. p. 646).

Ibn Rushd completes his book on *sharika* with a final chapter entitled "Discussion of the *aḥkâm* (modalities) of the valid (*saḥîḥ*) partnership." He says that the partnership is a revocable contract and not a necessary or binding one; each of the partners can "withdraw from the partnership whenever he likes" (Ibn Rushd, p. 305, orig. p. 646). The contract should ensure the interests of the contractors and it could not restrict the contractors' liberty to withdraw from the contract. Each contractor still retains the right to withdraw from the partnership without consulting the other and getting his consent (except in the case of partnership by delegation). Concerning the question of partnership, we observe that the criteria of the lawfulness of the contract also reside in the notions of *majhala* and *gharar*. This is particularly true in the case of the evaluation of labour regarding capital and thus for the determination of the part the contractor who brings labour can draw from the profit realised in the partnership. When it is a question of labour, immediately a factor of *majhala* is involved. How can precisely be measured the value of such a labour compared with another? How can the contribution of such a labour to the final production, and thus to the profit, be determined? The concept of ignorance is inseparable from the concept of labour and ignorance necessarily generates *gharar*: the contractors run the risk to suffer serious prejudices. A contract exposed to *gharar* must be seriously examined to see if it can be considered as *jâ'iz*.

Concluding remarks

What is there to be learnt from our brief reading of Ibn Rushd's economic analyses? A close look at them reveals that they rigorously cross-check the scholastic Doctors' view on the overall economic reality. The Doctors never conceived this reality as some coherent system, obeying any internal logic, which would make all the elements of the system interdependent from one another.[12] The Doctors' as well as Ibn Rushd's attention focuses on *particular facts*. De Roover expresses it with extreme clarity (in a French written text):

> While modern economists consider the economic system as a mechanism where each element interconnects with the others, this idea is foreign to the Scholastics who addressed other economic issues focusing on distributive and contractual or commutative justice. Their concern is principally centered on examining the validity of a series of contracts, some of them being licit and others illicit (...). They did not take [economic problems] as a whole, but one by one within the framework of contracts seemingly not interrelated and freely concluded between parties. (De Roover 1971, p. 17, our translation)

This observation significantly reflects Finley's judgment on the ancient Greeks' perception of economic problems:

> Of course they [ancient Greeks] farmed, traded, manufactured, mined, taxed, coined, deposited and loaned money, made profits or failed in their enterprises. And they discussed these activities in their talk and their writing. What they did not do, however, was to combine these particular activities conceptually into a unit, in Parsonian terms into "a differentiated sub-system of society". (Finley 1973, p. 21)

In the final analysis, for an ancient thinker such as Ibn Rushd, an economic problem boils down to the nature of the contract. The contract issue addresses the relationship between two subjects or two wills. Therefore, what matters most is the nature, the "health" of that relationship. Such is the "relationality", to put it that way, which did matter to the ancients. The health of a society lies in the health of contracts that bring individuals together. Attention should be paid to ensuring the preservation of the interests of both parties in a contractual relationship. What is just for scholastic Doctors as well as for Ibn Rushd is "the other's good", as ancient Greeks defined justice. If the Ancients' approach of economic phenomena is ethical it is because their principal concern is to avoid that "the other's good" be disregarded. Hence, their extreme concern about the uncertainty and/or risk in a contract. As mentioned above, the

12 Obviously, we do not mean here that the Doctors' conception of the world does not suppose any general order. But the latter is a *moral order*, governed by religious principles which govern also economic activities. What we mean is that medieval Doctors didn't conceive economic activities making up a "sub-system" having its relatively autonomous and coherent principles.

Ancients' writings are casuistic by nature. Their concern is not to elaborate a general theory of the economic activity but to examine the lawfulness, the *ethicity* of specific cases. It is no doubt this concern which led them to focus their attention on *exchange relations* and not on *modes of production*.

The final learning of this brief foray into Ibn Rushd's economic writings is as follows: when we endeavour to reading Ancient thinkers's analyses on economic matters, we progressively realise that the practical reason they all share, whatever their culture or religion, leads them to similar observations, similar results. This reading experience entices us to take some distance from such global and encompassing concepts as the Jewish or Christian or Islamic thoughts or traditions. Indeed, whether they were Jews, Christians or Muslims, when authors tackled economic problems in scholastic times, they felt the need to appreciate them in terms of licit or illicit, lawful or unlawful. What is at stake here is the question of ethics, i.e. the question of justice. And the inquiry we continue in the field of ethics and justice led us to subscribe to the idea that the just, in the final analysis, is "the good of the other", as ancient Greeks formulated (Ege 2009, 2015; Ege and Igersheim 2008). Irrespective of their specific culture and religion, when the Doctors are engaged in an analytical interrogation on the conditions of possibility of a valid contract, i.e. of a just contract, they progressively converge on this ethical principle that the licit contract is the contract which takes into account the good of the other, saying differently, which is found on the "mutual consent." Not only did the ancient Greeks but all thinkers who wonder on the conditions of justice share this same conviction. Divergences arise when it comes to define the *identity* of the "other." We believe that the main question of ethics is: "who is the 'other' whose good matters to me?"

Acknowledgements

I would like to express my gratitude to my friend Daniel Rottenberg who did his best to meticulously and carefully proofread this paper. I thank also my shadow referees for their very useful and constructive recommendations, suggestions and criticisms which allowed me to correct, clarify and improve my argumentation.

Disclosure statement

No potential conflict of interest was reported by the author.

References

Akalay, O., 1998. *Histoire de la pensée économique en Islam du 8e au 12e siècles.* Paris: L'Harmattan.

Aquinas, T., 1948. *Somme théologique: La justice,* vol. I: IIa-IIæ (trans. by M. S. Gillet with notes and appendices by J. Th. Delos). Paris, Tournai, Rome: Société Saint Jean l'Evangéliste, Desclée et Cie.

Bazzana, A., Beriou, N., and Guichard, P., ed., 2005. Averroès et l'averroïsme. Un itinéraire historique du Haut Atlas à Paris et à Padoue. *In: Actes du colloque international organisé à Lyon,* les 4–5 Octobre 1999. Lyon: Presses Univesitaires de Lyon.

Baloglou, C.P., 2012. The tradition of economic thought in the Mediterranean world from the ancient classical through the Hellenistic times until the byzantine times and Arabic-Islamic world. *In:* J.G. Backhaus, ed. *Handbook of the history of economic thought. Insights on the founders of modern economics.* New York, Dodrecht, Heidelberg and London: Springer, 7–91.

Belo, C., 2013. *Averroes and Hegel on philosophy and religion.* Farnham, Burlington: Ashgate Publishing Limited - Company.

Benmakhlouf, A., 2007. *Le vocabulaire de Averroès,* Paris: Ellipses.

Calvin, I., 1545. De Usuris. *In:* E. Cunitz, J.W. Baum, and E.W.E. Reuss, eds. *Ioannis Calvini opera quae supersunt omnia.* Publication Brunsvigae: C.A. Schwetschke, 1863, University of Geneva, Col. Corpus Refermotarum, vol. X, 245–9, Available from: http://archive-ouverte.unige.ch/unige:650

Chaplygina, I. and Lapidus, A., 2016. Economic thought in scholasticism. *In:* G. Faccarello and H.D. Kurz, eds. *Handbook on the history of economic analysis.* vol II. Cheltenham, UK: Edward Elgar Publishing, 20–42.

Daiber, H., 1999. *Bibliography of Islamic philosophy.* vol. 1: Alphabetical List of Publications. Leiden, Boston and Cologne: E.J. Brill.

De Roover, R., 1955. Scholastic economics: Survival and lasting influence from the sixteenth century to Adam Smith. *Quarterly journal of economics,* 69 (2), 161–90.

De Roover, R., 1971. *La pensée économique des scolastiques. Doctrines et méthodes.* Montréal: Institut d'Etudes Médiévales and Paris: Librairie J. Vrin.

Devellioğlu, F., 1970. *Osmanlıca-Türkçe ansiklopedik lûgat.* Ottoman-Turkish Encyclopedic Dictionary. Ankara, Doğuş Ltd. Şti. Matbaası.

Ege, R. and Igersheim, H., 2008. Rawls with Hegel: The concept of liberalism of freedom. *The European journal of the history of economic thought,* 15 (1), 25–47.

Ege, R., 2009. La place de la société civile dans la philosophie politique de Hegel et la question de l'économie politique. *In:* C. Diebolt and A. Alcouffe, ed. *La pensée économique allemande.* Paris: Economica, 27–46.

Ege, R., 2014. La question de l'interdiction de l'intérêt dans l'histoire européenne: Un essai d'analyse institutionnelle. *Revue économique,* 65 (2), 391–417.

Ege, R., 2015. La question de la justice chez Proudhon. *In:* V. Gioia, S. Noto, and A. Sanchez Hormigo, eds. *Pensiero ciritico ed economia politica nel XIX secolo: Da Saint Simon a Proudhon.* Bologna: Societa Editrice in Mulino, 222–37.

Essid, Y., 1987. Islamic economic thought. *In:* S.T. Lowry, ed. *Pre-classical economic thought from the Greeks to the Scotish enlightenment.* Boston: Kluwer, 77–102

Essid, Y., 1995. *A critique of the origins of islamic economic thought.* Leiden, New York and Cologne: E.J. Brill.

Finley, M.I., 1973. *The ancient economy.* Berkeley and Los Angeles: University of California Press.

Gauthier, L., 1909. *La théorie d'Ibn Rochd (Averroès) sur les rapports de la religion et de la philosophie.* Paris: Librairie Vrin.

Ghazanfar, S.M., ed., 2003. *Medieval Islamic economic thought. Filling the "Great Gap" in European economics.* London and New York: RoutledgeCurzon.

Hassan, M.K. and Mervyn, K.L., eds., 2007. *Handbook of Islamic banking.* Cheltenham, Northampton: Edwar Elgar Publishing.

Ibn Rushd (Averroes), [ca 1167] 2007. *Bidâyat al-mujtahid wa nihâyat al-muqtaṣid,* (original text). Lebanon: Dar Al-Kotob Al-İlmiyah; *The distinguished jurist's primer. A translation of Bidāayat Al-Mujtahid.* (translated by K.N. Imran Ahsan), Lebanon: Garnet Publishing Limited, 1996, vol. II; *Bidâyetü'l-Müctehid ve Nihâyetü'l-Muktesid. Mezheblerararsı Mukayeseli İslâm Hukuku.* (translation in Turkish by A. Meylâni). İstanbul: Beyan Yayınları, 1991, vol. III.

Islahi, A.A., 2014. *History of Islamic economic thought. Contributions of Muslim scholars to economic thought and analysis.* London, New York: Springer.

Kazimirski, A. de B., 1860. *Dictionnaire arabe-français.* Beyrouth: Dar Albouraq.

Kerridge, E., 2002. *Usury, interest and the reformation.* Burlington: Ashgate Publishing Limited.

Langholm, O., 1992. *Economics in the Medival schools.* Leiden, New York and Cologne: E.J Brill.

Lapidus, A., 1992. Une introduction à la pensée économique médiévale. *In*: A. Béraud and G. Faccarello, eds. *Nouvelle histoire de la pensée économique.* Paris: Ed. La Découverte, vol. I, 24–70.

Le Bras, G., 1947. La Doctrine ecclésiastique de l'usure à l'époque classique (XIIè-XVè siècle). *In: Dictionnaire de théologie classique,* Fascicules CXLII-CXLIII. Paris: Librairie Letouzey et Ane.

Leaman, O., 1988. *Averroes and his philosophy.* Oxford: Clarendon Press.

Libera, A. de, 1991. *Penser au Moyen Âge.* Paris: Seuil, "Chemins de pensée",.

Libera, A. de, 2000. Pour Averroes, Introduction to Averroes. *L'Islam et la raison. Anthologie de textes juridiques, théologiques et polémiques* (texts translated by M. Geoffroy). Paris: Flammarion, 9–76.

Noonan, J.T., 1957. *The scholastic analysis of usury.* Cambridge, MA: Harvard University Press.

Quran in English and Arabic, Available from: http://www.quranful.com/

Reig D., 2006. *Dictionnaire Arabe-Français, Français-Arabe As-Sabil.* Paris: Larousse.

Renan, E., 1852. *Averroès.* Lonrai, Koutoubia: Editions Alphée 2009.

Tamer, G., 2011. Averroism. *In*: K. Fleet, G. Krämer, D. Matringe, J. Nawas, and E. Rowson, eds. *Encyclopaedia of Islam, THREE.* Online, Available from: https://doi.org/10.1163/1573-3912_ei3_COM_24253

Taylor, R.C. and Omar, I.A., eds., 2012. *The Judeo-Christian-Muslim heritage: Philosophical and theological perspectives.* Milwaukee: Marquette University Press.

Thomas, A., ed., 2006. *Interest in Islamic economics. Understanding ribâ.* London, New York: Routledge.

Urvoy, D., 1998. *Averroès. Les ambitions d'un intellectuel musulman.* Paris: Flammarion.

Abstract

In the Middle Ages the major concept through which economic matters are analysed and evaluated is the "lawful", in Arabic *jâ'iz,* concept. It claims to establish whether a gain, a profit, a contract is lawful or not: that is the main question theologians examine when they are addressing the issue of appreciating any economic fact. In our study, we analyse the criteria of the "lawfulness" as found in the economic parts of Ibn Rushd's work entitled *Bidâyat al-mujtahid wa nihâyat al-muqtaṣid* (English translation: *The Distinguished Jurist's Primer*). Our thesis is inspired essentially by Raymond De Roover's studies on the economic thought in the Middle Ages. De Roover shows that the criteria for lawfulness are to be found in the nature of the contract between partners: a gain is lawful if the contract which generates it is lawful. Our study essentially consists in a text analysis.

The necessity to work, according to John Calvin's duty of stewardship

Caroline Bauer

1. Introduction

Analysing the way Calvin insists on unlimited effort in work in the search for prosperity, while paradoxically condemning the quest for personal enrichment and the pursuit of one's own interests, recent doctoral research[1] has demonstrated that in Calvin's thought, one's duty to work is based on a duty of stewardship. In the present context, this means that every man and woman has the responsibility to act as God would have done in his or her place. The goods which are thereby awarded, and which lead to prosperity, are a sign of the divine providence which requires a just and contented society. Calvin thus affirms, at the same time, a necessity to commit to unlimited work, the importance of the search for individual performance, and a duty of social responsibility.

John Calvin was the first reformer to develop a complete doctrine of the Christian faith from a Protestant point of view. In so doing, he paid particular attention to moral considerations. He praised strong worldly commitment, and consequently assigned a notable importance to the management of goods. Although he cannot be considered an economist, but rather as a preacher and theologian, his fine understanding of economic realities has been pointed out (Hauser 1931, Tawney 1922). Few scholars have deeply examined his social and economic thought,

1 Caroline Bauer, "Work and responsibility according to John Calvin, an interpretation by the duty of lieutenancy," PhD Diss., 2015.

however,[2] even though it is generally accepted that his doctrine contributed to the development of the modern economy.[3]

To this day, insufficient attention has been paid to the Calvinian justification of work, and the literature contains no proposals regarding a general interpretation of his idea of the duty of stewardship which mobilises anthropological, theological, economical, or philosophical arguments. Yet, such an interpretation could lead to a new understanding of the absolute moral necessity to create wealth without enjoying its fruits, and the unlimited injunction to work and reinvest. This article explores his justification for this position, and so draws out the implications for the concept of work from the principles expounded by John Calvin.[4]

Our analysis of this issue leads us to contrast Calvin's own justification of work with Max Weber's interpretation of the later Calvinism in his famous study *The Protestant ethic and the spirit of capitalism* (Weber 2005). The debate provoked by his analysis was huge, as is well known (e.g. Lüthy 1965, Besnard 1970, Disselkamp 1994). It is clear in Weber's text that his project is not to discuss Calvin's thought: indeed, he insists that it is impossible to attribute his description of later Calvinism to Calvin himself, even though he often quotes Calvin, presenting some of his ideas as lying at the origin of ascetic Calvinism. The gap between the early and later Calvinian ethics was already described in Weber's time by Ersnt Troeltsch (1991, 1994), and this opened up an enduring debate: but the nature of the connection between Calvin's own thought and the later ascetic Calvinism described by Weber remains an open research question.[5]

Our purpose is not to evaluate Weber's contribution, but to emphasise the specific nature of Calvin's approach. Weber described a concept of work

---

2 A remarkable exception is a work by the Swiss theologian André Biéler (1959), translated into English in 2005 (2005).

3 In the French theological field, we may mention: Ashley (1966), Biéler (1959), Bolliger (2009), Clavairoly (2010), Doumergue (1917), Hirzel and Sallmann (2008), and Krumenacker (2009).

4 All quotations translated by the author except those from Weber's *Protestant Ethic* and Calvin's *Institutes of Christian Religion.*

5 For example, André Biéler (1959, p. 514): "It is then honestly impossible to attribute to Calvin the responsibility of the evolution of capitalism *in its historic form.* Capitalism was only able to develop under this shape, among the Protestant populations, thanks to a loosening of the reformed doctrine and morality. Nowhere in Calvin's papers or acts, it should be possible to insert, for example, the text of Benjamin Franklin quoted by Weber, without letting appear, in all its violence, the contrast between Calvin's morality and that of the Puritans." Among other contributions, this question has been recently discussed in Willaime in Clavairoly (2010); Körtner in Hirzel and Sallmann (2008). For the analysis of Weber's idea of Puritanism, see Ghosh (2008, pp. 5–49).

rooted in a Calvinist ascetic praxis: yet, our description of the duty of stewardship, set out below, shows that the justification of work in the early Calvinism is based on very different presuppositions from those retained by the later ascetic Protestantism, although some points of convergence can be found.

In first section of this article, we present the principal features of the duty of stewardship according to Calvin's writings. This duty consists in managing all goods so that they testify to the plentiful and generous character of the world as creation. The prosperity thereby engendered should be understood as building towards a fraternal society in which people work for the common good.

In the second section, we draw out a characterisation of work from the perspective of stewardship. The concept of work is based on the necessity to realise cooperation between God and men so as to pursue God's project of a providential, creative and social life. We go on to define the nature of this creation.

In the third section, we list certain points of convergence and certain profound differences between the justification of work in the ascetic Calvinism described by Weber, and that found in our interpretation of Calvin. Our aim here is not to evaluate Weber's description of Puritanism. Our purpose is to show that the concept of work in Calvin's thought relies on theological, anthropological, and philosophical arguments which the account of ascetic Calvinism does not take into consideration.

The impossibility of interpreting Weber's essay as a general definition of a Protestant ethic is well established: even the concept of the "ascetic Protestant" is considered a "purely Weberian concept" (Ghosh 2008, p. 8). It is interesting, however, that the early and later interpretation of Calvinism can both lead to a justification of commitment without limit in work in search of prosperity, alongside a renunciation of one's own interests: yet, the frameworks underpinning these justifications differ profoundly.

2. Stewardship as justification of work

The basis for this analysis of Calvin's thought is the existence of a duty for believers to manage all goods as God would have done in their place, in the service of "the advancement of all the company of the believers in common" (Calvin 1854, p. 525). We call this the duty of *stewardship*. One definition of this term is given in *The Institutes of the Christian Religion*:

> Scripture, moreover, has a third rule for modifying the use of earthly blessings. [...] For it declares that they have all been given us by the kindness of God, and appointed for our use under the condition of being regarded as trusts, of which we must one day give account. (Calvin 1845, bk III, chap. X, §5)

Humans are then the administrators of the goods in God's stead; they hold the place of God, hence the term "lieu-tenant" in French ("holding the place of")[6] to express this duty of stewardship. They will have to report to God on how they discharge this duty.

And "all has been given" denotes the extent of this duty: any good and skill is given to serve the advancement of society. In its continuation, the text specifies that this quest for utility has to "be ordered to the charity": the goods are intended to produce social utility, with a requirement of efficiency expressed by the twice-repeated order to give account of this management.

Another definition in the commentary on the book of Genesis reveals that this duty of administration is associated with the idea of increasing the capacities of production, generation after generation. Calvin remarks on the verse where God gives the order to newly created man to keep and to cultivate the garden:

> that one who possesses a field receives the annual fruit from it so that he does not allow that the fund deteriorates by carelessness, but that he makes the effort to pass it on to those coming after him so well or better cultivated than when he received it [...] that each one thinks that he is the steward [*économe* in French] of God in all he possesses. (Calvin 1978, p. 54 on Gn 2, 15)

The steward has to administrate the properties on God's account, with the aim of increasing the fertility of the land. The duty to increase this productivity is inherent to human nature.

Let us see how the necessity to work is associated with this duty of stewardship. The necessity to work is constantly asserted by Calvin: "Those

6 Because it contains very clearly the idea of "taking the place of", the term "lieutenant" in French seems more adapted to Calvin's thought than the English term "steward". For a modern English reader, the term "lieutenant" is associated with its military meaning, a junior officer, which obviously deviates from Calvin's usage. But according to *The Oxford English Dictionary*, the earlier meaning of "lieutenant" was "one who takes the place of another [...], a representative, substitute, vicegerent" (1989, vol. VIII, p. 909). This sense is cited in examples dated from the fourteenth century to the end of the seventeenth century pertaining to religious representatives. The military meaning of the word, which appeared at the end of the sixteenth century (and so after Calvin's death), has supplanted the earlier one. At the same time, the term "steward", first understood as the official supervising the service of the master's tables, and later becoming an official administrative title, took on after the mid-eighteenth century a dimension of personal responsibility and representation, specifically acquiring the sense of one managing affairs on behalf of a lord or an employer (1989, vol. XVI, p. 665). Because of this inversion of sense, preference is here given to the word "stewardship" to translate the Calvinian lieutenancy.

whom the Lord has chosen and honoured with his intercourse must prepare for a hard, laborious, troubled life, a life full of many and various kinds of evils" (Calvin 1845, bk III, chap. VIII, §1). Nevertheless, Calvin abandons the argument that there is a curse attached to work, and on the contrary develops a dynamic justification of work: work is a way to develop a specific form of cooperation between man and God. Now, even if work is painful, it is a means to choose a life devoted to God: Calvin claims there should be a personal commitment by the believer in favour of work (Cf. Vol. XXVI, Calvin 1863, p. 301 on Dt 5).

At first, at the time of the creation of the world and before humanity was deformed by sin, work was "joyful and pleasant". At this early stage of humanity, "humans were created to employ themselves to do something and not to be lazy and idle" (Calvin 1978, p. 53). Work is part of human nature. To work is the way to recognise divine providence and God's continuous generosity. Creation is then described as a harmonious ensemble, fertile and plentiful. The abundance of goods and the productivity of assets then enter this logic as testimony to the abounding character of nature.

Yet, let us note that even in this perfect order, there is no possible symmetry between God's actions and human action. Man has been created as *imago dei*, but for Calvin this means a "portion" of this image, and indeed a "very small" one. But this very asymmetry gives a foundation to the idea of stewardship: Calvin notes that Chrysostome is right when he "relates this image of God to the lordship which was given to man to be as the steward [Fr. *lieutenant*] of God to govern the world: it is actually some portion of the image of God, but very small" (Calvin 1978, p. 36).

The introduction of original sin considerably increases this distance between God and man. Man is then described as being thirsty for a restoration of the lost harmony (p. 37). Let us note here that this idea of restoration of a lost harmony does not mean a return to a previous order, but rather a progress towards a renewed world where the harmony will have been restored. God continues to be creative through man's work and needs man to realise it. The fruits of labour are the result of this continued creation.

"Only apply to serve me, and let me do", says God according to Calvin, and in exchange "I shall make the whole [creation] produce" (Vol. XXV, Calvin 1863, pp. 625–626 on Dt 1, 3–8). The idea of stewardship is explicit here. God acts through the action of man. Work is a co-creation through which God gives his power of creation to the gesture of man. "God appropriates what he is doing in us" (Vol. XXVI, Calvin 1863, p. 655). The idea for supplying to God what he himself gives us justifies the search for prosperity: through man's work, God both gives abundance and shows his generosity. The steward is thus a representative of God on earth.

Economic prosperity is not an end in itself, and is senseless unless it serves the development of a fully human life for all on earth. We mentioned in the introduction a condition raised in *The Institutes of the Christian Religion* regarding the definition of stewardship: "[God] who approves of no administration but that which is combined with charity" (Calvin 1845, bk III, chap. X, §3). This charity does not only have the sense of the individual consideration of the poor (which Calvin encourages nevertheless), but also means to develop occasions to share the wealth and to multiply exchanges within the human community: it is this charity which is the end of work.

So the responsibility of the steward is to act for social justice: economic prosperity is therefore a necessity in order for there to be goods to redistribute. Nevertheless, Calvin does not call for social egalitarianism. The social hierarchy is a divine order that must be respected. But the more the steward is elevated in this hierarchy, the more intense is the duty to be a steward of God. Growing rich is legitimised, provided that this enrichment is correlated with a stronger service to others and to the community. Calvin understands society as a body where each member is dependent on the others. Society is seen as a body, no part of which can survive without the contribution of others, where each contributes what he has in surplus, to what the others are missing.

Work and the management of tangible assets are also considered by Calvin as a school for leading a spiritual life. Calvin argues that one who behaves in a non-virtuous way in material life cannot reach spiritual wealth (Calvin 1854, p. 372). No action on earth can be separated from its spiritual meaning, and Calvin describes the bad use of goods as a "desecration of the grace of God" (Calvin 1854, p. 627 on Luke 12, 48).

But even here God is at the side of man. When in the book of Genesis God condemns man to get his bread only through the hard work of his hands (Gn 3, 19), although this is a punishment, God "does not consider what they deserved but what will be profitable to them in the future, and therefore he rather acts as doctor than as judge" (Calvin 1978, p. 87). In this way, work is understood in terms of a logic of personal cure (and not of condemnation), of restoration, and of spiritual growth.

The logic of lieutenancy is based on the idea of a necessary alliance between man and God so that life blossoms. This covenant can be lived by various degrees of commitment. The basis of this alliance engages every man, whatever the degree of consciousness he has of it: God by his providence gives all the necessities for life, but in return, he asks man to be an actor in this continuous creation. Man must tend to the improvement of productivity and to the global increase of wealth. The aim of this commitment is to provide a full human life for all. In exchange, God promises happiness, sufficiency of goods, and the contentment of man. Already at this first level, the alliance with God has to be understood by the lieutenant as an alliance with all men, because the project of a fair and abundant society is only possible if man feels dependant on and responsible for others.[7]

The duty of stewardship defines the framework within which the nature of work for Calvin has to be understood. We now focus on the concept of work in order to outline its specific features.

3. The concept of work ensuing from stewardship

As described earlier, the end of work in Calvin's thought is the continuation of God's creative process. Concretely, work is the means ordained by God to create wealth and to jointly implement social justice. And to work in relation with God and others is the only way to be a good steward. We can consequently describe more precisely the nature of work for Calvin. We will successively emphasise the creative character of work, the universality of the concept, and the nature of this creation.

Work is first defined by its creative character. Calvin uses the term "profit" for that which is to be generated, and "fruiting" to describe the results of work. Work appears as the locus of an implementation of God's power of creation by the procurement of a surplus contributing to a general prosperity. But his action is not visible. Human work can then be defined as the action testifying the continuous providential presence of God in the world.

Work is therefore not reduced by Calvin only to the job itself. Calvin understands it rather as in opposition to idleness, which is coherent with the idea of testifying to the active presence of God, refusing the eventuality of an absent God. Work includes therefore all the socially creative activities in life. The care a father takes to educate his children, a voluntary activity, an activity of leisure – any action is work when it may contribute to an abundant and fraternal society. In the logic of stewardship, any

7 This is the universal side of the alliance, which anybody can interpret as the intent of a providential God. But the Scriptures reveal a much larger sense. It can mean an individual call, for the believers, to be faithful to God and let him guide their lives. Confronted with the divine Law, a law of perfect love, humans appear fragile and incapable of doing good by themselves, unable to satisfy their desire of harmony and communion. To the believers, God promises a spiritual regeneration, the forgiveness of sins, and a renewal of understanding. Man's fragility can thus be understood from a perspective of healing.

creative action contributing to harmony and communion between humans is work.

Nevertheless, there is indeed a promotion of the idea of *professions* within stewardship, because a professional activity has the obvious characteristic of returning a surplus, or creating value. For that reason, Calvin often draws examples from the world of the professions to illustrate the abundance of God's creative action through the work of man. The *job* is the most important occupation for men and is an illustration of the dynamics of creation. But it is certainly not the only place where this dynamic manifests itself.

How is this power of creation implemented through work? We can ask, for instance, whether the creative character of work depends on man's action, or rather on a joint but external divine action? In other words, is man alone responsible for setting up an environment favourable to creation? If so, man's action would be only a receptacle of God's grace. Or is this creative character a characteristic of human work? If so, the responsibility of man is to create value.

> Possess the earth. God does not say simply to his believers: come, look at what you can do, examine your strengths, and however he leaves them without support there, no: but he says to them: come to possess. As if he said: only apply to serve me, and let me do: because I shall work such kind that the one who strives to follow me will not lose his efforts, he will not work of one useless labour, I shall make the whole fruit. (Vol. XXV, Calvin 1863, col 625–626, second sermon on Dt 1, 3–8)

This quotation from Calvin's sermon on Deuteronomy shows that cooperation between God and man is to be understood within the framework of a common mission to develop the creation. God and man have *jointly* to "possess the earth." This "co-creation" cannot be understood in terms of parts distributed between God and man, with some efforts – or some fruits – coming from God, the others produced by men. The collaboration is rather to be understood as a joint presence of God's power in any concrete action of man, in any task – in coherence with the idea of an alliance to be concluded. There is no possible distinction between God's part and humanity's part in this co-creative process. Because God is invisible in these acts of creation, the steward, as God's representative, will necessarily have to maximise his efforts to produce as much as possible. From this definition of work proceeds a specific human responsibility to develop the prosperity of society.

This involvement in work is an answer to God's calling. But the idea of *vocation* in Calvin's thought is also more spiritual than a simple assignment to a given job. Calvin distinguishes different senses of vocation. Vocation, in its universal sense, means that every man is called to discover God as the provider of any good. In its particular or individual sense, it means that God calls the believer to faith (Calvin 1845, bk III, chap. XXIV §8) and to live his life in conformity with his faith. In the treatise *On the Christian life*, a part of *The Institutes of Christian Religion* devoted to ethics, Calvin invites each one to recognise his or her vocation, in the sense that each one is called to a life in compliance with God's will (Calvin 1845, bk III, chap. VI, §2). He interprets this calling as an order to accept the social limits of one's life, without any specific mention of profession.

Moreover, Calvin specifies that fidelity in a calling provides the possibility of changing jobs (Calvin 1855, p. 375), even for material reasons, where another job would bring more money and then allow a better life. If Calvin thus grants a certain importance to the vocation, it is because it expresses the necessity of persevering in one direction and of not losing one's sense of life: "Every man's mode of life, therefore, is a kind of station assigned him by the Lord, that he may not be always driven about at random" (Calvin 1845, bk III, chap. X, §6). The vocation helps the believer to persevere in the mission God entrusts, whatever it is.

In the treatise *On the Christian life*, as mentioned earlier, vocation and stewardship are bound together to justify a commitment to work with zeal. Undoubtedly, there is in Calvin's thought a specific Christian understanding of work as a spiritual path. But the call to stewardship is universal and describes the condition of any man, believer or not.[8] God acts through the action of each man. Certainly, he calls the believer to have a specific spiritual attitude: but nothing formally distinguishes the work of a believer from a non-believer. If work aims at providing all the goods necessary for humanity, the believer does not benefit from any particular privilege, authority, or superior knowledge which would apparently make him a better representative of God on earth, or a creator of goods justified by God. The creative character of work applies to any work and the sense of work described here is universal. This understanding of work as universal is in compliance with a very common idea in Calvin's time, that God has installed a particular order in the world which immutably includes the whole of humanity.

We need now to be more precise about the nature of the creation that is attached to work. We noted that, for stewardship, creation is defined as a participation in the acquisition of a general prosperity. Being prosperous signifies experiencing the abundant nature of creation. This abundance is evidenced through the sufficiency of goods, as seen in the first part: in the commentary of the book of Genesis, the creation in Eden, so fertile and

8 In his commentary on the New Testament, Calvin takes the example of the two virtuous men of Antiquity whose lives testified that God acted through them in spite of their absence of faith (Calvin 1854, pp. 498–499 on Mc 10, 21).

prosperous, is presented as a perfect world that man seeks to restore. "We learn here for which purposes all things have been created: so that men miss nothing in all their material needs and in all necessities of their life" (Calvin 1978, p. 37).

The increase of general wealth becomes an aim. But the term *prosperity* is not only understood in the economic sense of an increase of wealth. The true nature of prosperity is linked with the idea of harmony. Thus, the treatise *On the Christian Life* begins with this sentence:

> We have said that the object of regeneration is to bring the life of believers into concord and harmony [*symmetria et consensus* in the Latin edition] with the righteousness of God, and so confirm the adoption by which they have been received as sons. (Calvin 1845, bk III, chap. VI, § 1)

And the commentary on Genesis insists on the universality of this quest for restoration and harmony, because a harmonious world was what God had decided in Eden as the best for humanity. So the quest for harmony is not only a spiritual quest, but has to come about within economic and social life. This horizon of harmony helps us to understand that there is no idea of necessary economic growth in this ideal of an abundant society. The notion of accumulation is absent from Calvin's thought. So to increase the quantity of goods in order to allow a better life for all does not mean for Calvin any justification of a duty to become richer. On the contrary, Calvin asserts that a search for enrichment brings about greed, and greed destroys the harmony between humans:

> And then, let us not try to be rich. Because as soon as this greed to win will be in us, it is certain that we shall become thieves, there is no other possible consequence. [...] miserliness has to be knocked down, that is, the appetite to enrich us. (Vol. XXVI, Calvin 1863, p. 350 and 351)

Enrichment may be necessary to cover all needs. Enrichment itself is not condemned, but *appetite* is, as engendering a search for always more and more.[9] It is thus necessary to learn to be rich, writes Calvin. And this paradoxically means learning to content oneself with what one has – i.e. the contrary to a logic of unlimited economic growth.

> Paul says that we shall have taken great advantage, when we shall have learnt to be rich, that is, when we shall not try to acquire more [...] And then it is not enough

9 "In brief we see that most of the rich, when God would have given them all the earth in ownership, yet it would not be enough" (Vol. XXVI, Calvin, 1863, p. 352).

> that a rich man doesn't desire to become bigger, but we have to be poor in our hearts, that is, that no pride leads us to put trust in our wealth [...] Finally let us be ready to be impoverished, when it will please God. (Vol. XXVI, Calvin 1863, p. 352)

The prosperity that comes out of work is thus not a question of the quantity of goods, but of the quality of relations. At first, we may see only the relations to goods; but the only real good is God's love, and moderation is required so as not to be fascinated by material goods. It is difficult to be rich without idolising goods. The advice given in the treatise *On the Christian life* is first to receive the goods as a gift of God, for our "delight" (Calvin 1845, bk III, chap. X, §2), and second to introduce measure so to enjoy it in full good consciousness. This "measure" is to use the goods of this world as if not using them, according to an expression of Paul's Epistles (§4) (Cf. Dermange in Bolliger 2009, pp. 219, 220). Without praising a renunciation of wealth,[10] Calvin defends a detachment from material conditions. Certainly "the rule for a good use of the gifts of God is sobriety", but the latter consists in finding a "just position toward the goods" (Biéler 1959, p. 215). Being neither strict asceticism nor excess, the just criterion for the use of goods is to remain attentive to the needs of fellow man, in an attitude of renunciation of one's own desires. The prosperity resulting from work is not only wealth, but wealth under the condition of sobriety as a necessary condition to retain one's attention to others. So the quality of relations to goods aims at just relations with others, which Calvin understands as a real responsibility towards others.

We have already noted Calvin's restriction here: "God approves no administration but that which is combined with Charity" (Calvin 1845, bk III, chap. X, §3). Here, Calvin does not mean a duty to distribute alms after having earned some money. This combination of administration and charity is intrinsic to work. We could then define work as acts of charity by means of a creation of wealth benefiting all the society.

That is why Calvin's recommendation to the rich is finally to spend their money. This order is directly bound to the obligation of stewardship which consists in behaving as God would have done Himself, that is in distributing the profits of the wealth produced. Calvin proposes this description of God as a model for men:

10 In *On the Christian life*, for example, Calvin praises the existence of marble, ivory, and gold, because they stimulate an admiration for creation. However, some productions are illicit for Calvin because they do not correspond to the simplicity required by God – for example, certain luxury goods as the refinements of the table and of the garment (Vol. XXVIII, Calvin 1863, p. 33).

> As a man who would think of his household, he will get up every morning to work: and then having made his job, he still looks if there is some rest to set in order: and then he dares to spend what is given to him, so that the profit returns to all his household. So God is as a father for us. (Vol. XXVII, Calvin 1863, p. 105)

So work includes both production and distribution according to the responsibility of being a representative of God:

> All the rich thus when they have enough to do something good, it is certain that they are as officers [Fr. *officier*] of God, and that they exercise what belongs to Him, that is to help their fellow men to live. (Calvin 1863, XXVIII, p. 205. sermon CXLI, Dt 24, v. 19–22)

But, in order to help our fellow men to live, this distribution should preferably not be a direct gift. Calvin understands society as a body within which all the members are interdependent on each other. In that sense, it is more charitable to give work to the poor than to give money, if he or she is able to work. It is also more charitable to invest than to consume, if needs are first covered. So the creation occurring through work is, first, creation of economic activities and implementation of social justice, so that each can become an active steward, and also contribution to a fraternal communion in society.

The creative character of work is fundamental to understanding the concept of work in Calvin's thought. Work, despite its painfulness, is the way to experience God's generosity and to favourably answer the imperative responsibility of acting as God would have done in one's place. Work gives a coherence to the spiritual and material dimensions of life by giving a sense to life in conformity with God's will.

4. Work for Calvin in comparison with an ascetic protestant ethic

We have defined the concept of work in Calvin's thought, describing it as deriving from a responsibility to be a representative of God – a steward – in all dimensions of one's life. In the third section, we now propose to contrast this Calvinian interpretation with the Weberian concept of work, describing an ascetic Calvinist attitude, set out in his famous study *The Protestant Ethic and the Spirit of Capitalism* (Weber 2005). The two understandings find their origins – at least partially – in an interpretation of Calvin. In the Puritan case, Calvin's legacy has been profoundly transformed through time and through a pietistic influence, so it is no surprise to note profound differences in the justifications of work therein. And, methodologically, one account has issued from the analysis of doctrinal texts, while the other is a description of the ideal typical figure of the Puritan animated by psychological motivations sometimes distant from the doctrine itself.

The interest of such a comparison may lie in enlarging our understanding of the influence of a Protestant ethic in the interpretation of work, since, on this matter, Weber's thought is today much better known than Calvin's own. It is therefore relevant to highlight that the Calvinian concept of work, although built on very different arguments, can nevertheless find common points with a later Puritan ethic.

This also leads to our highlighting the originality and also the modernity of Calvin's thought on this subject. A goal in future research should be to furnish a more precise analysis concerning the interpretations of these differences or points of convergence.

We begin by briefly recalling the impossibility of disqualifying any one interpretation of work because of differences in justifications: the reader will therefore have to keep in mind the reasons why we disjoin Calvin's and Weber's perspectives. Second, we will note the similarities in the two attitudes to work according to Weber's or Calvin's position. Finally, we turn to focus on the differences between the two approaches.

It is well known that Weber's objective was not to describe Calvin's ethics, but rather to try to explain the historic coincidence between a sharp sense of business, exercised with virtuosity, and the demonstration by the same people of an intense piety. This combination exists according to Weber where Calvinism dominated and where conditions favourable to economic development were found.

Weber describes the influence of religious ideas, and the way they were able to be transformed into powerful motivations which contributed to the development of capitalism. He proposes an "understanding of the manner in which ideas become effective forces in history" (Weber 2005, p. 48). In that sense, Calvin appears as a theologian who proposed religious ideas which, combined with other ideas pre-existing him, were themselves transformed under the pietistic influence into psychological motivations for a rational control of the thirst for wealth. Weber tries to demonstrate how, through the rational conduct of life, religious motivations were able to overcome the deep irrationality of an unlimited commitment to profit while refusing its enjoyment.

Weber keeps a certain distance from dogmatic theology. On the one hand, he asserts that we cannot abstain from understanding the dogmatic foundations of ascetic Protestant morality in order to understand the capacity of this morality to influence people's behaviour (Cf. Weber 2005, p. 55). On the other hand, he notes that the dogmatic aspects are not handled in an exhaustive way, and will seem "hasty and superficial" (p. 56) to a theologian.

He consciously focused on certain aspects of the Reformation which, from the point of view of the religious consciousness, might seem at least secondary, and for some of them external. It is as "certain correlations between forms of religious belief and practical ethics" p. 49) that religious influences mark the capitalist spirit.

It is also essential to note that Weber focuses on the seventeenth and eighteenth centuries, and not on Calvin's own period; thus, the ideas with which he deals could well have been profoundly transformed through time.

Finally, we note a last gap between the Weberian perspective and that of Calvinian ethics. Weber does not describe the ideas of the whole Calvinist movement but only of a couple of denominations, described as "ascetic Protestantism." As Weber writes, they consist of "Calvinism in the form which it assumed in the main area of its influence in Western Europe, especially in the seventeenth century" (Weber 2005, p. 53), Pietism, Methodism, and churches stemming from Anabaptism. Weber observes that these four movements all endorsed a very rigid moral conduct in life, whatever their dogmatic disagreements may have been.

So Weber and Calvin invite the reader to consider two interpretations of Protestant ethics from two different angles. We will now highlight the main points of convergence in their understandings of work and in the responsibilities attached to work in the two conceptions.

Ascetic Calvinism, according to Weber, seems coherent with the Calvinian ethics when he describes the duty of the believer as being to please God in worldly actions. Weber notes that this is opposed to Catholic thought which valued the search for holiness by detachment from the world, as found in monasteries. Calvin's thought, as we have seen, invites us to adopt a discipline which can be challenging, and to direct all the acts of life according to the duty of stewardship. Work, if understood in the broad sense of a process of economic and social creation, is a necessity in both ethics. From this discipline, a favourable attitude emerges towards the search for profit and economic development. To become rich is a mark of success, in the sense that it is testimony of divine action. This idea is in correlation with Weber's thesis, although Weber interprets the motivation of the believer as an answer to an anxiety about salvation, a motivation which is absent from Calvin's argument.

The justification of work through stewardship also recommends the rejection of excessive consumption and of sterile savings. Investments and gifts are thus the only two possibilities for using a surplus of earnings exceeding the needs. To give work to others is the best answer to fighting poverty. Alms are suspect; investment in an economy of production is valued. This argument is also coherent with Weber's description.

The notion of the division of labour is coherent with the understanding of society as a body, where each person is complementary and interdependent. Therefore, the optimisation of productive capacities by distributing human forces according to the skills is in compliance with the requirements of stewardship.

By extending Calvin's ideas, we can thus conceive that this discipline can take the form of a rational conduct of life which justifies working without limit without any motivation to enjoy the fruits of work. However, work cannot be considered by the steward as an end in and of itself, and the pursuit of a profession is only one way among others to carry out one's responsibility.

Finally, the renunciation of one's own interest, required for the steward, can be interpreted as a sort of worldly asceticism, even if in reality it implies no renunciation of enjoyment. This asceticism is not motivated by a moral refusal of enjoyment, as it would be in Puritanism, but by the conviction that only the happiness received as a gift from God is good.

We have discussed the implications for worldly actions, the necessity to reinvest, the division of labour, work as a discipline for life, and personal sobriety: all these similarities between the two conceptions of work show that work can take a very similar form and application in the two ethics. However, after these concordances, we come to the points of disjunction between the justifications of work.

In so far as it defines work as an end in itself, the ascetic Calvinism according to Weber is not founded on the most fundamental justification of stewardship: the duty to contribute through work to a fair and prosperous society. The end of work according to stewardship is the common construction of a world enlivened by fraternity and communion between humans. This humanity comes about through the implementation of social justice. We will not develop the meaning of justice for Calvin in this paper, since it would need more development than we can provide here. But Calvin himself summed up the duty of justice in one formula, the golden rule in a positive formulation: "to do unto others as you would have done unto yourself." This is a justice based on a necessity of equity which has to be interpreted in the framework of liberality and attention to others. Work is a medium for the implementation of this justice. This end of work is absent in the ascetic Protestantism, for at least one reason. Charity is not a motivation: Weber underlines clearly that work has an exclusive "objective and impersonal character" (Weber 2005, p. 64) in the Puritan ethics.

It is because society is understood as a body whose members are both interdependent and weak that a society can only emerge through continuous and shared creation. In stewardship, the dimension of alliance is necessary to overcome man's incapacity to build a harmonious society. God gives what is missing to men. Sharing the goods is then a necessity to be a representative of God. The concept of alliance gives a contractual structure to the society, formalises the interdependence, justifies the inequality between humans, and gives an acceptability to differences in skills or capacities. It appears as a basis of the justification of work according to Calvin. On the contrary, Weber underlines that the leading contractual principle committing the Puritan to work is more the vocation than the alliance. It is an individual calling, an individual partnership with God, to which the ecclesial community can at most be a witness.

Third and last, there is no possibility of assigning any value to individual success in the Calvinism of Calvin himself. It is more comfortable to be rich than to be poor, but it is more difficult to be rich, because the rich man has a bigger responsibility than a poor one. Yet, man is incapable of undertaking any good action without God's participation, so he is invited to attribute all his results to God as if no merit could be ascribed to himself. In Weber's demonstration, the Puritan ethics is based on the anthropological understanding that man has the capacity to evaluate and control his level of holiness through the result of his actions, so that the rational conduct of life can lead to the certainty of being sanctified, blessed, and saved. Of course this link between results and sanctification is rejected in Calvin's argument. The anthropological premises on which the duty to work is built in the two Calvinist ethics are radically different.

Despite some convergences in the way work shapes social life, we can conclude that there are profound differences between three of the grounding arguments for the justification of work in Calvin's duty of stewardship as opposed to Weber's presentation of ascetic Protestantism. The definition of the end of work, the principle regulating social relationships, and the level of autonomy of man before God: these three bases of the understanding of work are incommensurable. These discrepancies profoundly change the nature of the concept of work, although both are rooted in a Calvinist faith.

5. Conclusion

We have tried to describe the originality of the concept of work proposed by John Calvin.

Grounded on the principles of the continuous generosity of providence and the necessity for men to carry on God's action, work is defined as the set of actions which implement the creative and redistributive process necessary for a harmonious society.

Even though such creation is ultimately dependent on God's power, this understanding of work attributes to men the responsibility to reconcile the will towards collective enrichment with the imperative of social justice. This conception is a consequence of a duty of stewardship, a mission falling upon all men (and women) to be, depending on their skills and means, representatives of God acting as God would have done in their places.

This creation is not foremost a project of creating economic value, illustrating the absence of any logic of growth in Calvin's thought. Rather, it is intended to lead to the creation of a humanity which finds, within the horizon of a social harmony, the restoration of the world as God could have thought perfect. But this quest legitimises an active search for economic prosperity, in so as far as it contributes to meeting all needs in society.

This humanity is conceived as a body, in which every individual is interdependent upon others. The weakness and dependency of men legitimises a necessary alliance between humans, based on a principle of complementarity.

All these original traits are absent from the later ethic of ascetic Protestant as described by Max Weber. Yet, some features of the Calvinian necessity to work can be found in the later ascetic Calvinism: a commitment to work as hard as possible, the search for economic success, and discipline in life leading to moderation of enjoyment and consumption. But the justifications for these features are radically different.

Acknowledgements

I would like to thank the two referees for their remarks and constructive suggestions, which led to extensive and useful revisions. And I am also particularly grateful to Ragip Ege and François Dermange for their expertise, encouragement, and advice throughout the period of this research.

Disclosure statement

No potential conflict of interest was reported by the author.

References

Ashley, W., 1966. *An introduction to English economic history and theory.* New York: A. M. Kelley.

Besnard, P., 1970. *Protestantisme et capitalisme* [Protestantism and capitalism]. Paris: Armand Colin.

Biéler, A., [1959] 2008. *La pensée économique et sociale de Calvin.* [The economic and social thought of Calvin]. Chêne-Bourg: Georg.

Bieler, A., 2005. *Calvin's economic and social thought.* Genève: WCC Publications.
Bolliger, D., 2009. *Jean Calvin: les visages multiples d'une réforme et de sa réception* [Jean Calvin: the multiple faces of a reform and its reception]. Lyon: Olivétan.
Calvin, J., 1845. *The institutes of the Christian religion.* Grand Rapids, MI: Christian Classics Ethereal Library. Available from: http://www.ccel.org/ccel/calvin/institutes
Calvin, J., 1854. *Commentaires de Jehan Calvin sur le Nouveau Testament.* Vol. 1 [Commentaries by Jehan Calvin on the New Testament]. Paris: Meyrueis.
Calvin, J., 1855. *Commentaires de Jehan Calvin sur le Nouveau Testament.* Vol. 3 [Commentaries by Jehan Calvin on the New Testament]. Paris: Meyrueis.
Calvin, J., 1863. *Ioannis Calvini opera quae supersunt omnia. corpus reformatorum* [Ioannis Calvini opera quae omnia. Reformed body]. Brunvigae: Apud Schwetschke et filium.
Calvin, J., 1978. *Commentaires de Jean Calvin sur l'Ancien Testament.* Vol. 1: *Le livre de la Genèse* [Commentaries by Jean Calvin on the Old Testament. Vol. 1: The book of Genesis]. Aix-en-Provence: ed. Kerygma; Fontenay-sous-Bois: ed. Farel.
Clavairoly, F., 2010. *Calvin: de la réforme à la modernité.* [Calvin: From Reform to modernity]. Paris, France: Presses Universitaires de France.
Disselkamp, A., 1994. *L'éthique protestante de Max Weber.* [The Protestant ethic of Max Weber]. Paris: Presses Universitaires de France.
Doumergue, É., 1917. *Jean Calvin, les hommes et les choses de son temps.* Vol. 5 [John Calvin, the men and things of his time]. Lausanne: G. Bridel.
Ghosh, P., 2008. *A historian reads Max Weber: essays on the protestant ethic.* Wiesbaden: Harrasowitz Verlag.
Hauser, H., 1931. *Les débuts du capitalisme* [The beginnings of capitalism]. Paris: Librairie Félix Alcan.
Hirzel, M.E. and Sallmann, M., 2008. *Calvin et le calvinisme: cinq siècles d'influences sur l'Église et la société* [Calvin and Calvinism: five centuries of influence on Church and society]. Genève: Labor et Fides.
Krumenacker, Y., 2009. *Calvin: au-delà des légendes* [Calvin: beyond the legends]. Montrouge: Bayard.
Lüthy, H., 1965. *Le passé présent* [The present past]. Monaco: Editions du Rocher.
Tawney, R.H., 1922. *Religion and the rise of capitalism: a historical study.* Harmondworth (GB); Ringwood: Penguin Books.
Troeltsch, E., 1991. *Protestantisme et modernité* [Protestantism and modernity]. Paris: Gallimard.
Troeltsch, E., 1994. *Die Soziallehren der christlichen Kirchen und Gruppen: Neudruck der Ausgabe Tübingen 1912* [The social teachings of the Christian churches and groups: reprint of the Tübingen edition of 1912]. Tübingen: Mohr.
Weber, M., 2005. *The Protestant ethic and the spirit of capitalism.* London: Routledge.

Abstract

This article analyses John Calvin's argument for the necessity of hard, lifelong work. Paradoxically, his argument runs alongside a condemnation of the quest for personal enrichment and the pursuit of self-interest. This apparent contradiction can be resolved if it is understood within the framework of a duty of stewardship, according to which every man has to act as God would have done in his place. Our description of this duty leads us to outline the concept of work in Calvin's thought, and to locate it within the context of Max Weber's understanding of the ascetic Calvinist interpretation of work.

Liberal Jansenists and interest-bearing loans in eighteenth-century France: a reappraisal

Arnaud Orain and Maxime Menuet

1. Introduction

The late twentieth century saw a challenge to the earlier interpretation of a secularised eighteenth-century France in which the "philosophical" spirit was triumphant. Studies by Dale Van Kley (1975, 1986, 2006), Roger Chartier (1990), Peter Campbell (1996), Catherine Maire (1998), and Monique Cottret (1998, 2016) have shown how the philosophical and political debates of the years 1750–1790 were deeply impregnated by Christian beliefs and how the religious movements themselves were active participants in those debates.

This was particularly the case of Jansenism, which was the most influential and intellectually the richest Christian protest movement in France, Holland and Austria in the seventeenth and eighteenth centuries. Jansenism – named after the Bishop of Ypres, Cornelius Jansen (1585–1638) – arose out of a reform within the Catholic post-Tridentine Counter-Reformation. It was a complex and protean movement that drew its substance from the teachings of Saint Augustine. The writings of Jansen and Jean Duvergier de Hauranne (1581–1643), better known as abbé de Saint-Cyran, sought to develop a very austere form of Christianity with a pessimistic view of human nature. For Jansen and Saint-Cyran, only *grâce efficace* [effective grace], which was distributed sparingly by God to His faithful, could save the soul. In this world, the corruption of humankind necessarily led men into evil, and the only life worth living was one of constant struggle against sin and fully dedicated to the salvation of the soul.

The nuns of the Port-Royal abbeys in Paris and the Chevreuse valley, their friends the *solitaires* [the lonely men], freed from worldly thoughts, and their go-betweens in Versailles and Paris, relentlessly advocated the teachings of Jansen and Saint-Cyran, often to the detriment of their own freedom. The movement was regarded with suspicion by the royal authorities from the outset. The Jansenists were too independent, too egalitarian, and overly critical of the Jesuits and their ostentation and pomp. Ultimately, the Jansenists were not in tune with the construction of Louis XIV's monarchy and were persecuted as heretics and sedition-mongers. Many of them were imprisoned or forced into exile. Having become all but extinct in the early eighteenth century, the movement "owed" its salvation to the deep-seated grudge Louis XIV held against it. Shortly before his death, the Sun King secured the famous papal bull *Unigenitus* (1713), launching fresh persecutions against the Jansenists, many of whom had to go underground. This persecution made this dissident theological movement an unrelenting and tireless opponent of monarchical authority until the Revolution.

Intellectually, in early modern times, Jansenism left an indelible impression on theology, politics, and what in the second half of the eighteenth century was to become "political economy." The pioneering works of Jean-Claude Perrot (1984) and Gilbert Faccarello ([1999] 1986) have highlighted how early Jansenism, and especially the works of Jean Domat (1625–1696), Pierre Nicole (1625–1695) and Pierre de Boisguilbert (1646–1714) were influential in the emergence of a proto-"invisible hand" theory. The idea that self-interest could produce a social optimum was one of the major contributions of Jansenism at the turn of the seventeenth and eighteenth centuries.[1]

However, twentieth-century historiography disregarded Jansenism when discussing economics in France and Europe in the decades preceding the Revolution. Despite the pioneering work by René Taveneaux (1960, 1977), researchers appeared to consider that religion no longer played a role in the economic thinking of the "Enlightenment." This view has been challenged in recent years by Vanhoorne (1996), Cottret (2002), Faccarello and Steiner (2008), Van Kley (2008), and Orain (2014). These authors have attempted to show that eighteenth-century Jansenists, such as theologian Jacques-Joseph Duguet (1649–1733), historian and professor Charles Rollin (1661–1741), or doctor of canon law and man of letters Étienne Mignot (1698–1771), in many respects prepared the way for the economic ideas of Melon, Montes-

1 See also concerning the early Jansenism of the seventeenth century, the discussions around Bernard de Mandeville's intellectual background by Kaye (1988), Dickey (1990), and, more recently, Seigel (2005).

quieu, or the Gournay circle. It appears from those studies that the question of interest-bearing loans was central to this story. Following Taveneaux (1977), Orain (2014) has attempted to sketch the repercussions of Jansenist thinking on the matter outside of the movement itself.

Early research on this issue ("usury" in the terms of the period) has revealed at least two opposing views within the Jansenist movement: the one rather strict, the other more liberal. This label, "liberal", was given by Taveneaux to a circle of Jansenists who were not only in favour of interest-bearing loans, but who, more generally, were known to "proclaim the exclusive rights of reason" against the mystery of faith (Taveneaux 1977, p. 181). Meeting within a Parisian seminary, that of the *Trente-Trois*,[2] the members of this circle openly spoke out against the mystical enthusiasms and superstitious beliefs of the Jansenist party, especially the convulsionary enterprise[3] and the *figurisme*, a doctrine that allowed for an interpretation of the events of the present based on the Old Testament. Opposed to the authority of the Pope and the bishops (even the Jansenists's), they were reputed among the movement to produce bold ideas and were accused to be close to the *parti des philosophes* (*Histoire de l'Académie Royale des Inscriptions* 1777, XXXVIII, pp. 248–56) (*L'ami de la religion* 1820, XXV, p. 149) (Courtin 1828, XVI, p. 92) (Michaud 1821, XXIX, pp. 23–4) (Picot 1825, IV, p. 245). An overview of the role played by the liberal Jansenists in the economic debates concerning interest-bearing loans in the eighteenth century is lacking. This issue is twofold.

First, as noted by Taveneaux (1977, p. 77), the social base of Jansenism changed during the course of the Enlightenment. After gaining a firm foothold among the lower clergy and regular communities during the seventeenth and early eighteenth centuries, the movement subsequently reached out to justice officers, artisans, merchants and traders during the ensuing decades. Now, it is well known that, among the latter, "merchant credit" (Gervais 2012) became the rule, and lending money at interest was an almost daily practice. In a recent book, Lyon-Caen (2010, p. 274 ff.) defended the idea that Jansenist merchants simply did not "think" about the prohibitions professed by the theologians of their movement on the issue. This interpretation is unsatisfactory from both a psychological and an historical point of view. Psychologically, the Jansenists were probably more concerned than any of their contemporary Christian believers with the salvation of their soul. It is therefore very likely that Jansenist theologians, writings, and sermons legitimising interest-bearing loans would have

2 Concerning this seminary, see Taveneaux (1977, pp. 180–1).

3 After the death of the deacon François de Pâris (1727), a mystical crisis would take place every night in the cemetery of Saint-Médard in Paris.

eased the consciences of Jansenist merchants. Historically, it has yet to be established that the liberal Jansenist movement was a tiny minority within the party. Cottret (2002) and Lyon-Caen (2010), who make this claim, fail to adduce any evidence to accredit it.

Second, Taveneaux (1977) reports very lively debates on the subject of interest-bearing loans among Jansenists in France and Holland. Furthermore, contrary to Lyon-Caen's mistaken claim, Taveneaux provides evidence that the liberal view triumphed in Holland in the early eighteenth century. Taveneaux also offers illuminating insights into the repercussions of the liberal Jansenist tendency in Enlightenment France. His 1977 collection of texts outlines the idea that the work of the Jansenists led the Christian teaching to accept the world (and not the other way round), that the Jansenists contributed decisively to squaring Christian faith with Modern Natural Law, and that they lent theological arguments to certain economic thinkers of the period.

This paper takes up matters where Taveneaux left off. Our study is an attempt to prove that although the liberal Jansenists were not the first and the only ones to address the prohibition of interest-bearing loans, their writings on the question shifted and fuelled the debate during the French Enlightenment.

Part 2 sets out the arguments of the late Scholastics that led to the progressive relaxation of this prohibition. Whereas the Jesuits of the sixteenth and seventeenth centuries extended the notion of extrinsic titles, that is, an idea inherited from the Middle Ages which allowed the payment of interest in certain cases (interest as an opportunity cost), the liberal Jansenists refuted this very logic. On the question of interest-bearing loans, Raymond de Roover (1955, p. 174) states that "[w]henever the *Philosophes* refer to the Doctors, they call them 'casuists' with an undertone of scorn and contempt." The liberal Jansenists had preceded the Enlightenment philosophers in doing exactly that. For Jansenist theologians, the arguments about titles, damages, risk of loss, risk of liquidity, and all the discussions of the unfortunate "casuists", were nothing short of ridiculous. From Jean Le Correur (?-1693) in the seventeenth century, through Dom Thierry de Viaixnes (1659–1734) and especially the *Traité des prêts de commerce* by Philippe Boidot (?-1751), Balthazar Aubret (1679-1754),[4] and Étienne Mignot in the eighteenth century, the Jansenist movement made a sharp distinction between two kinds of loans: "consumer" loans for the poor and which were necessar-

4 The first edition of the *Traité* (1738) is anonymous, signed by "M. ***", but copies carry a handwritten note signed "Aubray" and others even a printed name "Aubray" beside the designation "M.***". The name appears to have been added, it is slightly tilted, and does not have the same script. Taveneaux (1977) spells the name as "Aubert". We are following the *Bibliothèque Nationale de France* by using the spelling "Aubret". All the editions were anonymous and the *Traité* is a collective work attributed to Boidot, Aubret and Mignot.

ily interest-free; and "producer" loans to merchants, which legitimately bore interest. Relying more on reason than on faith, re-interpreting the Holy Scriptures and condemning the errors of all the authors since Thomas Aquinas, the liberal Jansenists simply redefined "interest" as the price to be paid for the use of money (Part 3).

Part 4 shows how these works by the liberal Jansenists actively participated in the French economic Enlightenment. Whether in the entry on "usury" in Diderot's *Encyclopédie*, the articles of other scholars on the question in the 1760s, or the books by Turgot and his Jansenist friends over the following decades, it was the *Traité des prêts de commerce* which was quoted, discussed and dismissed, and through it the tradition begun by Le Correur and Thierry de Viaixnes.

2. Scholastic Tradition and Interest-Bearing Loans

In the Middle Ages, the Scholastics drew on the exegesis of Aristotelian philosophy combined with the Holy Scriptures and Roman Law to prohibit the practice of lending at interest (see Bernard 1950; Noonan 1957, 1966; Finley 1973; Taveneaux 1977; Langholm 1983, 1984). After Aristotle, Thomas Aquinas considered money in itself as sterile; it was not a living thing, and its procreation was unnatural because it was without limit. As for time, it belonged to God alone. The usurer was not only idle; he was also a thief because he stole the fruit of the borrower's labour. Following Roman Law, money was, for Thomas, a fungible and consumable item, like grain. In this respect, the lender was no longer the owner of his money. It was the borrower who became the owner and who "consumed" the lender's money. Thus, the lender had no claim to interest for something that no longer belonged to him.[5]

5 "To take usury for money lent is unjust in itself, because this is to sell what does not exist, and this evidently leads to inequality which is contrary to justice. In order to make this evident, we must observe that there are certain things the use of which consists in their consumption: thus we consume wine when we use it for drink and we consume wheat when we use it for food. Wherefore in such like things the use of the thing must not be reckoned apart from the thing itself, and whoever is granted the use of the thing, is granted the thing itself and for this reason, to lend things of this kin is to transfer the ownership. Accordingly if a man wanted to sell wine separately from the use of the wine, he would be selling the same thing twice, or he would be selling what does not exist, wherefore he would evidently commit a sin of injustice. On like manner he commits an injustice who lends wine or wheat, and asks for double payment, viz. one, the return of the thing in equal measure, the other, the price of the use, which is called usury" (Aquinas 1265–1274, II-II, q. 78, a. 1).

However, there were exceptions for special cases. Damage could warrant an amount of money being received in excess of the principal. We enter here into the realm of extrinsic titles, that is, cases that were independent of the loan in itself but that arose during the period of time for which the loan was made. The three most common cases were very famous. These were *poena conventionalis* or the charge for late repayment, *damnum emergens* or the occurrence of damage, and *lucrum cessans* or the loss or cessation of profit. The first title, accepted by a broad range of scholastic theologians, allowed compensation to be paid when the money lent was paid back late with respect to the deadline stipulated in the contract. The second could occur when the lender, during the loan, no longer possessed the means to remedy any serious loss or injury that befell him. In this case, he was allowed to force the borrower to pay more than he had received. This title was not readily accepted by Thomas Aquinas, and the third, cessation of profit, was even more litigious.

Lucrum cessans approved of a monetary allowance in the event that the money granted to the borrower caused a loss of income for the lender during the same period. This was an opportunity cost. Theologians maintained considerable ambiguity towards this until the fifteenth century (Lapidus 1987, pp. 1106–7), but under pressure brought about by the renewal of commerce and the expansion of trade, as well as the development of nation states in the early modern period, the ecclesiastical doctrines were relaxed: *damnum emergens* and *lucrum cessans* were increasingly readily accepted, and states began to create (perpetual) annuities, the famous *rentes constituées* in France (see Langholm 1983, 1984).

Some Catholic theologians favoured this trend, in particular within the new order (recognised by the Pope in 1540), the Society of Jesus. Among them, two great theologians of the late scholastic movement, Luis de Molina (1535–1600) and Leonardus Lessius (1554–1623),[6] "contributed largely to accredit particular forms of usury" (Taveneaux 1977, p. 34). The role of the latter was essential. John Noonan (1957, pp. 350–1) and Toon Van Houdt (1995, 1998a, 1998b) have shown how Lessius, while still in keeping with the tradition of Thomas Aquinas, first extended the definitions and the number of extrinsic titles. *Damnum emergens* became in Lessius's way of thinking a "risk of loss", a guarantee against any damage

6 Lessius was a Flemish Jesuit and a theologian of great repute. He is best known for his treatise *De iustitia et iure* (*On Justice and Law*) of 1605 that went through more than 20 editions in the seventeenth century alone. This book was probably the first in-depth moral theological approach to economic and financial questions. In particular, Lessius went to Antwerp to study the banking system and the workings of commerce. For more details, see De Roover (1969) and especially Van Houdt (1995, 1998a, 1998b).

during the term of the loan that could be stipulated on entering into the contract, and paid by the borrower even if no loss occurred (Van Houdt 1995, p. 20). Concerning *lucrum cessans* or "cessation of profit", the lender no longer had to make complex calculations of what he would have lost. He could henceforth make an informal claim for a loss, but that claim, according to Lessius, "had to be real" (Van Houdt 1995, p. 25). Indeed, the title was explicitly requested by Lessius because to his mind the lending of money did not automatically lead to a loss of profit.

Instead of providing "a too broad and imprecise use of the title [*lucrum cessans*]", Lessius preferred to make an addition to this opportunity cost argument by "the creation of a new title" (Van Houdt 1995, p. 24) in the form of *carentia pecuniae* or "loss of liquidity", something close to a time preference.[7] He stressed that "the person who lends money relinquishes his liquidity. He uses ready money to buy the right to money in the future; in other words, he exchanges 'present money' (*pecunia praesens*) for 'absent money' (*pecunia absens*). As 'present money' is more valuable than 'absent money', the lender is permitted to ask more in return than he actually gave" (Van Houdt 1995, p. 24).

The religious prohibitions on specific forms of interest-bearing loans were relaxed through the work of Jesuit theologians. But this occurred within the scholastic framework. Lessius did not want to create any conflict with the tradition of Aquinas, but rather to extend the range of action of extrinsic titles. "A loan was not equivalent to a sale of (productive) *capital* but an exchange of (unproductive) *coins* for similar coins at some future date. In other words, a loan is an intertemporal exchange of two sets of goods which are fungible or interchangeable (Lessius 2. 20. 1. 13)" (Van Houdt 1995, p. 19). Although Lessius began to alter the meaning and number of extrinsic titles, although he opened the door to the idea that any amount of money has a price, "[t]his step would only be definitively taken in the 18th century" (Van Houdt 1995, p. 22). The liberal Jansenist theologians of the seventeenth and eighteenth centuries played a major role in taking that step, and they did it precisely by rejecting the scholastic arguments and the very idea of extrinsic titles.

3. The Liberal Jansenists and the Upheaval of the Scholastic Tradition

By wanting to set themselves apart from Calvinism, the early Jansenists and all the prelates who supported *Port-Royal* were unbending on the issue of interest-bearing loans. The most rigorist ideas were disseminated. First,

7 G. Faccarello stresses that "[i]t is also to be noted that the reasoning in terms of time preferences seems to have been widespread among confessors and casuists during the seventeenth century" (Faccarello 2016, p. 81).

Jansenist theologians applied the writings of Thomas Aquinas to the letter, granting *lucrum cessans* and even *damnum emergens* with the utmost reluctance. Second, they categorically refused any form of interest for annuities (*rentes*) without alienation of capital.[8] Nevertheless, by the mid-seventeenth century, things were becoming more complicated.

Among the great Jansenist theologians of this century, Pierre Nicole (1625–1695) and Antoine Arnauld (1612–1694) condemned the interest-bearing loan by referring to the ecclesiastical tradition, although they did acknowledge that reason did not forbid it (Taveneaux 1977, p. 123). They thereby opened a breach into which their successors were quick to step. The earliest elaborate analysis of interest-bearing loans to follow this line of reasoning came from a book by a close friend of the Jansenists of Port-Royal, priest and theologian Jean Le Correur. His *Traité de la pratique des billets entre les négociants* (1682) laid the foundations of liberal Jansenist doctrine for the next hundred years.

3.1 The Seminal Work of Jean Le Correur (1682)

After stating that interest is "a fair compensation" and that money "produces profit by the use made of it in trade" (Le Correur [1684] 1682, p. 21 and p. 38), Le Correur drew a sharp distinction between loans made by the rich to the poor and loans made by the rich to the rich. In the first case, things were clear: "the rich must lend free-of-charge to the poor in order to help them in their necessity, & not rush them too much to repay what they have lent to them" (Le Correur [1684] 1682, p. 14).[9] Interest-

8 In the case of the annuities, we are not speaking of a "loan" but of a "sale": an individual or an institution sold an amount of money to the Crown or to another individual. During his life or for perpetuity, the seller received interest. The buyer (the State or the borrower) was allowed to reimburse the capital to the seller, but the seller could not compel the buyer to reimburse it, whether at a fixed date or at any time.

9 Concerning a famous passage of the Book of Deuteronomy (XXIII, 20), "You may charge a foreigner interest, but not a fellow Israelite, so that the LORD your God may bless you in everything you put your hand to in the land you are entering to possess", Le Correur advocated that "[t]he law commands to lend free-of-charge to brothers, who are poor; in addition it orders the practice of *Billets* [with interest] with regard to foreigners who are rich, because it would be unfair and cruel to exercise it with regard to the poor" (Le Correur [1684] 1682, p. 116). He discussed other passages from the Old Testament and then came to the famous words of Jesus according to Luke (VI, 35), "lend to them without expecting to get anything back". For Le Correur, this was the charitable loan to the poor that was at issue (Le Correur [1684] 1682, p. 151). This passage is part of a series of commandments ordering Christians to lend to, help and assist not just the poor but also one's enemies. It forms part of the famous "evangelical counsels" (Le Correur [1684] 1682, p. 160).

ingly, this notion of the "poor" was rather elastic for Le Correur since it could include the "rich in difficulty" or the "ruined." In addition, the rich could also lend their money without interest to individuals "who have a surfeit", or in certain circumstances out of gratitude or generosity. The same did not apply for loans granted for the purposes of trade. In such instances, "neighbourly charity does not require me to give the use of my property free-of-charge to someone rich, and even less so the use of property that is useful, such as cash" (Le Correur [1684] 1682, p. 51).

In his reasoning, the theologian explained that since one rich man (a merchant) who received money in the form of a loan granted by another rich man (another merchant) was going to become richer through this loan, it was perfectly justifiable that the lender should receive interest, in other words a part of the profits of the borrower. Money "produces a profit indirectly through the industry of a rich & cautious merchant" (Le Correur [1684] 1682, p. 184). It would be unfair not to pay back to the lender more than he gave when his money had generated a profit. There was no need for "the pretext of a society" among merchants, that is, a company of commerce: interest payments were completely legitimate since "they are nothing but the value of the use of money, which is a useful good" (Le Correur [1684] 1682, p. 41). By this line of reasoning, money became "capital" (*ibid.*) and interest the price paid for money lent.

Le Correur sought to vilify annuities (*rentes constituées*), instruments that were supposed to be not merely tolerated but actually legal. Le Correur praised an ordinance that had been issued by Charles IX in 1567 in which the King

> condemns those who lend their money in annuities by a disturbance of manners. This King blames their laziness & their idleness, because having left work, they stayed without any occupation, & exposed themselves to all the evils that idleness ordinarily produces. He blames them also by a pure principle of police, because they have abandoned without necessity trade, which is necessary to his subjects & to foreigners.

Le Correur concluded that annuities were the instrument that produced "this dual evil" of putting "an end to commerce" and creating "idleness." His reasoning was subtle: interest-bearing loans were acceptable if made between two rich men in order to create a future benefit in agriculture, manufacturing or trade, in other words, in some productive activity. This was not the case with *rentes constituées* (Le Correur [1684] 1682, pp. 312–5).

This led Le Correur to dismiss the whole argument of those he invariably referred to as "the casuists" (see for instance Le Correur [1684] 1682, pp. 257–60). He considered *damnum emergens, lucrum cessans*, and their so-called extrinsic titles as mere "inventions." They were the inconsistent arguments of a "corrupted morality" (Le Correur [1684] 1682, p. 225). According to Le Correur, the very logic of titles was false. Whether there existed a risk of loss or an opportunity of profit for the lender, he put forward that if a merchant planned a future loss (a house falling into ruin) or a future profit (the arrival of a merchant ship), "he should not lend it [his money]." If the loss or the profit were not planned, it was the same, the merchant "puts himself voluntarily into powerlessness." In both cases, he was an "unwise" person and it was not possible to compensate "the harm he did to himself, by his pure and own fault" (Le Correur [1684] 1682, pp. 260–1). Le Correur purely and simply rejected the arguments of the Scholastics by refusing to consider the position of the lender. Interest was legitimate "not as compensation to make good the damage done, or to replace the gain for which opportunity arose, but only as the price or the value of the use of money (Le Correur [1684] 1682, p. 211). This was the "fertility" of money which "produces profit by the sorrows and attentions of a Merchant, who works constantly at his trade" (Le Correur [1684] 1682, p. 43).

In short, loans for trade or "production" were loans made between merchants, whereas loans to the poor were mere "consumer" loans. The former were related to the use of money in trade and charging interest was perfectly legitimate, whereas the latter were made out of charity and had to be free of charge. Money was productive as capital and the reasoning of the late Scholastics in terms of titles (damage, cessation of profit, risk, and so on) had to be dismissed out of hand.[10] This line was to be common and implicit throughout the liberal Jansenist tradition. Thus, Taveneaux concludes that "Le Correur announces a way of thinking, a method of analysis and moral concepts which were to inspire, some decades later, the Jansenists of the Church of Utrecht" (Taveneaux 1977, pp. 50–1).

3.2 Dom Thierry de Viaixnes and the Submission to Temporal Authorities

If we accept with Taveneaux that Le Correur actually established the method and tools of the liberal Jansenists for the century to come on the matter of interest-bearing loans, it was the French rather than the Dutch school that followed his example most closely.

Through the Jansenist theologians educated in Leuven and the influx of Port-Royalists fleeing persecution, the Netherlands and particularly the region of Utrecht, where a strong Catholic minority subsisted, became a hotbed of Jansenism in the late seventeenth century. Taveneaux claims that conflict arose at that time between the exiles and the French Jansenist bishops on the one side, and the faithful and the Catholic Dutch clergy on

10 Le Correur did not deal with time preference.

the other, over the matter of interest-bearing loans. His interpretation is both sociological and political. In keeping with the prevailing Calvinism and the spirit of commerce of the Republic, the vast majority of the faithful and the low clergy became favourable to the interest-bearing loan, in virtually all its forms. However, the Archbishop of Utrecht, Barchman, puppet of the French Jansenists, and the circle that included some renowned exiles – especially the rigorists Nicolas Le Gros (1675–1751) and Nicolas Petitpied (1665–1747) – opposed interest-bearing loans and in particular the so-called annuity contracts that were "redeemable on both sides" [*rentes rachetables des deux côtés*].[11] This was a dangerous stance for the Archbishop to take, because rejecting the legitimacy of interest-bearing loans would imply both cutting himself off from his base and endangering the survival of the Jansenist Church of Utrecht, which was merely tolerated by the authorities.

This stand-off between the Archbishop of Utrecht and the rigorists on the one hand, and the low clergy and the liberals on the other, lasted nearly forty years, and ended, contrary to what Lyon-Caen argues, in a resounding victory for the liberals in Holland.[12] However, the issue was mostly a debate among French Jansenists rather than between any would-be "Dutch party" versus a "French party." Indeed, it was French exiles and a Parisian seminary that provided the intellectual support for the Dutch low clergy. The sociological and even "patriotic" explanation of the struggle is therefore not entirely convincing.

Le Correur actually wrote to Pierre Bayle on 16 March 1685 to inform him of the publication of the second edition (Mons, 1684) of the *Traité de la pratique des billets*. Le Correur asked Bayle to insert the announcement in his journal *Nouvelles de la république des lettres*.[13] He spoke in this letter of the substantive agreement that prevailed among several French theologians concerning the legality of interest charges. Indeed, in a letter first published in 1729, but dating from the 1670s, two handwritten copies of

11 Without alienation of the capital, the seller – the lender – could oblige the buyer to reimburse the capital at a fixed date. This was no longer a "sale" in the sense of the theologians, this was "usury".

12 "During the eighteenth century, debates are quite lively within the Church of Holland, very close to Parisian jansenists. Under their pressure, it ends up rejecting the usury, it had, for a time, considered favourably" (Lyon-Caen 2010, pp. 270–1). On the contrary, Taveneaux has shown that in Holland the rigorists were placed in the minority at the beginning of the eighteenth century and that things were settled in the 1740s: the Church of Utrecht took a position very similar to that of the Calvinists concerning interest-bearing loans, see Taveneaux (1977, pp. 65–71).

13 http://bayle-correspondance.univ-st-etienne.fr/?Lettre-391-Jean-Le-Correur-a. An excerpt from the letter announcing the book was indeed inserted into the May 1685 issue of the *Nouvelles de la république des lettres*, p. 570–1.

which are preserved in France,[14] the famous Gallican and Jansenist sympathiser theologian Jean de Launoy (1601–1678)[15] took up Le Correur's analysis. He did not pay attention to the "distinctions of the Casuists", that is, the extrinsic titles, except very briefly in the case of loans to the poor. De Launoy considered *damnum emergens, lucrum cessans*, and so on, as quibbles masking a terrible usury. Trade in money was, in contrast, perfectly legitimate among merchants, "like any other good" (de Launoy 1729, pp. 2–3):

> And indeed I do not see what this heroic virtue of the evangelical counsel would consist of, namely, to lend without interest to people often richer than us, and this in order to acquire new landed estates, or to raise them to dignities and to public responsibilities. God's law looks to the help of the needy, and not the increase of fortune, which it has never advised, although never forbidden. (de Launoy 1729, p. 3)

The debate was fuelled by two works: a letter from Jean Opstraët (1651–1720), a doctor of theology and professor at Leuven University, published in 1710,[16] and the *Tractatus brevis reditibus utrimque redimibilibus* (1729) by Nicolas Broedersen (?-1772), a minister in Delft. Opstraët's letter affirmed the distinction made by Le Correur and de Launoy between charitable loans to the poor, which were necessarily interest-free, and loans granted to merchants, who made a profit from this use of money. Broedersen's *Tractatus* followed the same reasoning and included de Launoy's letter in French in an appendix. What is more, Broedersen's book was preceded by an important letter from a famous French Jansenist exiled in Holland, Dom Thierry de Viaixnes.[17] Sent to Archbishop Barchman in March 1728, it caused a big stir. A copy sent to a Parisian doctor (probably Philippe Boidot) was intercepted on the French border a few weeks later and immediately published by the enemies of the Jansenists in order to draw attention to the divisions in the Church of Utrecht.[18]

14 "Lettre d'un théologien à son amy au sujet de l'usure. Attribuée à de Launoy par Thiébaut de Berneaud; réfutée par M. du Tertre en 1697". Bibliothèque de l'Arsenal, Manuscrits français, 2248, and Bibliothèque Mazarine, Ms 4520 (2456).

15 About de Launoy, see Grès-Gayer (2009).

16 *Lettre d'Opstraët à un chanoine d'Utrecht*, 21 September 1710, cf. Taveneaux (1977, pp. 143–5).

17 Belonging to the congregation of Saint-Vanne. On his arrest in 1703, his imprisonment and subsequent exile, see Taveneaux (1960, pp. 156–65).

18 See Targny (1728). This letter sparked violent opposition from the most rigorous proponents of the Jansenist movement, see *Les Nouvelles Ecclésiastiques* (1728, p. 531). *Les Nouvelles Ecclésiastiques* between 1713 and 1728, in the edition of Paris, are published in the same volume.

Dom Thierry spoke of internal politics and defended the interest-bearing loan,[19] but his letter especially, after Le Correur, provided a tremendous supply of arguments for the liberal Jansenists on the issue. After long being favourable to the rigorist opinions of the Sorbonne, Dom Thierry asserted that he had changed his mind further to reading a "secret writing of Mr. de Launoi [...]." He added that "[i]t was not his authority that determined me to embrace his sentiment, but the solid & fundamental reasons it rested upon" (in Boidot *et al.*, 1759, IV, p. xxij). Although Dom Thierry did not quote Le Correur, he blamed the same "*Sorbonnistes*", a highly pejorative term, whose "ridiculous disputes" did not shed "any light" on the issue (Boidot *et al.*, 1759, IV, p. xxxiv). Unfortunately, he made no mention of their extrinsic titles.

According to Dom Thierry, interest-bearing loans between merchants were made to "support and enrich" trade and were "very useful" to the public (Boidot *et al.*, 1759, IV, p. xliv).[20] He examined the question of annuities (*rentes constituées*) with alienation of capital at greater length than either Le Correur or de Launoy. Dom Thierry discovered that perpetual annuities had been authorised by the Sorbonne to meet the needs of French kings since the sixteenth century thanks to a subterfuge: the idea that it would be a "sale", and not a "loan." For him, this was a major loophole. "That has always seemed to me very ill-founded, and even ridiculous" (Boidot *et al.*, 1759, IV, p. xxxvj), because if interest was no longer paid to the lender "he has every right to demand this return, even in the court of justice. He is no less the master of this money than if it had remained in his coffers" (Boidot *et al.*, 1759, IV, p. xxxvij).

More interesting still was the submission by Dom Thierry to the temporal authorities regarding commerce, in all cases. Those who truncated the quotations of Holy Scripture in order to prohibit the interest-bearing loan:

> could at most prove in this way that this prohibition was an ecclesiastical law; but in this case they would gain nothing: for the rules of trade for civil society are not the responsibility of the Church & its ministers, but come only within the jurisdiction of the Sovereigns, be they pagans or heretics. They have their power from God himself, as St. Paul teaches us so strictly. They are responsible for it only before the Almighty; & all their subjects should obey them, without excepting the pope or bishops, in all that is not formally contrary to his divine law. (Boidot *et al.*, 1759, IV, p. xl)

In

19 The Archbishop of Utrecht, Barchman, refused to consecrate a bishop in Harlem who was favourable to interest-bearing loans.

20 Dom Thierry made the same distinction as Le Correur and asserted of the Old Testament that "the loan for usury or interest was not only allowed towards foreigners, but even ordered [...]. This loan was even allowed towards brothers, when they borrowed without being in poverty & real necessity" (Boidot *et al.*, 1759, IV, p. xxv). He brushed aside the passage of the Gospel of Luke: "one need only read what precedes and what follows to see that it has not the slightest relation thereto [to the interest-bearing loan]" (Boidot *et al.*, 1759, IV, p. xxvj).

this, the Jansenist theologian took a crucial step on the issue. Religion became a matter of counsels, not of moral obligations. We can also detect a break with the idea of Christendom and a shift towards the idea of Nation, which was a key feature of eighteenth-century Jansenism.

Other French theologians supported the Dutch low clergy in the debates with the Church of Utrecht on the subject of interest-bearing loans. This was especially the case of Philippe Boidot, a superior of the Jansenist seminary of the *Trente-Trois* in Paris. He published in 1730 in The Hague a *Réponse aux difficultés proposées à un théologien sur les prêts de commerce de Hollande* defending the opinions of Broedersen and Dom Thierry de Viaixnes. Moreover, Boidot and the latter were friends, as shown by their extensive correspondence between 1723 and 1728 (Taveneaux 1960, p. 26). Boidot therefore drafted with Aubret, and probably already with Mignot, the *Traité des prêts de commerce*, first published in 1738 in Lille by Pierre Mathon. This book, the bible of the liberal Jansenists in the eighteenth century, was revised and reprinted under Mignot's guidance in 1759 and 1767 in four volumes, with a fifth volume published in 1770.[21]

3.3 A Bible for the Liberals: The Traité des Prêts de Commerce

The book was divided into three parts. The first examined the issue of loans to the poor. The general idea was to show that not only did they have to be free of charge, but the rich were also obliged to lend to the poor in need. The second part, *De l'usure à l'égard des riches* [Usury towards the rich], concerned, in order, the texts from the Old and New Testaments already discussed, the writings of the Church Fathers and the Church Councils, and the civil laws from Clovis to Louis XIV. In fact, this second part sought to prove that none of those texts condemned interest-bearing loans among merchants who used the money to make profit through trade. Since men were exhorted to treat their brothers as they wanted to be treated by them, it was clear that between the rich who lent to each other for trade, interest could be charged in addition to the principal.[22] The third part focused on the Scholastics. The authors actually pointed out different opinions and contradictions among various Doctors. Finally, the book concluded with the letters of de Launoy, Dom Thierry, and the excerpt from Le Correur's letter to Bayle published in *Nouvelles de la république des lettres*. The great merit of the work was to generalise the ideas

21 *Traité des prêts de commerce et réponse Aux six Lettre de l'Auteur des* Principes Théologique, Canoniques & Civils sur l'Usure, Tome cinquième, Paris, Knapen, 1770.

22 Indeed, "[I] would not want another to appropriate the profit of the money that I shall have lent to him, & which he would have used to increase his wealth; therefore I must not want to appropriate the profit of the money which my friend lent me, & which has served to improve my condition" (Boidot *et al.* 1738, p. 64).

of the liberal Jansenists on the issue, while seeking to give clear definitions and to be exhaustive as to "proofs."

The main idea was to establish "usury" as a simple "profit", "which one derives from the use of money" [*que l'on retire pour l'usage de l'argent*], and so to eliminate any negative connotations associated with the term and its practice (Boidot *et al.*, 1738, p. 6). The authors explicitly rejected the teaching of the "casuists." They spoke of them with disdain, and this was particularly the case concerning their invention of the extrinsic titles. As far as *lucrum cessans, damnum emergens,* and so on were concerned, the casuists had not only been "up to now, unable to find the slightest basis [for these titles] in the text of the Scriptures" (Boidot *et al.*, 1738, p. 101), they were also simply irrelevant. Like Le Correur, the authors of the *Traité des prêts de commerce* were not really interested in and did not discuss in depth these so-called titles, simply because they did not reason in terms of costs for the lender. The notions of cessation of profit or risk of loss were for the Jansenists useless "inventions" which only served to confuse a very simple question. In the case of a consumption loan made to a poor man, there were no possible exceptions, the charging of interest was strictly forbidden; in the case of a productive loan made to a merchant, there were no exceptions here either, interest being perfectly legitimate (Boidot *et al.*, 1738, p. 381).

Like Le Correur, they also had doubts about the validity of the *rentes constituées* [annuities]: if the rich lent money to the poor by this means, it was unlawful. The arguments of the "sale" versus the "loan" were anything but valid: annuities had to bear interest only if they were invested in a productive activity (Boidot *et al.*, 1738, pp. 44–7). Money was "a tool", "the instrumental cause of profit", and if this tool was used for those productive actions, among traders, the lender should be granted interest as if he were a partner in a company (Boidot *et al.*, 1738, p. 90). If not, if the money was consumed by a poor person in difficulty, this was usury and should therefore be prohibited.

More generally, the salient feature of the *Traité des prêts de commerce* of 1738, as well as in Mignot's editions and additions, was to demonstrate that Holy Scripture[23] conformed to the demands of natu-

23 When Moses allowed interest-bearing loans to foreigners, this meant that this type of loan was always allowed among the rich, because "a thing that is bad in its nature & contrary to natural law cannot be permitted under any circumstances: it cannot be damnable in one case & innocent in the other" (Boidot *et al.* 1738, p. 65). The passage from Luke suffered from an error in the Greek translation into Latin; it should supposedly have read "lend, never despairing" [*prêtez, sans laisser désespérer personne*] (Boidot *et al.* 1738, p. 106). And even if the translation of the *Vulgate* was adopted, it was only a simple precept of charity and generosity towards the poor, "from which one cannot infer anything as regards loans granted to the rich" (Boidot *et al.* 1738, p. 106).

ral law,[24] reason, and the temporal authorities. But what exactly did this mean? The Scholastics also referred to natural law and reason. Thomas Aquinas could have written that the "natural law that God has engraved in the heart of all men, compels us to love our brothers as ourselves, & to treat them in the same way that we would like to be treated" (Boidot *et al.* 1738, p. 10). But beyond these generalities, the authors of the *Traité des prêts de commerce* tended to adopt a more recent view, that of Modern Natural Law. Following Grotius and Pufendorf, they first took an anthropocentric vision of natural law. Contrary to the Scholastics, there were no more references to a cosmo-theological world in their book, no more ideas about the natural laws of animals, plants and other living creatures. Second, and more importantly, they tended to base morality only on human reason and even to subject the authority of divine law and Holy Scriptures to the criticism of reason. Since the edition of 1738, the Jansenists stated that "reason makes obvious to anyone who endeavours to think carefully, what is good or what is bad; what has to be done and what must be avoided" (Boidot *et al.* 1738, p. 75). Mignot confirmed the claim in 1759: "[A]ll the precepts of Morality are founded in reason" (Mignot 1759, p. x). What is striking in the *Traité des prêts de commerce* and shocked the contemporary Jansenist rigorists, is that in many passages the authors reason, like Grotius, as if God does not exist. Worse again, the Jansenists did not hesitate to write that men must use "the tribunal of reason [*le tribunal de la raison*] to judge the fairness of the precepts of Christian religion" (Boidot *et al.* 1738, p. 57). This expression, "the tribunal of reason", seemed to make human beings the judges of the Christian dogma, and even to question the revealed truths.[25] While Mignot later tried to defuse that interpretation of the *Traité*, he maintained the notion of "tribunal" and praised "the lights of reason, and that anyone who makes use of his reason, that is, anyone who abandons biases and shuts down passions, looks inside himself to listen solely to the voice of conscience" (Mignot 1770, p. 175). That was enough to accuse him of being a "faithless" [*un incrédule*] (*Journal Œconomique* 1772, p. 233)

24 The *Traité des prêts de commerce* referred both to "natural law" (mainly) and "natural right" (more rarely). The first is inscribed in human nature ("to treat our brothers in the same way that we would like to be treated"), while the second governs human beings ("it is forbidden to kill"). On this issue, see Goyard-Fabre (2002).

25 In his *Analyse de toutes les verités enseignées et professées dans la religion chrétienne* (1754), Mignot did not hesitate to declare: "It is for *reason* to examine whether the *authority* presented to it deserves to be listened to" (Mignot 1754, pp. 1–2).

and "modern philosopher" (see Part 4 below). Lastly, a third element brought the liberal Jansenists closer to the theory of Modern Natural Law, namely the submission of the religious authorities to temporal authorities, or more precisely, to civil laws. We have seen that this idea was important for Dom Thierry de Viaixnes, whose letter was reproduced in the *Traité des prêts de commerce.* Mignot defended this point of view in further work. In *Des Droits de l'État et du prince sur les biens du clergé* (1755), he blasted the claim of the Church to avoid paying taxes. Mignot stated that the alleged immunity of the divine law must give way to natural law because "those involved in the advantages of a society must share the burden with those who are members of the same society" (Mignot 1755, p. 336). Although he denied it (but finally rather weakly), Mignot actually preached a sort of natural moral law, in which God could be absent (see also Mignot, 1753).

To conclude, from the end of the seventeenth to the second half of the eighteenth centuries, some Jansenists tried to justify the charging of interest on loans. Their arguments, based on Modern Natural Law, prevailed over a dogmatic approach. More broadly, the reactions triggered by the question of interest-bearing loans among the Jansenists were different from the reactions of the Jesuits. In the Scholastics' doctrine, only the person of the lender was concerned, it was what could happen to him during the loan that was considered. On the contrary, Le Correur and the liberal Jansenists insisted on the borrower, or, more precisely, the purpose of the money borrowed (for profit or charity). In this way of thinking, interest was legitimate because the money lent generated a benefit; what happened to the lender – his own losses or damages – was never considered. Put another way, for the Jansenists, the analysis of interest-bearing loans through the concept of costs was simply irrelevant. They shifted the ground of the whole argumentation of the Scholastics on the issue without much ado, and this is probably one reason that explains the relative indifference of historians of economic analysis (no anticipation of cost concepts) toward this tradition until nowadays. This shift is important, however, because, as we will see, the Jansenist approach to the issue fuelled the debates of the French Enlightenment on the subject of credit.[26]

26 We have shown elsewhere the confluence of the rigorous Jansenist tradition and the reflections of some authors of the Gournay circle on the subject of interest-bearing loans (Orain 2014, pp. 477–80).

4. The Jansenist Tradition and the Economic Representations of the Enlightenment

4.1 The Traité des Prêts de Commerce *and Diderot's* Encyclopédie

In 1819, *L'ami de la religion*, a Catholic journal, suggested that "the *Traité [des prêts de commerce]* seems to have been used by all those who have written along the same lines since then" (*L'ami de la religion* 1819, p. 355), and Taveneaux states that the book "fed, during the century, all comparable productions" (Taveneaux 1977, p. 81). The first version of the *Traité des prêts de commerce* (1738) was reported in the *Journal des Sçavans* (1738, pp. 755–6) and in the *Mercure de France* (December 1738, p. 2846), but without any critical review in both cases.[27] What, then, was the future of the book? Taveneaux does not support his intuition, but *L'ami de la religion* did provide some information. It claimed that the same argumentative structure as that of the *Traité* supported the works of German journalist and contributor to Diderot's *Encyclopédie*, Johann-Heinrich-Samuel Formey (1711–1797), and merchant and Secretary of the Academy of La Rochelle, Jean-Baptiste Gastumeau (1697–1763). It is true that Formey's *Examen de l'usure suivant les principes du droit naturel* (1751) and Gastumeau's *Dissertation sur la légitimité des intérêts de l'argent* (1756) both mocked the "casuists" and the notion of titles, considering the matter in the same way as Boidot *et al.* (the rich-production/poor-consumption distinction and interest as the price paid for the "use" of money). Neither work, however, made any reference to the *Traité*. Not so, though, for Diderot's *Encyclopédie*, the "flagship" of the French Enlightenment, in which the influence of the work by Boidot *et al.* ran deep. This is an important point that has not attracted the attention of commentators until now.

The article "Usure (*Morale*)" [Usury] by Joachim Faiguet de Villeneuve (1703-1781) was published in one of the final volumes of the great dictionary in December 1765 but had been written in 1758.[28] This regular contributor to the *Encyclopédie* (he wrote some fifteen articles for it) deserves our attention. Born into a poor family from Moncontour in Brittany, Faiguet became a schoolmaster in Paris and also a pig merchant, which exposed him to a degree of ridicule. He submitted his first articles to

27 Also note that the bookseller and printer of the *Traité des prêts de commerce*, Pierre Mathon, from Lille, seems to have specialized in Jansenist publications on the subject of usury, whether favourable or unfavourable to loans with interest, since in addition to Boidot, Aubret and Mignot, Mathon also published rigorist Jansenists (Barbier 2002, pp. 386–7).

28 *Encyclopédie* 1765, t.17, pp. 529–53. At the end of the article "Usury", we find "*Article de M. Faiguet. (1758.)*". Written and probably delivered in 1758, it cannot refer to the new edition (that of 1759) of the *Traité des prêts de commerce.*

Diderot and d'Alembert in 1753 and participated in the encyclopaedic enterprise until the end. He became *Trésorier de France* (a very expensive *office*) at Châlons-sur-Marne in 1760 and a member of the Royal Agricultural Society of Brittany in 1761. As a contributor to the *Journal Œconomique* from the 1750s, Faiguet often addressed subjects of an economic nature. He notably published *Économie politique, projet pour enrichir et perfectionner l'espèce humaine* (1763),[29] *Mémoires politiques sur la conduite des finances et autres objets intéressants* (1769), and *Légitimité de l'usure légale* (1770), which was actually a reprint of his – very long – article in the *Encyclopédie* (Hecht 1959, pp. 79–80).

In all his work, Faiguet constantly referred to religious elements, and it was he who wrote the entries "Fêtes des chrétiens [Christian Holidays] (*Hist. ecclés.*)", "Fidele [Faithful] (*Théol. & Hist. ecclés.*)", "Sanctification [Sanctification] (*terme de théologie*)", "Dimanche [Sunday] (*Hist. et Discipl. Ecclés.*)", and "Moraves ou Frères Unis [Moravians]" in the famous dictionary. In those articles he came across as a "strict Christian" and very much aware of the Catholic Counter-Reformation (Shusterman 2010, pp. 102–3). Grimm did not hesitate to describe Faiguet as a "Socinian."[30] Although the adjective was often used in the eighteenth century to describe the enlightened trend of Jansenism (the one hostile to the *convulsionnaires*) (Maire 2005, pp. 85 and 88), was there sufficient evidence to describe Faiguet as a Jansenist writer, or at least a Jansenist sympathiser?

First, in the entry "*Études*", he criticised the education in Jesuit colleges, presenting in a very favourable light the Christian communities of Central Europe, notably the "Moravians", who followed the teachings of the Gospel in their daily lives. This praise for the Moravian Church was reminiscent of the life of the recluses of Port-Royal and assimilation between Moravians and Jansenists was commonplace in the eighteenth century.[31] Second, again in the *Encyclopédie* but also in his *Économie politique*, Faiguet strongly opposed the dissipation and idleness generated by religious holidays and preferred Sundays to be pious and laborious. Seventeenth- and eighteenth-century Jansenist bishops and priests specifically defended the same policy in this regard.[32] Lastly, it was the references used by Faiguet that testified to his Jansenist sympathies. In the article "Sanctification", he cited the Old and New Testaments using only the translation by the

29 Republished with another title in 1766.

30 "He wrote, for the *Encyclopédie*, the article *Dimanche*, and some others which were noticed among the good ones. They say he is a usurer and Socinian; but these two qualities can very well be consistent with the duties of a schoolmaster and a pig merchant" (*Correspondance littéraire*, III, 1 June 1763, pp. 240–4).

31 For example, in Rousseau's *Julie ou la Nouvelle Héloïse* (Part VI, Letter VII).

32 On this point among the Jansenists, see Taveneaux (1973, pp. 108–21).

famous Jansenist Louis-Isaac Lemaître de Sacy (1613–1684). In "Christian Holidays", it was the Jansenist priest Jean-Baptiste Thiers (1636–1703) who was mentioned, and in "Usury," which is of particular interest to us, he cited in support of his ideas the names of Dumoulin, Grotius, Pufendorf, Saumaise and Montesquieu,[33] but also the Jansenists Domat, Pascal, and Seguenot. When it came to actually quoting works, he constantly used the *Conférences ecclésiastiques sur l'usure* (1718) by Jansenist sympathiser Jean-Laurent Le Semelier (1660–1725), conferences held "under the cardinal of Noailles [a prelate very favourable to Jansenism], in other words, during the reign of the healthy & scholarly morality" (Faiguet de Villeneuve 1765, p. 538). At the very end of the article he highly recommended

> the anonymous author, who, at the end of the last century gave us the *pratique des billets*; another who recently published an *in -4° sur les prêts de commerce*, a book that outweighs the first, and which was printed in Lille in 1738. [...] All these great men have regarded as legitimate the modest interest charged to the wealthy, and they saw nothing in this commerce which was contrary to justice or charity. (Faiguet de Villeneuve 1765, p. 553)

The "anonymous" author of the *Traité de la pratique des billets* was none other than Jean Le Correur. Regarding the "*in -4° sur les prêts de commerce*", this was naturally the work of Boidot *et al.* in its first edition. And the article "Usury" by Faiguet was finally a summary, with a few variations and additions, of this latter work.

None of the late Scholastics is quoted, precisely because Faiguet did not think in terms of extrinsic titles. Like Le Correur and the authors of the *Traité des prêts de commerce*, he was very harsh with the "casuists", and especially with Thomas Aquinas. He attempted to prove that they were constantly "in contradiction with themselves" (Faiguet de Villeneuve 1765, p. 541). While seeking to combat usury, they actually promoted it. On the one hand, the annuities [*rentes constituées*] were not a good way to use

33 After his famous passage of *The Spirit of the Laws*, "[t]o lend money without interest is certainly an action laudable and extremely good; but it is obvious that it is only a counsel of religion, and not a civil law" (Montesqieu [1748] 1949–51, XXII, 19), Montesquieu had been attacked by the rigorist Jansenists in the *Nouvelles Ecclésiastiques* (October 1749, p. 164). He replied to these charges in his *Défense de l'esprit des lois* (1750) (Lauriol, 2013; Maire, 2013), which gave rise to new attacks from the journal of the rigorists (see *Nouvelles Ecclésiastiques,* April 1750, p. 72). Montesquieu did not quote the Traité des prêts de commerce, and his own logic and arguments were different from those of the liberal Jansenists. Equally, Mignot never referred to Montesquieu in the editions of 1759, 1767 or 1770 of the *Traité*. Montesquieu is quoted twice in the long article by Faiguet de Villeneuve, but very briefly (and not the famous passage of the Book XXII). Neither Jaucourt (1765) nor Laforest (1769 [1776]) referred to Montesquieu.

money if it was lent to the poor; quite the contrary, it was sinful. On the other hand, lending money to the poor, if the lender then invoked *lucrum cessans, damnum emergens,* and so on, was also a sin (Faiguet de Villeneuve 1765, p. 537–8). What mattered were not those false "scruples" but the light, again, of "natural law":

> Well-informed borrowers mock the scruples that one would want to attribute to those who lend to them. They feel & state that no harm is done to them in commercial loans. Accordingly, one sees everyday traders & businessmen, who, as neighbours, even as relatives, mutually lend to each other with interest; in this they are faithful observers of equity, since when they lend they only demand what they give without reluctance every time they borrow. They recognize that these conditions are also fair on both sides; that they are even indispensable to support trade. The alleged wrongs done to us, they say, are only imaginary wrongs; although the lender makes us pay legal interest, we are well compensated by the gains that he provides us, & by the trades that we make with the sums borrowed. In short, in the business of lending for profit, they sell us a good that it is useful to buy, that we sometimes sell ourselves, that is to say the use of money, and we find in this active & passive trade the same benefits that we find in all other trades. (Faiguet de Villeneuve 1765, p. 532)

Thus it could not be contrary to the law of God to lend to someone who would get rich with this money by increasing his trade, and who would also enrich the lender (Faiguet de Villeneuve 1765, p. 532). Interest was merely the price of "the use of money", nothing more.

As in the *Traité des prêts de commerce,* Faiguet argued on the one hand that it would be unfair if the lender did not share in the profit that the borrower generated with his money. On the other hand, he insisted that it was obvious that lending with interest to a poor man who was in need was forbidden by the sacred texts.[34] As in the letter by Dom Thierry de Viaixnes and the book by Boidot *et al.*, Faiguet refuted the idea that the loan was a "sale", as argued by the scholastic theologians, paraphrasing the idea of Thierry de Viaixnes about legal action enabling one to recover the principal.[35] Regarding the law of Moses, Faiguet maintained that free loans only applied to siblings and relatives, and that since God did not defend lend-

34 "Indeed, God's intention that is revealed to us in Scripture is that we treat our neighbour, especially if he is in distress, as our brother and our friend, as we would ask to be treated ourselves in such cases; that therefore we lend to him *for free* in his need of money, grain, clothes and anything else, *quamlibet aliam rem,* says the sacred text, therefore lodging when it is necessary. It is said in Leviticus, *xxv. 35* fear your God and your brother shall find refuge with you, *time Deum tuum vivere possit frater tuus apud te*" (Faiguet de Villeneuve 1765, p. 539).

35 "[I] still retain the ownership of what I lent you, & from this continuous ownership is born the right that I have to claim this thing in court, if you do not pay it back yourself after the term of the loan" (Faiguet de Villeneuve 1765, 535).

ing with interest to foreigners, whom he loved and cherished, this was by no means a prohibited practice but "a practice less favourable than the loan of friendship that He establishes between the Israelites." Regarding Luke's Gospel, "lend to them without expecting to get anything back", this could only be a maxim about charity (Faiguet de Villeneuve 1765, p. 545). He reviewed the exegesis about the translation of "despair" [*désespérer*] by referring to the same authors: "This observation is seen more in the *Traité des prêts de commerce, p. 106.*" After the Old and New Testaments, Faiguet moved on to the Church Fathers, etc., by reviewing again a similar if not identical argument to that of the liberal Jansenists, which it is unnecessary to detail again. But that was not all.

In Volume 13 of the *Encyclopédie*, published in 1765, the article "Interest-bearing loan (*Natural, civil and canon law*)" signed by Louis de Jaucourt (1704–1779), one of the great contributors to Diderot's dictionary, was much shorter and resumed most of the arguments prevailing among the Jansenists (and not those of the late Scholastics). However, it seems that Jaucourt, who was able to read Faiguet's entry (dated as we have seen from 1758) or the *Traité des prêts de commerce*, sought to go further:

> When a poor man borrows from a rich man, if this poor man borrows in case of great necessity, & with all his industry he is not able to pay any interest, charity probably requires the rich man to be satisfied with the repayment of the capital only, & even sometimes that he [the rich man] extinguishes it [the debt] in whole or in part: but if the poor man borrows to make windfall profits, I know of no reason why the rich man may not legitimately ask for a small portion of the profit that will be generated by the one to whom he provided the means to earn so much. (Jaucourt 1765, XIII, p. 334)

What was a "poor" man and what would he do with the borrowed money? Have we not seen "poor" merchants getting rich quickly thanks to the money that they were able to borrow? If there was mutual agreement, if the poor man was not in extreme need, then Jaucourt argued that lending at interest was lawful.

It was into this breach that the parish priest of Sainte-Croix and general vicar of the diocese of Lyon, Paul-Timoléon de Laforest (1708–1782), stepped with his *Traité de l'usure et des intérêts*. The book was first published in 1769 and republished appropriately at the beginning of 1776,[36] before Controller-General Turgot's disgrace. Again, the writings from the liberal Jansenist tradition were discussed, and even provided a focus for debate.

Thus, Laforest discussed the letter from Thierry de Viaixnes and the

36 The censor Coqueley de Chaussepierre gave his approval on 20 January 1776 (Laforest [1769] 1776, p. xi).

Traité des prêts de commerce in the first edition (1738).[37] After detailing the different parts of this book and ironically praising "the most talented erudition", he criticised the rich/poor distinction:

> It is moreover impossible to base the legitimacy or illegitimacy of interest only & specifically on the poverty or on the wealth of those to whom the money is lent or entrusted. These qualities of poor or rich are not easy to determine, and over three-quarters of men are truly & precisely neither the one nor the other. (Laforest [1769] 1776, pp. 135–6)

According to Laforest, it was the use made of the loan that was crucial. Of course, charity required not demanding interest when the poor man was in "extreme peril" (Laforest [1769] 1776, pp. 237–8), but lending one's money at interest when there was free mutual consent was perfectly legal. However, the lender had to know in advance how the funds were to be used. If they were used by "Traders, Bankers, Buyers, Entrepreneurs, in a word, those who use the money for a truly profitable purpose" (Laforest [1769] 1776, p. 261), then there was no problem. In contrast, when "the one to whom the money is provided does not use it in a fruitful manner, then one does not make with him a contract different from a loan, as it has been explained. But these cases are very common: they characterize and have always characterized usury and usurers." So when the loan money was "consumed" for purposes that "yield nothing", "that is usury" (Laforest [1769] 1776, pp. 225–6). We find in Laforest, in another way, the traditional distinction between a consumer loan and a production loan. But contrary to Formey, Gastumeau, Faiguet and Jaucourt, Laforest recognised the validity of the notions of extrinsic titles. According to him, money was not a commodity like others,[38] and his book was clearly an attempt to reconcile the arguments of Le Correur's tradition and that of the Scholastics on the issue. Now, at the time Laforest published his essay, the *Traité des prêts de commerce* had already been reissued several times, the last edition of 1767 (and the fifth volume of 1770) having again put the liberal Jansenist tradition in the spotlight.

4.2 The Last Editions of the Traité des Prêts de Commerce *and the Jansenist Legacy*

Despite the irony of a Jansenist theologian of Montpellier, Jean-Baptiste de

37 Which he incorrectly dated 1730.

38 "Money is sometimes *sterile*, sometimes *fertile*: *sterile*, when it is consumed: *fertile*, when its value persists and increases: it is not its nature that decides, but how it is used" (Laforest [1769] 1776, p. 235).

La Porte (1699–?), wondering in 1769 whether it was appropriate to "talk about a book that never made any sensation in this country and which, at the moment it appeared, was forgotten" (de La Porte 1769, III, p. 31), there is every reason to believe, instead, that the book met with real success.

To begin with, there were no fewer than three editions of the new *Traité des prêts de commerce* by 1767: the first two in 1759 and another in 1767, all by bookseller-publisher Jacques Vincent. Vincent was "a real Jansenist" (Lyon-Caen 2010, p. 237) and therefore the publishing of the book by Boidot *et al.* raised more questions about the alleged divisions within the party and the idea that the liberals were a completely isolated minority.[39] In any event, these three editions were a sign that the book was not stillborn. Moreover, it was reviewed by the major journals of the time, but in two stages. Although the *Journal de Trévoux* and the *Année littéraire* showed interest on the day of its publication in 1759, the *Mercure de France* merely reported it (*Mercure de France* April 1759, pp. 144–5). The latter, the semi-official government periodical, did however review it at length in 1767. The review was so glowing that *Nouvelles Ecclésiastiques*, the "rigorist" Jansenist journal, was moved: "We would have willingly left [the *Traité*] in the obscurity it deserves, if the *Mercure de France* had not announced that it was an important, solid & accurate book" (*Nouvelles Ecclésiastique* 14 October, 1767, p. 168). Let us begin by examining the views of the declared opponents of the Jansenists, the Jesuits, and then the two main French journals of the 1760s.

The *Journal de Trévoux* devoted a long review in August 1759 to the book by Boidot *et al.* After outlining the changes and additions with respect to the first edition, the Jesuit periodical argued that the *Traité des prêts de commerce* was the direct extension of the letter by Dom Thierry de Viaixnes (1728). After these few remarks on the Jansenist doctrine, the Jesuits were actually rather embarrassed.

In the *Traité* the authors "claim to draw implications favourable to trade loans" from passages of Holy Scripture and from the works of the Church Fathers (*Journal de Trévoux* August 1759, p. 1927). The journalist mainly discussed loans granted to "rich people." Being globally hostile to this practice, he recognised that it "does not impoverish them [the rich]" but that by increasing their wealth, it disturbed social welfare by rewarding "idleness" and "greed" (*Journal de Trévoux* August 1759, p. 1937).

On the doctrine of the Church, the journalist was very careful. Although Moses allowed usury when lending to foreigners, did he want to forbid it

39 This is the thesis put forward by Cottret (2002), and especially by Lyon-Caen (2010).

to the Jews only when lending to their poor brothers? It was not clear. This was in fact probably a "hazardous interpretation" of the text. The journalist did not mention the Gospels but simply noted that "Jesus Christ" always spoke "in terms so clear & so strong" in favour of free loans that sacred texts "powerfully resist the violence done to them by bending them to the system of usury or moderate interest" (*Journal de Trévoux* August 1759, pp. 1940–1). Only Saint Ambrose and Saint Jerome were cited as authorities against interest-bearing loans. But ultimately, while the journalist returned repeatedly to the prohibition on lending at interest to the poor, he did not make a clear statement about loans between the rich, or trade loans. He was highly embarrassed in this regard and preferred to stand by the scholastic tradition of extrinsic titles. What interested him was to lambaste a book stemming from Jansenism, as testified by the end of the review. "In closing this article, we are obliged to warn that there are other reprehensible proposals in this *Traité des Prêts de Commerce*", the journalist quoting a passage that supposedly undermined the Immaculate Conception of the Blessed Virgin. The author of the *Traité* allegedly "ignored or renounced the doctrine of this School [the Sorbonne]" (*Journal de Trévoux* August 1759, p. 1947–8). This was undoubtedly his main crime.

Fréron's *L'Année littéraire* discussed the book in 1759. The journalist was grateful to the author of the *Traité des prêts de commerce* for successfully clarifying the disputes among theologians and for dispelling, by using "natural law & the Divine Law", any clouds the "Schools" had spread on the issue (*L'Année littéraire* 1759, p. 135). He readily acknowledged that interest-bearing loans could not be made to the poor, but that it was permissible to demand interest "which is not costly to the borrower" when the latter made a profit from the money lent. The journalist then summarised in detail the arguments of Boidot *et al.* and exposed how the Church Fathers and the Scholastics had had to struggle in their time against loans with "excessive interest" that ruined families and entire cities. It was for these reasons that the Councils and Princes published ordinances against usury, "that is where the misconceptions we have had [about usury] stem from" (*L'Année littéraire* 1759, pp. 138–9). *L'Année littéraire* was full of praise for the *Traité* in a review that wholly adhered to the main arguments of the liberals since the Jansenist Le Correur, namely that lending to a rich man who used the money to increase his wealth did not infringe any law. A review so laudatory and so complete in "the most important and the most interesting periodical of the XVIIIth century" (Balcou 1991, n° 0118) was far from insignificant.

This applied even eight years later in the most widely read journal of the time, the *Mercure de France*, which devoted a critical note in July 1767 to the new edition of the *Traité*. The opening lines set the tone: "We know of no books more useful than this one, nor the use of which can be more universal, more practical, more daily" (*Mercure de France* 1767, p. 99). Its main merit was to have succeeded in opening a middle way between the zealous partisans (the "Doctors") of the ban on interest-bearing loans on the one hand, and the upholders of uncontrolled freedom on the other. For the journalist, by going to the roots of the debate (namely the Old and New Testaments), rather than exegesis by the casuists, the authors of the *Traité* had finally settled the issue. By separating lending to the poor, which was charity and for which interest could not be claimed, and lending to the rich, who were working towards their own success, the authors had allegedly dissipated "with a light that seems to leave nothing to be desired, all the clouds that the school's disputes spread on this issue" (*Mercure de France* 1767, p. 102). The rave reviews received by the *Traité des prêts de commerce* in the leading journals of the time were not without effect. Two contradictory trends stood out.

The first was the counter-attack by the "rigorist" Jansenists. The most comprehensive response by this camp came from Jean-Baptiste de La Porte. The author devoted a whole volume (vol. 3) of his *Principes théologiques, canoniques et civils sur l'usure* (1769) to criticising the *Traité des prêts de commerce.* But what was very interesting was the way in which de la Porte tackled his opponents. He maintained that annuities [*rentes constituées*] were a "sale", not a "loan" (de la Porte 1769, III, pp. 153–4), and he argued in terms of extrinsic titles, and as such *damnum emergens* or *lucrum cessans* were "legal titles of compensation" [*des titres légitimes de compensation*] (de la Porte 1769, III, pp. 165–6). However, de La Porte was trying to limit the spread of those titles. The "damage" needed to be reported and the lender had to have suffered genuine loss because "every profit which plays in the lender's favour, which enhances his wealth [...] is designated by all the laws as an injustice named usury" (de la Porte 1769, III, p. 167). Next, de La Porte objected to the idea that one could judge the validity of interest-bearing loans by "natural law" or, worse still, the authority of "human reason" (de la Porte 1769, III, pp. 185–278). This was an outrageous suggestion worthy of the "*philosophes*", who "reject the authority of the revelation" (de la Porte 1769, III, p. 210), an accusation taken up again in 1772 by the *Journal Œconomique* in a very positive critique of de La Porte's book (*Journal Œconomique* 1772, pp. 231–8). Finally, de La Porte tried to demonstrate how, contrary to being the normal price of the use of money, interest was harmful to agriculture, trade and industry (de la Porte 1769, III, pp. 279–519).[40] Credit removed money from the land because it was easier to become rich through usury than by farming. With insufficient investment in land, agriculture declined and the countryside was impoverished. As far as trade was concerned, the interest of money led to a rise in the price of goods when merchants were forced to borrow. This was devastating for the people (de la Porte 1769, III, pp. 426–9).

Mignot answered this attack by publishing a fifth and final volume of the *Traité des prêts de commerce* in 1770, one year before his death. This volume once again returned to the texts of the Church Fathers, the Scholastics and other theologians, but it also referred to another controversy. Mignot recalled the scandal provoked by the publications of Nicolaus Broedersen's *De usuris licitis et illicitis* (1743) and Scipione Maffei's *Dell'impiego del Denaro* (1744) in favour of interest-bearing loans, and the reaction of Pope Benedict XIV (1675–1758) through the encyclical letter *Vix Pervenit* (1745). Curiously, neither Faiguet de Villeneuve nor de Jaucourt in the *Encyclopédie* referred to this affair. Laforest mentioned the name of Maffei only in passing, but spent a few pages on the Letter of the Pope.[41] Mignot did not discuss the substance of the case, but he quoted Maffei and explained that his book was perfectly in tune with the *Traité des prêts de commerce* (with the same poor/merchants distinction). The interesting thing was that without discussing the encyclical letter (which reasserted the traditional doctrine and the exceptions of extrinsic titles), Mignot welcomed the fact that the Pope had appeared to accept the printing of *Vix Pervenit* in the second edition of Maffei's book (Mignot 1770, pp. 59–62). Not surprisingly, the rigorists, and especially the *Nouvelles Ecclésiastiques*, condemned the weakness of the Pope in this affair, whom they considered should have much more firmly censured Maffei's book (*Nouvelles Ecclésiastiques*, September 1745, pp. 106–7). De La Porte and Gabriel-Nicolas Maultrot (1714–1803) in their *Le défenseur de l'usure confondu* (1782) were less severe than the *Nouvelles Ecclésiatiques*: they praised *Vix Pervenit* and condemned Maffei's ideas in a book that was a reaction against the last volume of Mignot's *Traité* and the new group of publications from Turgot's entourage.[42]

We will not return here to the connections between the Traité des prêts de commerce on the one hand and two other Turgot's *Mémoires sur le prêts à intérêt et le commerce des fers* ([1770] 1789)[43] or the *Théorie de l'interet de l'argent* (1780, 1782) by Jansenists Rulié and Gouttes, helped by Turgot, on the other (see Orain 2014, pp. 481–4). What is important here is the transformation of the Jansenist legacy.

40 Concerning this idea in Duguet's *Institution d'un Prince*, see Orain (2014).

41 See Laforest (1769 [1776], pp. 6–8). This is the same in Rulié, Gouttes and Turgot's *Théorie de l'intérêt de l'argent*, book in which only the name of Maffei (spelled "Maphéi") is briefly mentioned (see Rulié, Gouttes [and Turgot] 1780, p. xiv).

42 For more details about the significance of *Le Défenseur de l'usure confondu*, see Orain (2014, pp. 42–3).

Indeed, the second trend was to take liberal Jansenist ideas to extremes. As in the tradition of Le Correur, Boidot, Aubret and Mignot, Turgot's supporters treated money and its price (interest) like any other commodity. But they also sought to prove that if generosity and charity were required in some severe cases, lending for free "is never the order of strict justice" (Turgot [1770] 1789, p. 34). In a perspective similar to that adopted by Laforest, Turgot explained that for a century or two:

> it resulted that borrowing by the poor to survive is scarcely perceptible in the total sum of loans; that the majority of loans are made to the rich, or at least to the industrious, who hope to obtain great profits by using the money they borrow. Therefore lending at interest must have become less heinous. (Turgot [1770] 1789, pp. 66–7)

But he went further. While acknowledging that there were very high-interest loans granted by usurers to poor artisans or small retailers, Turgot did not condemn them since they were useful to people who could not survive without them. The pledge loans, even to the poor, were no more blameworthy since it was impossible to enslave anyone who could not repay (Turgot [1770] 1789, pp. 68–9). For Turgot, only those loan sharks who lent to young people from good families were really harmful to society. Such loans "facilitated" and "encouraged" the "disorders" of families since they could lead the fathers to dishonour and ruin (Turgot [1770] 1789, pp. 71–2). The famous *Théorie de l'intéret de l'argent* compiled the *Traité des prêts de commerce* in Mignot's version, Montesquieu, and the works of Condillac and Turgot on interest-bearing loans (see Orain 2014). A shift compared with the earliest works of the Jansenists was therefore very apparent. The editors of the *Théorie* resumed the passages by Turgot about the now marginal loans to the poor (Rulié, Gouttes [and Turgot] 1780, p. 217 ff.) and the fact that only usury practised against the profligate sons of the well-to-do was actually dangerous (Rulié, Gouttes [and Turgot] 1780, pp. 170 ff.). This therefore meant the demise of free loans to the poor on which Dom Thierry, Boidot, Aubret, Mignot and Faiguet had so insisted. Nevertheless, by refusing the "errors" of the Scholastics and the rationale of extrinsic titles (Rulié, Gouttes [and Turgot] 1780, pp. 17–20), Rulié, Gouttes and Turgot pushed the logic of the liberal Jansenists to the limit: the "fair price" of the loan was "the annual interest of my capital, according to the current rate" (Rulié, Gouttes [and Turgot] 1780, p. 109).[44] Money, one century after Le Correur (1682), had well and truly become a commodity like any other.

43 Two texts are combined in this edition of 1789. Gustave Schelle has published separately the "Mémoire sur les prêts d'argent" (Turgot [1770] 1913–1923, III, pp. 154–202) and "La marque des fers. Lettre au Contrôleur général" (Turgot [1773] 1913–1923, III, pp. 617–26).

5. Conclusion

The principal innovation of the liberal Jansenist tradition is to have considered the issue of interest outside of the late scholastic framework. From Le Correur in the late seventeenth century onwards, they all rejected the very idea of extrinsic titles. In this respect, interest on money was no longer the result of any "damage", "cessation of profit", or, in a broader sense, any opportunity cost. Because it created profit through productive activities, money had to be remunerated. "Interest" became only the price to be paid for the "use" of a "capital." In reaching this conclusion, the Jansenists tried to reconcile Holy Scripture and Modern Natural Law. On their claim, credit transactions belonged to the sphere of free voluntary contract when they occurred among merchants. In this respect, they prepared the ground for the subsequent conceptualisation of credit as a normal market. Consumer loans to the poor were excluded from this, as they fell within the domain of Christian charity.

In the pre-Revolutionary period, the debate shifted. "Interest" became clearly a market price and not the result of a bilateral transaction, and the rich/poor dichotomy posited by the Jansenist theologians faded. The rich were no longer "obliged" to lend to the needy poor because the boundaries between unproductive consumer loans and productive trade loans had been blurred. Nevertheless, it was the Jansenists who had introduced the points for a debate that lasted nearly a century. This finding requires us to reassess the position of this religious current in the economic thinking of the Enlightenment. Contrary to the point made by Cottret (2002, pp. 65–6), there was no "ideological handiwork" involved here. In speaking of Rulié and Gouttes, she evokes a "synthesis, to suit them", a scattershot of ideas, without any connection between them. From the essay by Le Correur to the *Théorie de l'intérêt de l'argent*, including the crucial input by Dom Thierry de Viaixnes, this paper has attempted instead to show the great coherence of the liberal framework. The changes were minimal over a century, and although this current perhaps did not dominate the Jansenist movement itself (and again, what do we know about the conscience of the faithful on the question after 1760?), it did impose its vision and its arguments on the rising political economy of the Enlightenment.

---

44 We have seen that the Jansenist tradition did not deal with time preference because from Le Correur to Mignot; they dismissed the idea of any costs for the lender. Turgot, on the contrary, insisted on this argument and used it in order to justify the rate of interest in conjunction with his subjective theory of value. Concerning this important issue in economic theory, see Faccarello (2016, pp. 80–1).

Acknowledgements

We are grateful to the two anonymous referees and for comments received on an earlier draft of the paper from Arnaud Berthoud, Muriel Dal Pont-Legrand, Gilbert Faccarello, Philippe Steiner and Keith Tribe.

Disclosure statement

No potential conflict of interest was reported by the authors.

References

Aquinas, T., *Summa theologica.* 1265–1274.

Balcou, J., 1991. L'Année littéraire (1754–1776). *In*: J. Sgard, ed. *Dictionnaire des journaux.* Paris: Universitas, n°0118.

Barbier, F., 2002. *Lumières du nord.* Paris: Droz.

Bernard A., 1950. La formation de la doctrine ecclésiastique sur l'usure. *In*: A. Vacant, E. Mangenot et F. Amann, eds. *Dictionnaire de théologie catholique,* t. XV (2). Paris: Letouzey et Ané, 2316–2336.

Boidot, P., 1730. *Réponse aux difficultés proposées à un théologien sur les prêts de commerce de Hollande.* La Haye.

Boidot, P., Aubret, B., and Mignot, É., 1738. *Traité des prêts de commerce, ou l'on compare la doctrine des scholastiques sur ces prêts, avec celle de l'Ecriture sainte & des saints Pères.* Lille: Pierre Mathon.

Boidot, P., Aubret, B., and Mignot, É., 1759. *Traité des prêts de commerce, ou de l'intérêt légitime et illégitime de l'argent, nouvelle édition, augmentée.* 4 vols. Amsterdam and Paris: Vincent.

Boidot, P., Aubret, B., and Mignot, É., 1767. *Traité des prêts de commerce, ou de l'intérêt légitime et illégitime de l'argent, nouvelle édition, augmentée.* 4 vols. Paris: Vincent.

Broedersen, N., 1729. *Tractatus brevis de reditibus utrimque redimilibus.* Delphis: Bernardi van Holzen.

Broedersen, N., 1743. *De usuris licitis et illicitis.* (N. pl., n. publ.)

Campbell, P., 1996. *Power and politics in old regime France, 1720–1745.* London and New York: Routledge.

Chartier, R., 1990. *Les origines culturelles de la Révolution française.* Paris: Seuil.

Courtin, E., 1828. *Encyclopédie moderne ou Dictionnaire abrégé des sciences, des lettres et des arts.* La Haye: Lejeune, vol. XVI.

Cottret, M., 1998. *Jansénisme et Lumières. Pour un autre XVIIIe siècle.* Paris: Albin Michel.

Cottret, M., 2002. Du jansénisme au libéralisme : itinéraire de quelques abbés du siècle. *Dix-huitième siècle,* 34, 53–66.

Cottret, M., 2016. *Histoire du jansénisme.* Paris: Perrin.

Correspondance littéraire, philosophique et critique de Grimm et Diderot, depuis 1753 jusqu'en 1790. Paris: Furne, tome III (1761–1764).

Dickey, L., 1990. Pride, hypocrisy and civility in Mandeville's social and historical theory. *Critical review,* 4 (3), 387–431.

Faccarello, G., [1986]1999. *The foundations of Laissez-faire: the economics of Pierre de Boisguilbert.* London: Routledge.

Faccarello, G. and Steiner, P., 2008. Interest, sensationism and the science of the legislator. French 'philosophie économique' 1695–1830. *European journal of the history of economic thought*, 15 (1), 1–23.

Faccarello, G., 2016. Anne-Robert-Jacques Turgot (1727–1781). *In*: G. Faccarello and Heinz D. Kurz, eds. *Handbook on the history of economic analysis*. Vol. I. Cheltenham and Northampton: Edward Elgar, 73–82.

Faiguet de Villeneuve, J., 1763. *L'économie politique: projet pour enrichir et perfectionner l'espèce humaine*. Londres et Paris: Moreau.

Faiguet de Villeneuve, J., 1765. Usure (*morale*). *In*: D. Diderot, ed. *Encyclopédie ou Dictionnaire raisonné des sciences, des arts et des métiers, par une Société de Gens de lettres*. Paris: Briasson, David, Le Breton, Durand, Vol. 17, 529–53.

Faiguet de Villeneuve, J., 1770. *Légitimité de l'usure légale, où l'on prouve son utilité; que les casuistes sont en contradiction avec eux-mêmes. Monts de piété. Pratique injuste de la poste. Où l'on discute les passages de l'Ancien et du Nouveau Testament sur l'usure*. Amsterdam: Marc-Michel Rey.

Finley, M., 1973. *The ancient economy*. Berkley and Los Angeles: University of California Press.

Formey, J.-H.-S., 1751. Examen de l'usure, suivant les principes du droit naturel. *In*: *Choix de mémoires et abrégé de l'histoire de l'Académie de Berlin*. Berlin: Haude, vol. III, 324–51.

Gastumeau, J.-B., 1756. *Dissertation sur la légitimité des intérêts de l'argent*. La Haye.

Gervais, P., 2012. Crédit et filières marchandes au XVIIIe siècle. *Annales. histoire, sciences sociales*, 67 (4), 1011–48.

Grès-Gayer, J., 2009. L'électron libre du gallicanisme: Jean de Launoy (1601–1678). *Revue de l'histoire des religions*, 226 (3), 517–43.

Hecht, J., 1959. Trois précurseurs de la sécurité sociale au XVIIIe siècle: Henry de Boulainvilliers, Faiguet de Villeneuve, Du Beissier de Pizany d'Eden. *Population*, 14 (1), 73–88.

Histoire de l'académie royale des inscriptions et belles-lettres. Paris: Imprimerie Royale.

Jaucourt, L. de, 1765. Prêt à intérêt (*Droit naturel, civil, & canon*). *In*: D. Diderot, ed. *Encyclopédie ou Dictionnaire raisonné des sciences, des arts et des métiers, par une société de gens de lettres*. Paris: Briasson, Le Breton, Durand. Vol. 13, 333–6.

Journal des Sçavans. Paris: Chaubert, décembre 1738.

Journal de Trévoux ou Mémoires pour servir à l'histoire des sciences et des beaux-arts. Paris: Chaubert et Hérissant, août 1759.

Journal oeconomique ou Mémoires, notes et avis sur l'agriculture, les arts, le commerce. Paris: Boudet.

Kaye, F. B., 1988. Introduction. *In*: B. Mandeville, ed. *The fable of the bees or private vices, publick benefits*. Indianapolis: Liberty Fund.

L'ami de la religion et du Roi: journal ecclésiastique, politique et littéraire. Paris: Le Clère.

Laforest, P.-T. de, [1769]1776. *Traité de l'usure et des intérêts, augmenté d'une défense du traité, & de diverses observations sur les écrits qui l'ont combattu*. Lyon: Pierre Bruyset Ponthus.

L'Année littéraire. Paris: Lambert, 1759.

Langholm, Odd., 1983. *Wealth and money in the aristotelian tradition*. Oxford: Oxford University Press.

Langholm, Odd., 1984. *The aristotelian analyses of usury*. Bergen: Universitetsforlaget.

Lapidus, A., 1987. La propriété de la monnaie: doctrine de l'usure et théorie de l'intérêt. *Revue economique*, 38 (6), 1095–110.

La Porte, J.-B.-B. de, 1769. *Principes théologiques, canoniques et civils sur l'usure.* Paris: Delevacque, 3 vols.

Launoy, J. de, 1729. *Lettre de M. Jean de Launoy, docteur de la Maison de Navarre, à un de ses amis, sur le sujet de l'usure.* Delft.

Lauriol, C., 2013. Querelle de l'*Esprit des lois. In*: C. Volpilhac-Auger and C. Larrère, eds. *A Montesquieu dictionary.* Available from: http://dictionnaire-montesquieu.ens-lyon.fr/en/home/

Le Correur, J., [1682]1684. *Traité de la pratique des billets entre les négociants, seconde édition revue et augmentée.* Mons: Gaspard Migeot.

Le Semelier, J.-L., 1718. *Conférences ecclésiastiques de Paris sur l'usure.* Paris: Estienne.

Lyon-Caen, N., 2010. *La boîte à Perrette. Le jansénisme parisien au XVIIIe siècle.* Paris: Albin Michel.

Maffei, S., 1744. *Dell'impiego del denaro.* Verona: Giannalberto Tumermani.

Maire, C., 1998. *De la cause de Dieu à la cause de la Nation. Le Jansénisme au XVIIIe siècle.* Paris: Gallimard.

Maire, C., 2005. Les querelles jansénistes de la décennie 1730–1740. *Recherches sur Diderot et sur l'Encyclopédie,* 38, 71–92.

Maire, C., 2013. Jansénisme. *In*: C. Volpilhac-Auger and C. Larrère, eds. *A Montesquieu dictionary.* Available from: http://dictionnaire-montesquieu.ens-lyon.fr/en/home/

Mercure de France. Paris: Cavelier, Pissot, de Nully. Décembre 1738 and Avril 1759.

Michaud, L.-G., 1821. *Biographie universelle ancienne et moderne.* Paris: Michaud, vol. XXIX.

Mignot, É., 1753. *Discours sur l'accord des sciences et des lettres avec la religion.* Paris.

Mignot, É., 1754. *Analyse de toutes les vérités enseignées et professées dans la religion chrétienne.* Paris: Vincent.

Mignot, É., 1755. *Des Droits de l'État et du prince sur les biens du clergé.* Amsterdam: Arkstée et Merkus. 4 vols.

Mignot, É., 1759. Préface. *In*: P. Boidot, B. Aubret, and É. Mignot, eds. *Traité des prêts de commerce, ou de l'intérêt légitime et illégitime de l'argent, nouvelle édition, augmentée.* 4 vols. Amsterdam and Paris: Vincent. Vol. 1, iii–xx.

Mignot, É., 1770. *Traité des prêts de commerce et réponse aux six lettres de l'auteur des Principes théologiques, canoniques & civils sur l'usure, Tome cinquième.* Paris: Knapen.

Montesquieu, C.-L. de Secondat de., [1748]1949–51. *De l'esprit des loix. In*: C.-L. de Secondat de Montesquieu. *Oeuvres complètes de Montesquieu.* Paris: Gallimard, 2 vols.

Noonan, J. T., 1957. *The scholastic analysis of usury.* Cambridge and London: Harvard University Press.

Noonan, J. T., 1966. Authority, usury and contraception. *Cross currents,* 16 (1), 55–79.

Nouvelles ecclésiastiques ou Mémoires pour servir à l'histoire ecclésiastique de la Constitution Unigenitus. Paris, 15 vols. 1713–1803.

Orain, A., 2014. The Second Jansenism and the rise of French eighteenth-century political economy. *History of political economy,* 46 (3), 463–90.

Picot, M.-J.-P., 1825. *Mémoires pour servir à l'histoire ecclésiastique pendant le dix-huitième siècle.* Bruges: Félix de Pachtere, vol. IV.

Perrot, J.-C., [1984]1992. La Main invisible et le Dieu caché. *In*: J.-C. Perrot, ed. *Une histoire intellectuelle de l'économie politique (XVIe-XVIIIe siècle).* Paris: EHESS, 333–54.

Roover, R. de., 1955. Scholastic economics: Survival and lasting influence from the sixteenth century to Adam Smith. *The quarterly journal of economics,* 69 (2), 161–90.

Roover, R. de., 1969. Léonard Lessius comme économiste. Les doctrines économiques des casuistes dans les Pays-Bas espagnols au début du XVIIème siècle. *In*: *Mededelingen von de K. Vlaamse Academie voor Wetenshappen Klasse des Letteren,* XXXI, 2, Bruxelles.

Rulié, P., Gouttes, J.-L., and Turgot, A.-R.-J., 1780. *Théorie de l'intérêt de l'argent tirée des vrais principes du droit naturel, de la théologie et de la politique, contre l'abus de l'imputation d'usure.* Paris: Barrois.

Seigel, J., 2005. *The ideas of the self. Thought and experience in Western Europe since the seventeenth century.* Cambridge: Cambridge University Press.

Shusterman, N., 2010. *Religions & the politics of time. Holidays in France from Louis XIV through Napoleon.* Washington, DC: The Catholic University of America Press.

Targny, L. de., 1728. *Mémoire sur l'état présent des réfugiez françois en Hollande, au sujet de la religion.* Paris: Mazieres et Garnier.

Taveneaux, R., 1960. *Le jansénisme en Lorraine (1640–1789).* Paris: Vrin.

Taveneaux, R., 1973. *La vie quotidienne des jansénistes aux XVIIe et XVIIIe siècles.* Paris: Hachette.

Taveneaux, R., 1977. *Jansénisme et prêt à intérêt. Introduction, choix de textes et commentaires.* Paris: Vrin.

Turgot, A.-R.-J., [1770]1789. *Mémoires sur le prêt à intérêt et sur le commerce des fers, par M. Turgot, ministre d'État.* Paris: Froullé.

Turgot, A.-R.-J., [1770]1913–1923. Mémoire sur les prêts d'argent. *In:* G. Schelle, ed. *Œuvres de Turgot et documents le concernant.* Paris: Alcan, vol. III, pp. 154–202.

Turgot, A.-R.-J., [1773]1913–1923. La marque des fers. Lettre au Contrôleur general. *In:* G. Schelle, ed. *Œuvres de Turgot et documents le concernant.* Paris: Alcan, vol. III, pp. 617–626.

Viaixnes, Dom T. de., [1728]1759. Lettre de D. Thierry de Viaixnes, Religieux Bénédictin de la Congrégation de S. Vanne; à M. Corneille-Jean Barckman, Archevêque d'Utrecht, au sujet des prêts à rente usités dans la République de Hollande, selon les loix. *In:* P. Boidot, B. Aubret, and É. Mignot, eds. *Traité des prêts de commerce, ou de l'intérêt légitime et illégitime de l'argent, nouvelle édition, augmentée.* Amsterdam and Paris: Vincent. Vol. 4, xix–lx.

Vanhoorne, F., 1996. Du jansénisme au mercantilisme: la politique de l'abbé Du Guet. *Revue d'histoire ecclésiastique,* XCI, 41–65.

Van Houdt, T., 1995. Money, time and labour. Leonardus Lessius and the ethics of lending and interest taking. *Ethical perspectives,* 2, 11–27.

Van Houdt, T., 1998b. Tradition and renewal in late scholastic economic thought: the case of Leonardus Lessius (1554–1623). *Journal of medieval and early modern studies,* 28 (1), 51–73.

Van Houdt, T., 1998a. "Lack of money": a reappraisal of Lessius' contribution to the scholastic analysis of money-lending and interest-takin. *The European journal of the history of economic thought,* 5 (1), 1–35.

Van Kley, D., 1975. *The Jansenists and the expulsions of the Jesuits from France, 1757–1765.* New Haven and London: Yale University Press.

Van Kley, D., 1986. The Jansenist constitutional legacy in the French prerevolution, 1750-1789. *Historical reflections/réflexions historiques,* 13, 393–453.

Van Kley, D., 2006. *The religious origins of the French revolution.* New Haven and London: Yale University Press.

Van Kley, D., 2008. Religion and the age of 'Patriot' reform. *Journal of modern history,* 80, 1–44.

Abstract

This article is an attempt to prove that although the liberal Jansenists – Jansenism being the most powerful Christian protest movement of the seventeenth and eighteenth centuries – were not the first and the only ones to address the prohibition of interest-bearing loans, their writings on the issue shifted and fuelled the debate during the French Enlightenment, especially among the *Encyclopédistes* and the economists. By refuting the very logic of "extrinsic titles" of the Scholastics and their extension later on by the Jesuits, the liberals Jansenists redefined "interest" as the price to be paid for the use of money.

Defending free trade after physiocracy: On Dugald Stewart's architectonic of passions, reason and Providence

Thomas Ruellou

1. Introduction

Much has been written about the free market policies which came to be advocated in reaction to what is nowadays commonly called mercantilism. Yet, such a free-market policy programme might originate from manifold and divergent theories, and these would remain implicit, if not indeed entirely ignored, should the focus be placed solely on the practical applications to which they led. This article studies the approach followed by Dugald Stewart (1753–1828), the biographer of Adam Smith (1723–1790), and the first teacher of Political Economy in the British Isles. He believed that individuals automatically advance the public interest when following their own interests, in virtue of a harmony of Nature conceived in teleological and theological terms. According to him, there is a kind of natural order which allows for these beneficial consequences of self-interested economic activities. The study of his approach provides crucial insight into the arguments used to support freedom of trade at the beginning of the nineteenth century.

Generally speaking, economic liberalism and the drive to open markets presuppose that self-interested individuals perform actions that will eventually contribute to the public interest. In other words, a link between actions fostered by specific motives (typically, self-interest), and the public consequences of such actions, must implicitly be granted. In this respect, we can refer helpfully to the famous framework for analysing the relation between private and public interests proposed by Halévy in *The Growth of Philosophic Radicalism.*

Three kinds of interactions between private interests can be identified, namely a "fusion", a "natural identity", or an "artificial identity". Halévy's reading of British philosophers in general – and utilitarians in particular – has of course been criticised.[1] However, provided it is framed in sufficiently extensive yet unambiguous terms, I believe his framework remains useful for interpreting arguments developed by both philosophers and economists.

According to the "natural identity" of interests, individuals, "without desiring or knowing it, and while pursuing each his own interest, are working for the *direct* realisation of the general interest" (Halévy 1901–1904, p. 16, my emphasis). Halévy's implied argument can be analysed into three steps:

(i) individuals know what their interest is and follow it as a motive of action;
(ii) such self-interested individuals undertake actions to fulfil that motive;
(iii-a) achieving these actions necessarily leads to a better state of society for everyone.

This proposed identity between public and private interests can either be "immediate" or "progressive and gradual" (Halévy 1901–1904, p. 16). Thus, its "direct" nature does not mean it is instantaneously observed nor actually realised; it may rather be "ultimately" (Halévy 1901–1904, p. 17) observed, provided self-interest gains a "predominant influence on human action" (Halévy 1901–1904, p. 15). Hence, the link between (ii) and (iii-a) is "automatic" (Halévy 1901–1904, p. 15) and realised on its "own accord" (Halévy 1901–1904, p. 15), that is to say, realised without any institutional mediation, although it may take some time. The "artificial identity" also involves (i) and (ii), but presupposes:

(iii-b) unintended harmful consequences upon the whole.

1. According to Vergara (1998, pp. 99–101), Halévy confounded the positive side of utility (e.g. individuals seek pleasure and flee pain) with its normative one (e.g. the moral criteria ought to increase pleasure upon the whole). Besides, he thought that all philosophers he interpreted would have claimed that individuals act upon selfish motives. Halévy would have thereby claimed selfishness was the *only* motive individuals followed, thereby merging motives (selfishness, self-interest, self-love) which were different for most British philosophers (Vergara 1998, pp. 98–9). Although some of Vergara's criticisms do not apply to Jeremy Bentham's utilitarianism (Mongin and Sigot 1999), Halévy's focus on selfishness remains problematic regarding other philosophers he read, especially Adam Smith. For instance, Halévy's understanding of the "invisible hand" as evidence of an identity of interests is problematic, as will appear. Consequently, I confine myself to delineating a framework encompassing the public consequences of what individuals consider to be their self-interest, although what "self-interest" denotes of course depends on the author.

In that case, the link between private and public interests is neither "progressive and gradual" (Halévy 1901–1904, p. 16) nor instantaneous, but *indirect*: some "artifices" (Halévy 1901–1904, p. 17) are needed to make individuals choose specific actions "in spite of their avarice" (Halévy 1901–1904, p. 17, see Frobert 2003, pp. 25–31). A crucial role is here granted to the legislator. By exogenously influencing the benefits individuals may draw from their actions, he may make them choose specific actions which avoid harmful consequences. For example, he may set a maximum price on a market to prevent merchants from seeking a monopoly gain, or may establish legal restrictions, such as fees on some commodities to discourage people from consuming it. Therefore, the legislator does not prevent individuals from following what they think is best for them, nor does he force them into undertaking specific actions, but only channels individuals' choices into what leads to the best public interest. In this respect, "individual[s] … must submit to constraints in order that the interest of each should be artificially identified with the interest of all" (Halévy 1901–1904, p. 144).

In the case of the free-market economy with which I deal in this article, the "fusion" of interests is not relevant. Because it presupposes a spontaneous identification between private and public interests which takes place "within each individual conscience" (Halévy 1901–1904, p. 13), fusion would entail that an individual was interested "directly in the happiness of [his] neighbour" (Halévy 1901–1904, p. 13). In other words, all individuals would have an interest in directly fulfilling the interest of others. Thus, everyone would have the same interest in step (i) and cooperate to make the same decision in step (ii). This not only obviously fails to account for self-centred decisions, but also ignores the remote unintended consequences of decentralised actions.[2]

2. Defining such a cooperative interaction between individuals is the only logical way to understand a "fusion" of interests. In fact, Halévy's (1901–1904, p. 14) own explanation grounded on the association of ideas, according to which it is "only through sympathy that the happiness of a stranger can affect us", is ultimately fallacious. It can of course refer to the idea that we are pleased hence interested to see our fellow happy, as the opening sentences of the *Theory of Moral Sentiments* may intend (Smith 1759, I.i.1.1). Halévy, however, forgets that one can sympathize with grief as well as with joy (Smith 1759, I.i.1.4–5). The concord of sentiments being in both case agreeable (Smith 1759, I.i.2.1), there is no reason the misery of a stranger would not "affect" us. Despite this minor ambiguity, Halévy's argument can also mean that sympathy leads us to estimate the objects our fellow pursues and hence to desire them too. Yet, pursuing the same object as our neighbour for this reason is not a "fusion" of interests, for it does not mean we are "interested directly in the happiness *of our neighbour*" (Halévy's 1901–1904, p. 13, my emphasis), but only in the object to which *our happiness* is subservient. This confusion comes from the "associationist psychology" (originally advocated by Hartley) Halévy (1901–1904, p. 477) uses to understand "egoism" as "the primitive motive of which all the affections of the soul are the

I therefore focus on the natural and artificial identities. Besides, picturing Stewart as a philosopher arguing for "the public or general interest ... as opposed to the particular interests of merchants and manufacturers" (Kubo 2014, p. 941), or reaching an "impartial and disinterested stance" as a neutral judge could have done (Poovey 1998, p. 271), is unfortunately not of much help here. Indeed, such an impartial philosophical standpoint does not shed light on what specific connections private interests might bear to each other, and could thus imply either conflicts of private interests or an "identity of interests".

The conceptual distinction displayed above, along with Stewart's potential inheritance from François Quesnay (1694–1774) and Adam Smith, helps to understand why his analysis of the link between interests has until now not been consistently spelled out in the literature. In his process of shaping the doctrine of the recently established chair of Political Economy in Edinburgh, Stewart would have endorsed an original synthesis between physiocratic and Smithian theories (see Hyard 2004, Milgate and Stimon 2009, pp. 97–120). He indeed had a high admiration for both, and in his *Lectures on Political Economy*[3] very often compared them in pursuit of the

successive complications". In other words, Halévy considers the association of ideas subservient to self-interest, and therefore considers "sympathy" as a selfish principle (Vergara 1998, pp. 110–1). Although this may be coherent with Bentham's thought (Mongin and Sigot 1999, pp. 280–1), Smith (1759, VII. iii.1.4) explicitly rejected it. Similarly, although Stewart (1792–1827, II, p. 337) stressed that the association of ideas could lead to seek objects for their own sake whereas they were originally only means, he also criticised both Gay and Hartley for their "selfish system" (1792-1827, II, pp. 336–7). Stewart (1792–1827, II, pp. 252–347, 1815–1821, pp. 520–2) dealt with the association of ideas as a particular way that ideas occur in the human mind only, which does not mean being interested in our fellow's happiness as such. Consequently, the association of ideas cannot found a "fusion" of interests.

3. Henceforth, *Lectures*. These were not published during Stewart's lifetime, although he improved his manuscripts until the end of his life in the view of publishing them. Unfortunately, they were partly burnt after his death by his son Matthew Stewart. Consequently, we can only witness what message he spread during these *Lectures*, thanks to the remaining fragments of his manuscript and to two sets of students' notes taken during the session 1809–1810, published together in the eighth volume of his *Collected Works* (see Hamilton *in* Stewart 1855–1856 [1809–1810], VIII, vii–xii). In this article, I prefer confining myself to Stewart's moral philosophy contained in his published books and to parts of his *Lectures* published from the manuscripts, that is to say to give priority to what Stewart wrote with his own hand. However, the few quotations from the students' notes I use are always mentioned as such. These remain quite reliable insofar as Stewart himself read them (Hamilton *in* Stewart 1855–1856 [1809–1810], VIII, xxi-n) and as his editor considered them "remarkably copious and accurate, frequently corresponding word for word with" Stewart's own

best theoretical principles, especially concerning the productivity of agriculture or the doctrine of free trade. However, the incorporation of Quesnay's and Smith's concepts in Stewart's own *Lectures* is quite tortuous. Although Stewart (1855–1856 [1809–1810], VIII, p. 306) claimed that "with regard to the freedom of commerce ... both systems agree", Quesnay and Smith respectively relied on two opposite frameworks (Steiner 1987, pp. 1114–5). Quesnay assumed the existence of an order whose harmony ensures a priori the coherence of economic decisions; in this respect, the market only validates interactions which are in themselves mutually beneficial (Larrère 1992, p. 213). Smith, on the other hand, considered the market as a device which counterbalanced opposite private interests, which are thus made a posteriori compatible; in other words, although the market somewhat neutralises private interests by confining them to the production of wealth, they nevertheless remain in latent conflict (Winch 1978, pp. 80–1). It is in fact well known that Smith (1776, I.xi.p.10) had disseminated the advice that, by trying to reduce the number of sellers, "[t]he interest of the dealers ... is always in some respects different from, and even opposite to, that of the publick". The profit of merchants is indeed never as high as when the wealth of society is declining (Smith 1776, I.ix.1–2, p. 13). Thus, according to Smith, merchants do have an interest in opposing free trade and hence reducing the "opulence" of a country (Smith 1978, LJ(A), vi.88, see Winch 1978, pp. 140–5). Since Smith took for granted that some sectoral interests are fulfilled at the expense of others, or, to put it the other way round, that the general interest is reached by thwarting the merchants' interests, his view of the economy does not fit into the harmony implied by Halévy's framework. On the contrary, according to Quesnay, subservience and conformity to a "natural order" would allow mankind to reach its most beneficial condition. Indeed, the natural laws of such an order would "abundantly multiply the riches necessary to the subsistence of men" (Quesnay 1765, p. 123), whereas violating them would only make the exercise of individual liberty harmful to everyone's interest. No one could really gain by a restriction of trade, as recalled in the eighteenth *Maxime* for an agricultural kingdom: "disette et chertéest misère. Abondance et chertéest opulence" (Quesnay 1767, p. 570; see also Quesnay 1757, p. 209). This identity of interests must eventually be secured by a "legal despot" who transcribes natural laws into positive laws, and ensures the ensuing freedom of trade. Such a constitutional device is the only one that is coherent with the natural order, and thus leads to the best situation for everyone (Le Mercier de la Rivière

manuscripts (Hamilton *in* Stewart 1855–1856 [1809–1810], VIII, xxi–xxii). For a recent study of Stewart's *Lectures*, see Rendall (2012).

1767, p. 136). The despot is also co-proprietor of the soil in order to buttress his structural position – as illustrated by the *Tableau Economique* – and compel him to enforce the natural order (Le Mercier de la Rivière 1767, pp. 142–50, see Weulersse 1910, pp. 74–5).

In this overall perspective, Hyard (2004, 2006) and Demals and Hyard (2007) provide an interpretation of Stewart's writings that, according to me, implies he would have sided with Smith by rejecting the physiocratic identity of interests. After an early eulogy to physiocracy and legal despotism (Hyard 2004, p. 48, 2006, pp. 118, 125), Stewart would indeed have called for a mixed government. This stance verges on a rejection of the identity of interests to the extent that it would stand on an ensuing belief in the existence of conflicting social classes (Hyard 2004, pp. 181–5, 193, 2006, p. 134, Demals and Hyard 2007, pp. 65–6) in the Smithian sense explained above. Political troubles fostered by the French Revolution and the parliamentary reform movement in Great Britain, together with Stewart's Whig convictions, are said to have pushed him to distance himself from physiocracy, which was regarded with suspicion by public opinion.[4] This contextual interpretation thus entails a change of stance on Stewart's part. Although I do not deny that Stewart was under pressure in the aftermath of the French Revolution, I believe this contextual reading leaves open a twofold issue. First, it focuses on a public stance which does not imply a perfect coherence with Stewart's own philosophical beliefs. In other words, Stewart's defence of the British constitution may not have stemmed from a proper philosophical belief but may only be a disguise to escape governmental suspicion. Second, it supposes that Stewart actually believed that private interests needed to be counterbalanced, whereas his moral philosophy and his concept of interest may prove the contrary. All in all, Stewart's own philosophical theory may provide arguments opposing legal despotism independently from the political troubles to which he is said to have reacted.

Interestingly, Haakonssen (1984, 1996, pp. 235, 237, 240) has shown that Stewart's moral philosophy espouses a harmony between private and public happiness, a point that gains importance insofar as Stewart quoted Quesnay's *Droit Naturel* (1765) to strengthen this idea. That Haakonssen

4. This contextual reading is also provided by Rothschild (2001, pp. 56–61), Jones (2004), Milgate and Stimson (2009, pp. 97–120) and Kubo (2013, pp. 70–4) according to whom Stewart wanted to avoid suspicion by framing a separation between "political economy" and "theory of government", the legal despotism of physiocracy not being part of their "political economy". It must be noted that Stewart never uses the term "legal despotism", but "unmixed despotism" (Stewart 1792–1827, II, p. 240) only; yet, this latter expression unequivocally refers to the political dimension of physiocracy, which both Quesnay and modern scholars usually denote by "legal despotism".

does not mention legal despotism when describing Stewart's praise reinforces the issue above. Unfortunately, though, Haakonssen does not lay sufficient emphasis on the link between happiness, the motives of action, and their remote collective consequences. Hence, given the scholarly literature, we are left with a great paradox:

(a) A rejection of the identity of interests supposed by the physiocrats and the legal despotism that enables it;
(b) A belief in a harmony in terms of happiness that could be supported by, and inherited from, Quesnay.

I claim this paradox arises from proposition (a): the link between the identity of interests and legal despotism does not actually make sense in Stewart's writings. In fact, the physiocrats justified legal despotism as a solution to the fact that the majority does not correctly perceive the natural order. Most individuals are only driven by a "liberté animale", that is to say, they are subject to passions and body dysfunctions preventing them from adopting optimal economic behaviour. Only a minority possesses a "liberté d'intelligence" enabling acknowledgement of and obedience to natural laws (Quesnay 1747, 1765, Goutte 1985, pp. 154–9, Steiner 1992, pp. 229–30). The complete knowledge of this order and the conviction of the identity of interests therefore remains the despot's task, who aims at "containing" men on the right path (Quesnay 1747, p. 53, see Steiner 1998, pp. 94–5, Fischman 1998, pp. 91–2). For Quesnay, the identity of interests is thus artificial (iii-b). Accordingly, Stewart's repudiation of legal despotism does not, as such, imply a denial of the identity of interests it encompasses, for it may simply suggest that this identity is natural (iii-a), and not artificially implemented by constitutional devices channelling the choices of self-interested individuals. Stewart's moral philosophy in fact shows that despite a struggle between the different motives of action within each individual, private interests directly concur with that of the public. Thus, not only is the providential order he dealt with a priori harmonious, but it does not call for a despot. As it happens, Stewart tried to rid economic thought of references to conflicts such as those found in Smith's texts, as if they would uselessly obstruct the promising new science of Political Economy. In this perspective, Stewart's writings may well be considered as forming part of the early nineteenth-century movement of Christian moralists who, as Magnusson (2004, p. 53) put it, defended free trade on a ground alternative to the "conflict-ridden form of economics" inherited from Smith.

The three following sections develop this argument. I start by unfolding Stewart's depiction of a providential order, in the light of which all his economic ideas may be understood vis-à-vis Quesnay's and Smith's. I argue that at the private level, self-love (or "self-interest") cannot be fulfilled by individuals without accommodating themselves to the will of God made intelligible through the laws of Providence. They must reach what I call their *enlightened interest* by restraining their passions. Second, I argue that at the collective level, actions fostered by *enlightened interests* are mutually beneficial. However, the practitioners' passions and partial perceptions lead them to act contrary both to their interests and the public interest. This will lead me to assert in the last section that Stewart's endorsement of *perfectibility* and his defence of religious education is the condition for harmonious economic activity driven by self-interested individuals. Hence, his rejection of legal despotism is independent from the link he claimed to exist between private interests.

2. Dugald Stewart's providential dichotomy between passions and reason

Let us begin by scrutinising Stewart's account of the motives of human action, and the means by which individuals can pursue their own interest. From the *Elements of the Philosophy of the Human Mind*,[5] the first volume of which was published in 1792, to *The Philosophy of the Active and Moral Powers of Man*[6] published in 1828, Stewart mapped the complex frame of the human mind and its faculties.[7] I first examine how Stewart's moral philosophy rests on a providential depiction of the universe (Section 2.1). I then explain how individuals may accordingly pursue their interest by aligning themselves with Providence, that is to say, with the will of God. They must temper their passions in order to fulfil their self-love (Section 2.2), but may lack the skills of abstraction necessary to perceive Providence (Section 2.3).

5. Henceforth, *Elements*.
6. Henceforth, *Powers*.
7. Stewart's philosophy is in fact divided into three parts. As his editor William Hamilton reminded in the first volume of the *Elements*, these are "—the phaenomena of Knowledge or Cognition,—the phaenomena of Feeling or of Pleasure and Pain,—and the phaenomena of Conation or of Will and Desire" (Hamilton *in* Stewart 1792–1827, II, vii). The *Elements* only deal with the first part, while the two others, "the Feelings and the Conations, are treated … in subsequent books" (Hamilton *in* Stewart 1792–1827, II, vii). All his books then form a whole because they concur to the same philosophical project. That Stewart referred to the *Elements* in *Powers* indeed proves his constancy when studying these topics, the structure and coherence of which having been, by the way, settled as soon as 1793 in his *Outlines of Moral Philosophy*.

2.1 Dugald Stewart's providential naturalism

Stewart held a theological and teleological conception of the world. Political societies and human action fit inside this comprehensive order, in which everything conspires to a determinate end, "wisely calculated for human happiness" (Stewart 1792–1827, III, p. 354, 1815–1821, pp. 491, 520).[8] This conception, quite widely shared in the Enlightenment, is one of a benevolent order created by God in order to secure human happiness, thanks to the laws of Providence. Theology thereby pervades Stewart's thought, as Waterman (1991, pp. 113–4, 191) and Haakonssen (1996) have shown.

Stewart took part in the reaction both to Augustinism (Viner 1972, p. 7), and to dominant Calvinist thought according to which evidence for God was to be found in the Scriptures (Viner 1972, pp. 8–13, Stewart 2006, p. 35). Accordingly, Stewart rationally addressed theological arguments by considering that the actual world – created by God – is what should be interpreted, thanks to reason. Relying in part on Samuel Clarke (1675–1729) (Stewart 1828, VII, pp. 8, 29), Stewart distinguished two separate arguments which at that time were often merged by philosophers – namely, the existence of God, and His attributes. Accordingly, the existence of God is argued for a priori on the basis of the nature of causal chains, whereas His attributes are inferred a posteriori by observing the workings of the created world. Stewart thus expounded a priori "metaphysical suppositions" (Stewart 1828, VII, p. 7) of the existence of God, the truth of which is assumed by common sense. An a posteriori proof strengthens the former proof by determining that all phenomena are subservient to general laws promoting an end to which all means are perfectly adjusted (Stewart 1828, VII, p. 7). The a posteriori analysis is said to be "more satisfactory" (Stewart 1828, VII, p. 11) than the a priori one, because it is "simple and obvious" (Stewart 1828, VII, p. 11). Not only "everything which begins to exist must have a cause" but such "a combination of means conspiring to a particular end implies intelligence" (Stewart 1828, VII, p. 11). The harmonious operation of the world thus implies it was created by some sort of intelligence, whose attributes are thereby discovered. In other words, various efficient causes stirring the universe are adjusted by, and are subservient to, a final cause which can be considered the will of God. Contrary to early uses of the *Design* argument, this analysis was not confined by Stewart to an explanation of the purpose of human organs and body. Indeed, he extended the *Design* to the whole material

8. This may be why Forget (2001) and Blaug (2008) identified a belief in a "spontaneous order" in Stewart's writings.

world (Stewart 1828, VII, pp. 54–9, pp. 63–77) by way of analogy with man-made machines that perform a particular purpose (Becquemont 2010, pp. 84–5). Furthermore, the laws of Providence discovered by reason that Stewart alludes to do not refer to the physical world only, for he makes an analogy between the physical and the moral realms, both being directed by a final cause.[9] Indeed, according to Stewart (1828, VII, p. 157), "God exercises over the world not merely a government but a moral government", so that individuals ought to perceive and follow the final cause, thanks to reason:

> ... all that human wisdom ought to attempt, is to study the ends which she [nature] has apparently in view, and to co-operate with the means which she has provided for their attainment (Stewart 1828, VII, p. 324).

This divine will that transcends individuals provides the objective towards which they should aim. In this respect, there seems to be a lineage from Francis Hutcheson (1694–1746), through George Turnbull (1698–1748) and Thomas Reid (1710–1796), to Stewart. Indeed, they belong to the moral realism tradition of the Scottish Enlightenment, according to which moral judgements are not grounded on the subjective assessment of a spectator but refer to objective moral qualities. Given such an objectivity granted to the outer world, these philosophers would then inquire into the order and coherence the world may display. Hutcheson held that God's love of mankind was exhibited throughout the general laws of the universe, which could become effective through the moral benevolent behaviour of mankind. Turnbull inherited this providential approach, and both saw evil not as a proof of imperfection in God's creation, but rather a challenge for individuals to wisely choose what course of action is best fitted to God's benevolent purpose (Anhert 2014, pp. 48–57). Similarly, Stewart believed evil was not a "fault" (Stewart 1828, VII, p. 131) because free will and human agency render the existence of evil compatible with the *Design* argument, a point for which he found support in Joseph Butler (1692–1752) (Stewart 1828, VII, pp. 133–6).[10] Stewart's approach nevertheless differs from Hutcheson's and Turnbull's regarding the role granted to reason. Hutcheson indeed held a sentimentalist knowledge of the outer world, and Turnbull still believed in the importance of revealed religion (Stewart 2006, pp. 35, 40). When claiming that the "knowledge of the laws of nature is entirely

9. I am grateful to the anonymous referee for helping me clarify this point.
10. Stewart (1828, VI, pp. 391–2) criticised the Stoics on that point: although they made the idea of order compatible with that of freewill, they would have sometimes tended to exaggerate the former at the expense of the latter.

the result of observation and experiment" (Stewart 1793b, II, p. 6), or, as in his *Lectures*, that "the intentions of nature may be easily collected from facts which fall under our daily observation" (Stewart 1855–1856 [1809–1810], VIII, p. 73), Stewart was rather inheriting from Reid. In fact, Stewart introduced in the *Elements* the concept of "abstraction" as a power of the mind to perceive general laws (1792–1827, II, pp. 159–251). Abstraction relies on two main principles: analysis and synthesis. The observation of facts is followed by an analysis of them, that is, their reduction to general principles expressed as laws. Synthesis refers to the further deduction of conclusions given particular circumstances operating under these laws.[11] Abstraction thus helps the understanding of particular facts and reveals thereby their subservience to God's intentions.

Meanwhile, regarding the causal chain argument, Stewart opposed both David Hume (1711–1776) and Adam Smith. On the one hand, Stewart parted company with Hume's scepticism, according to which the relation between cause and effect can never be definitely ascertained. Although Stewart agreed that the truthfulness of a proposition cannot rest on experience alone, he maintained that common belief grants to the human mind a knowledge of truth and thereby of causality, allowing phenomena to be actually apprehended by their "final causes" (Stewart 1793b, VI, pp. 44–75, 1828, VII, pp. 15–119). On the other hand, although Stewart (1792–1827, III, pp. 351–2) referred to Smith's distinction between efficient and final causes,[12] the latter did not grant these concepts the same significance. Indeed, Smith assumed that Providence hid the final cause from individuals who are only driven by efficient causes without knowing the end to which they contribute (Keppler 2010, pp. 132–5). Accordingly, individuals wrongly believe their own reason to be the basis of the final cause, that is to say that what they "imagine … to be the wisdom of man" is "in reality the wisdom of God" (Smith 1759, II.ii.3.5; see Kleer 2000, pp. 23–5). However, despite this divergence from Stewart regarding individuals' awareness of the final cause, Smith's metaphor of the "invisible hand" seems evidence that individuals' actions contribute to an overall plan. Indeed, though the sole end which they [the rich] propose from the labour of all the thousands whom they employ, be the gratification of their own vain and insatiable desires, … without intending it, without knowing it, [they]

11. For a closer scrutiny of this topic, see Laudan (1970). For the influence of this mode of reasoning on British economists in the early nineteenth century, see Corsi (1987), Prasch (1996) and Depoortère (2008, 2013).
12. According to Smith (1759, II.ii.3.5), efficient causes are "various motions [that] conspire in the nicest manner to produce [an] effect", while the final cause is the "spring, which intends the effect it produces".

advance the interest of the society, and afford means to the multiplication of the species (Smith 1759, IV.1.10).

Whether Smith countenanced a providential scheme or if his analyses are purely secular is a highly debated issue.[13] Raphael and Macfie (1976, p. 7) notably infer that the Stoic doctrine of "cosmic harmony" has echoes in Smith's own opinions, especially in his "system of natural liberty" (Smith 1776, IV.ix.51). Yet, in my opinion, Smith's use of terms such as the "machine" or "system" of the universe in this respect calls this reading into question and rather supports the secular view. By equating philosophical systems with a kind of "imaginary machine invented to connect together in the fancy those different movements and effects which are already in reality performed" (Smith 1795, IV.19), Smith is likely to have only dealt with their "plausibility" (Smith 1795, II.12, IV.5, IV.8). In fact, he left no definite proof that such providential explanations could be anything but mere conventions (see Prasch 1996, pp. 1114–5, Haakonssen 2006, p. 207), and therefore whether final cause explanations of phenomena could be true. The latter ultimately remain "vacuous" for Smith (Haakonssen 1996, p. 259). Given this, the general rules of conduct, "promulgated by those vicegerents which he [the Deity] has thus set up within us" (Smith 1759, III.5.6) allow society to maintain itself without collapsing into chaos, albeit not being designed in view of a final cause. Indeed, if there is something like an order, it is neither imposed from above (Young 2002, pp. 21–2) nor rests on a kind of causality proper to *Design* arguments (Clavé 2005). Furthermore, there is no perfection in the outcome of social interactions. The most striking example is the declining state of society naturally brought about by the accumulation of capital, which is detrimental to the body of the people (Alvey 2004). Consequently, Smith actually granted a wholly different epistemological status to efficient and final causes than Stewart did.

Interestingly, the role Stewart grants to reason, and his distance from Hume and Smith, hint at his relative proximity with the physiocrats. Indeed, Quesnay (1747, p. 17) explained that individuals have the idea of the existence of the "Supreme Being", thanks to their external perceptions. Reason enables them to discover the natural laws they are subservient to, even though they cannot properly understand the very intentions of this

13. For instance, Kleer (1995), Hill (2001) and Oslington (2011) support the former interpretation, whereas Alvey (2004) supports the latter. Aspromourgos (2009, pp. 47–8) carries the secular view defended here a step further by claiming theological conceptions found in Smith's texts would only be rhetorical devices, so that "providence plays no role in any of his causal explanations of economic processes and outcomes". Viner (1927, pp. 219–20) long ago observed that "the significance of the natural order in Smith's economic doctrines has been largely exaggerated".

"Supreme Being" (Quesnay 1765, p. 115). There is an order which is the best by definition, "evidently the most advantageous to mankind" (Quesnay 1765, p. 121). However, the physiocrats followed Quesnay (1765, p. 121) in deriving moral laws from, and making them subservient to, physical laws. As explained above, Stewart rather holds a unity of *Design* in the universe, and did not conceive the moral realm to be a mere appendage to the physical realm. We nevertheless arrive at Haakonssen's (1996, p. 260) own conclusion, that "once the crucial moral problem in society becomes that of the relationship between individual actions and an over-all order, the moral goodness of which is divinely assured, the organizing principle for all study becomes this order, and Stewart saw his 'political economy' as the all-encompassing discipline which would study the natural order as a whole". This leads me to turn to individual motives in the following sub-section.

2.2 The human mind and the contending motives of action

Stewart's moral philosophy provides a classification of the motives of action regarding their relative ability to lead to happiness (the final cause). The key role Stewart granted to reason as opposed to passions is crucial when considering self-interest. In the second volume of the *Elements*, published in 1814, Stewart (1792–1827, III, p. 350) wrote that "the motives by which men are stimulated to action" aim at the "happiness and improvement both of the individual and of society". Yet, when driven by these efficient causes, individuals seek happiness without "any reflection ... on the purposes to which they are subservient", "in the *first* instance at least" (1792–1827, III, p. 350 original emphasis). There is thus a *secondary* element enabling individuals to properly secure their own happiness and that of society, as shown below.

In his later book *Powers*, Stewart opposed two distinct realms of the human mind, that of the "instinctive principles", and that of the "rational and governing principles". The former comprehend the "animal appetites" (that arise from the body), "desires" and affections (which come from, and refer to, social intercourse). As they do not presuppose an active reasoning in order to be followed, they are common to man and animals (Stewart 1828, VI, p. 207).[14] Most of all, they do not aim at happiness (Stewart 1828, VI, p. 212). On the contrary, "self-love", part of the rational principles, does so aim (Stewart 1792–1827, IV, p. 255, 1828, VII, p. 284). Self-love is also taken as synonymous with self-interest (Stewart 1828, VI,

14. Accordingly, "[t]he operations of the bee, when it begins, for the first time, to form its cell, convey to us a striking image of the efforts of unenlightened Man" (Stewart 1792–1827, II, p. 248).

p. 223). Given this, reason first defines what must be aimed at, and then evaluates all the contending motives described above regarding their ability to fulfil the interest so defined. It leads the individual to choose self-love as his ruling motive, driving him into action. In other words, will and action ought to be driven by the rational realm, contrary to Hutcheson's, Hume's and Smith's theories according to which passions – to which reason is only subservient – select the end towards which the individual aims. For Stewart, passions are opposed to reason, insofar as instinctive principles can become "a complex passion" exercising its "tyranny" (Stewart 1828, VI, p. 127) when they come to "pass the bounds of moderation" (Stewart 1793b, VI, p. 16) and lead the individual to sacrifice his "noble pleasures", his "permanent enjoyments of health, reputation and conscience" to a "pleasure of the moment" and "the meanest gratifications" (Stewart 1828, VI, p. 128). When they govern human conduct, passions prevent individuals from being happy:

> Our animal appetites, our affections, and the other inferior principles of our nature, interfere as often with self-love as with benevolence, and mislead us from our own happiness as much as from the duties we owe to others (Stewart 1828, VII, p. 284).

Moreover, passions can make individuals selfish. The description of selfishness below shows again how passions without reason prevent the fulfilment of interest:

> [T]he blame we bestow on those pursuits which are commonly called selfish, is founded, partly, on the sacrifice they imply of our true interest, to the inferior principles of our nature. When we see, for example, a man enslaved by his animal appetites; *so far from considering him as under the influence of an excessive self-love,* we pity and despise him for neglecting the higher enjoyments which are placed within his reach (Stewart 1793b, VI, p. 20, original italics omitted, my emphasis).

Misery does not arise here from an untempered self-love, nor from an "excessive regard to our own happiness" (Stewart 1793b, VI, p. 19), but from other motives that prevent it. Interest is "a calm regard to our own happiness" (Stewart 1828, VI, p. 222), depending on a balance between motives which is achieved, thanks to reason. This is different from Butler's philosophy according to which self-love must be constrained and moderated by the authority of conscience (see Butler 1991, pp. 332–3). For Stewart, self-love must be protected from the influence of the passions. Indeed, even if self-love is chosen for action, it can fail to reach its objective if reason does not sufficiently constrain the passions. Hence the major flaw of self-love is that it cannot by itself lead to happiness and thus fulfil the final cause of Providence.

Consequently, individuals must follow a "plan of conduct" (Stewart 1828, VI, p. 208) which allows them to depart from what I call an *unenlightened interest* suffering from the influence of the passions, and to shape an *enlightened interest* that matches the intentions of Providence. This plan of conduct is twofold. First, a moderation of the passions, thanks to reason and "self-government" (Stewart 1828, VI, p. 208) is needed. Therefore, appetites and desires must not be sated, but rather subjected to reason (Stewart 1828, VII, p. 286). Second, as self-love is by definition a self-centred regard – a concern for an individual's own happiness – generating a biased judgement of the happiness of his fellows,[15] one must thus look beyond one's own self:

> One set of men ... while they do what they can to improve their fellow-creatures, consider it as their chief business to watch over *their* own characters ... they study to accommodate their views and feelings to the order of Providence ... This indeed I apprehend is the great secret of happiness, – to study to accommodate our own minds to things external, rather than to accommodate things external to ourselves (Stewart 1828, VII, pp. 311–2, original emphasis).

Stewart states that "the most effectual way of promoting it [*self-interest*] is to observe religiously the obligations of morality; and these are ... very striking instances of that unity of design which is conspicuous both in the moral and natural world" (Stewart 1828, VII, p. 236, original emphasis). Accordingly, individuals driven by self-love ought to converge towards a "sense of duty". They must seek what is interesting for them and what is at the same time right. For instance, the motives and character of others must be taken into account,[16] in order to fulfil the duties owed to them, such as benevolence and justice. Paradoxically, it is thus rational for an interested individual to act disinterestedly (Stewart 1828, VI, p. 224, 1792–1827, III, p. 353).[17] We therefore return to the point mentioned at the beginning of this sub-section: *after* the efficient cause of self-love is chosen by reason, the final cause must be taken into account as a moral standard. Thus, "a fallible and short-sighted creature" (Stewart 1792–1827, III, p. 354) such as man must not merely calculate the "*expediency* of his own actions" (Stewart 1792–1827, III, pp. 353–4, original emphasis) – that

15. This bias increases with the interference of passions with self-love, as will be illustrated in Section 3.2.
16. For instance, Stewart (1828, VII, p. 309) underlined the necessity to accommodate ourselves to the real moral character of others, and not to an ideal one. Duties are divided into three categories: "duties with respect to the Deity", "duties to men" and to "ourselves".
17. "[A] sense of duty, and an enlightened regard to our own happiness, conspire in most instances to give the same direction to our conduct" (Stewart 1828, VI, p. 223).

would only be a partial self-centred view – but also ought to follow the will of God (Stewart 1792–1827, III, p. 357). However, individuals do not realise that acting morally has an impact on others: they just fit into the providential laws in order, as if through a "by-product" of morality (Haakonssen 1996, p. 235), to be happy in themselves. Again, here is a reason for putting aside the "fusion of interests": individuals follow the will of God because of its morally right quality, and not in view of its consequence for the happiness of society. Respecting moral duties is a moral prescription from God which does not entail that one is interested by what interests others. Therefore, from a theoretical point of view, happiness is the result of the knowledge of the normative prescriptions of a divinely instituted order. Nevertheless, this can fail in practice, because individuals do not perfectly perceive the laws of Providence. Abstraction, as a power of the human mind, is thus a means to complete the plan of conduct.

2.3 Abstraction as a guide to human conduct

Although the knowledge of the laws of Providence is based on observation, Stewart was sceptical about the capacity of ordinary individuals to perceive the whole of this harmonious order. Theoretically, an individual can pursue his *enlightened interest,* thanks to a plan of conduct, but the circumstances that correspond to the whole society can prevent him from doing so for they are too general to be correctly perceived. Reason, when employed to regulate private conduct or public policy, must indeed rely on a perception of the interests of the community which become more and more complex as society develops (Stewart 1792–1827, III, pp. 355–6, 1828, VII, 238, 271). The reason of individuals, isolated in their private activity, is not sufficient when facing such a complexity. While being driven by the search for happiness, they may fail to conceive an efficient plan of conduct to reach it because they ignore what the will of God is exactly.

In this respect, Stewart ascribed different degrees of perception to individuals. Abstraction, needed to perceive the laws of Providence, is shared by all, but to different degrees (1792–1827, II, p. 203; IV, p. 185). Stewart thus draws an distinction between philosophers and what can be labelled practitioners[18] of "business life". Practitioners make up the "bulk of

18. Stewart does not always use the same term to denote that latter class as individuals, but they are generally "non-educated" (Stewart 1793b, II, pp. 6–7) or "unenlightened" (Stewart 1792–1827, II, p. 215). For the sake of simplicity, I use the term "practitioners" which conveys the idea of practical activity in contrast with that of the philosopher. Such a distinction between two kinds of knowledge used by two respective classes of individuals has already been

mankind" (1792–1827, II, p. 67), the "multitude" (1792–1827, II, p. 215) of "common drudges in business and the arts" (1792–1827, II, p. 214), "who are occupied only about their own personal concerns" (1792–1827, IV, p. 190). In order to achieve their daily activities, they mostly rely on practical skills. In the *Lectures*, these skills are equated with "practical knowledge" "which is to be acquired in workshops" (Stewart 1855–1856 [1809–1810], VIII, p. 13), as opposed to that of the *Political Economist* who, assuming the role of a philosopher,[19] is "acquainted with the nature and condition of man".[20] Philosophers thus "move in a higher sphere" (1792–1827, IV, p. 190) and are guided by "systematical views" (1792–1827, IV, p. 188). Of course, abstraction is still necessary in order to achieve daily activities, as information from the external world could not otherwise be correctly interpreted by individuals (Stewart 1792–1827, IV, pp. 214–7). Practitioners simply do not engage much in abstraction. The distinction between these two classes therefore turns on whether they tend to handle particular or general facts:

> That there are many *particular facts*, a knowledge of which tends only to disturb our tranquillity, without bringing any accession of good to compensate the uneasiness which it occasions, our daily experience is sufficient to demonstrate. But the *general* laws of nature, as far as they have yet been traced, appear all ... wisely and beneficently ordered ... it is the business of a calm and enlightened philosophy in this, as in every other instance, to consult as an oracle the laws and intentions of Nature (Stewart 1815–1821, pp. 520–3, original emphasis).

The philosopher, contrary to practitioners, can therefore understand how the actions of individuals are subservient to a providential world (Poovey 1998, p. 274). Stewart indeed stated that the philosopher "takes a deeper interest in the universal drama of human affairs" (1792–1827, IV, p. 200), and that "in the moral world, as well as in the material, *the farther our observations extend*, and the longer they are continued, the more we shall perceive of order and of benevolent design in the universe" (1792–1827,

confirmed by Depoortère (2008) and Depoortère and Ruellou (2016). That various individuals are classified under the term "practitioners" does not prevent us from analysing differences among them. They do not all perform the same activity, and therefore may have different characters. This is not to the point here, however; Stewart's discussion on this matter (Stewart 1792–1827, IV, pp. 185–249) is addressed by Tannoch-Bland (1997).

19. The two figures are also mingled in Stewart (1792–1827, III, p. 331).
20. "To judge of the intentions of nature, requires in many cases ... *a comprehensive view of the constitution of man*, of the *circumstances of his external condition*, and of the mutual relations which these two parts of his destiny bear to each other" (Stewart 1855–1856 [1809–1810] , VIII, p. 72, my emphasis).

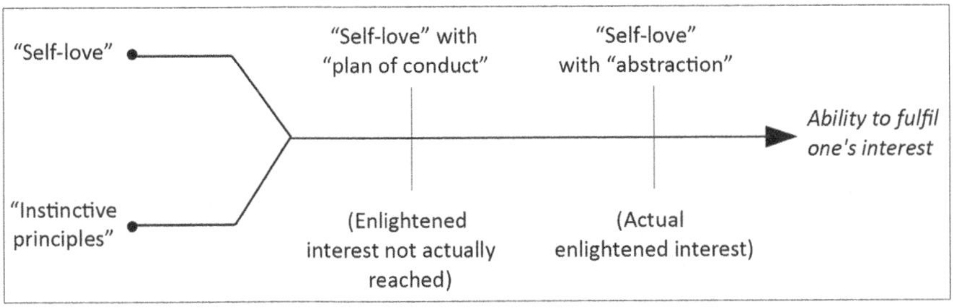

Figure 1 Stewart's classification of human motives and conducts

II, p. 247, my emphasis). As Depoortère (2008, p. 80) wrote, practitioners cannot deal with "abstract science". Their "unenlightened practice" (Stewart 1793b, p. 23) and "laborious occupations" prevent them from forming "their own opinions on some of the most important subjects that can employ the human mind" (Stewart 1792–1827, II, p. 67).[21] They are not "formed for the uncommon" (Stewart 1792–1827, II, p. 215) and their skills cannot be applied to "new combinations of circumstances" (Stewart 1792–1827, II, p. 216) for they do not have "general views" (Stewart 1792–1827, II, p. 218). They do not handle abstraction to a sufficient degree to achieve what they want in a complex world. Yet individuals could fulfil their interest had they a comprehensive view of it; and, hopefully, philosophy may help to overcome such a partiality:

> The ultimate object of philosophical inquiry is the same which *every man of plain understanding proposes to himself,* when he remarks the events which fall under his observation, with a view to the future *regulation of his conduct.* The more knowledge of this kind we acquire, the better we can accommodate our plans to the established order of things, and avail ourselves of natural Powers and Agents for accomplishing our purposes (Stewart 1793b, II, p. 6, my emphasis).

By extending his views beyond what practitioners directly perceive, and by exposing in general terms the laws of Providence, the philosopher can provide the means of happiness, e.g. to satisfy interests. In the *Lectures,* Stewart (1855–1856 [1809–1810], VIII, p. 15) explained that in order to

21. On the contrary, Coleman (1995, pp. 147–51) wrote that for Stewart, every individual may reach immediately and on his own the principles of Political Economy thanks to daily observations. According to Depoortère (2013, pp. 25–31), this would rather be the opinion of Nassau Senior. Moreover, Coleman confounds true axioms from which conclusions could be deduced, and general beliefs in the laws of Providence. More generally, Coleman does not deal with the topic of abstraction.

frame expedient laws, the statesman could not rely on the "*quick-sighted regard* to personal interest which commercial pursuits communicate" (my emphasis), because practitioners only address particular facts (1855–1856 [1809–1810], VIII, p. 17). The *Lectures* thereby confirmed the *Elements*, in which Stewart (1792–1827, II, p. 240) held that the statesman should not be "led astray" by "more limited views of temporary expedience". The different motives of action, and consequent different levels of perception of the means to happiness, are summarised in Figure 1.

The left part of the figure with two distinct branches shows how motives compete before action takes place. The right part shows what happens if self-love is pursued as an *enlightened interest*. In other words, the right part concerns an individual who has managed to overcome his passions and therefore correctly follows his interest: this refers to steps (i) and (ii) of Halévy's framework. Note that the first *enlightened interest* is "not actually reached", the lack of abstraction preventing an individual from reaching real happiness.[22] Having examined Stewart's account of the means of fulfilling private interests, the public consequences of these motives remains to be analysed. The following section explains whether private actions driven by *enlightened interests* have (iii-a) beneficial or (iii-b) detrimental public consequences. I show that if conflicts exist, they do not involve these interests – contrary to what scholars have written – but rather the prejudices of individuals.

3. A natural identity of interests hidden by prejudices

This section aims at showing that an identity of interests is depicted in Stewart's writings. The collective consequences of actions are highly dependent on the motive that gave rise to them. I will first argue that actions hindering the public interest actually stem from passions, that is to say *unenlightened* and misconceived interests (Section 3.1). These prejudices conceal *enlightened interests*, and the connection between the latter and the public interest. I then explain how an identity of *enlightened interests* in fact exists beyond the prejudices (Section 3.2).

22. Quesnay, however, claimed that individuals driven by a "liberté animale", although not as happy as those driven by a "liberté d'intelligence", were actually happier than mere passionate ones thanks of the use of reason and of useful knowledge provided, for instance, by memory. Indeed, as opposed to animals who are driven by instinct only, men can make use of their "intellectual" active volition (Quesnay 1747, pp. 18–25) to seek pleasures. The knowledge of the natural order then enables to *increase* these enjoyments (Quesnay 1765, p. 123, Steiner 1998, pp. 57–8, Lapidus 2005, p. 549).

3.1 Practitioners' passions and partial perceptions against the public interest

In the economic sphere, the public interest[23] is checked in the sense that an optimal level of happiness is not met. That practitioners do not necessarily follow motives conducive both to private and public happiness does not mean that their interests are opposed to that of the public. The public interest is in fact checked precisely because individuals fail to fulfil their own interest (that is, they do not achieve step (i) of Halévy's framework). Two flaws in the plan of conduct may be considered: practitioners may be subjected to passions; or they may lack skills of abstraction.

To start with, the public interest may be checked because of passions that oppose private interests, echoing the opposition Hirschman (1977) drew. In fact, practitioners are mostly led by their passions, especially avarice, which remains the immediate source of action for the bulk of the people (Stewart 1793b, VI, p. 9). Although merchants may have "enlarged views of their own interest" as called for by the "operations of extensive commerce" (Stewart 1855–1856 [1809–1810] , IX, p. 54), they nevertheless remain practitioners (Stewart 1855–1856 [1809–1810], VIII, p. 14) and in this respect, may still be led by "*immediate prospects of interest* and ambition, by the force of passion, by the caprice of the moment" (Stewart 1792–1827, IV, p. 188, my emphasis). The evidence suggests that they may even suffer from selfishness (Stewart 1792–1827, IV, p. 189). Accordingly, Stewart criticises monopolies because they proceed from the passions of merchants. In the students' notes we are left with, we read that regarding the "enlightened ideas" (Stewart 1855–1856 [1809–1810], IX, p. 36) of Political Economy,

23. Stewart uses various expressions such as "general interests", "common interest", "public interest", "public happiness", "general happiness" as synonymous. Indeed, a system of Political Economy, that is to say of legislation, must aim at the "general interests" (Stewart 1855–1856 [1809–1810], IX, pp. 376, 430), which are elsewhere called "the public happiness" (Stewart 1855–1856 [1809–1810], VIII, p. 288), the "general happiness" (Stewart 1855–1856 [1809–1810], VIII, p. 22), the "happiness of the people" (Stewart 1855–1856 [1809–1810], VIII, p. 21), or the "happiness of society" (Stewart 1855–1856 [1809–1810], VIII, p. 24). "[T]he happiness of millions" is entrusted to the legislator (Stewart 1855–1856 [1809–1810], VIII, p. 208), as the "greatest amount of happiness" is secured by the politician (Stewart 1855–1856 [1809–1810], VIII, p. 209). In this respect, the *Elements* clearly equate "human happiness" with the "interests of humanity" (Stewart 1792–1827, II, p. 247) or the "best interests of mankind" (Stewart 1792–1827 II, p. 71). The final cause of Providence, the "public interest" and "general utility" are, in a same passage of the *Lectures* (Stewart 1855–1856 [1809–1810], IX, pp. 378–84), described as the end at which every government should aim. For the sake of clarity, I choose to use the single expression "public interest" throughout this article.

> it is only of late years, and particularly since the publication of the *Wealth of Nations*, that they have obtained a complete triumph, in the judgment of all candid and well-informed men, over the *selfish* but deep-rooted *prejudices* of the ancient system (Stewart 1855–1856 [1809–1810], IX, p. 36, my emphasis).

Monopolies and exclusive corporations, obtained by prejudice, are therefore contrary to merchants' interests. Passions and greed prevent them from satisfying these interests. This is confirmed by another quotation from the students' notes, which encapsulates the whole spirit of the *Lectures*:

> The progress made in Political Economy during the course of the last century ... has discovered to the world some delusive project or erroneous opinion, counteracting human happiness, *and even counteracting the partial interests of those by whom the project or opinion was fostered and encouraged* (Stewart 1855–1856 [1809–1810], IX, p. 348, my emphasis).

Hirschman (1977, p. 32) contrasted "the favorable effects that follow when men are guided by their interests to the calamitous state of affairs that prevails when men give free rein to their passions". Stewart's condemnation of monopolies matches this contrast. This also concurs with Quesnay's framework, according to which restrictions of trade do not lead to true and permanent gains both for consumers and producers (Steiner 1998, p. 60). The regulation of trade is not a permanent or real benefit for merchants, but only, to use an expression already quoted above, a "temporary expedient". In the case of the corn trade, accordingly, the government should not listen to people who have a "partial or *mistaken* view of their own interests" (Stewart 1855–1856 [1809–1810], IX, p. 49, my emphasis). Consumers indeed call for a lowering of prices, while "inferior sets of dealers" who are victims of "popular prejudice" (Stewart 1855–1856 [1809–1810], IX, p. 54) act contrary to both their interest and that of the public. In order to protect "the general and permanent interests of the community" (Stewart 1855–1856 [1809–1810], IX, p. 49), the government must thus defend the freedom of trade against the "prejudices and passions of the unenlightened multitude" (Stewart 1855–1856 [1809–1810], IX, p. 53; see also Stewart 1855–1856 [1809–1810], IX, p. 118).[24] Although

24. Hilton (1988, p. 183) states that "Stewart ... approved his [Butler's] argument that self-love could be a virtuous emotion quite distinct from selfishness, and that the world would be a better place if more self-love, properly controlled and moderated, were practised. Indeed, it seems likely that, during the first half of the nineteenth century, the doctrine of 'enlightened self-interest' was envisaged more often in a Butlerian than in a Benthamite context, more with an eye to individual probity than to public benefit". The last sentence appears

Stewart directly quoted Smith and sought his authority on these matters, their accounts of the "mercantile system" were in fact opposed. In the *Wealth of Nations,* Smith asserted that merchants were perfectly conscious of their interest, even – or, consequently – in cases of monopoly (see for instance their interest in reducing the number of sellers: Smith 1776, I.ix. p.10, IV.ii.21, IV.ii.43, IV.vii.b.49, IV.vii.c.10, IV.vii.c.103). Smith indeed distinguished restrictions of trade called for in virtue of "private interest and the spirit of monopoly" (Smith 1776, IV.ii) from other mercantile policies that originate from "national prejudice and animosity" (1776, IV.iii). The former entails that merchants benefit highly from restrictions in competition.

In addition, Stewart added that monopolies are against the "general interests" because they tend to raise prices above their "intrinsic value" (Stewart 1855–1856 [1809–1810], VIII, pp. 151–2). Although he does not make any explicit reference here to the physiocrats, the logic of Stewart's argument is similar to that of the "*bon prix*" for which they called. Indeed, according to the physiocrats, reaching the "*bon prix*" for agricultural commodities secures the public interest in the agricultural realm (Quesnay 1757, p. 211). Stewart thus shares with the physiocrats the idea of a price level determined by sectoral interdependencies and the coherence of an overall order, thanks to which a common interest between all parties is met. All deviations from this "*bon prix*" would in fact benefit a sectoral interest only, yet to a lesser extent than if everyone obeyed the natural order. On the contrary, Smith's concept of natural price – provided a sum of revenues labelled "component parts" (1776, I.vi) has anything to do with some "intrinsic" value – is not a means to further the public interest. For example, a decline in the wealth of society combined with a growth of the population tends to reduce the natural wage rate (1776, I.viii.24–7). In that case, the natural price would be linearly reduced (1776, I.vii.33; I. viii.57) and market prices may still converge to it; yet the majority of the population would barely be subsisting.

In Stewart's thinking, the public interest may also be hindered because practitioners do not directly know the final cause of Providence, even when they are not selfish or driven by passions. Of course, as monopolies rest on passions, they necessarily suffer from a lack of abstraction, as Figure 1 shows. Accordingly, mercantile policies arise from the "first apprehensions of the mind" (Stewart 1793a, p. 89) dealing with trade, and "disturb the order of nature" (Stewart 1793a, p. 61). More generally, each

to be somewhat incorrect. Indeed, although Butler and Stewart were – as noted in Section 2 – close in some respects, the latter argued for the opposite public consequences of passions and *enlightened interests.*

profession judges its interest only with "partiality" (Stewart 1855–1856 [1809–1810], VIII, 16-n), as other examples confirm.[25] Thanks to their practical skills, the cultivators of the soil know by experience what to produce according to the available lands. Thus, "the husbandman is the best judge of his own interest" (Stewart 1855–1856 [1809–1810], VIII, p. 111). However, they cannot always advance the public interest because their situation "precludes them, in a great measure, from all information but what is supplied by the narrow circle of their professional employments" (Stewart 1855–1856 [1809–1810], VIII, p. 181). They are victims of "the inveteracy of *local prejudices and practices*" (Stewart 1855–1856 [1809–1810], VIII, 181-n, my emphasis) for they do not "listen to any ideas that are new" (Stewart 1855–1856 [1809–1810], VIII, 181-n) and hence cannot cope with "new combinations of circumstances" (Stewart 1792–1827, II, p. 216). New practical skills and knowledge of the world in which practitioners find themselves must be obtained, thanks to abstraction in order to achieve their daily activities. Accordingly, the role of government is to assist agriculture "by promoting the circulation of useful knowledge" (Stewart 1855–1856 [1809–1810], VIII, p. 181).[26] This may help them to actually fulfil their interest. Furthermore, regarding manufacturers, Stewart asked how far the legislator could help them to invest in "one part of a country in preference to another" (Stewart 1855–1856 [1809–1810], VIII, p. 12) "by roads, canals, harbours, and other public works" (Stewart 1855–1856 [1809–1810], VIII, p. 13). The similarity with the situation of the husbandman is confirmed by the fact that "[t]he multiplication of high-roads, and the establishment of regular posts and couriers" have "extend[ed] and quicken[ed] the circulation of knowledge" (Stewart 1855–1856 [1809–1810], IX, p. 344), as students' notes recall. I infer that both manufacturers and cultivators lack information about distant markets and therefore do not always employ their capital in a way as to produce the greatest value. Consequently, they do not perfectly advance their own interest. On the contrary, the legislator possesses all this information and allows it to filter down and circulate, thanks to these infrastructures, so practitioners can fulfil their interest. The legislator's top-down position is confirmed by the fact that he must "second the benevolent intentions of Providence in the administration of human affairs" (Stewart 1792–1827, II, p. 87).

25. Stewart (1815–1821, p. 97) considered John de Witt's writings to be the first in which "commerce is treated of as an object of national and political concern, in opposition to the *partial interests* of corporations and monopolies" (my emphasis). This implies that some monopolies do not rest on merchant's passions and selfishness, although they still fail to fulfil their own interest.

26. I return to this in Section 4 with the topic of education.

The following sub-section aims at showing why this top-down position does not imply an artificial identity of interests.

3.2 The natural side of the identity of interests

Now that we know that obstacles to public happiness arise from the passions of practitioners and/or their lack of abstraction, the linkages between their *enlightened interests* (e.g. interests actually fulfilled) may be easily inferred. In other words, this section aims at showing that self-interested individuals (steps (i) and (ii)) directly advance the public interest (step (iii-a)). This presupposes a specific way of promoting the public interest, that is to say of enhancing public happiness, although individuals may not always understand it.

3.2.1 Promoting the public interest. *Enlightened interests* are harmonious in the sense that they all contribute to the same end. Indeed, when Stewart argues that Political Economy should aim at the happiness of the whole society, he does not distinguish it from individual happiness (Stewart 1855–1856 [1809–1810], VIII, p. 23). This is not a coincidence. In fact, he also explicitly claimed that individuals "are most likely to advance both the public interests and their own, when they exercise freely their private judgment concerning the most effectual means of bettering their fortune" (Stewart 1855–1856 [1809–1810], VIII, p. 181). Indeed, "the morally right action coincides with what is publicly useful" (Haakonssen 1996, p. 258). This can be understood as the fulfilment of steps (ii) and (iii-a). In a footnote to his *Account of the Life and Writing of Adam Smith*, Stewart (1793a, p. 93) quoted Turgot, whom he considered a physiocrat, to support this opinion:

> Following from this, M. de Gournay concluded that when particular interests are precisely the same as the general interest, what we can do best is to leave every man free to do whatever he wants. Yet he thought it impossible that in free trade, particular interest could not lead to general interest.[27]

The fact that Stewart quotes Turgot is significant, as will become apparent later. According to Stewart, when an individual fulfils his *enlightened interest*, he carries out duties providentially imposed on him, and thereby

27. My translation. The original text reads: "De la M. de Gournay concluoit, que lorsque l'intérêt des particuliers est précisément le même que l'intérêt général, ce qu'on peut faire de mieux est de laisser chaque homme libre de faire ce qu'il veut. Or il trouvoit impossible que dans le commerce abandonné à lui-même, l'intérêt particulier ne concourut pas avec l'intérêt général".

unintentionally increases the happiness of his fellows (Stewart 1828, VI, p. 336). Because of the collective beneficial consequences of the plan of conduct, the greater the number of individuals who fulfil their *enlightened interest*, the more positive cross-effects there will be on the interests of others. The public interest can accordingly be apprehended as an increasing function of individual interests. Everyone indeed directly benefits from the fulfilment of interests, because they all contribute to the will of God. As it was for the physiocrats, the free scope allowed to private interests leads to a better situation in Paretian terms (Lapidus 2005, p. 550). Given this, if a legislator wished to foster the public interest, a crucial remark must be made. Public happiness can be increased only if everyone's happiness increases too. In other words, everyone's happiness ranking must be higher, in agreement with this increase of public happiness. Stewart therefore differs altogether from Smith's approach and from what is nowadays considered the classical utilitarian account. As already noticed, the former entails that merchants fulfil their interests at the expense of the public interest; the latter assumes that the collective sum of happiness can be increased at the expense of diminishing one's own happiness. For Stewart, on the contrary, no one can fulfil his *enlightened interest* and at the same time diminish the happiness of his fellows. Refraining from one's own search for happiness would indeed ultimately have an indirect negative impact on others, because of the cross-effects described just above.

Consequently, the fact that the legislator enables the circulation of knowledge, thanks to "roads, canals, harbours, and other public works" (Stewart 1855–1856 [1809–1810], VIII, p. 13), cannot be considered a proof of an artificial identity of interests. Indeed, it does not channel interested individuals from one action to another, but simply helps them to correctly fulfil their own interest (condition (ii)). As stated at the end of the previous sub-section, by having a better knowledge of the providential order, the legislator only helps manufacturers, merchants and farmers to be the happiest in themselves. Investing in "one part of a country in preference to another" (Stewart 1855–1856 [1809–1810], VIII, p. 12) is one of the means to do so. Collective happiness (condition (iii-a)) directly follows. This is why Stewart described Political Economy as the study of

> all those speculations which have for their object the happiness and improvement of Political Society, or, in other words, which have for their object the great and *ultimate ends* from which Political regulations derive all their value; and to which Wealth and Population themselves are to be regarded as only *subordinate and instrumental* (Stewart 1855–1856 [1809–1810], VIII, p. 10, my emphasis, original italics omitted).

Individuals' free search for wealth is a means to the final cause. The complete freedom of trade is therefore a way to give free reign to those efficient causes fitted for human happiness. In other words, the joint fulfilment of private interests and that of the public implies that the production of wealth should be undertaken through the "freest competition" (Stewart 1793a, p. 60). The "general interests" would indeed be fulfilled by the promotion of the commerce in land, and the end of primogeniture (Stewart 1855–1856 [1809–1810], VIII, p. 152). Moreover, as already noted regarding the corn trade, "the general interests of all the different parts of the world would be best attained by leaving" it "perfectly open" (Stewart 1855–1856 [1809–1810], IX, p. 118), that is, if the "course of imports and exports" were "regulated entirely by the interested speculations of individuals" (Stewart 1855–1856 [1809–1810], IX, p. 121). Freedom of trade between nations increases productivity and thus general opulence (Stewart 1855–1856 [1809–1810], IX, pp. 35–6). In opposing the fixation of a maximum legal rate of interest, Stewart was confident that "[t]he natural course of trade is too powerful to be controlled by laws which are at variance with the interests of private parties, and ... prejudicial to the interests of the public" (Stewart 1855–1856 [1809–1810], IX, p. 188). All in all, the "freedom of industry" increases "the happiness ... of the community" (Stewart 1855–1856 [1809–1810], VIII, p. 13).

Nevertheless, Stewart seemed to assume there would be this identity of interests, rather than to expressly analyse the mechanisms supposed to yield it. But this is because he may not have had to do so, for two reasons at least. First, since he allowed teleological arguments, it is thus normal, if not indeed trivial, that individual actions fostered by *enlightened interests* in accord with Providence are mutually harmonious. From the point of view of *Design*, to conceive of an entity or mechanism having a final cause, and at the same time to allow that there are efficient causes preventing this final cause, would be an absurd and self-contradictory proposition. This line of thinking recalls that of Quesnay concerning the indivisibleness of the general interest (Weulersse 1910, p. 51), and men who, as rational beings, experience the same determinations and thereby pursue the same good (Ege 2007, p. 116). Second, and as a consequence, Stewart did not seek to demonstrate the identity of interests, for it ultimately rests on a leap of faith, thanks to which he drives out conflicts of interests from his depiction of the mercantile system.

3.2.2 The biased judgements of practitioners regarding the congruence of interests. Because practitioners do not always follow their *enlightened interest*, they often wrongly assess the link between their interest and that of the public. The *Lectures* afford a good comparison between the contending beliefs of the Political Economist and practitioners who "think *merely* of their individual interests" (Stewart 1855–1856 [1809–1810], VIII, pp. 11–2, original emphasis), that is to say who neglect their moral duties imposed by Providence and thus do not follow long-run interests allowed by a plan of conduct. Each class focuses on short-run price fluctuations, and so buys or sells wrongly believing they are following their real interest. Thus, "[t]he manufacturer, ... and the various orders of annuitants and stipendiary labourers, exult when the farmer repines, and repine when the farmer exults" (Stewart 1855–1856 [1809–1810], VIII, p. 12). Following from this,

> In the midst of this conflict of contending interests and prejudices, it is the business of the *Political Economist* to watch over the *concerns of all*, and to point out to the Legislator the danger of listening exclusively to claims founded in local or in partial advantages, to remind him that the pressure of a temporary scarcity brings along with it in time its own remedy, while an undue depression of prices may sacrifice to a passing abundance years of future prosperity (Stewart 1855–1856 [1809–1810], VIII, p. 12, original emphasis).

Hyard (2004, p. 161) took this paragraph as proof that the legislator, advised by the Political Economist, has to arbitrate opposite interests, in the sense of framing laws which acknowledge such an opposition of interests. The legislator would therefore have to side with one of these interests, or counterbalance them.[28] I propose a different interpretation. The interests of manufacturers and farmers Stewart deals with here are called "partial advantages", that is to say partial interests, conceived in the short run. The conflict does not therefore concern the *enlightened interests* that would have been defined, thanks to reason. Consequently, an opposition between "interests" is only apparent because of a misconception of the purposes of Providence, that is to say "prejudices" that reveal a lack of reason, blurring the real interests.[29] This is why Stewart distinguished these partial visions from the "the *real and permanent* interests of proprietors, cultivators, and consumers" (Stewart 1855–1856 [1809–1810], VIII, p. 12, my emphasis).

---

28. She translates "watch over the concerns of all" by the French "*regarder au delà des différents intérêts*", which would read "*look beyond the various interests*". The French for Stewart's sentence would actually be "*surveiller les préoccupations de tous*". It is, in addition, surprising that she translates "concerns" by "*intérêts*" whereas Stewart explicitly dealt with interests *and* prejudices at the beginning of the same sentence. Her translation thereby confirms her vision of conflicting interests that must be mediated or counterbalanced.
29. Dixon (2008, p. 240) notices the opposition between short-run and long-run interests in this paragraph, but curiously seems to quickly conceal the "prejudices" that are yet remarked in the same sentence. Consequently, the definition of the "conflict", which is in my opinion an illusion, is less evident.

Stewart's moral philosophy confirms my reading. A selfish individual, for instance a miser, is unconcerned with the happiness of others while failing to be happy himself. He is even led "to state his own interest in opposition to that of other men" (Stewart 1793b, VI, p. 19). In the corn trade, once again, Stewart's opinion was clear enough as, relying on a sentence from the *Wealth of Nations*, he claimed that:

> the interests of the inland corn dealer ... and that of the great body of the people, *how opposite, soever, they might at first sight appear* ... must be at all times, even in years of the greater scarcity, exactly the same.... The truth of this principle ... is not self-evident; on the contrary, it is very strongly opposed by popular *prejudices* (Stewart 1855–1856 [1809–1810], IX, p. 49, my emphasis).

In fact, the practitioners' own activities and their immediate knowledge prevent them from seeing the real link between interests:

> the same circumstances which bestow on practical knowledge so inestimable a value in managing the little concerns of agricultural improvement, have a tendency to *bias or warp the judgment* in whatever relates to *the general interests* of an extensive country, diversified by numberless causes both moral and physical (Stewart 1855–1856 [1809–1810] IX, p. 124, my emphasis).

Depoortère (2008, p. 81) notes the biased judgements on the part of practitioners, but does not seem to deal clearly with the link between interests. In fact, although he acknowledges that practitioners wrongly perceive their interest, he adds they are thereby apt to "confound" it with that of the public. He seems to mean that private interests are opposite to the public interest. Another way of putting this is that, according to Depoortère, individuals believe in an identity of interests which does not in fact exist. In my opinion, Stewart's position is in reality the opposite. In fact, it has been highlighted that individuals are often not aware of the link between their interests and the public one: they do not believe in an identity but in an opposition. The following sentence also insinuates that the identity of interests is possible, and is not rejected as a matter of principle:

> The truth is that no wise statesman will reckon much on the disinterested benevolence of any one order of individuals; and the only occasions on which their *professional knowledge* is likely to be turned to national advantage, is when the interest of their order, and the interest of the community, are one and the same (Stewart 1855–1856 [1809–1810], VIII, p. 15, original emphasis).

Stewart nevertheless added here that "this is *less* the case with manufacturers and merchants than with farmers and country gentlemen"

(Stewart 1855–1856 [1809–1810], VIII, p. 15, original emphasis).[30] However, I believe that this is because of their passions and partial views, which I studied earlier. In fact, Stewart then quotes Josiah Child, writing that the "eyes" of merchants, by being "continually fixed on what makes for their peculiar gain or loss", prevent them from "turn[ing] their thoughts to what is most advantageous for the kingdom in general" (Stewart 1855–1856 [1809–1810], VIII, p. 15). This is another way of describing *unenlightened interests*. The hope that Political Economy would erase such a prejudice can be noted at the end of the students' notes:

> ... in proportion as its general principles assume somewhat of a systematical form, *the connexion between the interests of individuals and the national prosperity*, and the still more unexpected connexion between the prosperity of nations and that of neighbouring communities, *becomes more and more apparent* (Stewart 1855–1856 [1809–1810], IX, p. 348, my emphasis).

The "connexion" between these interests is therefore real and independent from observation, for it becomes "more apparent". According to Stewart, there is no opposition between social classes. The classical tripartition between labourers, owners of capital and landlords, acknowledged by Stewart, neither implies nor rests on an opposition of their interests. The conflictual aspects of economic relations – the aspects which so concerned Smith – disappear because of Stewart's theology. In fact, his influence on early nineteenth-century economists resided in raising the question of the congruence between the individual and national interest (Brown 1994, pp. 198–206),[31] such that his successors would inherit this new approach

30. Although Stewart here claimed to be following the argumentation Smith had laid down in the *Wealth of Nations* (Stewart 1855–1856 [1809–1810], VIII, p. 15), the emphasis he himself puts on the word "less" reveals that he is obviously distorting Smith's thought. Indeed, it is as if Stewart wanted to introduce some circumstantial considerations, enabling the merchants' actions to concur sometimes more or "less" with the public interest, depending on the situation. This is confirmed by his *Account of the life and writings of Adam Smith*, where he wrote that, according to Smith, the interest of merchants would "*not always*" (Stewart, 1793a, pp. 60–1, my emphasis) be the same as that of the public. Smith (1776, I.xi.p.10) had actually claimed this was "never" the case: it is "always ... opposite". Similarly, Stewart often borrowed Smith's expression the "mercantile system" (1776, IV.i–viii) to highlight that, just as Smith did, he attacked "prejudices" (Stewart 1793a, p. 88), although Stewart could not help adding that Smith also targeted "powerful bodies of men *interested* to defend" that system (Stewart 1793a, p. 89, my emphasis). On the emphasis Stewart put on prejudices rather than on sectoral interests, see Magnusson (2004, pp. 81–2).
31. Unfortunately, Brown (1994) does not explain whether this "congruence" was actually endorsed by Stewart and his successors. Nevertheless, a glimpse of the

even when they went on to throw out its religious features. Now that the direct link between private motives and the public interest has been settled, I can explain why Stewart actually rejected legal despotism.

4. "Perfectibility of mind" against "legal despotism"

Thus far, I have shown that although an identity of interests exists, its conditions are not automatically met. Every individual must first reach the utmost level of perception drawn in Figure 1 in order to fulfil his interest. Yet this faculty which enables individuals to reach a comprehensive view also explains Stewart's criticism of legal despotism (Section 4.1). The perfectibility of the human mind and religious education are prerequisites for the pursuit of private interests rather than passions (Section 4.2).

4.1 A reconsideration of Stewart's account of physiocracy: natural order without legal despotism

Stewart rejected legal despotism because he believed it was unnecessary with respect to the natural order. Showing this requires us to examine his very personal and partial reading of physiocracy. Stewart in fact rejected legal despotism because he dismissed the physiocrats' theory of knowledge and focused rather on the argument concerning the final cause. As shown below, from 1792 onwards, his texts constantly show the same standpoint.

In 1814, Stewart explained that a belief held in common between him and physiocrats was that of a benevolent order aiming at a given final cause. He focused on their account of Nature by emphasising that

> the title of *Physiocratie* ... affords a strong presumptive proof ... [of] the frequent recurrence made ... to the physical and moral laws of Nature, as the unerring standard which the legislator should keep in view in all his positive institutions. ... [I]n the statement of them given by their original authors, it is taken for granted as a truth self-evident and indisputable, not merely that benevolent design is manifested in all the physical and moral arrangements connected with this globe, but that the study of

---

answer is possible thanks to McCulloch (1845, p. 13), who would later state that "[s]o long as Dr. Smith confines himself to a statement of the advantages resulting from the freedom of industry ... his principles and reasonings are equally sound and conclusive, but they are less so in other instances. He does not say that such branches of industry as are found to be most for the advantage of individuals are *necessarily, at the same time,* most for the advantages of the public. ... *A state being nothing but a collection of individuals,* it follows that whatever is most advantageous to them individually *must* be so also to the collective body" (my emphasis).

> these arrangements is indispensably necessary to lay a solid foundation for political science (Stewart 1792–1827, III, p. 348, original emphasis).[32]

In this respect, "[w]hen Stewart lauded Free Trade as a means of moving 'nearer and nearer to the order of nature', he looked at 'nature' through mainly physiocratic eyes" (Hilton 1988, p. 68). What strikes the reader here is that although he deals with the legislator's aim, Stewart does not make any reference to legal despotism. This can be explained by an interesting claim he had made earlier, in 1802. Stewart classified Quesnay and Turgot with physiocrats, as authors whom he broadly called Economists. According to Stewart, they

> began to speculate about the natural order of political societies ; or, in other words, about that order which a political society would of itself gradually assume, on the supposition that law had no other object than to protect completely the natural rights of individuals, and left every man at liberty to pursue his own interest in his own way, as long as he abstained from violating the rights of others. *The connexion between this natural order and the improvement of mankind*, has been more insisted on by the biographers of Turgot than by any other authors (Stewart 1792–1827, II, p. 489, my emphasis).

We today know that Turgot's opinions are specific and that he was not a mere zealous defender of Quesnay's thought. What is important here is that Stewart shared Turgot's account of perfectibility, as did Condorcet (Winch 1996, p. 169). Stewart saw a "connexion between M. Turgot and M. Quesnay" because of a "coincidence of their opinions about the most essential principles of legislation" (Stewart 1792–1827, II, p. 489). Since those "principles of legislation" are based on final causes, I infer that Stewart believed that the physiocrats' final cause could be grasped, thanks to perfectibility. In fact, according to Stewart, there is not *one* theory of knowledge (Quesnay's, for instance) on which the study of the natural order would stand, but rather several. In this respect, he rejected from 1792 onwards the "doctrine" (Stewart 1792–1827, II, p. 119) of sensationalism which, "although it has for many years past been a subject of controversy in England, ... continues still to be implicitly adopted by the best philosophical writers in France" (Stewart 1792–1827, II, p. 119). Regarding the French authors, Stewart remarks:

> [t]his doctrine ... has been employed by some of them to support the system of materialism, and by others to shew, that the intellectual distinctions between man and

32. That Stewart (1792–1827, III, p. 349) then also ascribed to Smith a theory based on final causes proves his continuing focus on that point, although in this respect he missed Smith's actual point (see Haakonssen 1996, pp. 259–60).

> brutes arise entirely from the differences in their *animal organization*, and in their powers of external perception (Stewart 1792–1827, II, p. 119, my emphasis).

This may very easily be thought to apply to physiocracy, and to Quesnay in particular, whom Stewart read closely. According to Quesnay, the different degrees of perception among individuals in fact result from the malfunction of an organ or the physical characteristics of their body.[33] Legal despotism was thus advocated by the physiocrats because they claimed that not all individuals could perceive the "natural order". Stewart (1855–1856 [1809–1810], VIII, p. 308) in fact stressed that, according to them, only the despot would have the "intuitive conviction" of the identity of his interest with that of the nation, thereby enabling him to translate natural law into positive law. In Stewart's own mind, on the contrary, the perception of a benevolent order of Providence is achieved through an active power of the human mind, which mixes abstraction so as to apprehend particular facts with a common sense that recognises their truth. Knowing the final cause is not solely a result of the senses. As Stewart supposed the human mind to be something perfectible and theoretically capable of reaching comprehensive views of the final cause of Providence, the distinction between "liberté animale" and "liberté d'intelligence" did not make sense for him. Stewart believed that the final cause could be perceived, thanks to the perfectibility of the human mind, which would help overcome wrong original perceptions.

Stewart then advanced two arguments side by side: opposition to the physiocrats on the theory of knowledge, and praise for their study of a benevolently designed order. Stewart was particularly interested in this latter aspect of their theory. Consequently, his personal account of physiocracy implied that the natural order could be implemented without the intervention of a despot: this is why from 1792 onwards – that is to say, before the political troubles Stewart is said to have reacted to –he supposed that communities would approach the natural order by themselves:

> To delineate that state of political society to which governments may be expected to approach nearer and nearer as the triumphs of philosophy extend, was, I apprehend, the leading object of the earliest and most enlightened patrons of the economical system. It is ... an ideal order of things, to which they have a *tendency of themselves to approach*, and to which it ought to be the aim of the legislator to facilitate their progress (Stewart 1792–1827, II, p. 236, my emphasis).

---

33. Quesnay (1747) is quite eloquent on that point. The physiocrats' theory of knowledge is not strictly speaking "sensationalist", although they inherit ideas from Condillac (1714–1780) (see Weulersse 1910, pp. 120–2). Steiner (1992, pp. 227–30) calls it "normative sensationalism".

No despot here either. The compatibility Stewart claimed between the natural order and the perfectibility of the human mind reveals that he dismissed legal despotism from the start, for its justifications are overthrown by principle. He therefore *never* advocated it. Given the political context of course, it was important for Stewart to signal his awareness of the arbitrary side of legal despotism, its "dangerous tendency", and "unqualified" arguments (Stewart 1792–1827, II, p. 240, 1855–1856 [1809–1810], VIII, p. 308); but this is only a secondary argument, which reinforces his prior rejection of legal despotism. As perfectibility is depicted in his very first works (Winch 1983, p. 39), his adhesion to it and his reference to Turgot was not a strategy to distance himself from physiocracy and sweep away legal despotism either, even though the political context would have led him to do so. From Stewart's very first book, the "tendency" of societies is opposed to an artificial constitutional framework designed to make individuals comply with the natural order, thanks to a change in their choices. This proves that Stewart defended the natural aspect of the identity of interests, according to which the fulfilment of private interests automatically contributes to that of the public. Stewart selected physiocratic elements only when he considered them to be coherent with his thought.[34] Stewart (1815–1821, p. 380) indeed wrote that the physiocrats' "metaphysical system ... might have been useful in counteracting the gloomy ideas then so generally prevalent about the order of the universe ... With their practical tendency in a political view we are not at present concerned".

Besides, that Stewart did not advocate the co-property of the soil, as Hyard (2006) or Demals and Hyard (2007) note, does not imply that he rejected the identity of interests. This concentration of property was formerly advocated by the physiocrats to strengthen the despot's conviction of the identity of interests. Stewart pointed to the absence of such interested legislators in democracies, for instance (Stewart 1855–1856 [1809–1810], IX, p. 366). Yet this does not imply conflicts of interests. In fact, a legally interested sovereign does not imply individuals rationally complying with the public interest, for the former is not a necessary condition of the latter. Individuals led by self-interest may directly serve the public

34. The spirit of this selective reading also appears in a footnote of the *Elements* that Stewart (1792–1827, II, p. 237) added in 1802: "To some of my readers it may appear trifling to remark, that in availing myself of an occasional coincidence of sentiment with a contemporary author, I would not be understood to become responsible for the consistency of his personal conduct with his philosophical principles, nor to subscribe to any one of his opinions, *but those to which I have expressed my assent by incorporating them with my own composition*" (my emphasis).

good as in an identity of interests, with or without the physiocratic co-property of the soil.[35]

What fundamentally distinguishes Stewart from the physiocrats is not the form of government they eventually defend, but their account of how individuals may converge on the public interest. Stewart thereby stressed the importance of the perfectibility of mind and education, with which the last sub-section below deals.

4.2 The perfectibility of mind and the spread of knowledge

The lack of interest Steward paid to legal despotism is actually part of a general downplaying of the role of governments in achieving the identity of interests. Stewart distinguished the "municipal code" of Nations from the form of their government (Stewart 1793a, p. 55). According to him, the knowledge provided by Political Economy aims at influencing the former and not the latter. Neither a despot nor any other form of government is necessary to ensure happiness, which depends "not on the share which the people possess, directly or indirectly, in the enactment of laws, but on the equity and expediency of the laws that are enacted" (Stewart 1793a, p. 54). Indeed, as "inexpedient laws may, in consequence of ignorance and prejudice, be sanctioned for ages by a Government excellent in its constitution" (Stewart 1855–1856 [1809–1810], VIII, p. 22), the perfectibility of mind Stewart endorsed enables framing laws coherent with Providence. Indeed, "in proportion as public opinion becomes enlightened, the voice of people becomes the voice of reason" (Stewart 1815–1821, p. 524), for the "[p]rogress of reason necessarily accompanies the progress of society" (Stewart 1792–1827, II, p. 210). Stewart's recurrent praise of the invention of printing and the consequent spread of books shows his optimistic vision of social development. Furthermore, Stewart was confident in this respect that each individual will eventually follow his *enlightened interest.* In fact, education and the spread of knowledge can alleviate practitioners' perceptual errors.

The spread of knowledge first enables practitioners to moderate their passions. What is important here is that it is daily activities that shape an

35. Adam Smith (1776, V.i.d.17) himself explained that the Chinese sovereign had an interest in the prosperity of his country because he was co-proprietor of the soil. But he obviously did not share the physiocratic belief in an identity of interests. Consequently, it appears strikingly that describing an institutional framework or type of property that could interest the sovereign does not mean anything regarding the compatibility of interests. Hence, saying conversely as Stewart did that there are no interested legislators is not logically sufficient to reject physiocracy and the harmony entailed by the natural order.

individual's character, which is not innate. Yet, as "reason, considered as a principle of action, is of inferior force to habit" (Stewart 1815–1821, p. 522), the inferior classes must be educated early enough in order to counteract the bad habits they are liable to acquire. For example, education (Stewart 1855–1856 [1809–1810], IX, 330, pp. 346–7), especially that provided by religious establishments under the direction of the Presbytery, could prevent labourers from being profligate and intemperate, and help them develop habits of saving and of frugality.[36] Knowing the true laws of Political Economy designed by God would therefore enable them to have a correct plan of conduct and follow their *enlightened interest*, rather than their instinctive impulses. According to Stewart, education helps individuals manage their motives of action: philosophy enables them "to preserve a proper balance among all its [the human mind's] various faculties, principles of action, and capacities of enjoyment" (1792–1827, II, p. 66). This explains why Stewart advocated public education provided by religious establishments (Stewart 1815–1821, pp. 511–2), where supporting such institutions should be part of the duties of the Sovereign, alongside the administration of justice or public works (Stewart 1855–1856 [1809–1810], IX, p. 211).

Second, the spread of philosophical studies would allow the development of abstraction and make the pursuit of *enlightened interest* perfect. Every individual could indeed follow the final cause of Providence (Stewart 1815–1821, pp. 490–1).

> It is from this tendency of philosophical studies to cultivate habits of generalization, that their chief utility arises; accustoming those who pursue them to regard events, *less in relation to their own immediate and partial concerns, than to the general interests of the human race*; ... (Stewart 1815–1821, p. 520, original italics omitted, my emphasis).

Individuals would thereby consequently understand the "connexion between the interests" (Stewart 1855–1856 [1809–1810], IX, p. 348) which before was wrongly conceived. In other words, they would stop believing they could gain at the expense of others.

As an aside, we may note that Stewart claimed that the distinction between philosophers and practitioners is also produced by habit. Consequently, the gap between philosophers and practitioners regarding the skills of abstraction may be dramatically reduced, although a strict dividing line between them may remain (as we can guess from the students' notes;

36. Hyard (2004, pp. 177–80) points to this as a means to maintain the social order by rendering labourers obedient, at a time when the radical movement was shaking Great Britain. Without opposing this interpretation, I believe education is also a means to follow *enlightened interests* and not immediate passions.

see Stewart 1855–1856 [1809–1810], IX, p. 338). In fact, Stewart believed that practitioners should not totally replace their commercial activities with philosophical speculation, which must remain the preserve of the philosopher. As happy individuals, they would remain "useful member[s] of society" (Stewart 1792–1827, II, pp. 60–1).

Can this importance assigned to education be considered another top-down artificial means to achieve the identity of interests, as was the physiocratic despot? Quesnay (1765, pp. 122–3, 1767, pp. 566–7) indeed ascribed to government the primary task of teaching natural laws to citizens. At first sight, Stewart's claim that "[i]f the multitude must be led, it is of consequence, surely, that it should be led by enlightened conductors" (1792–1827, II, p. 67), may indeed seem similar. Yet his thought on this topic differs from Quesnay's for two reasons. First, education is not a constitutional device, and can be diffused under any form of government:

> Under *every* form of government, (*whatever* it may be,) provided its general spirit be favourable to liberty, and allows an unrestrained freedom of discussion, these enlightened views of Political Economy will gradually and slowly prevail in proportion to the progress of reason and the diffusion of knowledge (Stewart 1855–1856 [1809–1810], IX, p. 376, my emphasis).

Second, education does not channel the choices of self-interested individuals, but more precisely helps them to become interested in their own happiness (step (i)), and *actually* reach it (step (ii)). Indeed, the identity of interests is not always realised, because individuals must obviously seek their own interest in the first place. Education is for Stewart a *condition* for interests to steer society. When these interests drive individuals' conduct and are effectively fulfilled, the public interest is automatically realised (step (iii-a)). For Quesnay, education and the ensuing conscious respect of the natural order entails a modification of choices compared to what a mere "liberté animale" would have entailed, and thus helps interested individuals to reach a better outcome (step (iii-b)). Quesnay's analysis fits Halévy's idea that "by education individuals are taught to identify their interest with the general interest" (1901–1904, p. 20). On the contrary, Stewart takes for granted that as soon as individuals manage to seek their own interest, there is no need to talk them into pursuing the public interest, or the interest of others. This confirms that Stewart does not subscribe to an artificial identification of interests.

In the end, Stewart was optimistic about the effects of education, which may increase the happiness of all and thus fulfil the will of God. In this respect, "we ... may reasonably enjoy the satisfaction of considering ourselves ... as *fellow-workers with God* in forwarding the gracious purposes of his government" (Stewart 1815–1821, pp. 491–2, original emphasis). One can see here how Stewart's depiction of economic interactions serves a theodicy. Accordingly, the *end* is already determined, and all that remains is to advance more and more rapidly towards its completion, to which economic activities as such, assisted by religious knowledge, are the *means.* Progress is here synonymous with the discovery and achievement of a final cause, which, when not actually fulfilled, is thwarted because of prejudices. History itself is subservient to this theodicy, for all events may implicitly be linked to a final cause.

5. Conclusion

By outlining a distinction between different motives of action, and describing their respective private and public consequences, I have shown that Dugald Stewart advocated a natural identity of interests. In a providential world, individuals may be driven into action by self-love which is the search for individual happiness. Nevertheless, they have to form a plan of conduct in order to moderate their passions and overcome the partiality of self-love. The use of abstraction, by helping to make apparent the general laws of Providence that are beyond common and immediate knowledge, improves the plan of conduct. Only *enlightened interests* can help both the individual and society to be happy. Passions, prejudices, and the lack of abstraction hide *enlightened interests* and trap the economy in a non-optimal course. This distinction between the different motives of action in Stewart's thought, and the different degrees of perception of interest, has until now been absent from the scholarly literature. This explains the different and opposing answers proposed to the question of the connection of interests.

Stewart granted a crucial role to the spread of knowledge in order to secure a correct perception of these *enlightened interests.* The faith in such a perfectibility of the human mind entails a shift in what could be called social regulation: a form of regulation which eventually relies on economic agents themselves and no longer on government. Indeed, Stewart grounded Political Economy on a sort of "natural order" tantamount to that of the physiocrats, but for which a despot is not needed. Stewart thereby circumscribed an independent province for economics, of which he is the first lecturer. Because it serves a theodicy where mankind progressively fulfils the final cause of Providence and reaches happiness, Stewart's Political Economy also erases the very issue that mixed governments aimed at solving. In fact, what could possibly be checked and balanced if enlightened interests are, according to Providence, harmonious?

Acknowledgements

I would like to thank Thierry Demals, Christophe Depoortère, Knud Haakonssen, Alexandra Hyard, André Lapidus and the two anonymous referees for their comments and remarks on previous versions of this article. I am also grateful to Gilbert Faccarello and the participants of the workshop *Theology and Political Economy* (Labex Comod) held in Lyon in December 2014. I have also improved this paper, thanks to the advice of participants at the seminar *Les Après-midis de Philosophie et Économie* of PHARE held in June 2014, and those of the *17th Summer School in History of Economic Thought, Economic Philosophy and Economic History* held in Saragossa in September 2014. I am of course responsible for remaining mistakes.

Disclosure statement

No potential conflict of interest was reported by the author.

References

Ahnert, T., 2014. *The moral culture of the Scottish Enlightenment, 1690–1805*. New Haven, CT: Yale University Press.

Alvey, J., 2004. The hidden theology of Adam Smith: a belated reply to Hill. *European journal of the history of economic thought*, 11 (4), 623–8.

Aspromourgos, T., 2009. *The science of wealth. Adam Smith and the framing of political economy*. London: Routledge.

Becquemont, D., 2010. «Design», histoire du mot et du concept: sciences de la nature, théologie, esthétique. *In:* J. Gayon and A. de Ricqlès, eds. *Les fonctions: des organismes aux artefacts*. Paris: Presses Universitaires de France, 81–96.

Blaug, M., 2008. Invisible hand. *In:* S.N. Durlauf and L.E. Blume, eds. *The new Palgrave dictionary of economics*. 2nd ed. London: Palgrave Macmillan.

Brown, V., 1994. *Adam Smith's discourse: canonicity, commerce and conscience*. London: Routledge.

Butler, J., 1991. Fifteen sermons. *In:* D.D. Raphael, ed. *British moralists, 1650–1800*. Indianapolis, IN: Hackett, 325–86.

Clavé, F.U., 2005. Adam Smith face au «système de l'optimisme» de Leibniz. *Revue de philosophie économique*, 12, 19–72.

Coleman, W.O. 1995. *Rationalism and anti-rationalism in the origins of economics: the philosophical roots of 18th century economic thought*. Aldershot: Brookfield.

Corsi, P., 1987. The heritage of Dugald Stewart: Oxford philosophy and the method of political economy, 1809–1832. *Nuncius, annali di storia della scienza*, Anno II (2), 89–144.

Demals, T. and Hyard, A., 2007. James Mill et les «Économistes». *Revue Française d'Histoire des Idées politiques*, 25 (1), 61–88.

Depoortère, C., 2008. On Ricardo's method: the Scottish connection considered. *History of political economy*, 40 (1), 73–110.

Depoortère, C., 2013. William Nassau senior and David Ricardo on the method of political economy. *Journal of the history of economic thought*, 35 (1), 19–42.

Depoortère, C. and Ruellou, T., 2016. An insight on Dugald Stewart's interest and influence in political economy from a letter to Thomas Robert Malthus, 1820. *History of European ideas*, 42 (4), 534–40.

Dixon, W., 2008. Ricardo: economic thought and social order. *Journal of the history of economic thought*, 30 (2), 235–53.

Ege, R., 2007. Le concept de «lois naturelles» chez François Quesnay. *In:* A. Berthoud, B. Delmas and T. Demals, eds. *Y a-t-il des lois en économie?* Villeneuve d'Asq: Presses universitaires du Septentrion, 101–20.

Fischman, M., 1998. Le concept quesnayen d'ordre naturel. *Cahiers d'économie politique* (32), 67–97.

Forget, E.L., 2001. Jean-Baptiste Say and spontaneous order. *History of political economy*, 33 (2), 193–218.

Frobert, L., 2003. *Elie Halévy. République et économie (1896–1914).* Villeneuve d'Asq: Presses universitaires du Septentrion.

Goutte, P.-H., 1985. Évidence, ordre naturel et science économique dans l'œuvre de Quesnay. *In:* G. Klotz, ed. *Ordre, nature, propriété.* Lyon: Presses Universitaires de Lyon, 119–78.

Haakonssen, K., 1984. From moral philosophy to political economy: the contribution of Dugald Stewart. *In:* V. Hope, ed. *Philosophers of the Scottish Enlightenment.* Edinburgh: Edinburgh University Press, 211–30.

Haakonssen, K., 1996. Dugald Stewart and the science of a legislator. *In: Natural law and moral philosophy: from Grotius to the Scottish Enlightenment.* Cambridge: Cambridge University Press, 226–60.

Haakonssen, K., 2006. Natural jurisprudence and the theory of justice. *In:* A. Broadie, ed. *The Cambridge companion to the Scottish Enlightenment.* Cambridge: Cambridge University Press, 205–21.

Halévy, É., 1901–1904. *The growth of philosophical radicalism.* London: Faber and Faber Limited, 1928.

Hill, L., 2001. The hidden theology of Adam Smith. *The European journal of the history of economic thought*, 8 (1), 1–29.

Hilton, B., 1988. *The age of atonement: the influence of Evangelicalism on social and economic thought, 1785–1865.* New York: Clarendon Press.

Hirschman, A.O., 1977. *The passions and the interests. Political arguments for capitalism before its triumph.* Princeton, NJ: Princeton University Press.

Hyard, A., 2004. *Le Whiggism de Dugald Stewart. Une synthèse des visions britannique et française de la société commerçante.* Thesis (PhD). EHESS, Paris.

Hyard, A., 2006. Dugald Stewart, les «économistes» et la Révolution française. *Annales historiques de la révolution française* (345), 115–41.

Jones, G.S., 2004. *An end to poverty? A historical debate.* London: Profile Books.

Keppler, J.H., 2010. *Adam Smith and the economy of the passions.* New York: Routledge.

Kleer, R.A., 1995. Final causes in Adam Smith's *theory of moral sentiments. Journal of the history of philosophy*, 33 (2), 275–300.

Kleer, R.A., 2000. The role of teleology in Adam Smith's wealth of nations. *History of economics review*, (31), 14–29.

Kubo, S., 2013. George Pryme, Dugald Stewart, and political economy at Cambridge. *History of political economy*, 45 (1), 61–97.

Kubo, S., 2014. D. Stewart and J. R. McCulloch: economic methodology and the making of orthodoxy. *Cambridge journal of economics*, 38 (4), 925–43.

Lapidus, A., 2005. Physiocratie. *In*: M. Borlandi, R. Boudon, M. Cherkaoui, and B. Valade, eds. *Dictionnaire de la Pensée Sociologique*. Paris: Presses Universitaires de France, 549–51.

Larrère, C., 1992. *L'invention de l'économie au XVIIIe siècle: du droit naturel à la Physiocratie*. Paris: Presses Universitaires de France.

Laudan, L., 1970. Thomas Reid and the Newtonian turn of British methodological thought. *In:* R.E. Butts and J.W. Davis, eds. *The methodological heritage of Newton*. Oxford: Basil Blackwell, 103–31.

Le Mercier de La Rivière, P.-P., 1767. *L'Ordre naturel et essentiel des Sociétés politiques*. Paris: Desaint.

Magnusson, L., 2004. *The tradition of free trade*. London: Routledge.

McCulloch, J.R., 1845. *The literature of political economy: a classified catalogue of select publications in the different departments of that science, with historical, critical and biographical notices*. London: Longman, Brown, Green and Longmans.

Milgate, M. and Stimson, S.C., 2009. *After Adam Smith: a century of transformation in politics and political economy*. Princeton, NJ: Princeton University Press.

Mongin, P. and Sigot, N., 1999. Halévy's Bentham *is* Bentham. *Philosophy*, 74 (288), 271–81.

Oslington, P., 2011. Divine action, providence and Adam Smith's invisible hand. In: P. Oslington, ed. *Adam Smith as theologian*. London: Routledge, 2011, 61–75.

Poovey, M., 1998. *A history of the modern fact. Problems of knowledge in the sciences of wealth and society*. Chicago, IL: University of Chicago Press.

Prasch, R.E., 1996. The origins of the a priori method in classical political economy: a re-interpretation. *Journal of economic issues*, 30 (4), 1105–25.

Quesnay, F., 1747. Essai physique sur l'économie animale. *In*: F. Quesnay, *Œuvres économiques complètes et autres textes* (C. Théré, L. Charles, and J.-C. Perrot, eds). Paris: INED, vol. 1, pp. 5–60.

Quesnay, F., 1757. Grains. *In*: F. Quesnay, *Œuvres économiques complètes et autres textes*. (C. Théré, L. Charles, and J.-C. Perrot, eds). Paris: INED, vol. 1, pp. 161–212.

Quesnay, F., 1765. Droit naturel. *In*: F. Quesnay, *Œuvres économiques complètes et autres textes*. (C. Théré, L. Charles, and J.-C. Perrot, eds). Paris: INED, vol. 1, pp. 111–23.

Quesnay, F., 1767. Maximes générales du gouvernement économique d'un royaume agricole. *In*: F. Quesnay, *Œuvres économiques complètes et autres textes*. (C. Théré, L. Charles, and J.-C. Perrot, eds). Paris: INED, vol. 1, pp. 565–96.

Raphael, D.D. and Macfie, A.L. 1976. Introduction. *In*: A. Smith, 1759. *The theory of moral sentiments. The Glasgow edition of the works and correspondence of Adam Smith*. Oxford: Oxford University Press, 1–52.

Rendall, J., 2012. Adaptations: history, gender and political economy in the work of Dugald Stewart. *History of European ideas*, 38 (1), 143–61.

Rothschild, E. 2001. *Economic sentiments: Adam Smith, Condorcet, and the Enlightenment*. Cambridge, MA: Harvard University Press.

Smith, A., 1759. *The theory of moral sentiments. The Glasgow edition of the works and correspondence of Adam Smith*. D.D Raphael and A.L Macfie, eds. Oxford: Oxford University Press, 1976.

Smith, A., 1776. *An inquiry into the nature and causes of the wealth of nations. The Glasgow edition of the works and correspondence of Adam Smith*. R.H Campbell and A.S Skinner eds. Oxford: Oxford University Press, 1976.

Smith, A., 1978. *Lectures on jurisprudence. The Glasgow edition of the works and correspondence of Adam Smith*. R.L Meek, D.D Raphael and P.G Stein, eds. Oxford: Oxford University Press, 1978.

Smith, A., 1795. *Essays on philosophical subjects. The Glasgow edition of the works and correspondence of Adam Smith.* W.P.D. Wightman & J.C. Bryce, eds. Oxford: Oxford University Press, 1980.

Steiner, P., 1987. Le projet physiocratique: théorie de la propriété et lien social. *Revue économique,* 38 (6), 1111–28.

Steiner, P., 1992. L'économie politique du royaume agricole: François Quesnay. *In:* A. Béraud and G. Faccarello, eds. *Nouvelle Histoire de la Pensée Economique,* Paris: Editions La Découverte, vol. 1, 225–53.

Steiner, P., 1998. *La "science nouvelle" de l'économie politique.* Paris: Presses Universitaires de France.

Stewart, D. 1792–1827. *Elements of the philosophy of the human mind. The collected works of Dugald Stewart.* K. Haakonssen, ed., Bristol: Thoemmes Press, 1994, vol. II–IV.

Stewart, D., 1793a. *Account of the life and writings of Adam Smith. The collected works of Dugald Stewart.* K. Haakonssen, ed. Bristol: Thoemmes Press, 1994, vol. X, 3–98.

Stewart, D., 1793b. *Outlines of moral philosophy. The collected works of Dugald Stewart.* K. Haakonssen, ed. Bristol: Thoemmes Press, 1994, vol. II, 1–38; vol. VI, 3–108, and vol. VIII, 3–6.

Stewart, D., 1855–1856 [1809–1810]. *Lectures on political economy. The collected works of Dugald Stewart.* K. Haakonssen, ed., Bristol: Thoemmes Press, 1994, vol. VIII–IX.

Stewart, D., 1815–1821. *Dissertation: exhibiting the progress of metaphysical, ethical, and political philosophy, since the revival of letters in Europe. The collected works of Dugald Stewart.* K. Haakonssen, ed., Bristol: Thoemmes Press, 1994, vol. I.

Stewart, D., 1828. *The philosophy of the active and moral powers of man. The collected works of Dugald Stewart.* K. Haakonssen, ed., Bristol: Thoemmes Press, 1994, vol. VI–VII.

Stewart, M.A., 2006. Religion and rational theology. A. Broadie, ed. *The Cambridge companion to the Scottish Enlightenment.* Cambridge: Cambridge University Press, 31–59.

Tannoch-Bland, J., 1997. Dugald Stewart on intellectual character. *The British journal for the history of science,* 30 (3), 307–20.

Vergara, F., 1998. A critique of Elie Halévy: refutation of an important distortion of British moral philosophy. *Philosophy,* 73 (283), 97–111.

Viner, J., 1927. Adam Smith and Laissez Faire. *Journal of political economy,* 35, 198–232.

Viner, J., 1972. *The role of providence in the social order. An essay in intellectual history.* Princeton, NJ: Princeton University Press.

Waterman, A.M.C., 1991. *Revolution, economics and religion: Christian political economy, 1798–1833.* Cambridge: Cambridge University Press.

Weulersse, G., 1910. *Le mouvement physiocratique en France (de 1756 à 1770),* Paris: Alcan, vol. 2.

Winch, D., 1978. *Adam Smith's politics. An essay in historiographic revision.* Cambridge: Cambridge University Press.

Winch, D., 1983. The system of the North: Dugald Stewart and his pupils. *In:* S. Collini, D. Winch, and J. Burrow, eds. *That noble science of politics: a study in nineteenth-century intellectual history.* Cambridge, NY: Cambridge University Press, 23–61.

Winch, D., 1996. *Riches and poverty: an intellectual history of political economy in Britain, 1750–1834.* Cambridge: Cambridge University Press.

Young, J.T., 2002. Adam Smith and the physiocrats: contrasting views of the Law of Nature. *History of economic ideas,* 10 (3), 7–28.

POLITICAL ECONOMY AND RELIGION

Abstract

Dugald Stewart (1753–1828) defended free trade in light of a providential account of Nature, according to which there would be an "identity of interests" (Halévy 1901–1904). He thereby tried to rid economic thought of references to conflicts and thus pursued the physiocrats' programme rather than Adam Smith's. In fact, Stewart claimed that (i) self-love depends on an accommodation to Providence, by which individuals restrain their passions; (ii) self-love fosters actions that lead to a direct increase of public happiness; (iii) the perfectibility of mind allows to dismiss "legal despotism", which can be replaced by religious education.

Theological themes in Ricardo's papers and correspondence

Sergio Cremaschi

1. Introduction

I intend to reconstruct David Ricardo's philosophical and theological ideas concerning toleration, religion and morality, and the problem of evil. My reconstruction is carried out on the basis of evidence from the *Ricardo Papers*, the correspondence and his parliamentary speeches. I will highlight the context of statements he made on several occasions on such topics as the existence of a natural universal morality, the ethical essence of religion, the arbitrariness of any theological speculation and accordingly the uselessness of theology as such, unlimited toleration including even atheists, and the impossibility of theodicy or lack of any answer to the question why there is suffering in the world. I will argue that the claims Ricardo endorses are typical of an early-nineteenth-century 'rational Christian' and inspired by his experience as a Jew by birth and education, for a time fellow-traveller of the Quakers, and then a regular hearer at Unitarian services. I shall explore the implications of Ricardo's interest in the religious sceptic Pierre Bayle, and particularly his argument against theodicy, for his views on the scope and method of political economy. I shall suggest that his view of the function of economic science, more modest than Malthus's, is connected with a less optimistic attitude concerning the possibility of a more egalitarian and humane society. I will add that he believed that political economy should be a secular science precisely for theological reasons, namely that the anti-dogmatic kind of religious belief he declared to be rationally legitimate ruled out any kind of dogmatic 'a-theology' like the *Laissez-Faire* Metaphysics cherished by his friend James Mill.

The structure of the paper is as follows, Section 2 discusses the reasons why philosophico-theological themes in the correspondence and the '*Commonplace Book*' were overlooked, first by Sraffa and then by later commentators; Section 3 discusses the contents of a pamphlet on Christianity in India by Trower and Ricardo's comments; Section 4 reconstructs the context and contents of Ricardo's parliamentary speech on toleration; Section 5 is a reconstruction of Ricardo's reading notes on Bayle, Hume and other authors; then an examination of the discussion on theodicy in the correspondence with Mill and Malthus (Sections 6 and 7); finally, in Section 9, a few conclusions are drawn on Ricardo's views on theology, religious freedom, natural morality, theodicy, and their bearing on political economy.

2. A hidden agenda in Ricardo's *Nachlass*

Readers of recent monographs on Ricardo may have failed to notice the existence of Ricardo's '*Commonplace Book*' from the period between 1817 and 1819.[1] They may find some detailed, albeit scant, information in the *Works and Correspondence* (Ricardo 1951–1973, 10, pp. 393–8), but be left with the impression that nobody, since Sraffa, has looked at it again. As in the '*Commonplace Book*', consisting actually of a set of notebooks and loose papers containing notes and abstracts, Ricardo's reading plan is also documented in the correspondence with James Mill. Sraffa is as careful as ever in reporting the contents and, with some patience, the most gifted treasure hunters among readers might, for example, be able to reconstruct those passages from Pierre Bayle which Ricardo found of special interest. Yet, the criterion followed by Sraffa was to include in the *Works and Correspondence* just what is directly relevant to economic theory and nothing else. One consequence is, for example, that the Parliamentary discussion on the Christians' petition is reprinted but the text of the petition itself is omitted. Another is that Sraffa tends to underestimate the importance of non-economic topics in the correspondence; for instance, when Ricardo discusses Trower's pamphlet and the reader is left without any information about the contents of the publication under discussion; again, when the topic of theodicy emerges, namely in the notes on Malthus and the related correspondence with Mill, the reader is left without information either about the context or the co-text of the discussion. Perhaps the gravest consequence, however, is that information about the '*Commonplace Book*' is

1 Weatherall (1976) and Henderson (1997) completely ignore such readings; Milgate and Stimson (1991, p. 23) and King (2013, p. 33) do notice them but dismiss them in half a page.

packed into six pages. Nonetheless, what emerges clearly enough is the fact that 40% of Ricardo's readings consisted of modern history and travel journals and 60% of writings about the theory of knowledge and scepticism, the limits of human knowledge in religious subjects, the relationship of religion and morality, toleration, and theodicy or the problem of evil.

3. Natural and revealed morality in the correspondence with Trower

It has been remarked more than once that Ricardo's *Principles*, when compared with Adam Smith's *Wealth of Nations* and Malthus's *Principles*, looks much more like a scientific treatise than a philosophical work. The impression arises from the circumstance that no hint is given of connections either with a philosophical system as a whole or with philosophical or meta-economic claims of any sort. While agreeing that the impression is justified, I am not yet ready to endorse an unjustified inference from so shaky a basis, namely that the *Principles* look secular because Ricardo himself was 'secular', an 'unreligious mind' who professed 'atheism'.[2] I would object, first, that Ricardo never disclosed atheistic or agnostic leanings, secondly, that when he did discuss theological issues on a few occasions, the opinions he disclosed, far from providing evidence to his privately held atheism or agnosticism, are quite consistent with his public image as a 'rational Christian'.

One example is provided by a letter to Hutches Trower of 8 November 1813 where he comments on a pamphlet the latter had published reporting an exchange – letters to the Editor of the *Times* – between 'Laicus' (pen name of the lawyer and committed Evangelical, John Poynder) and 'an East India Proprietor', that is, Hutches Trower himself (Trower 1813). Ricardo, after writing that he had read the letters 'with very great interest' and that his own impression was that all that could be said on the subject had 'been ably said on both sides', concludes,

> My opinion coincided with yours before I read your letters and it is now very much strengthened by the facts and reasoning which you have brought forward. (Ricardo 1951–1973, 6, p. 96)

Poynder insists on the idea that Christianity is needed in India, as it is desirable that the faith of the Gospel should supplant the Hindu's absurd, cruel, and immoral superstitions which give room to infanticide, the

2 The phrases reported are by Depoortère (2002, p. 501) and Hartwell (1971, p. 36); Henderson (1997, p. 163) instead, somewhat more prudently writes that he was, if 'not atheist, an agnostic'.

burning of widows and human sacrifices (Trower 1813, pp. 3–4). He then adds that, in order to achieve this goal, the East India Company should establish an Episcopal Government in India while granting additional facilities to Missionaries to proceed there (Trower 1813, pp. 5–10).

Trower's rejoinders illustrate the alleged dangers carried by an Episcopalian establishment in India with a considerable flow of missionaries. He asserts that 'there are many reasons for deprecating any attempt to convert the Hindoos to Christianity' (Trower 1813, p. 48) as both impossible and counterproductive (Trower 1813, pp. 13–4), while rejecting the claim that the Hindus are 'in the most dreadful state of moral depravity' and addicted to 'every vice which can degrade our nature' (Trower 1813, p. 38), adding that 'their vices are not attributable to their religion' (Trower 1813, p. 14,39), that their moral character 'is not deserving of the severity with which it is censured' (Trower 1813, pp. 86–7) and that it 'may be improved without their conversion' (Trower 1813, p. 87).

From Ricardo's admission that his opinions coincide with Trower's something may be inferred, *not* his atheism, but rather that he shared the following opinions,

(1) people cannot and should not be forced to believe something whose truth they are not persuaded of;
(2) morality can be improved independently of adhesion to some given set of religious beliefs;
(3) the moral character of non-Christian nations is not necessarily perverse;
(4) the moral character of Christian nations does not necessarily correspond to the purity of the Gospel's teaching.

Another item from Ricardo's correspondence with Trower deserves discussion. In a letter of 26 January 1818, Ricardo mentions John Bird Sumner as 'a clergyman, the author of a clever book on the Records of Creations, in which Malthus's system is not only defended for its truth, but for its affording proofs of the benevolence and goodness of the Creator' (Ricardo 1951–1973, 7, p. 247). This carries more implications than any reader unaware of the context would draw. The 'clever book' was the *Treatise on the Records of Creation* (Sumner 1816). This was precisely a treatise on theodicy, trying to improve Paley's argument in his *Natural Theology* by proving that Malthus's principle of population could be read as one more application of the kind of 'arithmetic' approach to theodicy previously adopted by Paley. In the latter's version, the argument is that the total sum of good in the world may be proved to outweigh that of evil once we define good as pleasure and evil as pain, and we include the *total* amount of pleasure and pain in the world, that is, that of all sentient beings, even including insects (Paley 1802, p. 491; cf. Cremaschi 2014, pp. 90–4). Sumner's 'improved' version asserts that the same result is reached in a simpler and less extravagant way if we instead define evil as pain and good as moral improvement (Cremaschi 2014, pp. 135–9). In a nutshell, the solution is the following, (1) to some extent, evil will 'arise necessarily from the law of nature', and suffering is necessary in order 'to make men look beyond the present day and the present state of things' (Sumner 1816, 2, p. 258); (2) evil is to some extent the result of ineffective institutions which, even when they do not 'positively' teach 'improvidence', are so framed as to discourage the learning of 'prudence' (Sumner 1816, 2, p. 301); (3) the main 'cause of the greatest evil of the poor is ignorance' (Sumner 1816, 2, p. 292), but, as recent improvements in educational systems show, there is a possibility of great improvement in the human mind, and the 'only true secret of assisting the poor is to make them agents in bettering their condition, and to supply them, not with a temporary stimulus, but with a permanent energy' (Sumner 1816, 2, pp. 338–9).

Note that Ricardo, in his usual, calm manner, qualifies the book as 'clever', even though – being persuaded of the impossibility of any theodicy – he was obviously convinced that Sumner's argument was fallacious. Here is his charitable comment,

> I am sorry to hear that Mr Sumner does not intend writing any more on Political Economy – his whole attention in future is to be devoted to the study of Theology. Whether in this future pursuit he will have an equal chance of benefiting mankind, as in the former, I have great doubts, or rather have no doubt at all. (Ricardo 1951–1973, 7, pp. 247–8)

To the unaware reader, the latter sentence might sound like yet another revelation of an 'unreligious mind'. Instead, what Ricardo is implying here is that *theology* (not *faith*) is a vain pursuit. The clarification may be in order here that what was meant by 'theology' at the time was either *natural theology* (the discussion of the existence and attributes of the Deity on the basis of purely rational argument) or *revealed theology* (the discussion of the above topics in the light of assertions taken from the Holy Scripture combined with rational argument). Such twofold definition – it is as well to note – fails to overlap with current twenty-first century meaning, where historical and philological study of Biblical texts and related oral traditions is given pride of place. Theology, thus understood, had been the bête noire of eighteenth-century *Aufklärer* – that is, enlighteners – from all over Europe, including, besides fideist Bayle and deist Voltaire, also Adam Smith, arguably a theist and even a *bona fide* Presbyterian (Cremaschi 2017), and such an orthodox enough Lutheran as Kant. The point of the attack was that theology as commonly understood was an impure mixture of unwarranted metaphysical claims going beyond the reach of human knowledge and assertions about God allegedly found in the Bible which are in fact not there, for although the Bible does teach moral precepts, such as to love one's neighbour, it has a noncommittal attitude vis-à-vis inquiries into God's essence. Besides, while theodicy was a privileged chapter in post-Reformation theology, after the age of Leibniz and the Cambridge Platonists it was unanimously declared a vain enterprise by philosophers. Paley, Sumner, and Malthus were the rear guard in an irreparably lost war.

Let me add that Thomas Belsham, the Minister whose services Ricardo attended from 1814 to 1823 (Sraffa 1955a, pp. 39–40; Weatherall 1976, pp. 61–72; Cremaschi 2015), used to teach that faith is a *practical* attitude, not a theoretical one, that human knowledge is limited and it is useless to inquire into subjects 'without the grasp of the human mind' as Medieval divines used to do, for example into 'the mode of the divine existence' (Belsham 1826–1827, 2, p. 55) and that on 'the most important doctrines of natural and revealed religion' we should not require 'rational knowledge' but rest content instead with 'rational belief' (Belsham 1801, p. 110).

4. Toleration in a parliamentary speech

Milgate and Stimson deserve praise for having drawn attention to Ricardo's political theory as something more than an appendix to his economic theory (Cremaschi 1994). They have argued that his politics have little to share with Benthamite politics, that he 'reached his conclusions before the publication of James Mill's essay on *Government*' (Milgate and Stimson 1991, p. 18), that his argument for extension of political rights and religious toleration is not just a reformulation of Bentham's and Mill's arguments, and besides that, at least in his last years, he adopted a markedly pro-working class attitude (Milgate and Stimson 1991, pp. 61, 119).

I would add that he had alternative sources for his political ideas. For example, long before he first met Mill, his attendance at Hackney Chapel had offered him the opportunity to meet radicals and reformers of various tendencies. Note, in this connection, that Belsham complained, shortly after 1794, of abandonment of the Pulpit in favour of political militancy by fellow-Ministers (Williams 1833, p. 462). When Ricardo and Mill first met, the political scenario was changing, radicals were re-defining their political stance, and the idea of Reform was to become for many of them the catch-all formula for a new kind of liberalism, fostered by the Philosophical

Radicals allied with an assorted company of 'Friends of Reason' in a number of campaigns (Cremaschi 2004, pp. 384–5). In some of these – think of the anti-slave-trade campaign, whose leader was an Evangelical MP – the company was really an oddly assorted one.

Commitment to religious toleration was a matter of course for Ricardo for more than one reason, first as a Jew by birth, secondly as the husband of a Quaker, and thirdly as a Unitarian by choice. Toleration for every kind of religious opinion, including atheism, was the first point of the Unitarian agenda since Theophilus Lindsey founded the first Unitarian congregation in Britain. Unitarians campaigned for religious toleration for obvious reasons, anti-Trinitarianism was not covered by the Toleration Act of 1689, and up to 1813 still fell under the penal law, and it was not until 1829 that the Corporate and Test Act was abolished (a law depriving Dissenters of full rights) (Stuart 2003; Dave 1978, pp. 65–8; Watts 1998). Let me recall a remarkable comment by Ricardo on toleration for atheists. After a visit to Gatcomb by Sydney Smith, an *Edinburgh Review* editor, he writes to Mill on 9 September 1821 that Smith 'is always on the liberal side, but has a strong propensity to halt half way – he is for tolerating all religions, but is inclined to be intolerant to those whom he supposes to have no religion. I contended for Dr. Lindsey's principle, that even the Atheist should be heard' (Ricardo 1951–1973, 9, p. 60).[3]

On 26 March 1823, while supporting in Parliament a petition for the release of Mary Ann Carlile who had been imprisoned on the basis of an indictment to have sold atheist literature, he declares that 'a fair and free discussion ought to be allowed on all religious topics' (Ricardo 1951–1973, 5, p. 288). In a letter of 4 April 1823 to Isaac Lyon Goldsmid, a leading figure in the campaign for Jewish emancipation, he writes, 'I carry my principles of toleration very far; – I do not know how, or why any line should be drawn, and am prepared to maintain that we have no more justifiable ground for shutting the mouth of the Atheist than that of any other man' (Ricardo 1951–1973, 9, p. 278).

And in fact, Ricardo's Parliamentary Speech on religious freedom was occasioned by a 'Christians' petition against the Prosecution of Unbelievers', whose 'prime mover' was Aspland (Sraffa 1955a, p. 41). The petition was

3 Theophilus Lindsey, the founding father of British Unitarianism, sternly campaigned for toleration, but apparently never discussed the issue of toleration for atheists, and besides he had no doctoral degree. It is probably the case that Sraffa's 'Lindsey' should be amended into 'Lindsay'. James Lindsay was a Unitarian Minister with whom Ricardo was acquainted and who had a doctoral degree and advocated 'not only for Toleration, but for that unbounded freedom of opinion, to which alone genuine Christianity must owe its future prevalence, and its permanent influence' (Lindsay 1813, 22).

presented to the House of Commons by radical MP Joseph Hume and supported by Ricardo. Starting with the argument that 'belief does not in all cases depend upon the will' (Aspland *et al.* 1823, p. 363), the petitioners asked the Honourable House to act in order to abolish the possibility of prosecution of unbelievers (Aspland *et al.* 1823, p. 364). Ricardo's speech, while referring to Paley and other Anglican authorities, claimed that the law should not establish *any* limit to discussion on theoretical aspects of religion and that the public authority has no competence to judge whether such discussion is conducted with respect or instead with 'levity and ribaldry', and he vindicated 'a more large and liberal spirit of toleration' (Ricardo 1951–1973, 5, p. 324), contending for 'the general right of self-opinion, and for the unfettered liberty of discussion' (1951–1973, 5, p. 331)

The first argument is that imposing profession of belief in a future state is self-defeating,

> what an absurd and immoral mode did the law provide for estimating the credit of a man's faith before his testimony was legally admissible! When the question was put to a witness, 'Do you believe in a future state?' If he were a conscientious man, entertaining seriously such an opinion, his answer must be in the negative, and the law said he should not be heard; but if he were an immoral man, and disregarded truth, and said, 'I do believe in a future state,' although in his conscience he disbelieved in it, then his evidence was admissible, and his hypocrisy and falsehood secured him credibility. Now, there would be some sense in the law, if it declined tempting the hypocrisy of the individual, or his fear of the world's hostility or prejudice, and let in other evidence to establish, from previous knowledge of the individual, whether or not he ought not to be admitted as a witness; but as it stood, it was absurd and ridiculous. (Ricardo 1951–1973, 5, p. 327)

One more argument advanced is that 'on so abstract religious subjects, upon which it was quite impossible to obtain universal assent, no man had a right to say to another, "My opinion upon religion is right, and yours is not only wrong when you differ from me, but I am entitled to punish you for that difference" (Ricardo 1951–1973, 5, pp. 324–5).

Another is that moral obligation does not arise exclusively from religion, and it has a previous source, the force of 'moral impressions'. Note that, besides being an assertion of the existence of a natural morality, this statement also alludes to a notion utterly incompatible with Benthamite ethics, namely the idea of 'moral impressions'.

The report adds that Ricardo declared that

> he firmly believed in the possibility of a man's being very honest for all the social purposes and essential obligations of the community in which he lived, and still not assenting to the belief of a future state. He fully admitted that religion was a powerful obligation, but he denied it to be the only obligation – it was, in fact, one which was superadded to the general force of moral impressions – it were a libel upon human nature to say otherwise. (Ricardo 1951–1973, 5, p. 327)

Then he reportedly repeated a neat distinction between opinions on theoretical matters and a capacity to grasp the moral quality of actions. He declared

> that the obligation of religion was not alone considered as the test of moral truth, and that a man might be very sceptical upon doctrinal points, and yet very positive in the control of moral impressions distinct from religious faith. (Ricardo 1951–1973, 5, p. 328)

At last, he introduced a distinction between positive sciences, where some unerring criteria for ending controversies exist, and other disciplines bound to remain forever – so to say – the battlefield of unending struggles. He said that there was

> not in polemics, as in astronomy, one unerring criterion to which the common credence of mankind bowed – it was not like the rising sun, or any of the other phenomena of nature, which were bound by indissoluble and indispensable laws; but, on the contrary, a subject open to conflicting opinions. (Ricardo 1951–1973, 5, p. 329)

To sum up, Ricardo's reasons in favour of unlimited religious freedom were typically those endorsed by 'rational Christians', namely, that (1) the essence of religion is morality, not speculative truth; (2) acceptance of theoretical claims is a matter of rational persuasion, not will; (3) the non-believer may enjoy as strong moral motivation, deriving from 'moral impressions' independent of opinions on theoretical issues, as the believer; (4) human nature is good enough to grant that even a non-believer may perceive such moral impressions; (5) to controversy on theoretical truths in religion, unlike astronomy, an end cannot be put by any unerring criteria; (6) no one has the authority to silence opponents in matters of religious opinion; (7) any attempt to force profession of religious belief upon non-believers as a proof of their moral accountability would be self-defeating and demoralising.

5. Natural morality, theodicy and toleration in the *Commonplace Book*

More evidence of Ricardo's interest in theological issues may be found in the '*Commonplace Book*', consisting of two notebooks and a few pages of notepaper containing reading notes from 1817 and 1818 (Ricardo unpublished). Part of this philosophical reading concerns the theory of knowledge and scepticism, including Locke, Hume and Dugald Stewart.[4] I have already mentioned that more than half of it verges on religious subjects. Sraffa, though as accurate as ever, seems to have been less than enthusiastic about

4 For a reconstruction see Cremaschi and Dascal (1996, pp. 496–7; 1998, pp. 246–52).

Ricardo's religious interests and did not allow much room for them. A rather more analytical reconstruction may be of some use.

In the 1817 notebook Ricardo wrote down a select list of titles of chapters with the addition of a number of excerpts copied in full from two of Pierre Bayle's works (Ricardo unpublished; cf. Ricardo 1951–1973, 11, p. 393). The first is *Pensées diverses sur la Comète.* The topics Ricardo deemed worth examining are, in chs. XLVI, LXXXIV, XCIX, C, CVIII, that opinions keep on being widely shared albeit contradicted by experience just because of their antiquity and generality, and that even visions firmly believed by several witnesses turn out patently false (Bayle 1682, 1, pp. 130–3; 1, pp. 219–21; 1, pp. 266–73; 1, pp. 292–3); in ch. LXIX, that right reason teaches us to honour God not by ceremonies, but rather through the practice of virtue (Bayle 1682, 1, pp. 179–82); in chs. LXXXI and XCI, that religion is constantly used by rulers either to defend themselves or to manipulate their subjects (Bayle 1682, 1, pp. 205–9; 1, pp. 242–4); in ch. LXXXVIII, that conversions obtained by force or bought with money are counterproductive (Bayle 1682, 1, pp. 228–35); in chs. CXX, CXXIII and CXLVI, that idolatry is more obnoxious than irreligion and atheism does not necessarily lead to corruption of morals (Bayle 1682, 1, pp. 315–8; 2, pp. 5–8; 2, pp. 37–9); in chs. CXXXIV – CXXXVIII, that experience shows that religion fails to correct vicious inclinations because, more than on principles they profess, men tend to act on particular judgements dictated by the passion prevailing at the moment (Bayle 1682, 2, pp. 8–18).

The second work is the *Dictionnaire historique et critique.* From this, just two excerpts are reported. The first, from note B in the entry 'Anabaptistes', reports that excesses by this sect offered the Roman party an occasion to defame Reformation, and that the Reformers, in order to confront competition, 'shouted with all their strength' against the Anabaptists (Bayle 1697, 1, p. 200). The other is from note 1 to the entry '*Gregoire I*' and it reports the anecdote of a monk at Pavia Chartreuse pointing to Giangaleazzo Visconti's burial place as that of a 'great saint', and justifying such qualification by the maxim followed in his own country, namely, to 'call saints all those who do us good'; Bayle comments that this maxim, far from being a typical Italian product, 'is followed at every time and in every country' (Bayle 1697, 2, p. 598).

Ricardo carefully read more entries. In letters to Mill of 12 September 1817 (Ricardo 1951–1973, 7, p. 190) and 9 Nov 1817 (Ricardo 1951–1973, 7, p. 206) he mentions those on '*Manichéens*' (Bayle 1697, 3, pp. 302–7), '*Pauliciens*' (3, p. 624–36), and '*Marcionites*' (3, p. 314–9). These discuss the doctrines of the sect of Manicheans or Paulicians – as they were named in Armenia – and of that of Marcionites. These sects used to set the merciful God of the New Testament against the allegedly merciless God of the Old Testament. The point Bayle wants to make here is that it is hard to account for the existence of evil without allowing for two original co-existing principles, and that to refute this idea is even more difficult for Christians than for the polytheists, since they are bound either to deny God's omnipotence or to make God the author of evil.

The second notebook, probably from 1818, includes an excerpt from ch. 14 of John Locke's *Reasonableness of Christianity* which declares that among the ancient Heathens some philosophers cultivated the knowledge of one God, but few went to their schools 'to be instructed in their duties', and most people rested content with sacrifices and services, while 'the priests made it not their business to teach them virtue' (Locke 1695, p. 147).

Besides, there are two excerpts from David Hume's *Natural History of Religion*. The first is from Section 12, declaring that in all ages religious conviction 'is more affected than real', and 'the assent in these matters is some unaccountable operation of the mind between disbelief and conviction, but approaching much nearer the former than the latter' (Hume 1757, p. 72); the other, from Section 14, declares that the virtuous man 'is drawn to his duty without any effort or endeavour' by the force of the natural ties he has with his family and community, to which a 'sentiment of order and moral beauty' is joined, without any 'pretence to religious merit; and the virtuous conduct is deemed no more than what we owe to society and to ourselves' (Hume 1757, p. 82).

Reading notes follow from two works by Richard Watson, the Regius Professor of Divinity at Cambridge and Bishop of Llandaff, *An Apology for Christianity* (1776), being a rejoinder to Edward Gibbon, and *An Apology for the Bible* (1796), being a rejoinder to Thomas Paine. The first excerpt from the former book says that it is 'just as illiberal in Divines, to attribute the scepticism of every Deist to wilful infidelity; as it is in the Deists, to refer to the faith of every Divine to professional bias' (Watson 1776, pp. 86–7). The next declares that Gibbon's polemics against miracles go beyond the point by relying on an idea of unchangeable laws of nature as if they were fully known (Watson 1776, p. 92–6), while there 'was a time no one was acquainted with the laws of magnetism; these suspend in many instances the laws of gravity; nor can I see, upon the principle in question, how the rest of mankind could have credited the testimony of their first discoverer; and yet to have rejected it, would have been to reject the truth' (Watson 1776, p. 92).

Three excerpts follow from *An Apology for the Bible*, the first on fairness in controversy, 'A philosopher in search of truth forfeits with me all claim to candour and impartiality, when he introduces railing for reasoning, vulgar and illiberal sarcasm in the room for argument' (Watson 1796, p. 29).

The second is a defence of prophecies from the Hebrew Bible (Watson 1796, pp. 160–2). The third is about Deism, arguing that it runs into the same difficulties as revealed religion (Watson 1796, pp. 367–9), among these 'the existence of evil, moral and natural, in the work of an infinite being, powerful, wise, and good' and 'the gift of freedom of will, when the abuse of freedom becomes the cause of general misery' (Watson 1796, p. 369).

The last notes are from *An Examination of the Bishop of London's Discourse concerning Prophecy* by Convyers Middleton, a Cambridge fellow with a taste for theological controversy. The first excerpt is again on fairness in controversy. It declares that the Bishop 'forgot surely that he was now discoursing from the Press, and not from the Pulpit, for though *Ipse dixits* may carry authority with them, where no body can contradict, yet they would never pass for arguments, where speech and debate are free' (Middleton 1750, p. 35). The second is about 'questions, wholly speculative, fruitless and inexplicable', arguing that 'the foundation of all religion' lies in 'those practical, social and real duties, which our reason and senses prescribe in common to all' (Middleton 1750, pp. 196–7).

To draw a balance, it would be a risky enterprise to try to evince Ricardo's own opinions from evidence of what he found noteworthy. Nonetheless, fixing a list of topics he deemed worth discussing would already be a result of some interest. A reasonable list might be as follows, (1) the existence of the tendency to believe whatsoever opinion on authority; (2) the need for mutual respect in religious controversy; (3) the ethical character of all true religious teaching; (4) the superstitious and immoral character of religion reduced to ceremonies and sacrifices; (5) the possibility of morality without a foundation on religious belief and falsity of allegations of immorality against atheism; (6) the irrelevance of speculative theology; (7) the irrelevance of Deism as an alternative to revealed religion as being just one more speculative theology leaving decisive questions unanswered; (8) the miscarriage of all philosophical trials in theodicy. This is no more than an agenda for discussion, and yet there is enough to refute a number of claims advanced by some commentators.

6. Theodicy in the correspondence with Mill

The last point listed above, namely the impossibility of any theodicy, was again discussed by Ricardo on other occasions, when he manifested his interest in the issue and expressed the opinion that all philosophical trials in theodicy had miscarried – note that among these were those staged by the young Malthus, Paley, Sumner, and the mature Malthus – thus taking a stance close to Kant's refusal of theodicy, of which he was obviously enough unaware. But he also rejected – as politely as ever – Mill's implication that the failure of any theodicy leaves atheism as the only option. In fact, while discussing Bayle in letters to Mill of 12 September 1817 (Ricardo 1951–1973, 7, p. 190) and 9 November 1817 (Ricardo 1951–1973, 7, p. 206) he writes,

> On these difficult points I keep my mind in a state of doubt from which *in this world* I never can be relieved. To account for evil in a world governed by a Being of unbounded benevolence and power is or appears to be impossible. It is as puzzling a question now as in the early times of which Bayle writes. Is it much different from the Manichean heresy to say that the Creator's benevolence is unbounded, but that his power is limited – and thus to account for evil? (Ricardo 1951–1973, 7, p. 206; my emphasis)[5]

Mill answers, on 3 December 1817, that he completely agrees with the last remark, for supposing that God's power is limited amounts to supposing 'that there is some power in the universe, which the Deity cannot controul, and which has a tendency to produce evil' (Ricardo 1951–1973, 7, p. 212). But, while Ricardo's implication was that all philosophical trials in theodicy will end up with miscarriage, and we can hope at most for an answer to the question on the causes of evil *in a world to come,* Mill typically presumes that this is a water-proof reason for atheism, and goes on attacking alleged hypocrisy by somebody else. In fact, he adds, 'Poor Mr. Malthus – If I am not mistaken, it is he who solves the difficulty about the existence of evil in this manner. What a misfortune – what a cruel misfortune, it is, for a man to be obliged to believe a certain set of opinions, whether they be fit, or not, to be believed!' (Ricardo 1951–1973, 7, pp. 212–3). That is, he presumes that Malthus, while being obviously aware of the undeniable conclusion he has presented, goes on – unlike virtuous Mill who consistently abandoned the career of 'a priest' for which he had been educated – teaching what he cannot obviously believe in order to keep his own 'prebends'. Besides the usual arrogance it betrays, the comment is particularly inept in failing to notice changes in Malthus's theodicy, from 1798 to 1803 and 1817 (Cremaschi 2014, pp. 79–81, 94–9, 145–51) and assuming that – plausible or implausible as it might be – it was still the 1798 one which invited precisely such criticism.

Note that Ricardo's answer of 18 December 1817 politely avoids comments on Mill's own presumptions and instead introduces what is perhaps an indirect objection. He shifts to a comment about religion within a dis-

5 King (2013, p. 32) writes that, even though we cannot establish Ricardo's views on religion, at least this letter proves that he was 'agnostic on the problem of evil'. The comment is misleading, for *agnosticism* is the claim that we cannot answer the question of *God's existence* while *theism without theodicy* is a respectable enough tradition.

cussion of Mill's recently published *History of British India* (Mill 1817) that he had started to read. He writes that Mill's own view of the manner in which 'mankind become acquainted with the idea of the Supreme Being is much the same as that of Hume' (Ricardo 1951–1973, 7, p. 229) and 'the adulatory expressions' with which primitives address him are no proof 'of any just or sublime conception of him' (Ricardo 1951–1973, 7, p. 229). This is perhaps a polite but malicious way of responding, for Mill did not admit of 'any *just or sublime* conception' of God but just rejected *any* conception of God.

Besides the opinions that both metaphysics and speculative theology are vain enterprises, the idea that theodicy is a risky business is something else that Ricardo had heard at Unitarian 'instructions'. Like every other eighteenth-century philosopher, Priestley had tried to solve the problem of evil, and his solution resembles Leibniz's solution. He writes that, since 'all evils and inconveniences have final causes', once the final cause has ceased to exists, 'evils tend to be eliminated by themselves' (Priestley 1762, p. 250), and even

> everything painful and disagreeable in the world appears to a philosopher [...] to be excellently provided as a remedy of some greater inconvenience, or a necessary means of a much greater happiness; so that, from this elevated point of view, he sees all temporary evils and inconveniencies to vanish, in the glorious prospect of the greater good to which they are subservient. (Priestley 1767, p. xvii)

Belsham writes, in a first phase, that philosophical necessitarianism is an appealing doctrine also in so far as 'it demonstrates the inseparable connexion between moral and natural evil, and proves that by the established course of nature every vice shall be followed by adequate punishment' (Belsham 1801, 310), that 'the preponderance of happiness' is 'very considerably on the side of virtue' and, 'generally speaking, every purpose of substantial justice is answered independent of a future state' (Belsham 1801, 351); this doctrine is also 'inseparably connected with that of optimism', showing that all events are 'necessary parts of a great system, which shall eventually produce the greatest possible sum of happiness and virtue, both to the universe and to individuals' (Belsham 1801, 313). Yet, later on, he writes that, when we consider the world as a whole, 'we see enough' to be satisfied

> that the result of it is a great preponderance of good [...] but when we consider the divine dispensations in detail, we shall immediately discover that they are far beyond the reach of human sagacity (Belsham 1826–1827, 2, pp. 36–7)

and the fact 'that evil, natural and moral, is unavoidable in the works of God, is a problem of very difficult solution' (Belsham 1826–1827, 2, p. 37).

To sum up, the only admissible argument to reconcile the Creator's goodness and what experience proves about the course of the world is that the amount of good may overwhelm the amount of evil in the long run, but we can neither prove this in a totally convincing way nor can we explain evil-in-the-short-run away as being merely apparent.

7. Theodicy in the correspondence with Malthus

In the *Essay on Profits* of 1815 Ricardo mentions Providence. He apparently wants to draw from one of Malthus's claims such further implications as to lead to implications opposite to the original ones. He notes that

> it has been remarked, in reference to a single country, that if the crops are bad in one district, they are generally productive in another; that if the weather is injurious to one soil, or to one situation, it is beneficial to a different soil and different situation; and, by this compensating power, Providence has bountifully secured us from the frequent recurrence of dearths. If this remark be just, as applied to one country, how much more strongly may it be applied to all the countries together which compose our world? Will not the deficiency of one country be made up by the plenty of another? (Ricardo 1951–1973, 4, p. 31)

To be fair, God is mentioned here in the context of a *tu quoque* argument, and thus his mention cannot be assumed to imply direct commitment to his existence.

A similar, but somewhat more committed, concession is made in his *Notes on Malthus*. His objection concerns the latter's qualification of rent as a 'bountiful gift of Providence' and the argument is that rent comes from limited resources such as land, but not from unlimited ones, and that it is scarcity, not intrinsic usefulness, to give a price to scarce resources. Thus, the problem for a political economist is not

> whether the Creator did not consult our real happiness by limiting the productive powers of the land, but whether the fact be not, that he has so limited it, – He has given us an unbounded supply of water, of air, and has set no limits to the use we may make of the pressure of the atmosphere, the elasticity of steam and many other services rendered to us by nature. (Ricardo 1951–1973, 2, p. 210; cf. pp. 337–8)

On balance, Ricardo's argument seems to be in favour of a less value-laden approach in economic theory. Note that he does mention the Creator here and in the previous quote he had not hesitated in mentioning Providence. It is true that both mentions are made for the sake of the argument, namely, that he is drawing implications from Malthus's own argument while trying to refute it by a *reductio ad absurdum*. Yet, he seems to mention the Creator or Providence without any special caution. It seems that the argument here is both of a *tu quoque* nature and one that Ricardo could seriously endorse, even though with opposite conclusions. His main concern seems to be exclusion not of religion but of 'metaphysics'; that is, he wants to rule out our capacity to detect an axiological and teleological order in the world and also wants to fix boundaries to the scope of human knowledge. In more detail, he wants to confine human knowledge to the discovery of correlations and formulation of general laws. This may depend in turn on *limited scepticism*, one of the doctrines taught by Belsham. In a word, he seems to favour a more 'secular' approach to political economy but, in more detail, he favours a more secular approach in so far as he favours a more 'modest' view of the science or a *more limited* view of its scope, amounting to the study of correlations between observable magnitudes. Thus, he seems to believe that political economy has – in Malthus's own words turned upside down – less 'resemblance to the sciences of morals and politics' than to 'the science of mathematics' (Malthus 1820, 2, p. 518; cf. Cremaschi 2010). This view in turn is inspired, rather than by a Cartesian or rationalist trust in the unlimited powers of human knowledge, by moderately sceptical awareness of its limits (Cremaschi and Dascal 1996, pp. 495–504; 1998, pp. 248–9). In turn, this did not result from the attitude of a 'true scientist' in contrast with the allegedly muddled, moralising attitude of priest Malthus; on the contrary, we face here one of the many billiard-ball effects with which the history of science at large is disseminated, namely, secularising consequences of a theological doctrine (Cremaschi 2002).

8. The impossibility of theodicy and its consequences for political economy

Ricardo's views on the possibility of faith and the impossibility of theology, the independence of morality from religion and unbounded freedom of enquiry are of remarkable interest for a reconstruction of both his biography, political views and activity as a politician and philanthropist and the intellectual background – natural science, philosophy, theology, political theory – against which his contributions to political economy took their course. This would be enough to make the present reconstruction of some interest to historians of economic thought too. But what is especially important for them is the most typically theological theme – and apparently most abstruse one – theodicy.

In 1798, Malthus had characteristically tried to square the circle of asymmetry between growth of resources and growth of population by means of a very particular kind of theodicy introduced in order to fill the gap.

He had been attacked on every side, one of them being Christian charity, and had carried out an egregious retreat in several steps, while claiming he had always been right. In Ricardo's Library, there was a copy of Malthus's *Essay on Population*, 5th ed. 1817 (Sraffa 1955b, p. 398). This suggests that he read this work in the 1817 edition and, by implication, that he may have been exposed to Malthus's own theodicy in its third version, which was different from the original as well as from the already revised 1803 one. Besides, as documented in the '*Commonplace Book*', it was precisely in 1817 that Ricardo started reading Bayle's work. The fact that the discussion of theodicy in the correspondence with Mill also dates from the last months of that year suggests that Ricardo's interest in theodicy did not arise from a sudden conversion from economic to religious interests, but was precisely occasioned by the tangle that political economists of the time were trying to untie, namely the growth of wealth and its link with poverty, that is, the causes of social evil or the viability of some kind of *social theodicy*. Let me add that Malthus's discovery of the principle of population occurred in the context of a refutation of a new kind of theodicy, that is, the atheistic anthropodicy centred on an idea of unlimited human perfectibility proposed by William Godwin and the Marquis of Condorcet (Cremaschi 2014, pp. 79–84). This was just one step in an on-going process transforming theodicy from a highly abstract discussion into 'applied theology', hardly any strange invention by Malthus himself. In fact, the eighteenth-century discussion of population was mainly of a theological kind, exploring the role of divine providence behind the growth and decrease of population, shifting from discussion of the causes of metaphysical, physical, and moral evil – or of human finitude, suffering, and wickedness – to that of the causes of misery and vice unavoidably going with misery (La Vergata 1990, pp. 20–40).

Let me recall briefly what Malthus' theodicy was originally and how it was restyled in its third 1817 version. The eighteenth-century Anglican ethics to which Malthus was exposed while at Cambridge elaborated on Richard Cumberland's attempt to mark a third way between the intellectualist and the voluntarist view of the law of nature, yielding a rational-choice account of natural law, where a law-giver God chooses from among a number of possible sets of laws on the basis of a *maximandum,* happiness for his creatures. Such a solution tried to settle at once the problem of evil and the foundation of moral obligation by proving that God's choice is justified in so far as it is the one that reduces the mass of suffering in the world to a minimum. Malthus's 1798 theodicy tried to prove that evils deriving from action of the principle of population were partial evils in so far as they enforced exertion by human beings, thus transforming matter into mind (Malthus 1798, pp. 97–101; cf. Cremaschi 2014, pp. 64–7). A second version, based on William Paley's *Natural Theology*, is presented in the 1803 essay. It contends that there is a moral order in the world, less tragic than the one of the first essay, and it depends on the possibility of avoiding evils carried by the principle of population through a combination of prudence and chastity. Once it has been proved that the passions may be dominated, and that a world where passions are under control would be a comparatively happy place, the world turns out to be not an evil place, and its Creator to be omniscient, benevolent, and perhaps also omnipotent (Malthus 1803, 2, pp. 88–95; cf. Cremaschi 2014, pp. 94–9). A third version is presented in the 1817 5th edition, arising from reaction to criticism by evangelical authors such as John Sumner and Thomas Chalmers. In this version, moral improvement becomes the variable to be maximised in the divine plan. The resulting new theodicy is more prudent than both former versions, amounting either to the Cambridge Platonists' optimism made softer or to a claim analogous to the Kantian one of the failure of any theodicy. The signs of this change are, first, that inequality and poverty are no longer accepted in a Paleyite fatalist spirit and that existing conditions of society are now justified on the argument, not that they are the happiest available, but that they are the most favourable to moral development; second, that population growth is now not an actual cause of social evil but just an always present potential cause, and that its negative effects can be effectively checked by *moral constraint*, that is, delayed marriage without irregular gratification, in turn made possible by, or going together with, more education, more self-respect, and more self-reliance (Malthus 1803, 1, p. 19; 2, pp. 214–5, p. 251; cf. Cremaschi 2014, pp. 145–55).

James Mill was far from immune from such concerns. If we are to believe his son's account, among the reasons for his decision to abandon the profession of Presbyterian preacher for which he had been educated, there was 'a state of perplexity' when facing 'a world so full of evil' that made it impossible to believe that such a world 'was the work of an Author combining infinite power with perfect goodness and righteousness' (Mill 1873, ch. 2). And, oddly enough, in his own *Elements of Political Economy*, apparently an axiomatic and deductive introduction to the economic science, he smuggles in an attempt to settle the problem of social theodicy. First he argues, in a factual tone, that, if the condition of 'the great body of the people' is not easy and comfortable, it can only be made so by one of two methods, either by quickening the rate at which capital increases, or retarding the rate at which population increases (Mill 1821, p. 44), and, if we cannot secure 'human happiness' by making capital increase as fast as population, the practical problem is to find a way to limit the number of births (Mill 1821, p. 65). He then goes on to argue that a sociological, not purely economic, fact should also be taken into account. The possibility that mankind may advance in knowledge and discover ways to take more command over the means of happiness depends 'upon the existence of a class of men who have their time at their command; that is, who are rich enough to be freed from all solicitude with respect to the means of living in a certain state of enjoyment. It is by this class of men that knowledge is cultivated and enlarged' (Mill 1821, p. 63). This would not be so bad, if Mill did not shift without previous notice, from cause-effect relationships to value judgments. In fact he adds,

> What is the class of men by whom the greatest happiness is enjoyed, [...] they who are raised above solicitude for the means of subsistence and respectability [...] the men of middle fortune [...] who, having their time at their own disposal, freed from the necessity of manual labour, subject to no man's authority, obtain, as a class, the greatest sum of human enjoyment. For *the happiness, therefore, as well as the ornament of our nature,* it is peculiarly desirable that a class of this description should form as large a proportion of each community as possible. (Mill 1821, p. 64; my emphasis)

Note that this is no longer value-free scientific consideration, being rather a moral evaluation of the condition of society. And here, after having applied the Malthusian principle of population in its original crude version, he also applies – without spelling it out – the Benthamite principle of utility also in its crude original formulation, where only the *total amount* of happiness is taken as a criterion of justice, with the twofold effect of transforming a purely theoretical discussion of economic laws into a normative theory of justice, and of introducing a Calvinist atheist doctrine of predestination according to which only a few – here, the middle class – are destined for salvation and everyone else should be happy and content for them.

Robert Owen too was no stranger to these problems. It is worth reporting a table-talk remark by Ricardo on Owen's views, reported in John Lewis Mallet's diary (14 January 1820) on free will, necessitarianism, theodicy, and, remarkably, the possibility to fight social evils. He writes,

> Ricardo knows Owen intimately. He says that he is a thorough necessitarian; but being at the same time Deist, he believes that all works for the best. It were to be wished, upon this principle, that he would be less pertinacious in his efforts to alter the state of society. (Ricardo 1951–1973, 8, p. 153)

If we try to spell out the full implications of this comment, we might – with due caution – head towards the conclusion that Ricardo was implying the following, (1) belief that all works for the best or, in eighteenth-century philosophical jargon, Optimism, or the claim that there is an answer to the question on evil, carries a paradox, the same as the one Adam Smith pointed out with regard to Stoicism, that is, it makes moral judgment and action unnecessary; (2) the above optimistic belief derives from a combination of necessitarianism and Deism. This comment, no less than Ricardo's comments in the correspondence with Mill and Malthus, and his reading notes in the *Commonplace Book* highlight the relevance theodicy had – in Ricardo's view – for the issues of population, the relationship of rent, profits and wages, poverty, the condition of the working class – namely the topics of his chapter on machinery of 1819 that will, by no means coincidentally, occasion Mill's complaint. The fact that our world is not a Panglossian one leaves nonetheless a hope that something better is possible.

His comment on Owen is telling. It points precisely to the link between theodicy and the social question and may shed additional light on the Malthus–Ricardo controversy in so far as it concerns precisely a decisive point in the controversy, namely, the status of political economy, either a science similar to mathematics or a part of 'the science of moral and political philosophy' (Malthus 1820, 1, p. 203; cf. Cremaschi 2010). Ricardo's limited scepticism, implying limits to moral knowledge, necessitarianism, the refusal of theodicy, played in favour of the former alternative.

Note that rejection of theodicy in general implied also rejection of Malthus's 1817 version, namely a *moral* theodicy where evil is justified not as means to more happiness but as a spring for moral improvement. That is, Ricardo's mature view may have been that such social evils as poverty *ought* to be reduced but – unlike Malthus's mature view – they are not made any more comprehensible by such considerations as that they are the spring of moral improvement, and indeed such considerations may border on blasphemy. Thus, waging war on poverty is still a moral imperative, but one that is still in force despite awareness of the tragic character of the human condition.

Ricardo apparently disagrees, for different reasons, with Mill, Owen and Malthus, although it is with Malthus that he has more in common. The claims he seems to reject are,

(a) all work for the best (in Voltaire's phrase, *tout est bien*);
(b) evil is out there as a means to our moral improvement;

while the claims he seems, instead, to endorse are,

(a) evil is a hard fact for which no account is available;
(b) yet we have a duty to do good, that is, to promote our neighbour's happiness.

Allow me to make a step forward and then come back. Max Weber, in his sociology of religion, points at one basic function of religions, namely providing an answer to the question of the origins of evil. In his famous '*Zwischenbetrachtungen*' he argued that, in a 'rationalised' world, the tension becomes obvious between a rationalised economy and a religion that has itself been rationalised. Thus, 'the religions of salvation have had a tendency to depersonalise and objectify love in the unique sense of acosmism. Yet [they] have watched with profound suspicion the deployment of economic forces which [...] have likewise become impersonal' (Weber 1915, p. 331). In such religions, typically, the precept of love becomes universalised and every human being becomes a brother or sister, but this is bound to clash with the logic of the market where every human being, in an analogous universal way, tends to become one more magnitude in the quantified world of the market. He adds that money 'is the most abstract and "impersonal" element that ever existed. The more the world of the modern capitalist economy follows its own immanent laws, the less accessible it is to any imaginable relationship with a religious ethics of brotherliness' (Weber 1915, p. 331). Ricardo somehow probably sensed Weber's tension and went looking for a way out of it, while keeping his conviction of the existence of severe limits to human knowledge in mind, and thus refused to accept any of the social theodicies or anthropodicies that had been formulated – Godwin's, the young Malthus's, Mill's – as intellectually arrogant and blasphemous. His final view was perhaps not too far, in terms of policies, from Malthus's last views but – we may speculate – still with one point of disagreement in terms of speculative issues. The point may have been that even a *moral* theodicy – that is Malthus's 1817 version – according to which social evil is there to provide an occasion for moral improvement would have been for him both intellectually unwarranted and morally repugnant. To the question why there are poverty, destitution, diseases, high rates of mortality the only intellectually and morally acceptable answer is, we do not know.

This attitude, resulting from awareness of the existence of serious *limits* to human knowledge – both theoretical and moral – and the preoccupation of *usefulness* of knowledge is what marks Ricardo's *modest* research program in political economy, a program whose spirit has been most of the time misunderstood by commentators as a kind of arrogant aprioristic deductivism mistaking idealised assumptions for the real world. It was precisely this attitude that was mistaken, shortly after his death, by his admirer Marx for a 'Stoic, objective, scientific' attitude (Marx 1965–1968, 2, p. 112) and by his detractor Leslie Stephen for lack of 'human feeling' (Stephen 1900, 2, p. 222).[6]

6 To tell the whole truth – one disgusting enough to deserve being confined to a footnote – he wrote that Ricardo 'was a Jew' and 'Jews, in spite of Shylock's assertions [...] are naturally without human feeling' (Stephen 1900, 2, p. 222).

9. Conclusions

(1) Ricardo was apparently neither an atheist nor an agnostic; but belief and disbelief are existential attitudes, not theoretical claims, whether Ricardo believed or rather doubted – after all, who does not doubt? – is not an appropriate question for historians; thus, the pertinent question is whether he admitted the possibility of religious belief or instead ruled it out as irrational, and the answer is that his own philosophy was a kind of limited scepticism leaving room for religious belief for whoever would like to avail himself of this option.

(2) He argued for toleration not on the basis of the crude argument that religion is a fake – and even less on the even cruder one that, since he was himself an atheist, toleration for atheists was to be defended – but on the more rational one that nobody is the owner of the truth, there are several sets of beliefs that reasonable persons may adopt, and that even those who adopt absurd beliefs cannot be forced to change their beliefs at will.

(3) He believed that speculative theology is impracticable and irrelevant in so far as it is an attempt to formulate what is unknowable in terms of a scientific truth; note that he was not declaring the impossibility of faith, he was just declaring that formulating theological doctrines is an impracticable task; he was not advancing an argument in favour of atheism but one more argument against dogmatism and intolerance.

(4) He believed that morality is independent of revelation, that there is a *natural morality* accessible to every reasonable mind independent of different religious beliefs; note that this is typical enlightenment staple shared by deist, theist, and liberal Christian thinkers; besides, that it is not a peculiarly 'modern' view, being just an old anti-Augustinian and anti-Calvinist doctrine defended in the Middle Ages by Aquinas and William of Ockham, and in modern Britain by every enemy of religious fanaticism, from the Cambridge Platonists to Richard Price, Francis Hutcheson, and Adam Smith.

(5) He concluded that theodicy is impossible for the same reasons Kant advanced in order to prove 'the miscarriage of all philosophical trials in theodicy' and, unlike James Mill, believed that such conclusion is no argument for unbelief but rather one more argument for moral responsibility vis-à-vis poverty, against the kind of dogmatic *laissez-faire* optimism Mill and others were prone to adopt.

(6) Besides, he believed that, even though what every religion has to teach is precisely morality, the latter comes before religion and it is 'autonomous' in a somewhat Kantian sense; that is, he rejected the prevailing Anglican doctrine shared by Malthus that the moral law is a path to happiness and that virtue will be rewarded; for him, a sense of

duty – including a duty to fight poverty – derives from reason, may be further confirmed by faith, but could hardly be grounded in the certainty that virtue will be rewarded.

(7) And he believed that social science should be a secular science precisely for theological reasons; in other words, leaving the biographical question aside, the anti-dogmatic kind of religious belief to which Ricardo *possibly* adhered, but that *certainly* declared to be fully legitimate, ruled out both Malthus's moral and political science and Mill's Laissez-Faire Metaphysics.

Acknowledgements

Most of the work for this paper was carried out while the author was a Jemolo Fellow at Nuffield College, Oxford. Several questions asked in the paper stem from conversations with Pier Luigi Porta. The author is also grateful to two anonymous referees for useful suggestions and to Grayson Ditchfield for discussion of Dr. Lindsey's identity.

Disclosure statement

No potential conflict of interest was reported by the author.

References

Aspland, R. et al., 1823. The Christians' petition to parliament against the prosecution of unbelievers. *The monthly repository*, 18 (210), 362–4.
Bayle, P., 1682. [1939]. *Pensées diverses sur la comète.* 2 vols. Ed. A. Prat. Paris: Droz.
Bayle, P., 1697. [1740]. *Dictionnaire historique et critique.* 4 vols. Amsterdam: Brunel.
Belsham, T., 1801. *Elements of the philosophy of the mind, and of moral philosophy. To which is prefixed a compendium of logic.* London: Johnson.
Belsham, Th., 1826–1827. *Discourses, doctrinal and practical; delivered in Essex street chapel.* 2 vols. London: Hunter.
Cremaschi, S., 1994. Review of M. Milgate and Sh.C. Stimson 'Ricardian Politics'. *The European journal of the history of economic thought*, 1, 622–4.
Cremaschi, S., 2002. Two views of natural law and the shaping of political economy. *Croatian journal of philosophy*, 2 (5), 181–96.
Cremaschi, S., 2004. Ricardo and the utilitarians. *The European journal of the history of economic thought*, 11 (3), 377–403.
Cremaschi, S., 2010. Malthus's idea of a moral and political science. *The journal of philosophical economics*, 3 (2), 5–57.
Cremaschi, S., 2014. *Utilitarianism and Malthus's virtue ethics. Respectable, virtuous and happy.* Abingdon: Routledge.
Cremaschi, S., 2015. Belsham Thomas and Ricardo. *In:* H. Kurz and N. Salvadori, eds. *The Elgar companion to Ricardo.* Aldershot: Edward Elgar, 14–7.

Cremaschi, S., 2017. Invisible beings. Adam Smith's lectures on natural religion. *The Adam Smith review*, 10, 230–53.
Cremaschi, S. and Dascal, M., 1996. Malthus and Ricardo on economic methodology. *History of political economy*, 28 (2), 475–511.
Cremaschi, S. and Dascal, M., 1998. Malthus and Ricardo, two styles for economic theory. *Science in context*, 11, 229–54.
Dave, D., 1978. *A gathered church. The literature of the English dissenting interest, 1700-1930.* Abingdon: Routledge.
Depoortère, Ch., 2002. On Ricardo's method, the Unitarian influence examined. *History of political economy*, 34 (2), 499–504.
Hartwell, R.M., 1971. Introduction. *In:* D. Ricardo, *The principles of political economy and taxation.* Harmondsworth: Penguin, 7–47.
Henderson, J.P., 1997. *The life and economics of David Ricardo. With additional chapters by J.B. Davis.* Dordrecht: Kluwer.
Hume, D., 1757. [2007]. The natural history of religion. *In:* D. Hume. *A dissertation on the passions. The natural history of religion.* Ed. T.L. Beauchamop. Oxford: Clarendon, 3–30.
King, J.E., 2013. *David Ricardo.* Houndsmill: Palgrave Macmillan.
La Vergata, A., 1990. *Nonostante Malthus. Fecondità, popolazioni e armonia della natura. 1700-1900.* Torino: Bollati Boringhieri.
Lindsay, J., 1813. *A Sermon on the influence of religious knowledge as tending to produce a gradual improvement in the social state.* London: Johnson.
Locke, J., 1695. [1999]. *The reasonableness of Christianity.* Ed. J.C. Higgins-Biddle. Oxford: Clarendon.
Malthus, Th. R., 1798. [1986]. An essay on the principle of population. *In:* E.A. Wrigley and D. Souden, eds. *The works of Thomas Robert Malthus.* Vol. 1. London: Pickering.
Malthus, Th. R., 1803. [1989]. *An essay on the principle of population. The version published in 1803, with the Variora of 1806, 1807, 1817 and 1826.* Ed. P. James. Cambridge: Cambridge University Press.
Malthus, T.R., 1820. [1989]. *Principles of political economy.* Ed. J. Pullen. Cambridge: Cambridge University Press.
Marx, K., 1965–1968. *Theorien über den Mehrwert.* 3 vols. Berlin, Dietz (Marx & Engels Werke, 26/1-3).
Middleton, C., 1750. *An examination of the bishop of London's discourse concerning prophecy.* London: Manby and Cox.
Milgate, M. and Stimson, Sh.C., 1991. *Ricardian politics.* Princeton: Princeton University Press.
Mill, 1821. [1995]. *Elements of political economy.* 3 ed. London: Routledge/Thoemmes Press.
Mill, J., 1817. [1997]. *History of British India.* 10 vols. Ed. H.H. Wilson. London: Routledge.
Mill J.S., 1873. [1981]. Autobiography. *In:* J.S. Mill. *Autobiography and literary essays.* Eds. J.M. Robson and J. Stillinger. Toronto: University of Toronto Press, 1–290.
Paley, W., 1802. [1970]. *Natural theology.* Westmead, Gregg.
Priestley, J., 1762. [1972]. A course of lectures in the theory of language and universal grammar. *In:* J.T. Rutt, ed. *The theological and miscellaneous works of Joseph Priestley.* New Yok: Kraus Reprint. Vol. 23.
Priestley, J., 1767. [1775]. *The history and present state of electricity with original experiments.* London: Bathurst.
Ricardo, D., unpublished. *Ricardo papers. Miscellaneous private.* Cambridge: Cambridge University Library.
Ricardo, D., 1951–1973. *The works and correspondence.* 11 vols. Ed. P. Sraffa. Cambridge: Cambridge University Press.

Sraffa, P., 1955a. Addenda to the Memoir. *In:* D. Ricardo. *The works and correspondence.* 11 vols. Ed. P. Sraffa. Cambridge: Cambridge University Press. Vol. 10, 18–64.

Sraffa, P., 1955b. Appendices. *In:* D. Ricardo. *The works and correspondence.* 11 vols. Ed. P. Sraffa. Cambridge: Cambridge University Press. Vol. 10, 355–98.

Stephen, L., 1900. *The English utilitarians.* 3 vols. London: Duckworth.

Stuart, A., 2003. *Unitarian radicalism. Political rhetoric, 1770-1814.* London: Palgrave Macmillan.

Sumner, J.B., 1816. *A treatise on the records of the creation and on the moral attributes of the creator.* London: Hatchard.

Trower, H., 1813. *Christianity in India. – Letters bewteen Laicus and an East India proprietor as they appeared in the Times newspaper in the months of August, September and October, 1813.* London: Rivington.

Watson, R., 1776. *An apology for Christianity.* Cambridge: Merrill.

Watson. R., 1796. [1799]. *An apology for the Bible.* London: Evans.

Watts, R., 1998. *Gender, power and the Unitarians in England 1760-1860.* London: Longmans.

Weatherall, D., 1976. *David Ricardo. A biography.* The Hague: Nijhoff.

Weber, M., 1915. [1975]. Religious rejections of the world and their directions. *In:* M. Gerth and C. Wright Mills, eds. *From Max Weber, essays in sociology.* New York: Oxford University Press, 323–59.

Williams, J., 1833. *Memoirs of the late Reverend Thomas Belsham.* London: Printed for the author.

Abstract

I review evidence from published and unpublished sources on Ricardo's theological ideas. The main focuses of interest are the existence of a natural morality independent of religious confessions, morality as the essence of religion, uselessness of theological speculation, justification of toleration for everybody, including atheists, and the miscarriage of any attempt at a philosophical theodicy. The paper explores also the connection between Ricardo's interest for theodicy and his views on the scope and method of political economy and suggests that his opinion that political economy should be a secular and value-free science close to mathematics depends precisely on theological reasons.

Religion and political economy in Saint-Simon

Pierre Musso

The project of Henri Saint-Simon (1760–1825) was to complete the French Revolution by a social change in order to eliminate the so-called "feudal-military" system and to bring about a new society which he named "the industrial system," while avoiding social disintegration and anarchy. To do so, it was necessary to "reorganise" the society and modify everything without removing anything. He thought that the French Revolution had not fulfilled its promise of social change; it merely changed men. Therefore, he wanted to rebuild everything, including Christianity, and he envisaged a post-revolutionary revolution. To this end, Saint-Simon instituted a new alliance, between scientific truth and the utility of productive labour, which he set against political illusion and theological superstition. After the French Revolution, "there was a widespread revival of religious sentiment in early 19th century France" (see Faccarello and Steiner 2008) and in this context Saint-Simon sought to answer two fundamental questions: one, which was put forward in 1793 by William Godwin in *An Inquiry concerning Political Justice*, was how to "aim for this happy time which will witness the dissolution of political power"; the other, posed in 1797 by Chateaubriand in his *Essai sur les Révolutions*, was: "What religion will replace Christianity?". Saint-Simon answered: politics has to be dissolved in the economy, and a "New Christianity" – the title of his last unfinished work of 1825 – has to be founded. This amounts to establishing an immediate link between the economy and religion by reducing politics to a sort of religious or moral economy freed from government mediation. He thus linked industry, production, and labour with a new ethic of fraternity.

Inscribed at the cornerstone of two centuries, the work of Saint-Simon,[1] made up of some 50 texts, pamphlets, or books, lies at the crossroads of philosophy, morality, and religion, but also of the nascent disciplines of political economy and sociology. If the religious question infused all of these works written between 1802 and 1825, the economic question, for its part, was linked to industrial concerns. It appeared in 1817–1818 in the work *L'Industrie*, which he oversaw, where it boiled down to the more ordinary problem of good budget management or administration. Our analysis of the relation between political economy and religion is organised into three stages: first, the recurring problem of religion, raised by Saint-Simon as early as his first text, namely the *Lettres d'un Habitant de Genève à ses Contemporains* (*Letters from an Inhabitant of Geneva to his Contemporaries*) of 1802–1803; second, the appearance of the economic problem of identifying production with politics in *L'Industrie*; and finally, the metamorphosis of the Christian religion into a moral and industrial religion in his later texts, notably *Nouveau Christianisme* (*New Christianity*).

1. Religion, a necessary social relationship

On his deathbed, Saint-Simon reportedly said to his last secretary, Olinde Rodrigues (1795–1851): "We thought we could say that every religious system had to disappear because we had succeeded in proving the obsolescence of the Catholic system. We were wrong. Religion cannot disappear from the world. It simply changes".[2] Reflection on religion runs through the work of Saint-Simon, for he sought its metamorphosis into a secular religion rather than its removal. Every society needs a religion, it cannot dispense with it, but it is transformed like any other institution. His definition of religion is dual, like the etymology of the word: *religere* (to interpret) and *religare* (to connect). It is both a philosophical system designed to explain the world and a social institution that works as a social bond. Religion is a system of representation of the universe comparable to science and it is the cultural foundation of any social organisation (see Françoise Fichet-Poitrey 1990). This dual definition of religion sheds light

1 Our references refer to the critical edition of Henri Saint-Simon's *Œuvres complètes*, published in 4 volumes under the supervision of Juliette Grange, Pierre Musso, Philippe Régnier, and Franck Yonnet (Saint-Simon 2013). Each reference is composed of the title or an abbreviation of the title of the work of Saint-Simon, followed by the volume and page numbers in the aforementioned edition of the *Œuvres complètes*. See also in English, *Henri Saint-Simon (1760–1825). Selected writings* (Saint-Simon 1975). See also Musso 1999, 2005, 2006, 2017.

2 *Le Globe*, 30 December 1830.

on the whole of Saint-Simon's work: as a representation of the world, religion is obsolete and has to be replaced by scientific knowledge; yet as a social bond, it is the fundamental moral foundation of the industrial system.

In a letter of 1811, Saint-Simon wrote "religions have never been and could never be anything but materialised philosophical systems"(*Correspondance,* I, p. 817). Religion is assimilated with a general idea equivalent to that of God, which acts as a moral and philosophical foundation for every society. Consequently, it is "a human invention" (*Lettres de Genève,* I, p. 127), a purely collective belief. Saint-Simon borrows his criticism from the "Ideologues," notably Charles-François Dupuis (1742–1809), one of the masters of anti-clericalism, who published a 12-volume essay on *L'origine de tous les cultes, ou la religion universelle* (*The origin of all cults or the universal religion*) in 1795. Saint-Simon says about him that he "clearly demonstrated [...] that all known religions were founded on the scientific system and that any reorganisation of the scientific system would consequently result in the reorganisation and improvement of the religious system" (*Mémoire sur la Science de l'Homme,* II, pp. 1081–2). Science was getting rid of religious superstition in the same way that astronomy and chemistry were replacing astrology and alchemy, respectively. The clergy who had exercised scientific power since the Middle Ages now had to be replaced by scholars. Indeed, "religion is ageing. Like other institutions, it needs to be renewed after a certain time" (*Sur les Sciences,* I, p. 401). Religion is useless to science, but necessary to politics for the organisation of every society, of which it is the indispensable foundation. For fear of disintegration and anarchy, Saint-Simon emphasised the importance of the bond that guarantees the social contract: "I believe in the necessity of religion for the maintenance of social order" (*Sur les Sciences,* I, p. 402). Religion, thus reduced to a unifying collective belief, even to an opinion, will ultimately be transformed into a "code of morality" (*Catéchisme des industriels,* IV, p. 2929). On this point, Saint-Simon joined Louis de Bonald (1754–1840) who, in 1796, published his *Theory of Political and Religious Power in Civil Society demonstrated by reasoning and history.* This work presents a conception of religion as the universal bond of intelligent beings, which science can fulfil in the religions of "Universal Reason."

Because he reduced religion to a social institution and a moral principle, he proposed to "consider religion as a human invention, which I shall regard to be the kind of political institution that comes closest to the general organisation of humanity" (*Lettres de Genève,* I, p. 127). As early as in his first text, Saint-Simon presented himself as "the founder" of a new religion built on a belief other than the belief in God, namely sacred knowledge. For divine law, he substituted the scientific law of universal gravitation as the unifying principle of the world's regulation. In the *Letters of an Inhabitant of Geneva to Humanity*, which he addressed "to his contemporaries" in a later edition, in the form of a divine revelation – "It is God who spoke to me" (*Lettres de Genève*, I, p. 127) – he represented the relation directly by associating Humanity with Science, embodied by Newton, through a subscription before the tomb of the great scientist. The new scientific religion was to be without institutional mediation: without church and especially without government. Humanity, represented by a "Council of Newton," would be directly enlightened by science: "Each council will have a temple built that will contain a mausoleum in honour of Newton [...]. Children will be brought there by their parents as soon as possible after their birth. Anyone who does not carry out this commandment will be regarded by the faithful as an enemy of religion" (*Lettres de Genève*, I, p. 124). This scientific religion would have its elect and its faithful, and even "its founder invested with great power," namely Saint-Simon himself, to whom this religion "was revealed". Religion is metamorphosed and transfigured because it is a collective belief in which men immerse themselves in order to sustain society. In a letter to his nephew dated 1810, Saint-Simon wrote: "Religion, my nephew, has always been and will always be used as a basis for social organisation. This truth is indisputable [...]. Religion has always been modified, and it will always change, so that it has always been proportionate to and will always be in proportionate measure to the state of enlightenment" (I, p. 598).

Saint-Simon distinguished the intangible foundation of religion for the maintenance of social order from its capacity to explain the world, evolving according to human knowledge. The fixed element of religion is the moral normativity intended to maintain social order, whereas its unstable element is its justification of the explanatory causes of the order of the Universe. Consequently, "the idea of God ought not to be employed in physical sciences, but I do not say that it ought not to be used in political combinations, at least for a long time to come. It is the best way that has been found to motivate the higher legislative provisions" (*Sur les Sciences*, I, pp. 404–405). The legitimisation of laws requires collective belief. This is why, as Saint-Simon stated as early as 1808, it was necessary to provide a "catechism," which is exactly what he wrote with Auguste Comte 15 years later, with *Catéchisme des industriels* (*The Catechism of Industrialists*). Such a breviary would have to be divided into two parts: one "teaches man how the world is formed" and the other "teaches him how he should behave" (*Sur les Sciences*, I, p. 406). The intra-religious dividing-line drawn by Saint-Simon in fact distinguishes between two dimensions of society that must equate two purposes of science: the first obeys the laws discovered by scientists such as Newton, the second obeys "laws" that he wanted to update by creating "a science of society" or "science of man," which Auguste Comte, who was his secretary for seven years as a young man, was to call "sociology" in his 47th lesson (§15) of the *Cours de Philosophie Positive* (*Course in Positive Philosophy*) (Comte 1975).

Therefore, religion is useless to science, but necessary to politics. Saint-Simon "dislocated" religion from the spiritual sphere and placed it in the temporal sphere, but maintained it at the heart of the society. Religion founds the social contract and all institutions, for it makes the social organisation homogeneous by providing it with a single principle, a general idea so to speak: "Every meeting of peoples and men has to be provided with common institutions and an organisation: without them everything is decided by force," for "the religious institution, from whatever aspect we consider it, is the main political institution" (*Mémoire sur la Science de l'Homme*, II, p. 1146). Saint-Simon transformed the idea of religion by invalidating it from the point of view of truth, but preserving it as an indispensable social belief: "It would be folly to want to suppress at present the moral institutions that still exist. That is to say, religious institutions" (*L'Industrie*, II, p. 1578). Religion no longer rules over the world, it becomes the "substratum" of the social fabric. Thus, Saint-Simon carried out a double inversion: he reduced religion to a human invention, and then sanctified this invention as a temporal institution vital to every society. Religion being indispensable to every society, it was therefore necessary to reformulate it after the Revolution and with the birth of industry. This is the founding operation of a new industrial religion, which was to combine the political economy with an "earthly morality."

2. The identification of politics with the economy

Unlike the religious question, economic issues emerged in Saint-Simon's work only after 1817 and first became central in *L'Industrie*. This marked a decisive turning point in his thinking. The development of industry was to become his constant concern and the economy was identified there. Even before the writing of his work, he had run companies and wanted to create a large industrial establishment. He concentrated his reflection on the political economy, which he criticised and in the domain of which he reinvested his concepts, just as he revisited his conception of religion. Thus, he announced in *L'Industrie*: "This is the set of the principles which we propose to stick to, and which we may call indifferently a general plan of finance, or a treatise on general economics, or an encyclopaedia of applied sciences. Such is the undertaking for which we propose that all industrialists ("*savants d'application*") should come together" (*L'Industrie*,

II, p. 1451). The new importance he attached to political economy is related to his meeting with Jean-Baptiste Say (1767–1832).

Like religion, the term "economy" has two main meanings: it is both a discipline and a practice of saving. In *L'Industrie,* Saint-Simon also explained the use he made of the term "economist": "We use the word "economist" to designate those who cultivate political economy [...], economists having been the true founders of Political economy" (*L'Industrie,* II, 1644n). They bring together economic and industrial issues. Because they are good managers, the "industrialists" – a substantive that he coined at the time – have the duty to direct the public economy, for they "form the class of citizens best able to save money while they administer" (*Système Industriel,* III, p. 2495).

Written and published between 1816 and 1818, *L'Industrie,* or *Political, Moral and Philosophical Discussions, for the benefit of all men devoted to useful and independent works,* carries the famous epigraph "Everything by industry, everything for it." This collective work includes two volumes containing several notebooks: Augustin Thierry (1795–1856), the historian who had become his "adopted son" in 1814, Camille Saint-Aubin (1758–1820), a former member of the Tribunat, and Jean-Antoine Chaptal (1756–1832), the famous chemist and former Minister of the Interior, took part in the writing of the first volume. The second volume was written by Saint-Simon and Auguste Comte, who became his new secretary in August 1817.

Saint-Simon resumed the problematic theories of the *Letters of an Inhabitant of Geneva.* Following Thomas Paine and William Godwin, for whom "the Government - even in its best forms - is evil",[3] like the latter he wanted to suppress the "useless intermediary and often dangerous government" (*L'Industrie,* II, p. 1472). But in *L'Industrie,* Saint-Simon replaced the distinction between the governing and non-governing (the pair constituting "Humanity" in the *Letters* of 1802) with a new, economy-based distinction between producers and "non-producers". In his famous "Parable" (*L'Organisateur*), he later compared producers to bees and non-producing consumers to hornets. Thus, he shifted his criticism of politics and government function into the economic field.

3 The formula of Thomas Paine – "Government, even in its best state, is but a necessary evil" – was repeated and radicalised by William Godwin and then by Saint-Simon who proposed the suppression of permanent armies (*Le Politique,* III, 1850). See Paine (1776) and Godwin (1793).

2.1. *Economics is the truth of politics*

The analysis of society in terms of the economy makes it possible to differentiate between two forms of economic policy: the good one – that of bees, in which consumers produce and money is obtained by labour – and the bad one – that of hornets which consume much without producing anything, as they obtain money through force and cunning. Just as there are two types of savings or currencies (the good and the bad), there are two forms of politics: "There are two kinds of fortunes: on the one hand, those which, generally speaking, are the result of hazardous operations or speculation, either by the government or by individuals, and which are consequently a kind of plundering, and on the other hand, another species of fortune which is acquired with the intention of putting it to a completely different use, and which is the result of hard labour and rigorous saving. The latter are always employed to perfect sciences, fine arts, and arts and crafts" (*L'Organisateur*, II, p. 2217). Bad politics is the money acquired by force and idleness, hence "noxious" money, a sort of loot, whereas the economy is the "good" money earned by labour and by economy (saving). Economics is the truth of politics, and a political system is only the application of morality. Saint-Simon often played on the double meaning of words: thus, the economy understood as a discipline (economics) must be the science of industrialists in the same way as the economy understood as good management is their practice. "At the stage now reached in the work which is to give industry the principles intended to govern it, there remains only one thing to be done to attain the goal: that is for the knowledge of political economy to become widespread among industrialists. It is difficult to understand, although it is only too true, that a science so useful, so necessary to industry as political economy, that a science which is the specific science of industry, should nevertheless be, of all the existing sciences, that which is by far the least widespread" (*L'Industrie*, II, p. 1637). Economy is politics and it is the science of industry. It even offers a general model for thinking about the circulation of flows within the society, particularly so as to define the "Industrial System".

2.2. *Economy, a model of the circulation of flows in society*

In the field of economic theories, the period 1760–1820 is marked by the search for models or images to represent the functioning of the society. Thus, the analogy between the physical body and the social body, and the comparison of the circulation of blood to that of money, was a recurrent theme with most economists: it is found both in the Physiocrats and in Rousseau. In his *Second Essay on Banks*, Scottish mercantilist John Law

(1671–1729), Controller General of Finances of France, wrote: "Money is to the State what blood is to the human body: without the one, one cannot live; without the other one cannot act. Circulation is necessary to one and the other, and credit appears in commerce like the mind or the most subtle part of blood. [...]. When blood does not circulate in all parts, the body decays, likewise when money does not circulate in the provinces, the State suffers and weakens". Following John Law, François Quesnay (1694–1774), a physician of the King and an economist, wrote in his *Economic Table* (1758): "In relation to finances, the bank is the very heart of the kingdom, towards which all the money must return in order to start the circulation again. Those who wish to amass or retain it are like parts or extremities of the human body that seek to stop the blood that waters and nourishes them: they would soon destroy the principle of life in the heart".[4]

Saint-Simon adopted this image, and if the analogy is down-to-earth, he used it to define circulation as the condition of the functioning and changing of society as a "true being." Saint-Simon applied the model of circulation that he had borrowed from hydraulics and physiology to political economy. If the economy guarantees the circulation of money, the government that levies taxes is equivalent to its disruption. Thus, the law of finance becomes a lever of social change: "The most important law of all is undoubtedly that which regulates the budget, for money is to the political body what blood is to the human body. Any part of the body where blood ceases to circulate languishes and soon dies. In the same way, any administrative function which ceases to be paid ceases promptly to exist" (*L'Industrie*, II, 1605). Establishing the immediate circulation of blood – the institution of money amounts to organising the social body like a human body – the physiological model of social relations is thus complementary to the political economy. Moreover, "it is economical to dispense with an intermediary" (*L'Industrie*, II, p. 1459).

2.3. The decisive influence of Jean-Baptiste Say

Jean-Baptiste Say's treatise (first edition in 1803; third edition in 1817) was the major treatise on political economy that dominated the early nineteenth century in France. It defended liberal theses according to which taxes should be reduced to the strict minimum. Saint-Simon's reading of this treatise and his meeting with Jean-Baptiste Say was essential for his conception of economics. Saint-Simon attended some of Say's courses in 1813 and, in fact, two years later, he joined the *Society of Encouragement for*

4 Texts quoted by Francine Markovits (Markovits 1986, p. 175).

the national industry of which Chaptal was president for life and Say was one of the most important activists.

Saint-Simon was inspired by Say's *A Treatise on Political Economy.*[5] "This work," he wrote, "contains all that political economy has hitherto discovered and demonstrated. It is presently the *nec plus ultra* of this science in Europe" (*L'Industrie,* I, p. 1497). He showered praise on it: "Out of all those who put their hands to the work, the scholars who wrote on political economy seem to me to have produced the most useful works, and M. Say's *Treatise on Political Economy* seems to me to be the book in which the greatest number of coordinated and positive ideas are found" (*L'Industrie,* II, p. 1496). Saint-Simon referred all the more readily to Jean-Baptiste Say since the latter was, like him, a cotton manufacturer during the First Empire. In the nascent era of economics, particularly with Smith and Say, the enterprise emerged as an autonomous social force, or even an institution, in relation to the State and the Church. Identified with modernity, the new century and the social system to come, Saint-Simon celebrated the enterprise in contrast to the "old institutions" of the feudal-military regime: the administrative apparatus, the Church and especially the government. Say severely criticised the increasing unproductive expenditure of the latter, because taxes slow down and divert the circulation of economic wealth. In his *Treatise* he wrote: "The unproductive expenditure of the government, far from being favourable to production, is prodigiously prejudicial to it. Taxes are an addition to production costs; they have an opposite effect to the progress of industry".[6] Say therefore recommended that the government should "studiously avoid all interference between individuals, lest it superadd the evils of administration to those of natural position".[7]

Saint-Simon took up this analysis by Say, together with his criticism of taxes, but he adopted a different point of view: not economic, but political. He emphasised the contribution of Say who distinguished economics as an autonomous science: "Mr. Say takes a step further than Smith in philosophical terms. At the start of his work he establishes that political economy is distinct and independent of politics; he says that this science has a basis that is entirely different from that of the science which is intended to organise nations" (*L'Industrie,* II, p. 1636). For sure, Say revealed the specificity of economics in relation to politics, but Saint-Simon wanted to go somewhat further in Godwin's footsteps and reduce politics to economics,

5 About Say and the relationship between politics, economy, and religion, see Whatmore (2000), in particular pp. 120–5 and pp. 213–4.

6 Jean-Baptiste Say, *Traité d'économie politique,* Livre III, ch. 9 "De l'impôt et de ses effets en général". (Say 2006, II, p. 986).

7 *Ibid,* vol II. p. 744. Livre II, chap. VII. "Des revenus industriels — Des profits de l'ouvrier".

that is to say to industrial production. Indeed, Godwin also defended the industry against politics: "When we look at complicated machines of human contrivance, various sorts of mills, of weaving engines, of steam engines, are we not astonished at the compendium of labour they produce? [...] In a state of equal labour their utility will be liable to no dispute" (Godwin 1793, II, p. 845). Saint-Simon concluded from his reading of Say's *Treatise* that "the author has vaguely felt, and in spite of himself, that political economy is the true and only foundation of politics" (*L'Industrie*, II, p. 1497). Saint-Simon politicised economics, and conversely he "economised" politics, defined as a science of production: "Politics is therefore — to summarise in two words — the science of production, namely the science whose purpose is the order of things most favourable to all kinds of production" (*L'Industrie*, II, p. 1498). Saint-Simon declared himself to be the founder of the new and "true" society, the "industrial society," of which science is the foundation and industry the application. He peremptorily multiplied founding assertions about industry and invented the "industrial society" formula: "Industry really possesses all the forces of society" (*L'Industrie* II, p. 1465). The definition of politics as a "science of production" relegated it to the second rank, behind the economy and management, paving the way for its marginalisation. Politics was thus projected outside of power and the State in productive, material, or intellectual work.

With this shift of policy towards production and industry, Saint-Simon found a lever to effect the change in the social system that was his main purpose. He compared the future government to a mere junior school supervisor or a factory shop manager. Unlike Say, who separated politics and economics, Saint-Simon unified them: "We think that to raise politics entirely to the level of science there is nothing else to do but to proceed in the same way, that is, to bring successively into the domain of political economy all the fractions of the former policy which have not yet been included" (*Le Politique*, II, pp. 2059–60). In other words, politics has no virtues other than cunning and strength. In the industrial system, it must turn into applied morality and productive economy. To deal with politics, we must make a double return: to morality and economy, that is, to a morality of production.

As early as 1818, in *Le Politique*, the term economy again refers to its ordinary meaning, namely good management and particularly savings in public spending. The economy is assimilated with the sound administration of the State. The government of men is useless: the only things that matter – according to Prosper Enfantin's formula – are, "the administration of things," management, and organisation. Politics no longer "fits" society like previous institutions, be they the State, the Church, or the Academies.

The only social cement, the only new institution, is the factory or workshop where the division of labour and the "morality of production" reign supreme. The reference point is the working community, which is the factory where everyone is associated with each other through their "capacities" or competences, and assigned to their places by the technical division of labour: "There is thus a perpetual and necessary trade between science and industry.... What has prevented us from seeing it clearly to this day is the fact that relations have not yet been direct between the two classes, as they took place only through government [...] Scientists and producers have common affairs to deal with. Why would they introduce a third party into their business?" (*L'Industrie*, II, p. 1461). Government is a third party to be excluded: it is arbitrary and expensive; it protects and serves the idlers who make it up and use it, so it is useless. For "the true Society" (with a capital "S"), industrial society must be considered a "society" (with a tiny "s"), that is a company, a workshop, or a factory, a place of cooperation between producers through labour: "Let us take a factory as an example. All those who contribute to production including entrepreneurs do really participate in society, in the true meaning of the word, though no one has thought of spending prodigious efforts with the purpose of maintaining the association. But they are only associated through their working together to achieve a common goal, and that is how we must consider nations if we are to have fair ideas in politics. Look at a nation as if it were a vast industrial workshop where the labours of each member are combined with those of others so as to achieve the improvement of everybody's lot!" (*L'Industrie*, II, pp. 1685–6, note).

Saint-Simon transfers politics from the State to production and the factory. There remains to be associated with it a collective belief to maintain it, that of cooperation in work. In 1822 Saint-Simon asserted, "Politics must be nothing other than the application of morality to the administration of public affairs" (*Système Industriel*, IV, p. 2762). He establishes the following equation: policy = morality + management (moral management and a morality of management) or, in another form, politics = morality + production (production of a morality of production). His reading of Say led him to place the truth of politics within economics and morality. A positive policy would be at the same time an enhancement of industry and the production of an industrial morality: "Morality gains in fact at the same time as industry improves" (*L'Industrie*, II, p. 1498). To deal with politics, we must make a double return to "principles" and to economy, that is to say to an "industrial morality" that "relates all morality to production, in the same way as we shall relate politics to it" (*L'Industrie*, II, p. 1578). "Political science" would thus be the sum of a morality and management or the production of an ideology resulting from industrial production. We then have a perfect definition of the concept of "industrialism," which he created in 1824. Henceforth, he became an "industrialist" activist and even wanted to create an industrialist party. He advocated "the formation of a new political party, a party ruled by the heads of industrial undertakings, and whose principal and direct aim is to activate production" (*Système Industriel*, III, p. 2616). He wanted to be the mouthpiece of "industrial doctrine" and declared himself to be the advocate of industrialists: "I have undertaken to assert industrialists' political rights; you know that I have made myself their advocate, their agent" (*Système Industriel*, III, p. 2617). Industrialist policy was based not only on economic rationality, but also on a new industrial religion.

3. A new industrial, secular and earthly religion

Saint-Simon's main aim was to "regenerate" the Christian religion, as in response to the question posed by Chateaubriand. This concern can be found in most of the industrialist philosophers of the early nineteenth century[8]: "we must recast the whole system of moral ideas. It must be based on new foundations. In a word, we must pass from celestial morality to earthly morality. [...] Christianity led morality to take a great step forward. It would be unfair and preposterous to deny it. But we must recognise with the same good faith that its reign is over and that the time during which it was useful is already far from us. The era of positive ideas is beginning. We can no longer give morality other motives than palpable, definite and present interests. Such is the spirit of the age and such will be, forever and increasingly, the spirit of future generations. This is the great step which civilisation will take; it will consist in the establishment of a positive and earthly morality" (*L'Industrie*, II, p. 1577). This formula of "earthly morality" created by Saint-Simon means a "morality of production," a phrase by Robert Musil in *The Man Without Qualities.* Addressing the industrialists, Saint-Simon said to them: "They founded the Christian religion, you must regenerate it" (*Système Industriel*, III, p. 2499). The problem no longer consisted in criticising the former "feudal-military" society in which the clergy held the spiritual power, but in building the new industrial society with the scientists rather than the clergy, and with the industrialists instead of the military and the nobility.

8 In early 19th century France, "political economy became more prominent among publicists [...] and political elites. These two developments greatly influenced those who sought to further a modern, post-revolutionary society, and who in their different ways expressed a new approach to economics and politics known as *industrialisme.*" (Faccarello and Steiner 2008, p. 26).

3.1. The "Industrial Society"

On the basis of the "principles of industry" which he discovered thanks to economic enlightenment, Saint-Simon was then able to review all the components of the social system and recast it according to his inaugural project. The alliance of industry and science – both at the service of production at the source of all wealth – is the foundation of the "industrial society": "Society as a whole rests on industry. Industry is the only guarantee of its existence, the sole source of all wealth and prosperity. On such grounds the most favourable state to industry is therefore the most favourable to society. This is at once the point of departure and the goal of all our efforts" (*L'Industrie*, II, p. 1444). Science has replaced religion and is invested with spiritual power in the industrial society, which will be founded on labour: "There are men who employ all their forces, all their means, to study the laws of nature. There are others — much more numerous — who are concerned with the application of acquired knowledge in order to produce useful or agreeable things" (*L'Industrie*, II, p. 1449).

Scientists and industrialists are the two great players in society: like spiritual and temporal powers, they cannot be dissociated. Science and industry are two sides of the same coin: "Science must relate to industry. It must never lose sight of their common goals, namely — production" (*L'Industrie*, II, p. 1458). In the name of production – a sort of new idol – Saint-Simon laid the cornerstone of industrial religion, as Friedrich Engels noted in the *Anti-Dürhing*: "According to Saint-Simon, science and industry, both united by a new religious bond, destined to restore that unity of religious ideas which had been lost since the time of the Reformation - a necessarily mystical and rigidly hierarchical "new Christianity" (Engels 1950 [1878], p. 254).

Saint-Simon maintained that it was not enough to defend a project of social change "scientifically" founded on political economy; it was also necessary to develop a new "religion" because religion – as he wrote as early as 1802 – is "the only sort of political institution that tends to the general organisation of humanity" (*Lettres de Genève*, I, p. 127). It is a secular religion, brought back into the temporal sphere – that is, excluded from the spiritual power where science replaced it – and thus religion as a mere institution. This earthly morality is intended to form a bond to avoid the triumph of selfishness, for the sole logic of economic interest leads to social disintegration and anarchy. This is why he set "industrialism" – a term he invented in 1824 – against liberalism. Indeed, Saint-Simon was well aware that the self-organisation of the workshop would not suffice to regulate industrial society. That is why politics needs a philanthropic morality to keep it going.

3.2. A Pauline morality of the workshop

What is this morality? The answer was that industrialism must re-energise itself from the primitive Christian religion of brotherly love towards neighbours. The epigraph to *Industrial System* (1821) is as follows: "God said, Love and succour each other" and in his last work, the *New Christianity*, it was the quotation of St. Paul from the Epistle to the Romans, "He who loves others has fulfilled the law. Everything is encapsulated in this saying: Thou shalt love thy neighbour as thyself". Considering that there is no moral progress in history, it is through a kind of circularity between the origin and the end of the history of Christianity that Saint-Simon based the forthcoming "industrial system" on Saint Paul's universal moral finality set from the beginning of Christianity. Such must be the key to the "industrial society": there could be no industrialist policy without an industrial morality inspired by the original Christian matrix. Modern economic rationality merges with the original Christian symbolism in a great historical loop.

The philanthropic aim of this new industrialist religion was to improve the lot of the "poorest class" by giving work to all, transforming nature through works of public interest, notably the construction of territorial networks. Thus, the primitive Christian religion of communion and fraternal love is appropriate to the kind of economic association found in the workshop and the factory. The religious practices of the disciples of Saint-Simon would consist in tracing on the body of France and around the Mediterranean, "material" networks of railways or telegraphy and "immaterial" financial or educational networks to ensure the generalised and accelerated circulation of all flows: of men and goods, of knowledge, and money. The industrial system is thus viewed as a living organism and as a true earthly paradise where everything flows and everything communicates. This program of major works is of interest on two accounts: to produce bonds and to develop work. Industrialisation therefore achieves a vast synthesis that connects the socio-economic finality of the workers gathered in the factory with the ethical–religious purpose surging from the religious communion of brothers. In "industrialism", everything is "combined" and unified by members' cooperation, coordination of work, association of skills, communication of flows, and fraternal communion. Every socio-political conflict dissolves in industrialist pacifism and in the association of "capacities" in the workshop.

"Industrialism" – understood essentially as the policy of industrialists – must be founded on a morality, that of original Christianity. The utilitarianism and rationality of industrialism are not enough. Here, Saint-Simon differs from Say and Bentham (see Allix 1910). Only a philanthropic aim –

an industrial morality, so to say – can constitute the social bond that prevents disintegration, the explosion of selfishness, and ultimately anarchy – the worst of all evils. Industrial religion is an integral part of the definition of industrialism, which in Saint-Simon cannot be reduced to simple utilitarianism. "Today God imposes on all Christians the sacred obligation to contribute with all their means to constituting the industrial and scientific system; which is merely the implementation of the divine principle" (*Système Industriel*, III, p. 2573).

3.3. The new Christianity

This unfinished work written in 1825, subtitled "Dialogues between a conservative and an innovator," is supposed to contain the essence of the Saint-Simonian religion, or even "the whole doctrine" according to Saint-Simon.[9] The *New Christianity* concluded his work as the *Geneva Letters* had begun, by the promise of the expected coming of the people of God who "always proclaimed that a great epoch would come to which he gave the name of Messiah, when religious doctrine would be presented with all the generosity of which it is capable; that it would also regulate the action of temporal power and of spiritual power, and that then the whole human race would have but one religion, one organisation" (*Nouveau Christianisme*, IV, p. 3187). Humanity would be united by a universal industrialist association and a unique morality of fraternity. A single social organisation – that is to say an industrial one – derives from a "general, universal and unique religion" (*Nouveau Christianisme*, IV, p. 3204). Saint-Simon assimilated the industrial and scientific system with the finality of history giving birth to: "definitive and complete Christianity, which is the same thing" (*Système Industriel*, III, p. 2573). This *new Christianity* celebrates industrial production and the fraternal communion of skills in the workshop. The value of work is the ultimate landmark of this world picture; it is "a religion which encourages and honours labour" (*Opinions Littéraires...*, IV, p. 3133). As with St. Paul and the Reformation, salvation is to be sought in work. The more this work is of general interest, the more it contributes to the new religion. This is why Saint-Simon asked artists, scientists, and industrialists to draw up a plan of major works for the appropriation and beautification of the country. This was done by Michel Chevalier (1806–1879) after the Saint-Simonians' retreat at Ménilmontant in 1832, and his

9 Saint-Simon is supposed to have said the following to Olinde Rodrigues concerning *New Christianity*: "All the doctrine is there". This is what Laurent (Ardeche) reports in his address "Aux Saint-simoniens, gardiens de leur foi au Nouveau Christianisme" (Saint-Simon and Enfantin 1865–1878, vol. 40).

project was then used by them as a guideline for action for half a century (see Chevalier 1832). Beyond salvation in work, this "definitive Christianity" makes it possible to establish paradise here below, on earth and in the future, that which was believed to be the lost primeval paradise. "The golden age which a blind tradition has hitherto placed in the past is before us," reads the epigraph to the *Literary, philosophical, and industrial Opinions* (*Opinions Littéraires...*, IV, p. 3025).

The establishment of the industrial system thus becomes a divine task: in this system, "Christianity itself becomes active and turns into a political constitution, as God ordered" (*Système Industriel*, III, p. 2572). Society cannot be limited to a community of interests. Its condition of success depends on sharing a common goal and on communing through the same industrialist faith: "A society cannot subsist without common moral ideas - this community is as necessary to the spiritual as the community of interest is to the temporal" (*Système Industriel*, III, p. 2480). A vast synthesis can thus be made which links the purpose of daily action, namely, to carry out major works of general interest; the social goal, namely, the economic association of workers in factories; and the religious–ethical finality, namely, the brothers' religious communion.

"Industrial society" would realise the promise of this *New Christianity*, which no longer carries the hope of another life but of an earthly happiness to come. Henri Desroche summarised this Saint-Simonian shift as follows: "What the old Christianity promised in the eternal form of a supernature, the new Christianity promises in the temporal form of a super-society" (Desroche 1969, p. 42). To achieve this, it is "sufficient" to reverse the symbolic axis of the Christian religion from its vertical earth/sky position to a horizontal temporal position built on a past/present/future axis. In such a flattened worldview, everything becomes earthly and unfolds at an attitude appropriate for man. Henceforth, industrial religion carries the happiness of humanity towards the future thanks to the great story of progress. With the heralding of a new society, the elements of industrial religion come together: science delivers "truth" and becomes belief; production and work are "useful" actions for humanity; and progress is the driving force of its history.

4. Conclusion

This *New Christianity* is a religion or industrial ideology in which politics is reduced to Pauline economy and morality. That is how Saint-Simon answered Godwin's and Chateaubriand's questions: on the one hand, politics is reduced to a "science of production"; on the other hand, it will be subjected to Pauline morality. Consequently, politics, reduced to a mere management function, will be the link between the economy and religion. Durkheim emphasised the inextricable link between this renewed Christianity, universalism, and industrialism: "Thus religion constitutes the principal part of the system, for it will render international association possible, and this is itself the necessary condition of industrialism" (Durkheim 1971 [1928], p. 213). Therefore, he concluded that "the Saint-Simonian religion can be nothing other than a pantheism". Admittedly, this religion is a "religion of immanence". However, Saint-Simon was not satisfied with "bringing" God back to earth. His new religion, celebrating human action for the transformation of nature and society, was universal humanism rather than pantheism. On the other hand, the question that Durkheim addressed to the new industrialist religion – which he even called "Saint-Simon's error" – is relevant: "Saint-Simon felt the necessity of raising something above the "purely economic order but encompassed by it at the same time" (Durkheim 1971 [1928], p. 229). This Durkheimian image of the superimposition of religion on the economy is to the point, because for Saint-Simon, it was necessary to compensate economic utilitarianism by philanthropic morality. There follows an essential question raised by Durkheim: "Where are these moral forces capable of instituting, making acceptable and maintaining the necessary discipline?" (ibid.). Who will enforce the moral norm superimposed on the industrialist economy, in a situation where the State is in the process of being extinguished? Does the general supervising State, providing a minimum police role, have enough power to do so? Saint-Simon attempted to answer such a question by defining industrialism as the combination of an economy and a morality of association in which the need for discipline has become marginal. This would imply either a kind of self-regulation inherent in society on a cooperative model of the ideal workshop, or a pure and simple fusion of morality and economy. In this case, morality – and therefore politics – is produced directly through work, in factories, and around industry. "Work" and "Fraternity" would be the operators of such a merger because they are both economic and moral values. The *New Christianity* was an ultimate reform after the Reformation that would pave the way for such a world vision. Saint-Simon heralded the entry into the modern era of the neo-Christian, post-revolutionary, and post-Reformation industrial religion, freed of all forms of institutional mediation. Such was his powerful answer to the two major questions of Godwin and Chateaubriand. Hereafter, this scientific, economic, and industrial religion – which the Saint-Simonians enriched and implemented – triumphed in the West. The government of things thus became the administration of men.

Acknowledgements

The author thanks the two anonymous referees of his text for their attentive reading and their valuable advice. He also thanks Gilbert Faccarello for his readings, corrections, and all the care he had given to the final version of this text.

Disclosure statement

No potential conflict of interest was reported by the author.

References

Allix, E., 1910. J.-B. Say et les origines de l'industrialisme. *Revue d'économie politique.* 24 (4), 303–13, and 24 (5), 341–63.

Bonald, L. de, 1843. *Théorie du pouvoir politique et religieux dans la société civile, démontrée par le raisonnement et par l'Histoire.* 3 vols. Paris: Le Clère.

Chateaubriand, F.-R. de, 1797. *Essai politique, historique et moral sur les révolutions, anciennes et modernes considérés dans leurs rapports avec la Révolution Française, à tous les partis.* London: J. Deboffe.

Chevalier, M., 2008. Le système de la Méditerranée. (*Le Globe,* January–February 1832), reproduced in *Le Saint-Simonisme, l'Europe et la Méditerranée.* Introduction and notes by P. Musso. Houilles: Editions Manucius.

Comte, A., 1975. *Cours de philosophie positive.* 6 vols. Paris: Hermann. (Re-printed in 2 vols., Paris: Hermann, 1998, Leçons 1 to 45 with a presentation by Michel Serres, François Dagognet, Allal Sinacoeur. Re-printed in 2012, Hermann, Leçons 46 to 51 by Michel Bourdeau, Laurent Clauzade and Frédéric Dupin.)

Desroche, H., 1969. *Le nouveau christianisme et les écrits sur la religion.* Selected and presented texts. Paris: Le Seuil, coll. "Politiques".

Dupuis, C.-F., 1822. *L'origine de tous les cultes, ou la religion universelle* [1795]. 3 vols. Paris: Emile Babeuf.

Durkheim, É., 1971. *Le socialisme: Sa définition, ses débuts. La doctrine saint-simonienne.* Posthumous ed., with an introduction, by Marcel Mauss. Paris: Presses Universitaires de France.

Engels, F., 1950. *Anti-Dühring.* Paris: Editions sociales.

Faccarello, G. and Steiner, P., 2008. Religion and political economy in early nineteeth century France. *In:* B. W. Bateman and H. S. Banzhaf, eds. *Keeping faith, losing faith: Religious belief and political economy.* Volume 40 of *History of Political Economy,* annual supplement, 26–61. Durham: Duke University Press.

Fichet-Poitrey, F., 1990. *L'idée de religion chez Saint-Simon: Religion et laïcité.* Paris: EHESS, *Les travaux de l'atelier Proudhon* (n. 9).

Godwin, W., 1793. *An inquiry concerning political justice, and its influence on general virtue and happiness.* 2 vols. London: G. G. J. and J. Robinson.

Markovits, F., 1986. *L'Ordre des échanges. Philosophie de l'économie.* Paris: Presses Universitaires de France.

Musso, P., 1999. *Saint-Simon et saint-simonisme.* Paris: Presses Universitaires de France (coll. "Que Sais-Je ?").

Musso, P., 2005. *Le vocabulaire de Saint-Simon.* Paris: Ellipses.

Musso, P., 2006. *La Religion du monde industriel. Analyse de la pensée de Saint-Simon.* La Tour d'Aigues: L'Aube.

Musso, P., 2017. *La religion industrielle. Monastère, manufacture, usine.* Paris: Fayard.

Paine, T., 1776. *Common sense; addressed to the inhabitants of America, on the following interesting subjects: I. Of the origin of government. II. Of monarchy. III. Thoughts on the present state of American affairs. IV. Of the present ability of America.* Philadelphia, PA: W. and T. Bradford.

Saint-Simon, H., 1975. *Henri Saint-Simon (1760–1825). Selected writings on science, industry and social organization.* K. Taylor, ed. New York, NY: Holmes and Meier.

Saint-Simon, H., 2013. *Œuvres complètes,* with introduction, notes and comments by J. Grange, P. Musso, P. Régnier and F. Yonnet. 4 vols. Paris: Presses Universitaires de France.

Saint-Simon, H. and Enfantin, P., 1865–1878. *Œuvres de Saint-Simon et d'Enfantin, publiées par les membres du conseil institué par Enfantin pour l'exécution de ses dernieres volontés et précédées de deux notices historiques.* Paris: E. Dentu.

Say, J.-B., 2006. *Traité d' économie politique ou simple exposition de la manière dont se forment, se distribuent et se consomment les richesses,* Variorum edition. C. Mouchot, ed. Paris: Economica.

Whatmore, R., 2000. *Republicanism and the French revolution. An intellectual history of Jean-Baptiste Say's political economy.* Oxford: Oxford University Press.

Abstract

The project of Henri Saint-Simon (1760–1825) was to complete the French Revolution by a social change in order to eliminate the so-called "feudal-military" system and to bring about a new society which he named "the industrial system". Everything had to be changed, including religion and its relation to political economy. In this paper, I examine: (i) the recurring problem of religion, raised by Saint-Simon as early as his first text; (ii) the emergence of the economic problem of identifying production with politics; (iii) and finally, the metamorphosis of the Christian religion into a moral and industrial religion.

A dance teacher for paralysed people? Charles de Coux and the dream of a Christian political economy

Gilbert Faccarello

> I would deeply regret it if your work for the journals induced you to stop or even simply suspend your course of political economy, which you could, more rightly than Vico, entitle *The New Science*. (Lamennais to Coux, 19 October 1833, in Dudon 1911, pp. 85–6)

> According to Zoroaster, ancient magi believed that the spirit of the seas would severely punish the least stain on his waters; they consequently detested navigation and, in the interest of their eternal happiness, they relinquished the incalculable advantages they could have drawn from it. With such a doctrine, trade could not flourish; a moral obstacle opposed its development and … Say and Sismondi, had they lived among the fire worshippers, would have been as useful to them as a dance teacher for paralysed people. (Coux 1830–1831, p. 104)

1. Setting the stage

In France like in other European countries, the question of poverty was often debated under the *Ancien régime*. During the French Revolution, it was thought that the problem could be more or less easily settled, but the different policies proved to be a failure. People may have thought for a while that the persistence of the phenomenon was due to one decade of dramatic political events. But at the beginning of the nineteenth century, after the fall of the Empire, there was no more room for doubt: not only did poverty persist, but the nature of the phenomenon seemed to have dramatically changed. Poverty turned into pauperism: it was permanent, massive, and intimately connected to economic growth and the new industrial society. Wealth and poverty developed at the same vertiginous rate.

The development of pauperism induced, from all quarters, an indictment of political economy. Not only were liberal economists incapable of curing the disease, but the evil seemed to be a direct consequence of the implementation of the policies they proposed. From that moment, debates never ceased during the century, first on pauperism, then on the "question sociale". This was the occasion for many currents of thought to emerge and develop. But while some of them, like the Phalansterians and the Saint-Simonians, are well known, others are relatively neglected today, despite the fact that they also played an important part in French politics. Christian political economy is one of them.

This approach emerged during the first half of the 1830s, powerfully initiated by Jean-Paul Alban de Villeneuve-Bargemont[1] (1784–1850) and his three-volume book: *Économie politique chrétienne ou Recherche sur la nature et les causes du paupérisme en France et en Europe et sur les moyens de le soulager et de le prévenir* (1834), but also, and before him, by Charles de Coux (1787–1864). Both authors called for the emergence of a new, Christian school of political economy, in opposition to both liberal political economy and socialism.

This current of thought developed in various directions – liberal Catholicism and social Catholicism in particular – during the following decades. Different associations were created, which played an important role in French economic and political life, and new political forces emerged, like the first "Démocratie chrétienne" in 1848. Popes Gregory XVI, Pius IX, and Leo XIII also intervened in the debates, especially through the publication of encyclical letters. They usually condemned the liberal tendencies of the movement but also retained some of the ideas being debated. It could thus be said that the theories put forth at the beginning of the 1830s in France later generated – through French and European debates among Catholics – what has been called the social doctrine of the Church, officially expressed in Leo XIII's encyclical *Rerum Novarum* published in 1891.

The analysis of what happened in France during the 1830s is thus of great interest. However, the emergence of Christian political economy[2] is a bit more complex than usually asserted. It is mainly the outcome of two different intellectual traditions, which, moreover, developed in different

1 Also called "Monsieur de Villeneuve" in the literature of the time.

2 It is to be noted that the phrase "Christian political economy" was used by the authors themselves, with the explicit aim to define a new school of thought – also called the "charitable" or "Catholic" school. For a different use of the expression "Christian political economy" in the British context, inaugurated by Malthus's *Essay on the Principle of Population*, see Waterman (1991, chapter 1).

directions. So far, only the work of Villeneuve-Bargemont has attracted the attention of scholars.[3] His 1834 book, in particular, created sensation because of its tone – a denunciation of the evil of pauperism and its supposed causes: the policies dictated by the political economy of the "English school" – and its length and content: three well-documented volumes. The present paper focuses instead on the writings of Charles de Coux, who also powerfully attacked the liberal system, and whose ambition was more theoretical. Before going deeper into the subject, however, three important remarks are required to explain the general religious context of the debates.

The first regards a distinction within the Christian churches in France, that is, between Catholic worship on the one hand, and Reformed worship – the Protestants – on the other hand, with their multiple variants. France had a very tragic religious past. During the sixteenth century, the Wars of Religion between Catholics and Protestants devastated the country. The 1598 Edict of Nantes, a treaty promulgated by King Henri IV – himself a Protestant who converted to Catholicism to accede to the throne – put an end to the wars and created a space for Protestants in the Catholic kingdom. However, this Edict was repealed in 1685 by Louis XIV, provoking new persecution of Protestants and the emigration of many of them. Protestant worship was later officially accepted in France under the 1789 Revolution. Religious liberty was, subsequently, redefined by Bonaparte in certain clauses he added to the Concordat signed in 1801 with Pope Pius VII. At the beginning of the nineteenth century, the Protestant Churches were still weak, and in the process of reconstruction. Moreover, under the Restoration, their action was hindered by the authorities – especially as regards the right of association and publication. This explains why, at that time, for the majority of the population, "Christian" meant "Catholic". While picking up some themes already put forth by such Protestant authors as Germaine de Staël and Benjamin Constant,[4] Christian political economy proper was developed by Catholic writers.

Second, one must be aware of the fact that, during the nineteenth century, strong anti-Protestant feeling existed among many Catholic writers. The Catholic Church, which saw its influence on the population greatly decline during the eighteenth century with the development of atheism, deism, and pantheism, was just starting to reconquer public opinion – with works like *Génie du Christianisme, ou Beauté de la Religion Chrétienne*

3 See, for example, Théry (1911), Festy (1919), Moon (1921, chapter 1), Ring (1935), Duroselle (1951, part I, chapter 1), Tiano (1993), and Tanaka (2001–2002).

4 On these themes, see Faccarello and Steiner (2008, Section 2).

(Chateaubriand 1802) – and did not appreciate the return of Protestantism in the national religious landscape. A strong anti-Protestant rhetoric developed, culminating at the end of the century in a racist discourse, with arguments that were to be found later in anti-Semitism. The important point to note is that, from the very beginning, Christian political economy – in various ways, depending on the authors – was part and parcel of the anti-Protestant arsenal.[5]

Finally, a third remark is in order. Among the many topics that might divide Catholics, an old question returned to the agenda: the opposition between Gallicans and Ultramontanes. The controversy was of importance because it involved the question of the relations between the spiritual power – the Church – and the political power – the State. Supporters of Gallicanism were in favour of the relative autonomy of the French Church vis-à-vis the Pope, and of a certain intervention of the State in religious affairs, for example in the nomination of bishops. On the contrary, Ultramontanes supported the idea of the pre-eminence of the Pope over the French Church. At the beginning of the nineteenth century, the largest part of the Catholic hierarchy was Gallican, but things changed some decades later. In addition, under the Restoration, most practising Catholics were also in favour of a strict monarchical political regime. The two great philosophers of the Counter-Revolution, however, Joseph de Maistre (1753–1821) and Louis de Bonald (1754–1840), were Ultramontane, and their ideas played a part in the intellectual formation of those who, in the 1830s, proposed a Christian political economy.

In the following pages, I first present the historical and intellectual circumstances of the intervention of Charles de Coux (Section 2). I then deal with his project (Section 3) and with his critique of political economy, his fundamental idea for an alternative approach, and his description of the logic of an industrial economy (Section 4). Finally, I examine the solutions he proposes to put an end to pauperism (Section 5). A brief statement of the significance of his work and legacy concludes (Section 6).

2. Charles de Coux's intellectual background

In strong contrast with Alban de Villeneuve-Bargemont's legitimist and conservative milieu scandalised by the new economic and social order,

5 This important point is a part of a wider debate on the respective merits of the "nations catholiques" and the "nations protestantes". On Protestantism and anti-Protestantism in France during the nineteenth century, see Leroy-Beaulieu (1902), Baubérot (1985), Encrevé (1985), Sacquin (1998), and Baubérot and Zuber (2000).

Charles de Coux was a member of a group of Catholic activists who, at the turn of 1830, gathered around the Abbé Hugues-Félicité Robert de Lamennais[6] (1782–1854) and who, in various fields, remained influential during the following decades.

2.1. *"God and Liberty"*

Lamennais was well known at that time, especially since the end of the 1810s when he published a series of writings that won him a reputation as a formidable theologian and polemist. He was an activist of the Ultramontane cause and a fierce critic of Gallicanism. He was also ultra-royalist, but during the 1820s, like François-René de Chateaubriand, he became more and more disappointed with the Restoration. He proposed an alliance between the Church and the liberals, called for the institution of certain fundamental rights – freedom of conscience, freedom of the press, freedom of teaching – and for the separation of Church and State. He had with him some young disciples, like Philippe Gerbet (1798–1864) and Louis-Antoine de Salinis (1798–1861), both abbots (and later bishops), with whom he published a periodical, *Le Mémorial Catholique.*

At the time of the July Revolution of 1830 that put an end to the Restoration, they were joined by a young Dominican monk, Henri-Dominique Lacordaire (1802–1861) and by some laymen – Charles de Coux and the young Charles Forbes de Montalembert (1810–1870). Together they founded a daily newspaper, *L'Avenir* – the motto of which was "God and Liberty"[7] – and the Agence générale pour la défense de la liberté religieuse (General Agency for Religious Freedom), the aim of which was to fight for the freedom of teaching and to serve as a publishing house.

L'Avenir was first published on 16 October 1830, and the publication stopped on 15 November 1831. Its life was short, but the ideas it campaigned for resonated strongly, especially among the younger members of

6 Robert was the family name. His father added "de Lamennais" – at that time also spelled "de La Mennais". I follow the (now) common spelling of "Lamennais" that the author adopted in the 1830s, and the usage of calling the author Lamennais instead of Robert de Lamennais.

7 "*L'Avenir* was founded ... just after a revolution, which had made evident the falseness of the way followed by the power, for the restoration of the society. When God strikes in this way, men's duty is to think about their faults, and to seek an understanding of what can save them" (Lamennais et alii 1831, i). On the approach followed by *L'Avenir*, see Lamennais (1830a, 1830b, 1831a, 1831b).

the clergy. However, they frightened conservative Catholics and most of the Catholic hierarchy. In the end, the progressive ideas of *L'Avenir* were condemned by Pope Gregory XVI in the encyclical *Mirari Vos* (15 August 1832). The Lamennais group accepted the judgment. However, Lamennais' submission did not last long and, after the publication of his celebrated *Paroles d'un croyant* (1834), he broke with the Church and moved towards socialism.

The other members of the group went on fighting in favour of Catholicism and progressively formed an important network of influence, with periodicals like *Le Correspondant*,[8] *Revue Européenne* (1831–1835)[9], and the daily *L'Univers* (1833–1919). Moreover, in 1836, Gerbet, Salinis, and Casimir de Scorbiac (1796–1846) started an intellectually ambitious periodical, *L'Université catholique. Recueil religieux, philosophique, scientifique et littéraire.*[10] Its aim was to foreshadow, in 20 volumes, what could have been the teaching in a Catholic university in France, if only such an institution were allowed. The lobby also had international connections: with the newly independent Belgium of course – the attitude of the Belgian clergy and its alliance with the liberals in order to obtain the independence had been a model for Lamennais – but also with the Irish and Polish Catholics fighting for their recognition.

The Lamennais group exerted a lasting influence on French intellectual life. The positions of its members, however, were not homogeneous, and they evolved over time in favour of, roughly speaking, either liberal political or conservative but social Catholicism. While the Catholic hierarchy progressively adopted the principles of the latter, the former was always

8 First published weekly (1829–1831), then monthly (1843–1868) after a long interruption, and then fortnightly (1869–1937).

9 Initially published with this mention: "Par les rédacteurs du *Correspondant*".

10 As *L'Université catholique* played an important part in the emergence of Christian political economy, it is interesting to note that, after the lively controversies over *L'Avenir* and Lamennais' ideas, the editors tried to calm things down. In 1836, the "Avertissement" to the first volume stated: "In religion, the editors are united in the same faith, the same and entire submission to the teaching of the Church and the judgments of the Holy See – in particular, the most recent ones – to which they subject all their works, either religious, or scientific: *in necessariis unitas*" (*L'Université catholique*, 1836, I, Avertissement). At the end of the same volume, a "Circulaire aux souscripteurs de *L'Université catholique*" emphasised this state of mind: "Some people … initially had doubts about the line we follow. Their fears soon vanished. They saw that neither the Holy See nor the Episcopate would have cause for complaint about our works …. They also saw that nobody was more far removed than we are from this spirit of rivalry and quarrel that might sow dissension among Catholic journals and disrupt their efforts for the defence of religion" (*L'Université catholique* 1836, I, p. 571).

condemned.[11] It is in this ferment of ideas that the origin of Christian political economy is to be found, four years before the publication of Villeneuve-Bargemont's book. This origin remained relatively unnoticed at that time, except by Villeneuve-Bargemont himself, probably because the other theological and political ideas of the group and the debates they generated eclipsed this topic.

2.2. *Toward a Christian political economy*

The economist of the group was Charles de Coux.[12] His career had been eventful. He was three years old when, at the beginning of the French Revolution, he emigrated to Great Britain with his mother and was brought up there – his father joining the counter-revolutionary Armée des Princes in Germany (Périn 1864, 1865; Thibeaud 1864). He came back to France in 1803, but he resumed travelling abroad: in particular, he worked for some years as an interpreter at the Legislature of Louisiana in the United States.[13] He settled in Paris in 1823 and on 20 February 1830, in a long letter to Lamennais, he proposed some critical reflections on political economy from a Christian perspective, for possible publication in *Le Mémorial catholique* (Coux 1830a). The same year, he took part in the foundation of *L'Avenir*, in which he published articles,[14] especially on politics, including two incisive papers entitled "Économie politique" (Coux 1830–

11 The liberal ideas expressed by Montalembert in *L'Église libre dans l'État libre* (1863) were vigorously condemned in 1864 by Pope Pius IX in his restatement of the conservative principles of the Catholic Church (encyclical letter *Quanta cura* and its companion *Syllabus* – a list of eighty propositions condemned by the Church). The economic field was not spared either. Pius IX condemned Coquelin and Guillaumin's *Dictionnaire de l'économie politique*, which was put on the *Index Librorum Prohibitorum* in 1856. The *Dictionnaire* was in good company: in the same year, J. S. Mill's *Principles of political economy* was also condemned.

12 "[A] writer who had since a long time meditated on the subject [pauperism and political economy], and who can use a vast set of carefully gathered and verified facts, intends to deal with it in *L'Avenir*, to the extent it deserves" (Lamennais 1831b, p. 84).

13 He sided with the Americans during the Anglo-American war of 1815, and took part in the defence of the city of New Orleans (Thibeaud 1864, p. 235). He also spent some time in Brazil.

14 In *L'Avenir*, many papers were not signed. Sometimes, those by Coux are indicated by "C. de C.". However, after the journal ceased publication, the editors re-published what they regarded as the main articles in a series of two volumes entitled *Mélanges catholiques extraits de L'Avenir* (Lamennais et al. 1831), in which the identity of the authors was disclosed (see Coux 1830b, 1830c, 1830–1831, 1831a, 1831b, 1831c, 1831d, 1831e, 1831f, 1831g, 1831h, 1831i, 1831j, 1831k, 1831l, 1831m, 1831n).

1831), probably those he first intended to publish in *Le Mémorial catholique.* In 1832, at the request of the young Antoine-Frédéric Ozanam (1813–1853) and his group of friends, the Lamennais group organised a series of lectures entitled "Conférences de philosophie catholique".[15] In this context, Coux started lecturing on political economy (8 March 1832), a course that was, it seems, appreciated by Catholic activists:

> M. de Coux started his course of political economy, so profound and interesting. I advise you to subscribe. His lessons are crowded, because in them, there is truth and life, a great knowledge of the wound that is eating away at society, and the only remedy that can cure it. (Ozanam to Ernest Falconnet, 25 March 1832, in Ozanam 1873, p. 59)

Coux soon had to stop teaching because of sickness (cholera was raging in Paris), but, from some allusions to be found in a letter by Lamennais (19 October 1833, quoted above as an epigraph to this paper), it seems that he resumed teaching after he recovered. While the whole course was supposed to be published in both Paris and Louvain (Belgium), only the first two lessons were published in 1832 by the Agence pour la défense de la liberté religieuse, entitled *Essais d'économie politique.*[16] The syllabus of the course (Appendix 1), published by the Belgian publisher as an advertisement to subscribe, was sent with the instalments of Gerbet's *Introduction à la philosophie de l'histoire* – also a part of the Conférences de philosophie catholique. Some echoes in the press brought Coux's ideas to the attention of a broader audience than the circle close to *L'Avenir,* and in this respect, two reactions are of interest. One is a critical review of the *Essais,* published by François de Corcelle in *Revue des Deux Mondes* (Corcelle 1833). The other is a paper by François Lallier published in *Revue Européenne* (Lallier 1835), which was of course very positive – Lallier was a friend of Ozanam,[17] and the *Revue Européenne* belonged to the Catholic lobby.

Coux's lectures played an important part in the formation of young intellectuals like Ozanam and Lallier.[18] Probably also thanks to Coux,

---

15 Eighty to a hundred people attended these lectures (Lallier 1835, p. 133).

16 An edition of the *Essais,* with the same title, only concerns the first lesson.

17 Lallier later published papers in *L'Université catholique* and took an active part in the Christian critique of political economy.

18 "In spite of the fact that we could listen to him [Coux] only during a short time, these lessons much impressed our minds, we young Christian men, still tired and hurt by being reproached for such a long time for failing to understand part of human nature, denying industry and destroying … the worldly civilisation" (Lallier 1835, p. 133).

Lamennais was starting to take an interest in political economy.[19] He encouraged Coux to develop his ideas. Referring to the *Essais*, he wrote:

> I cannot express how pleased I am. There is here a new thinking that contains the seed of the sole possible way to regenerate society. The whole set of your lectures will form one of the most beautiful books, and one of the most useful, that can be published in our time; and all sensible discourse on political economy in the future will only be an application or a development of it. (Lamennais to Coux, 27 April 1832, in Dudon 1911, p. 80)

An opportunity presented itself when the Belgian episcopate created a Catholic university, first located in Malines in 1834 and then, a year later, in Louvain. The chair of political economy was offered to Coux. He accepted it and, in his first lecture, praised "the glorious constancy of the Belgian episcopate who ... opens this refuge to the Catholic science in order to preserve us ... against the barbarism of false knowledge" (Coux 1836b, I, p. 90).

In Malines and Louvain, Coux's lectures on political economy – broadly understood as "social and political economy" (Coux 1835, p. 7) – involved two courses: one on social economics ("économie sociale"), and the other on "political economy in its strict sense" (Coux 1838b, p. 148)[20] sometimes also called "économie réglementaire" (regulatory economics) (Coux 1836a, p. 57). But some of his lectures reached a wider public, thanks to the above-mentioned *L'Université catholique*. This periodical, produced in Paris, published lectures in all fields, and one section, entitled "Sciences sociales", included political economy. From 1836 until 1840, some of Coux's lectures – the syllabus of his "Cours d'économie politique" (Appendix 2) and a great part of his "Cours d'économie sociale" – were published there (Coux 1836a, 1836b, 1837a, 1838a, 1839b, 1840a). Their publication stopped in 1840 without any explanation.

At the same time, *L'Université catholique* also published another course in economics: Gerbet and Salinis requested the collaboration of Villeneuve-Bargemont who, from 1836 to 1838, gave to the journal a "Cours sur l'histoire de l'économie politique"[21] (Lectures on the history of political

19 He himself published a paper on credit some years later (Lamennais 1838), a paper praised by Villeneuve-Bargemont (1841, II, p. 375).

20 On these distinctions, see Section 3.3 and Appendix 2.

21 Like many "lectures" published in *L'Université catholique* (Coux's being an exception) Villeneuve's lessons (1836, 1837, 1838) had never been read in front of a public. They were a simple series of papers, announced as being "the summary of a more extended book" (Villeneuve-Bargemont 1836, I, p. 83n). They were later collected and published in Belgium under the title *Histoire de l'économie politique, par Alban de Villeneuve* (Villeneuve-Bargemont 1839) but this was done without Villeneuve-Bargemont's consent: at that time, he had in fact temporarily abandoned the idea of a book because of the publication in 1837 of Jérôme-Adolphe Blanqui's *Histoire de l'économie politique en Europe, depuis les anciens jusqu'à nos jours*. The existence of an unauthorised edition of his own lectures prompted him to revise and enlarge the text and to publish it in Paris through Guillaumin (Villeneuve-Bargemont 1841).

economy). A third series of lectures in political economy was published in the journal between 1839 and 1842:[22] that of Louis Rousseau, a former Phalansterian, certainly as a complement to Coux's lectures. This new course[23] was introduced by the editors in the following way:

> Some of our subscribers have complained that in our works on political and social economy, we have not sought to inform our readers about the works of renowned modern economists like the *Fourierists* and the *Phalansterians.* They have expressed the wish that, in stating their doctrines, we should let them know their useful and commendable elements, and refute what is contrary to Catholic beliefs. This is precisely what M. Rousseau is going to do in the lectures we start today. (*L'Université catholique*, 1840, IX, p. 95n, italics in the original)

We must finally insist on an important but neglected point: during this period, Coux also wrote four long papers published in English. Some well-known Irish Catholics (Michael Joseph Quin, Daniel O'Connell, and Cardinal Nicholas Wiseman) founded a new and successful periodical, *The Dublin Review*, published from 1836 onwards. There were connections between the French and Irish Catholic activists, and Coux immediately contributed some papers,[24] the most important ones, for our purpose, being "Christian political economy" (1837b), on Villeneuve-Bargemont, and "Saint-Simonism" (1838b), on Claude-Henri de Saint-Simon and the Saint-Simonians – a paper also published in French some months later in *Revue de Bruxelles* (Coux 1839d), with the addition of a short introduction (Coux 1839c).[25]

In Belgium, Coux stayed in office 11 years, until 1845 when he came back to Paris as the director of the Catholic daily newspaper *L'Univers* (his disciple Charles Périn (1815–1905) succeeded him in the chair). He left this post in January 1848, disagreeing with the pro-Jesuit line of the editor,

---

22 It seems that after 1842, political economy was no longer of interest to the editors of the journal.

23 The substance of Rousseau's lectures was taken up in his book, *Croisade du XIXe siècle. Appel à la piété catholique à l'effet de reconstituer la science sociale sur une base chrétienne. Suivi de l'exposition critique des théories phalanstériennes* (Rousseau 1841).

24 Coux, like Montalembert, had a mother of English origin. Montalembert was born in London, and, as noted before, Coux spend his childhood in Great Britain during the French Revolution. Both spoke English and had connections with the English-speaking world.

25 The other papers are "The Archbishop of Cologne" (Coux 1838c), "Belgium and Holland" (1838d) and finally, and most probably, "Trade with France" (1839a). In the *Dublin Review*, the articles were published anonymously. However, research in archives could disclose the name of many contributors (see Russell 1893).

Louis Veuillot. During the February Revolution, together with Lacordaire, Ozanam, and Henry Maret (1805–1884, a theologian and a former supporter of *L'Avenir*), he participated in the foundation and editing of a new daily, *L'Ère nouvelle*, the organ of the first "Démocratie chrétienne", intended to support the new Republican regime.[26]

> The mission of *L'Avenir*, first, and then of *L'Univers*, was to prove in a practical way that we could be orthodox Catholics and stop being Legitimists. That of *L'Ère nouvelle* was to show in the same way … that the Church is not alarmed by the most advanced political doctrines. (Coux to Maret, 5 April 1849, in Bressolette 1977, p. 466, n. 36)

Coux, however, left *L'Ère Nouvelle* in September 1848[27] and withdrew from public life until his death in 1864.

3. Coux's project: "To give political economy what it is lacking"

3.1. An enigma?

"M. de Coux was the first to propose a complete system of political economy from a Christian point of view", Charles Périn wrote when Coux died (Périn 1864, p. 119; 1865, p. 371). He was "the founder of Christian political economy". But are things really so straightforward? While it is true that Charles de Coux pioneered a Christian conception of political economy before Villeneuve-Bargemont and tried to develop a general Catholic framework in which the principles of political economy could be embedded (see Section 3.3 and 4.5), we cannot find in his writings a clear statement of a "complete system of political economy from a Christian point of

26 This daily newspaper was an event, even if its life was short: the prospectus was published on 1 March 1848, the first issue on 15 April 1848, and the last on 1 April 1849.

27 Coux left in September, at the same time as Lacordaire, because he did not agree with some of the articles published in the journal. Contemporaries explained this departure in various ways. According to Falloux (1856, p. 457), Lacordaire and Coux left because of the democratic inclination of the journal. According to Périn (1864, p. 120; 1865, p. 372), they left because of the Gallican opinions expressed by the journal. Falloux is probably right for Lacordaire, but not for Coux. "There were enough disagreements between us [the editors] for me to go on accepting, as a founding member, the responsibility for all the articles; but, as long as your opinion prevailed … I usually agreed with you", Coux wrote to Maret on 5 April 1849 (in Bressolette 1977, p. 466 n.36) – and Maret's democratic opinions were well affirmed. Périn's opinion is probably correct as regards Coux, but it seems that the latter also left because of the less liberal, and more interventionist, economic flavour of some papers published in the journal.

view". In a way, Périn was echoing Coux's own assertions: in his letter-programme to Lamennais, Coux had written that he "had the project to give political economy what it is lacking, a foundation that could not be contested by anyone" (Coux 1830a, p. 85), and in his 1832 *Essais*, he had stressed that "the practical consequences of Catholicism form the most admirable system of social economics that ever existed on earth" (Coux 1832, p. 4).

Compared with other writers of the same period, Coux published relatively little. Unlike Villeneuve-Bargemont – or, later, Charles Périn himself – he did not write any great treatise. Yet it seems that he was preparing for such a task. In a letter to Coux, Lamennais mentioned the "book that you are preparing" (4 February 1835, in Dudon 1911, p. 87), but no such book was published. A manuscript exists however: that of Coux's Louvain lectures on political economy "in its strict sense", which many friends encouraged him to publish. But he always rejected this prospect. According to one of these friends, Hippolyte Thibeaud:

> He had composed a full treatise of political economy. To a friend …, on several occasions, he read some pages of the highest interest. Joint endeavours were made on more than one occasion to push him to publish the manuscript. His modesty always led him to refuse. In the end, he answered: "The person who replaced me in Louvain knows all my ideas. He must publish a treatise on political economy. They could be stated in a much better way than I could do it myself". (Thibeaud 1864, p. 241)

Charles Périn, to whom Coux alluded here, expressed the same regrets. Yet he was the custodian of Coux's papers and had in his possession the manuscript of the lectures, a 475-page document that he bequeathed to the Catholic University of Lille, in France. But he asserted that he did not find anything publishable in it (Périn 1881, p. 25). A first reason probably lies in the state of the manuscript (Coux 1844–1845) – in fact an unfinished draft, sometimes carelessly written, some chapters being moreover merely outlined and others not developed at all –, which would have necessitated serious rewriting and completion for publication. But there is perhaps a more fundamental reason. The manuscript is presented by Coux as his "last words" – "Novissima Verba!" is the epigraph on the cover page –, and if we refer to Coux's project, the statement of some new and pathbreaking principles in economics, from a Catholic perspective, could have been expected. However, on this point, the content is disappointing: while including many interesting historical developments, for example on the evolution of the forms of labour from slavery to wage-labour, and some pages on points already addressed in his published lectures on social economics, it is basically an introductory course on political economy in the

Say tradition (see for example Appendix 3) – rejecting, however, the law of markets. To understand this state of affairs, it is thus necessary to analyse Coux's project more precisely. What, then, was lacking in political economy, and how could Catholicism provide it with indisputable foundations?

3.2. A moral dilemma

In his 1830 letter to Lamennais, in his 1832 *Essais* and in the lectures published in *L'Université catholique,* Coux always told the same story. He wrote that when he was in England and in the United States, he was struck by – and suffered from – the contrast between these Protestant nations and many Catholic countries, the best example of which being Spain. He saw how the wealth of the former made such a strong contrast with the poverty of the latter, and he was shocked by the link which apparently existed between the religion prevailing in a country and the social and economic state of that country. All this seemed to confirm what had been suggested since the eighteenth century: that the Catholic faith and its institutions formed an obstacle to economic development, while the Protestant faith favoured it.

> I lived among Protestants, and you know that their financial and industrial supremacy has always been their favourite argument. When they compared, in my presence, England, so rich and anti-Catholic, with Spain, so faithful and poor, I could only acknowledge that a Church, the dogmas of which … had produced such disastrous results was missing one of the essential features of truth. (Coux 1830a, p. 81)

Coux's faith was shaken because he could not understand why the true religion – Catholicism, in his eyes – could put believers at such a disadvantage. It is true, he stressed, that the material consequences of a religion cannot be a proof of its truth:[28] it was the task of apologetics to develop this truth, with totally different arguments. But he thought that God could not have neglected these material aspects of worship, and that consequently the true religion should also possess some principles to ensure the prosperity of the community.

> Of course I knew that the aim of the true religion cannot and should not be the temporal happiness of man, but I also understood that it is obliged to ensure it … like an additional reward, granted without being promised, because otherwise the society in

28 This point of view is restated again and again in his published lectures: see for example 1836b, I, p. 278, 279; 1837a, IV, p. 82, 248, 254. See also 1837b, p. 188: "all [the Catholic writers] lay down the principle, that the truth of no creed is to be tested by the effect it produces upon the earthly happiness of its followers."

possession of the absolute truth would not be what it must be: the aristocracy of mankind. (Coux 1830a, p. 81)

The important economic problems that first arose in England during the first decades of the century were a kind of revelation to him, because they were not temporary, as was first thought, but structural, permanent, and intimately linked to the economic regime. "Unfortunately, destitution deceived all expectations and thwarted the calculations of the economists: it has grown according to a geometric progression and will end in dreadful chaos" (Coux 1830a, p. 81). The arrogant prosperity of the Protestant countries was just a delusion, and it became clear that the economic system at the origin of this delusion contained seeds of self-destruction. Societies based on it were unavoidably condemned to disintegration.

3.3. Towards a "social and political economy"

According to Coux, these events induced him to draw some conclusions. The first was that the economists were responsible for this situation, despite the fact that they tried to put the blame on the workers: "Philosophy itself admits that there is no remedy to the evil because it blames the superabundance of the population: it thus stresses a cause, the action of which cannot be changed but by means of a permanent famine" (Coux 1830a, p. 81).

Malthus's doctrine spread all the more easily as it pointed the finger at the people, who were suffering, as the real authors of their own destitution; and Malthus's followers believed they did all in their power in favour of the workers when they could tell them ...: "you would not be hungry, had you not been born". (Coux 1832, p. 46)

But the responsibility was that of political economy itself, because this awful economic system was its doing. It provoked "the plague of pauperism" through the implementation of its theories (Coux 1832, p. 56). "The language of the economists reveals the depth of the social scourge; their teaching made this scourge, since they govern the world. They are the priests of money" (Coux 1832, p. 50). In these conditions, economic theories can only be "deceptive" (Coux 1832, p. 53).

How is it possible to refuse to acknowledge that the industrial school, the school founded by Adam Smith, took a wrong turning ..., when we look at the present state of England and France? In both countries, amidst appalling distress ..., there are huge amounts of wealth; but all around a starving mob is rising up. (Coux 1832, p. 55)

Such a society cannot last and revolution is imminent (Coux 1832, p. 54). This is the reason why Coux tried to identify the conditions of a stable and lasting social relation on which the prosperity of a country could be built. In this perspective, he compared the material consequences of different kinds of religious and social belief – or unbelief – and came to the conclusion that Catholicism alone was able to generate such a desirable relation.

> The earthly value of the various beliefs will be … appreciated in money, since we will be able to evaluate them according to their material results. This point of view, which has nothing in common with theology, will allow us to compare them with each other …, and the one generating the greatest welfare on earth will be considered by its opponents themselves, if not as the *truest*, at least as the most *useful* doctrine. (Coux 1836b, I, p. 278, italics in the original)

Unfortunately, Catholics wrongly disregarded political economy and abandoned this field of study to their opponents. Their behaviour, Coux admits, can of course be explained. They acted in this way primarily because political economy "exclusively deals with human cupidity". Political economy is in their eyes the "theology of material interests" (Coux 1830–1831, p. 96): born outside the Church, "its first words were words of blasphemy" (Coux 1836b, I, p. 92). It was thus in conflict with their ethics of sacrifice and charity. But they also neglected political economy for another, less glorious, reason: discouraged, they started to raise doubts about their own religion. They believed in the end that its dogmas were unfavourable to any idea of material welfare and prosperity.

> Political economy has a great influence on the religious destiny of the people. Since it shows them all the wealth produced by industry, since it continuously invites them to the feast of fortune, they feel in the end tired of the resistance they oppose and they curse the worship that deprives them of all these goods. This is the part played by political economy, since its origin, vis-à-vis the Catholic nations. It did not attack its dogmas directly, but it blamed these dogmas for the alleged misery of their followers. (Coux 1830–1831, p. 105; see also 1836b, I, p. 92)

It was thus high time to react. But did all this mean that the entire corpus of political economy had to be rejected? It seems at first sight that this should be the case, especially if we remember how very harsh Coux could be with economists and economics.[29] However, a pure and simple

29 The theories of political economy are false and misleading. Smith, Say and Ricardo had "their reason polluted, first by Protestantism, and then by philosophy" (Coux, 1836b, I, p. 93).

rejection was not on his agenda. In his opinion, the prevailing economic theories could also be scientifically accepted, and express some truth: for example, they "unveiled the causes and the effects of credit, explored the maze of circulation, showed how capital is formed and accumulated" (Coux 1836b, I, p. 94), and Coux's developments in his manuscript lectures on political economy are in fact systematically based on the law of supply and demand. But these theories have to be put in the right perspective. According to the letter to Lamennais quoted above, one must "give political economy what it is lacking." Coux's idea was to include political economy "in its strict sense" – "which almost exclusively deals with exchangeable wealth ... and cannot encroach on the teachings of morals" (Coux 1844–1845, p. 22) – within a larger set of theoretical propositions that was supposed to give it its real meaning, and without which it would remain partial and therefore dangerous.

The production of wealth supposes the existence of a society, and society supposes sociability. "Social economics" studies this sociability and its object is to determine which form of society is the most capable of securing this sociability, that is, the most apt to favour the creation of wealth in a stable and durable environment. It must thus come first. "Its main object is the knowledge of the laws of society; it is ... the necessary prelude to political economy" (Coux 1836b, I, p. 95). It is of a higher order than political economy because it has something to do with the Law of God.

> It is difficult to believe that ... no voice ever arose to prove to the economists that all their most central theories ... are implicitly contained in Catholicism. Even a superficial study of their doctrines could have been sufficient to realise that they are but a collection ... of the consequences that naturally ensue from the application of the revealed truths. (Coux 1830–1831, p. 106)

Despite the fluctuations in Coux's use of the terms in his different writings, this approach remained unchanged. Lamennais accepted it, and expressed the idea in a striking way.[30] In the first issue of *l'Université catholique,* it is also clearly stated in Philippe Gerbet's "Discours

30 "It seems to me that political economy gains everyday a greater importance .... This science leads to all others, because, in the end, there is only one science. One usually deals with it like Medea with her father. She wanted to gather his limbs back together and make them younger. But I do not even see the cauldron in which our scientists could proceed in this operation with this science, out of which it could become one and alive again" (Lamennais, letter to Coux, 4 February 1835, in Dudon 1911, p. 87).

préliminaire."[31] And according to Coux, it is precisely the correct division of the science between "social economics" and "political economy" proper that the Saint-Simonians could be credited with:

> In their hands, political economy became divided into two distinct branches. To the first they gave the name of "social economy", because it is the science of all these institutions by the help of which societies subsist, beginning from the family and mounting up to the State; and because we learn from this science what should be the nature of those institutions, in order to secure the greatest possible quantity of general prosperity. The second branch, moving in a humbler sphere, was the science of Smith and Ricardo – political economy in its strict sense, – or, in other words, the science of the elements of the wealth of nations, and the means of increasing it, when a nation is constituted. This division, which at first seemed imperfect and obscure, but which was in fact a correct one, tended much to promote the birth of St Simonism. (Coux 1838b, p. 148)

4. The mistakes of political economy and the logic of industrialism

While the principles of political economy are thus not to be rejected, some of them have nevertheless to be criticised, amended or dropped in the perspective of social economics. Coux raised five major points.

4.1. Against the principle of population

The first critique concerns Malthus's principle of population – "Malthus the Protestant", the "married priest" and his "merciless" logic (Coux 1836b, I, p. 95) – so quickly adopted by the economists. "The existence of a superabundant population, when compared with the quantity of provisions we can command, is as great a fallacy as ever gained credit among mankind" (Coux 1837b, p. 169). The population of a country is never in the position of a crew on a boat, lacking food and not knowing when it will

31 "Political economy … states the laws of production, distribution and consumption of all that serves the material well-being. It deals in particular with the facts gathered by statistical history. It thus entails in the first place calculation devices: it establishes a kind of balance, of social equation, between needs and resources, and presents the mathematical theory of society. … Social science, in its more elevated part, links … all the facts to something superior to the idea of usefulness … it starts from the law of justice and charity, which is the soul of society, and is itself linked to the religious dogmas. Science then does not proceed by way of calculation, as political economy does, it does not rely only on simple experience to find out, through induction, the conditions of the political body: it deduces from religion the fundamental and absolute laws of human society" (Gerbet 1836, p. 32). A similar statement was made by the first rector of the Université Catholique of Malines/Louvain (De Ram 1840, p. 14).

be possible to stock up again: "we deny most absolutely that there is in Europe one single country, which, with the land already under cultivation, and by the assistance of the means of traffic which it derives from its industry, might not subsist a more numerous population than that which it now contains" (Coux 1837b, p. 168). Moreover, before discussing Malthus's views, both followers and critics should have checked whether or not a state of overpopulation really existed, which they never did.[32]

Finally, the principle of population is a real attack on divine wisdom because, were it true, it would mean that God, when he commanded "be fruitful and multiply", wished to punish men for a transgression they had not yet committed:

> ... one might be tempted to believe, that it was to punish Adam for the fault he had not yet committed, that God imposed on him the command to increase and multiply. Economists of both sexes combined their efforts in this crusade against marriage, – and certainly if the propagation of our species could be stopped by subtlety and talent, the works of Miss Martineau would entitle her to the especial gratitude of that posterity – whose existence she would have prevented. (Coux 1837b, p. 168; see also 1836b, I, p. 95)

Faced with their belief in an excess of population, moreover, economists propose absurd solutions, for example when they assert that a powerful check to procreation can come from the will of the workers themselves when they realise that a larger family would deteriorate their welfare. This kind of assertion, Coux stresses, could be adapted to those who already have some comfort in life, and who are afraid of losing it. But it is wrong when it is supposed to apply to poor people. They do not have anything to lose, and a family life constitutes the sole happiness they can hope for in this world (Coux 1837b, pp. 171–2).

> No doubt this perspective is a real check upon a young man whose personal situation would be made much worse by the necessity of providing for a young family; but then his situation must be one which is capable of becoming worse; that is to say, he must be in possession of some comforts which he must give up when he gives up celibacy. If, like the Irish peasant, he has reached the last pitch of human misery, what has he to fear? (Coux 1837b, p. 171)

32 "Yet this was the point at which they should have commenced .... If we are not mistaken, the disputants followed too closely the example of the learned men of the sixteenth century, who expended so much ink in proving on the one side, that men might be born with teeth of gold, and on the other, that such a phenomenon was impossible; they would have done better, in the first place, to open the mouth of the child who occasioned the dispute, and at once ascertain the fact" (Coux 1837b, p. 168).

Finally, "Malthus hardly deals with the question of the price of labour" – a central point for Coux (see Section 4.6 and 5.2) and "this is the radical flaw of his essay" (Coux 1844–1845, p. 339).

4.2. The neglect of the laws of the distribution of income and wealth

Hence a second critique. While there is no overpopulation with respect to food, it cannot be denied that there is one with respect to available jobs: "The superabundance of the population that eat must not be confounded with the superabundance of the population that work" (Coux 1837b, p. 168). The problem takes us back to the logic of the industrial society. But it also takes us back to the question of the distribution of income, since pauperism also concerns, for a great part, the population that works but whose wages are too low. It is therefore not enough to study the laws of the production of wealth, as political economy does, but it is also necessary to study the laws of its distribution – Villeneuve-Bargemont subsequently stressed the same point.

> Economists only dealt with the first of these two conditions .... They were only busy with one question: to determine the laws that most favour the production of material wealth, and these laws ... became the aim ... of the science. Exclusively devoted to this research, economists were careful not to ask whether the distribution of public wealth does not have at least the same importance as its increase. (Coux 1830–1831, p. 107)

4.3. A wrong concept of wealth

Hence also a third critique of political economy: economists "misunderstand" (1830–1831) the notion of wealth. Their concept is erroneous because it is unduly restrictive. As a matter of fact, most of them, following Smith, equate the elements of wealth with the material goods exchanged in markets and therefore having a price. But such a restrictive notion is wrong, for two main reasons.

First of all, wealth should normally refer to the well-being of a society, to the quantity of utility that can be derived from the goods it produces. The price is by no means a good indication of this utility. It depends on fluctuations in demand and supply, and varies more than proportionally to the imbalance between them (Coux 1832, p. 70). When the wealth of a country is only conceived in monetary terms, as economists do, then "a famine is a means to fortune, and the destitution of the people a proof of opulence" (Coux 1832, p. 71). One should distinguish, Coux stresses, between the price and the intrinsic utility of a good, between its exchangeable value and its value in utility.

> The latter exists by itself, it is, so to speak, the *substantive* of the public wealth, while the former, a simple *adjective*, only indicates the relations between two exchangeable goods in so far as they are exchangeable. (Coux 1832, p. 74, italics in the original)

Second, limiting the elements of wealth to goods that have a price unfortunately neglects a whole set of other elements that contribute in the same way, and to an even greater extent, to national prosperity. These non-tradable elements form the social wealth *par excellence*, the most important being the moral ideas and the virtue[33] they generate. In a given society, the entire set of beliefs underpinning the ideas of good and evil, just and unjust, and even its institutions, plays a decisive role in economic life and in the prosperity of the country. It cannot be excluded from political economy: "viewed in this way, any religion, any philosophical system falls within the province of political economy" (Coux 1832, p. 62).

> If the *price* is no longer considered as the sole measure of the prosperity of nations, everything that contributes to increase this prosperity — whether or not it is liable to have a monetary evaluation – must be viewed as an element of wealth. Then the wealth of nations will be estimated as much on their moral virtues as on their skills in banking activities – at least those virtues or vices that have an influence on agriculture and industry. (Coux 1832, p. 71, italics in the original)

What would be the future of the wine-growing activity, if religion were to prohibit the consumption of alcohol? Or the future of agriculture, or sea trade, were religion to forbid eating meat or seafaring (Coux 1832, p. 61)? Economic activities could not have developed properly in such contexts. Political economy would have been a useless science, and Say and Sismondi would have been no more useful to the population "than a dance teacher for paralysed people" (Coux 1830–1831, p. 104). Moral ideas and beliefs are themselves wealth, negative or positive, and a moral system that favours trade and industry, generating respect for others and a feeling of safety and liberty, would form, at the material level, an invaluable collective wealth.[34]

33 "Virtue is nothing other than the preference given to the just over the unjust, whatever the cost of this preference may be, and this is precisely why it is the principle that generates all human transactions" (Coux 1832, p. 85).

34 The liberal economist Charles Dunoyer developed similar ideas (see Faccarello 2010a, pp. 738–1).

4.4. *The wage question*

Charles de Coux also tackled a fourth theme that he placed at the centre of his analysis of pauperism: the wage question. At first sight, his critique seems odd. As he wrote in his letter-programme to Lamennais:

> ... while I was endeavouring to discover the causes of the distress that devastates the countries dominated by industrialism, a fact voluntarily neglected by the economists struck me as the alpha and omega of the question; the labour of the poor man is his commodity, the only one he has to sell, and ... the conditions that rule the value of all other commodities also apply in this case. (Coux 1830a, pp. 82–3)

The fact that labour, or its services, is a commodity had certainly not been "voluntarily neglected" by the economists. The point Coux stressed is rather the inverse relation that exists between wages and profits – an important element of his analysis, on which the future of society depends.

> [N]one of them [the economists] realised that labour is an instrument for the person who buys it, and a commodity for the one who sells it; and that consequently there are here two interests that cannot be opposed without threatening the very existence of society. (Coux 1832, p. 39)

Economists neglected the fact that labour is the sole source of revenue for the workers, and focused instead on labour as a means of production, as a cost: "economists, led by the desire to increase production indefinitely, took sides with the merchants of labour [those who demand labour, that is, the entrepreneurs]. All their theories ... evidently aim to reduce the price of wages" (Coux 1830–1831, p. 109). Moreover, labour is also the commodity subjected to the greatest instability: "Of all marketable commodities, that which is least sure of a demand, most variable in its price, and which makes to the producer the most unfavourable return, is unquestionably manual labour" (Coux 1837b, pp. 169–70). For all these reasons, the state of society that ensues can be worse than slavery: while the owners of slaves had the obvious interest and duty to feed them, the entrepreneurs, for their greatest benefit, do not have this worry with workers (Coux 1830a, p. 83; 1844–1845, pp. 317–22).

4.5. *Against the "outburst of all cupidities": how to found a Christian political economy?*

Last but not least, Coux's fifth critique is directed at the fact that political economy essentially deals with the "outburst of all cupidities" for earthly goods (Coux 1836b, I, p. 93), and takes this as its central behavioural hypothesis. Public prosperity is considered to result directly from the wealth of each member of the community: but the outburst of the passion to grow rich only generates calamities. "Instead of considering, with Catholicism, that the wealth of everybody lies in the wealth of all, they saw the wealth of all in the wealth of each of them. Instead of growing poorer to the benefit of one's neighbour, they wanted to grow rich at his expense" (Coux 1836b, I, p. 93). Human beings who are solely led by their self-interest can only join together "as wolves do when they are chasing the same prey" (Coux 1832, p. 84). Society cannot but fall into a state of anarchy.

> Each member of the large human family being endowed with boundless cupidity, his desires cannot be concentrated in the finite without an insatiable ambition, an ambition that inflates as his possessions grow. The uncontrollable strength of his lust will put him in a state of endless war against all his fellows. (Coux 1836b, II, p. 162).

It is, however, to be noted – and this is an essential point – that Coux never questioned the fact that political economy assumes the selfish behaviour of people as an axiom. After Original Sin and the Fall of Man, this kind of behaviour is unfortunately normal: "cupidity … is a passion inherent to the fallen man" (Coux 1836b, I, p. 96; see also 1830a, p. 85).

> We agree on this point with the Utilitarian school, and we start from the fact that self-interest is the strength that leads the will because, except in some very rare and exceptional cases, necessarily unknown outside the Catholic Church, man brings everything back to himself and only takes decisions with a view to his welfare as he understands it. (Coux 1836b, II, p. 161; see also I, p. 280)

As in Boisguilbert more than a century before (Faccarello 1986, 2014), this basic behaviour is explained by theology. As it is impossible to change it, Coux aimed at neutralising its effects. This neutralisation is the foundation of social economics or Christian political economy, and is based on the uncovering of the sole stable social relation capable of generating real prosperity. This relation is indicated by religion, and only by Catholicism. It is based on a fundamental ethical value: sacrifice. It is this point "that distinguishes fundamentally Christian political economy from anti-Christian political economy. The former considers sacrifice as the principle which generates wealth, but for the latter it [the principle] is cupidity" (Coux 1836b, II, p. 161; see also I, p. 280).

How should we understand this sacrifice? It is the Christian virtue, that is, the attitude which puts love for one's neighbour, charity, at the centre of action, and which makes men adopt a virtuous conduct – the respect of justice – even if this must have a detrimental effect on them. In such a way, a lasting social relation is created that excludes any hostility against others.

Moreover, Coux's argument stresses the fact that this virtuous behaviour is not only compatible with the material prosperity of a nation, but is in fact the only way to attain it. Any sacrifice for the benefit of others – or for the general interest – certainly at first impoverishes the person who makes it. But this person in turn receives the benefit of the sacrifices made by others, and Coux was convinced that this generalised attitude, far from being a zero-sum game, ultimately increases the general welfare.

> If the sacrifices of the Catholic were lost for society, if the hardships he endures, his unselfishness, his charity, his good faith, the purity of his mores, did not turn to the benefit of anybody, we would not have anything to answer to the anti-Catholic economists. But is it really so? ... The Christian sacrifice, while finding its principle in the love for God, always ... turns to the benefit of others, and if it impoverishes those who make it, it enriches others. But we are all the others of others, and, consequently, each member of a Catholic society finds in the sacrifices of the other members a great compensation for his own sacrifices. Nay, he is a hundredfold rewarded since, on the one hand, there is no lasting society without a reciprocal devotion of its members and, on the other hand, the more vigorous the spirit of sacrifice, the greater are the social advantages that are divided between all. (Coux 1836b, I, p. 93)

But what obliges the members of a community to adopt such a behaviour, so opposed to the nature of man after the Fall? It is, Coux states, not only the belief in a God, but in a "rewarding and vengeful God" who inevitably and infallibly rewards and punishes men during their eternal life. In a kind of Pascal's wager, men compare their immediate and temporal interest, which is always uncertain, with their eternal interest, which is certain. They are still led by cupidity, but by "the cupidity for the goods of another life, the craving for an imperishable wealth" (1836b, I, p. 96). Self-interest is still the prime mover, but "an enlarged, inflated self-interest, extended beyond the grave" (Coux 1836b, I, p. 280). This is obviously an essential point: "the most naive religions were never so stupid as to ask the believers for devotion without reward" (Coux 1836b, I, p. 280; see also 1832, p. 57). Sociability is based on this fact.

> Sociability is nothing other than this essential association of the individual with the Divinity ... whom he obeys at the expense, if necessary, of his immediate interest, because his well-understood interest demands it .... As a result, the belief in a rewarding and vengeful God does not unite directly men together, or in other words the association of the believer with his like is only a consequence ... of his association with the Divinity. (Coux 1836b, II, p. 410).

There is no state of nature, and no social compact. Only religion matters, and moreover a religion based on a Revelation, because what is just or unjust, good or evil, must be clearly stated from the outset and independent of the actions of men.

The lectures published by Coux in *l'Université catholique* develop this point of view extensively and propose a typology of societies – "unitary", "Catholic", and "transactional" societies – based on the possible combinations of two elements: what he calls the *legitimate* order (based on religious beliefs) and the *legal* order (based on political structures). Suffice it here to stress that the aim of these developments is to show that Catholicism is the only religion that can generate genuine and lasting prosperity. As an example, note how Coux denies Deists and Pantheists, on one hand, and Protestants, on the other hand, the notion of a "rewarding and vengeful God" which is so essential to the social relation:

> Socially speaking, there is no difference between the absolute negation of a Supreme Being, and the affirmation of a deity indifferent to his creatures or crushing them under the weight of a rule that they cannot change, through either their submission or their disobedience. Self-interest does not care about the carefree greatness of a God who leaves man to himself, who does not ask him anything, who does not establish any link between this life and the future life. If he accepts this doctrine … he will of course look for his happiness in the sole region where his efforts can have any success in his world, and his interest will be exclusively temporal, destructive of all society, all safety, all work and all wealth. (Coux 1836b, II, p. 162)

4.6. The logic of the industrial society: pauperism

What are the economic and social consequences of the behaviour imposed by anti-Christian political economy, and why is the phenomenon of pauperism unavoidable in this context?

Competition is the war of all against all. Coux describes it and stresses its negative effects. The maximisation of profits, he writes, is damaging not only because it is necessarily excessive, but also because it generates dishonesty (Coux 1836b, I, p. 93). In his analysis, the central variable is wages – the wages that he accuses economists of neglecting.

In the struggle for markets, Coux admits, competition can for a time be favourable to the entire society. Any State possesses what he calls "latent wealth",[35] and a first stage of the process of growth consists in its progressive exploitation: in this situation, the demand for labour increases with

35 "*Latent wealth* is formed of the common wealth not yet made fruitful by the labour of men, of industrial wealth that has not yet the shape of exchangeable goods, and generally of all the improvements still possible in science and legislation, in agriculture and in industry.… The clumsy worker made skilful, the forces of nature harnessed to increase the produce of his labour days, new ways will one day hasten the progress of the national wealth, and the working force needed by the development of these resources will give some affluence to the working class, at least for a time" (Coux 1832, p. 108, italics in the original).

the production, and the wage remains at a certain level or even increases. From the context, we understand that the exploitation of latent wealth corresponds to the realisation of the potentially most profitable investments of the moment. However, this exploitation is limited in time. The dynamics of investments weakens, profits erode under the effect of competition. To maintain the profitability of their activities, entrepreneurs must reduce their costs, and therefore wages. The reduction of the wage rate in turn increases the profitability of some investments that can now be made (Coux 1832, p. 108). This is how pauperism starts, with the dangers it entails.

> The Gods flee, chased away by the roaring of the worker. ... He no longer receives his daily bread, and while hunger kills him, who can hope that, in his agony, he will not interrupt the peace of everybody? (Coux 1832, p. 109).

This process is intensified by other remarkable phenomena, the first of which is a growing exposure to risk for the entrepreneurs. To increase their profits, they think up and realise ever more risky projects, the outcome of which is usually highly uncertain. They are encouraged by two important factors (Coux 1832, pp. 87–8). In the first place, there is the development of the capital market, which allows them to finance their projects thanks to the credit – the confidence – they inspire in lenders. In the second place, and even more important, there is a deep modification in mentalities, in public opinion, which gradually comes to consider failures and bankruptcies not as ignominious actions, but as normal events in economic life. This change of opinion in turn increases the willingness of the entrepreneur to realise risky projects, and the economy is transformed into a casino – "trade became a gaming table. Then came the disasters" (Coux 1832, p. 87). In this way, badly conceived productions are explained, together with the resulting gluts and crises, the negative consequences of which always fall on the workers. Even bankruptcies can be profitable: "when it was no longer shameful to suffer the reverses of fortune, some started to take advantage of this. Profitable bankruptcies succeeded ruinous bankruptcies. People went into liquidation in the same way as they might set up a factory" (Coux 1832, p. 88). The same logic also explains why a growing amount of capital leaves the sectors of production and commerce: "it concentrates in the stock exchange, and the capitalists speculate instead of making commerce" (Coux 1832, p. 86).

A second remarkable phenomenon is the mechanisation of production processes. Again with a view to reducing the costs of production under the pressure of competition, the massive and quick introduction of machines generates an important reduction in the level of employment, together with a simplification of the tasks and a general deskilling of labour. Hence an increase in the jobless, a reduction in the wages of those who are still employed, and an extension of pauperism.

> These wonderful machines ... provoked a complete revolution in society, a revolution which could have been happy, had their introduction been slow and progressive: the wages of the poor would not have been taken away.... When, with the aid of machines, it became possible to obtain from a single man the quantity of product that was formerly made by one hundred and fifty craftsmen, the least interruption in the sale of the products caused a fall in the price of wages. From this moment the worker lost all security in life. (Coux 1832, pp. 44–5)

The other negative consequences of the introduction of machines make the situation even worse. In the first place, because of the simplification of the tasks performed, entrepreneurs could resort to the massive employment of women and children: the supply of labour was considerably increased, wages decreased, and the number of paupers increased (Coux 1837b, pp. 172–3). In the second place, the working conditions considerably deteriorated, exhausting the workers and damaging their health.

> The employment of very young children, the vast workshops where men and women live together during sixteen hours per day, the lack of air, a temperature similar to that of the torrid regions, the corruption of the mores provoked by all these causes, the destitution which ensues, all concurs to destroy the body and deaden the mind of the worker. (Coux 1832, pp. 80–1)

Finally, two other points should be noted. First, greediness everywhere generates dishonesty, which destroys the confidence that is so necessary to economic activities – either the confidence of the entrepreneur in his collaborators (Coux 1832, pp. 85–6) or the confidence of the customers in the quality of the products they buy (Coux 1832, pp. 89–90) – and reduces profits: "the genius of the engineer does not produce enough to cover the embezzlements of the administrator" (Coux 1832, p. 86). Second, foreign competition intensifies the downward pressure on wages. In their struggle for markets, countries can only efficiently deal with costs, that is, with wages, since technology is disseminated more or less quickly among competitors. The country which gets the upper hand is the one where the workers can most tolerate a reduction in wages and endure hunger. "Competition between countries that have an equal abundance of capital and equally skilful workers is only competition between the stomachs of these workers" (Coux 1832, p. 72).[36]

The situation of the workers is thus desperate. They endure a double penalty: not only can they no longer satisfy their essential needs, but because of the industrial society, their needs increase in number – "what all others possess is lacking for each of us, and therefore each of us is just as poor because of the wealth of others as because of his own destitution" (Coux 1836b, I, p. 528).

> [T]hanks to the decay of religious feeling, and to the desire for the comforts of life …, the workman has contracted habits and acquired tastes which were formerly unknown to him. And thus he is doubly a sufferer, since his condition is worse, and his anxiety for its improvement greater. This is the wound which is so deeply seated in commercial countries, and which, if not healed, must in the end prove mortal. (Coux 1837b, p. 170)

Poor people must give up all prospect of improvement. The owners of capital form a new aristocracy, and it is impossible for anyone to grow rich solely with his or her labour. Hence the widening gap between the rich and poor, and the hate of the latter for the former (Coux 1832, pp. 88–9).

5. How to eradicate pauperism?

5.1. The wrong solutions

Once pauperism has been explained in this way, the main question remains: is it possible to eradicate it? How to put an end to the logic of industrialism, Coux asks, without adopting one of the many solutions proposed by various socialist writers, which all lead more or less directly to the abolition of private property and liberty?[37] The authors who belong, to one degree or another, to the Christian approach reject these solutions, and Coux is no exception. Private property takes its origin in present or past labour, it is a natural right that secures liberty. No law can justify confiscation – even a modest one, even through a simple tax – because any

36 "In the struggle that would then take place in every market in the world between her merchants and ours, supposing all else to be equal, success must depend upon the low price of labour ; or, in other words, that country whose workmen could longest and most patiently endure hunger must in the end carry off the victory" (Coux 1837b, p. 181).

37 In his manuscript lectures, Coux criticised the Saint-Simonians and the Fourierists and presented the communists as a kind of synthesis between the two (Coux 1844–1845, pp. 112–7, 344–7).

confiscation is simply bondage, "a retroactive bondage" (Coux 1832, p. 96).

Neither is the solution proposed by certain economists acceptable. From the writings of Say and Sismondi, Coux only retains a single idea: production must be "accelerated", one must always produce more in order to increase the demand for labour, and thus reduce unemployment or increase wages.

> According to Say and his immediate followers, the glut of manufactured produce which so frequently took place, and the almost periodical suspensions of the labours of the mechanics, were occasioned by there being still not a sufficiency produced. According to Sismondi and many others, the increase of population was the real cause of a distress which could no longer be disputed. All demanded fresh markets. (Coux 1837b, p. 174)

But, according to Coux, it is evident that this headlong rush into production cannot but worsen the situation in the long run, insofar as the search for new markets inevitably leads to downward pressure on wages in order to reduce costs. "This remedy ... has until now only provoked new disasters" (Coux 1832, p. 48).

Some proposals were also made by Villeneuve-Bargemont. Most of them were probably acceptable to Coux, but he did not say anything about them in his published lectures. However, in *The Dublin Review*, he criticised one of them, central to Villeneuve's approach: that which considers agriculture as a priority sector, that is to say, which subordinates the development of industry and trade to a growth process centred on land. This solution was obviously linked, in Villeneuve-Bargemont, to his proposal for the limitation and reorientation of human needs. Coux was certainly not against this limitation, but he thought that the model of development proposed by Villeneuve-Bargemont was not feasible and could not, therefore, solve the question of pauperism. He opposed the "blind antipathy to the factory system" (Coux 1837b, p. 179) developed in the 1834 book: "the preference which the Catholic school gives to agriculture, ... to say the least, is carried greatly too far" (Coux 1837b, p. 187).[38]

One reason for Villeneuve-Bargemont's proposal was his acceptance of what I have called the Montesquieu/Herrenschwand approach (Faccarello 2010b) – later also developed by Alexis de Tocqueville –, that is to say, the idea that the development of manufacturing makes the economy more

38 However, at the end of his syllabus (Coux 1836a, p. 57), he noted rather elliptically that, thanks to progress in industry, "the permanent decrease in the prices of ... [industrial] products will soon deprive industry of the main part of its influence on the wealth of peoples, and agriculture will regain its own".

vulnerable because the demand for manufactured products is subject to sudden and violent variations, and those who work in this sector are disconnected from agriculture and thus from food. Coux did not reject this hypothesis.[39] However, it was his opinion that a country cannot avoid autonomous industrial development. His ideas were extensively developed in his 1837 paper published in *The Dublin Review.* An excess supply of labour can perfectly exist in agriculture as in manufacturing, and the problem would remain unsolved. "Unhappy Ireland is a living proof of the utility, nay more, of the necessity of commercial industry." (Coux 1837b, p. 166) The Montesquieu/Herrenschwand model of development is here implicitly referred to:

> Whether ... the superabundance of labour exists in the fields, or in the factories, the effects is the same as respects the profits of the labourers... M. de Villeneuve admits this fact, and wishes to encourage ... what he calls national manufactories; that is to say, manufactories that are chiefly employed in working up the indigenous raw material. But ... that nation which has more hands and more capital than it can employ in agriculture or in national manufactures, must, upon pain of being exposed to a redundancy of labour, extend the sphere of its industry, so as to take in the raw material of foreign countries. Undoubtedly it will then find, that the only means of keeping up the rate of wages is by an immense exportation; and machinery will become indispensable: and then follow those giant factories where millions of workmen are congregated. In fact, it is impossible to command foreign markets, and to sell in them, under the form of merchandize, their superabundant labour of the country, without possessing the advantage of cheapness. Now, the factory system, superior machinery, and unbounded capital, can alone insure the necessary degree of cheapness to encounter the accumulated difficulties of freight, high duties, and foreign competition. (Coux 1837b, pp. 182–3)

A problem of coherence arises here because it seems that Coux is criticising Villeneuve-Bargemont for his rejection of the solution proposed by economists, which Coux had himself rejected. The context shows, however, that this contradiction is only apparent: Coux seems to isolate the idea of an agriculture-centred process of growth from the other proposals stated in *Économie politique chrétienne.* It therefore comes as no surprise that, in a market economy based on private property and competition, the idea he criticises is unrealistic and cannot suppress pauperism.

39 "There is some difference between the wealth of a people which only produces what is necessary and that of a people whose industry mainly produces what is superfluous. The revenue of the former possesses a fixity unknown by the latter, and while the agricultural nation will last through centuries without fearing anything other than bad weather, the manufacturing nation is exposed to all the dangers of competition" (Coux 1832, pp. 102–3).

5.2. Is there a remedy?

This apparent contradiction in Coux's reasoning, however, shows the existence of a dilemma in his own thought. For what are the solutions he himself proposed to eradicate pauperism? While his analysis eloquently states the evil that undermines modern societies, it seems that the remedies proposed prove in the end to be either derisory or unattainable. That being the case, his analysis petered out and this is perhaps an additional reason why Charles Périn did not discover anything publishable in the manuscript, of which he was the custodian.

For Coux, the problem of the distribution of income is undoubtedly central. It is possible, of course, to invoke charity. However, even if charity is abundant and well-managed, "it will never be sufficient to cover the ordinary needs of the worker" (1844–1845, p. 321). A high enough wage is needed, at least to allow those who have a job not to fall into destitution. But in a free market society, the level of wages depends on the supply and demand of labour, and the development of competition, machinery, and modern industry structurally produces an excess supply of labour. Some historical examples, Coux noted, confirm this. During the Empire, wages were high because labour was in short supply, owing to the needs for the army, conscription and high mortality on the battlefields. During the Restoration and the July Monarchy, on the other hand, war and conscription ceased, and the supply of labour became abundant: wages decreased continuously in spite of the economic development of the time (Coux 1837b, p. 173–4). Is there a remedy? How should we understand Coux's statement that "these machines, which at the same time have so prodigiously enriched and impoverished society, would have produced entirely different results, had Catholicism retained its ancient social power" (Coux 1844–1845, p. 343)?

Coux believed that the solution consisted in acting on the labour supply to reduce it and thus, all things being equal, increase wages. In this perspective, he found nothing better than to refer to the institutions of the Catholic Church, including the celibacy of the clergy (which avoids an increase in the population) and the religious feast-days (which are public holidays), supplemented by an ethics that holds luxury tastes and goods in contempt – thus reducing the needs of the workers (Coux 1830–1831, p. 106).[40]

40 Coux neglected the fact that contempt for luxury reduces the demand for this kind of good, thereby reducing their production and hence the demand for labour.

> Nor did the Church act less wisely with respect to the rate of wages. The old Dutch East Indian Company, in order to keep up the price of their spices, burned a part of those which they gathered in abundant years. The Church did the same; she consumed a part of the labour of the workmen by the multitude of her religious festivals; and the labourer then sold his remaining working days more dearly than he would have sold the whole year of labour, if he had consented to work all the year: and in the pomp of these festivals were held out to him unexpensive enjoyments, which turned his mind from more costly pleasures. The Church had nicely calculated that the labourer should *gain the most* and *expend the least* that was possible. The Catholic economists assert, that the Reformation, by suppressing ecclesiastical celibacy, has rendered powerless the different clergy which it has created; and that, by suppressing festivals, it has brought into the market that superabundance of labour which is now mistaken for a redundancy of population. (Coux 1837b, p. 197, italics in the original)

These points are developed in the manuscript lectures (Coux 1844–1845, part III, chapter 3), where Coux also made a case for the creation of workers' associations: they would have been led by devoted non-workers, for example priests, whose role would have been to discuss the level of wages with the masters (Coux 1844–1845, p. 347). During the 1848 Revolution, in some papers published in *L'Ère nouvelle*, this same approach led Coux to propose a reduction in the length of the working day, again with a view to diminishing the supply of labour and increasing wages.

A similar approach can be found in a paper Coux published in 1844 in *Le Correspondant*, "De l'économie politique nationale au point de vue de la France". There he supported a protectionist policy in favour of "national labour", avoiding the ordinary downward pressure on wages due to international competition. There is of course nothing original in this proposal, except for the ethical justification developed by the author, who refers to the values of Catholicism as opposed to those of "philosophy" and "Protestantism". In substance, the Catholic ethic of charity – helping one's neighbour – favours personal relationships with those who are helped, and thus the immediate neighbourhood of the believers. It is primarily an interpersonal relationship, and a feeling that grows weaker with the distance between human beings. It is the opposite of the ethic of philanthropy – the ethic of philosophy and Protestantism. The latter promotes a love for humankind, an abstract and intellectualised love which favours the masses and creates institutions that help human beings indiscriminately and automatically – like the English Poor Laws – and which can be counter-productive. It is Coux's opinion that true and efficient help comes from Catholic charity and its local institutions. It is this same charity that obliges us to prefer our fellow citizens to foreigners: "in the political sphere, one's neighbour is evidently one's country" (Coux 1844, p. 32). "I am far … from having any hostile feelings towards foreigners …; I do not hate them, I simply prefer our fellow citizens. Let the foreigners be happy and prosperous, as long as my fellow citizens do not suffer in consequence" (Coux 1844, p. 32). Hence the justification for the protection of "national labour".

> Considered as a pure theory, that is, disregarding the national constraints and the *faits accomplis*, the prohibitive system is eminently bad.... But prohibitions and protective duties are henceforth ... a necessary evil; an evil however that entails some compensations because, on the one hand, it places it [France] in the first rank among those peoples who want freedom for national labour and, on the other hand, it ensures the daily bread of its workers." (Coux 1844, p. 58)

"You see once more", Coux told his students, "that absolute solutions are impossible in political economy": all depends on the circumstances (1844–1845, p. 157). In his unpublished lectures, the opposition between the ethic of philosophy and Protestantism and that of charity and the justification for a protectionist policy are expressed, in a more neutral way, through the distinction between a "humanitarian political economy", which deals with the interests of humanity as a whole, and a "national political economy", which focuses on the wealth of the country (Coux 1844–1845, pp. 10–1, 422–26). Ideally, the interests of humanity benefit from an unlimited domestic and international competition, but with the emergence of machinery and modern industry "the negative effects of industrial competition start to be felt" (1844–1845, p. 423), the economies and peoples of many countries suffer and their interests no longer converge: in these circumstances, economic policy must protect the nation, and "national political economy" is just "the science adapted to the needs of the fatherland" (1844–1845, p. 426).

5.3. From hope to pessimism

Are these remedies efficient? Coux's answer is not so clear-cut, and he proved in the end to be rather pessimistic. For example, in the case of protectionism, while noting its necessity, in his unpublished lectures he also stressed that this policy, when (unavoidably) implemented by many countries, results in increased domestic competition between the national producers no longer able to sell on foreign markets, and ultimately increases pauperism. This is, he admitted helplessly, "a very serious question": "modern civilisation depends on its solution, but this is an enigma, whose answer is known by Providence only – as for me, I do not know it" (1844–1845, p. 426). The same is true for a possible reinstitution of the Catholic festivals. This would be helpful if all the countries did the same: but this is now unfortunately impossible, because a unity of belief among nations no longer exists (1844–1845, p. 324).

Coux must have felt that his emphasis on the strategic character of the level of wages, while accepting at the same time private property and free trade, was a derisory statement in the face of such huge a problem as pauperism. In a way, and in spite of the fact that he never abandoned this approach, he must have been aware of this from the beginning:

> As my ideas developed, political economy acquired, to my eyes, a new nature …: linked with God, it became Catholic; it borrowed something from the infinity of the religion that had just subjected it, and the question of the wages, to which I first decided to stick exclusively, seemed to me too narrow in the end. (Coux 1830a, p. 84)

This "something from the infinity" is what Coux developed later in his "social economics" and his apologetic attempt to prove that only a social relation based on Catholicism can be lasting and advantageous. However, in real life, this relation became looser and looser and the society ruled by Catholicism – an idealisation of the Middle Ages – evolved under the attacks of philosophy and Protestantism. Unbelief dominated and temporal interests gained the upper hand over eternal interests, provoking the situation that Coux had before his eyes. In this perspective, the only way to eradicate pauperism would be to restore the strength of the Catholic relation, that is, to provoke an authentic cultural and social revolution. Villeneuve-Bargemont did not hesitate to propose such a programme.[41] But was this restoration feasible? On this point, Coux's writings are ambiguous. Like Villeneuve, he sometimes dreamed of a reform in people's behaviour. As the problems are the result of the avidity for earthly happiness, is not a limitation on human needs to be hoped for?

---

41 "How to make labour, industry, the production of wealth, the progress of the civilisation, be in harmony with the welfare of the most numerous classes of society? The way exists … but it requires … a complete change in social doctrines. Instead of … being only guided by cupidity and the morals of material interests, one should consider all human beings – whose destiny is not limited to a short passage on this earth – as brothers destined to share the same legacy; one should demonstrate moderation, justice and charity in all enterprises; one should love and seek progress in everything, but with wisdom, … without greed; one should not neglect the acquisition of the commodities of life, but not get them at the expense of the happiness of others; one should regulate needs, desires, profits, so that labour, wages and the moral and physical betterment of the lower classes can go *pari passu* with the increase in wealth …. One should thus protect agriculture because it leads more certainly to this goal, encourage the machines which are useful to all but proscribe, by means of prohibitive rights, those [that are] harmful to the working class: such is the solution to our problem. Industrial selfishness will, no doubt, answer: *Master, your words are harsh!* … To you, they may seem so. But they are clear and soft to hearts that are not closed to justice and truth" (Villeneuve-Bargemont 1834, I, pp. 385–6, italics in the original).

> Happy those who know how to content themselves with exchangeable goods that suit their position! Nations live the last days of their material happiness when a senseless self-love presses them to want more. The worker only suffers distress when he seeks after goods that are not for him, and a reckless desire for luxuries lead the middle classes to their ruin. But how to repel the invasion of these artificial needs that arise from our pride? Has philosophy some of these magical words that charm the human heart and stop its aberrations? Religion alone speaks the language where these words can be found, and here again … the *usefulness* of Catholicism reveals itself in all its splendour. (Coux 1832, pp. 106–7, italics in the original)

But in the end, Coux's discourse was pessimistic. He rarely broached the subject in his publications and, on these occasions, the tone is negative. Ultimately, the present state of society cannot be changed and must therefore be accepted:

> This form of society, however, in spite of all the disadvantages it entails …, is the only possible one today. This is the reason why our duty, as Catholics, is to frankly accept it because we owe it the remnants of a more perfect sociability. (Coux 1839b, 8, p. 171)

As for the "social economics" that was supposed to place political economy in the right perspective, Coux twice played down its importance, as if its virtue could only be negative – in other words critical, but unfit for reconstruction.

> We should not delude ourselves, Messieurs, *qua* the importance of social or political economics. Dying societies can learn from its teaching the real cause of their fears, but there stops its power. The disease that kills them comes from above, and above lies the remedy. (Coux 1836b, I, p. 97)

> They [the Catholic writers] acknowledge frankly that the remedies they propose can scarcely by possibility be adopted in the present state of the world; and they hardly attempt to conceal the sadness of their forebodings as to the future destiny of society. (Coux 1837b, p. 198)

Coux felt powerless. That being the case, it is tempting to turn against him the judgment he expressed on Say and Sismondi. He probably felt that he himself was a "dance teacher for paralysed people".

6. Conclusion: a new school in political economy?

It would have been interesting to compare systematically Coux's developments with those of the main critical writers of his time, including Malthus, Sismondi, the Saint-Simonians, the Phalansterians, and even Tocqueville. But this would go beyond the scope of the present study, that is, a clear statement of his approach and analysis of his doctrine. To conclude, then, we must address a pending question: to what extent, at that time, was Christian political economy a new school of thought – Coux's dream – based on a corpus of specific theoretical propositions?

At the turn of the 1830s, in reaction to the mass pauperism created by the new industrial system and to the first modern economic crises, the project of a Christian political economy emerged in France from different branches of Catholicism, either politically liberal or conservative Legitimist. Charles de Coux belonged to the former, Alban de Villeneuve-Bargemont to the latter. Their critiques of the prevailing economic system were similar, but they did not necessarily agree on the remedies, except for the reaffirmation of Christian values, the role of charity and sacrifice, and the need to raise wages. Villeneuve is by far the more famous of the two nowadays: but Coux, whose intention was certainly more theoretical and ambitious, could claim priority. In *Économie politique chrétienne,* Villeneuve referred to him, acknowledging that he (Villeneuve) had "benefited from many of his observations" (1834, I, p. 83n).[42] Towards the end of his *Histoire de l'économie politique,* he stated again the convergence between his own preoccupations and those of Gerbet and Coux.

> The similarity between our ideas and those of the authors whose lectures today confer such great interest to *L'Université catholique* was for us an important encouragement, and also a source of hope. We are pleased to think that, thanks to the conscientious work of these Catholic philosophers and many political economists who go in the same direction … science will, sooner or later, become Christian and Catholic, and will lead the human race towards a better destiny. (Villeneuve-Bargemont 1838, 5, p. 335; see also 1841, II, pp. 360–1)

Both authors aimed explicitly at the creation of a new school in political economy – Villeneuve had probably been inspired by Coux on this point. Characterising such a school in his 1837 paper of *The Dublin Review,* Coux wrote:

> Catholic in its faith, and catholic in its manner of conceiving science, this school, little known in England, begins to develop its principles in France; and its existence is the necessary consequence of the entire contradiction which facts have given to the doctrines and to the promises of Protestantism and of philosophy. (Coux 1837b, p. 175)

Villeneuve dreamt of some new theoretical developments on a Christian basis – enrolling in the Christian school the "writers whose efforts

42 In January 1829, when he was still the prefect of the Department of Nord, Villeneuve sent an administrative report to the Minister of the Interior Jean-Baptiste Sylvère Gaye de Martignac. In it, he stressed the permanent state of destitution of part of the population and the necessity to find remedies, but without any notable developments (Villeneuve-Bargemont 1829).

tend to restore the moral and religious element of the economic science" (1844, p. 240). In a sense, Coux's and Villeneuve's attempts proved to be rather successful, because, despite the fact that Villeneuve was sometimes seen more as an "apostle" than "an economist or a statesman" (Blanqui 1837, II, p. 172), contemporaries who did not necessarily belong to this movement considered that the new school was now part of the theoretical landscape. François-Félix de Lafarelle-Rebourguil (1839, I, pp. 21–72), for example, counted three schools of thought in political economy: the "English or positive school" (Smith, Ricardo, Say, Destutt de Tracy), the "moral school" (Malthus, Sismondi, Droz) and the "charitable or Christian school." Charles Louandre wrote along the same lines, but proposing a slightly different classification:

> Like philosophy, political economy is divided into three schools: the Catholic school, the administrative school [the liberal economists], and the revolutionary school [the associationists and socialists]. The leaders of the Catholic school ... are MM. de Coux and de Villeneuve-Bargemont. (Louandre 1847, p. 278)

But listing the members of the school precisely was not an easy task. From the start, the delimitation of this current of thought was all the more vague because, for some authors, it still lacked doctrinal unity. François Lallier, for example, who had been greatly impressed by Coux's lectures in Paris in 1832, and whose paper in *Revue Européenne* was a eulogy of Villeneuve's 1834 book, recognised that the new school was, "if not de facto and really united, then at least united in spirit, hope and heart" (Lallier 1835, p. 135). Lafarelle-Rebourguil (1839) just mentioned a few names, and other writers could not clearly state who belonged to the school – Villeneuve, rather arbitrarily, tried to include in the movement certain authors who had written before him or approximately at the same time. Obviously, in the 1830s and at the beginning of the 1840s, the "école charitable ou chrétienne" was only a hope for those who felt close to this sensibility.[43] For Villeneuve himself, the constitution of a new current of thought was, in the end, a simple wish (1834, I, p. 83 n.1, 89 n.1; 1841, I, p. 360). It is with this hope that, in

43 The topography of this sensibility remained vague for a long time. In the 1850s, the names put forth by Alfred Nettement – a Conservative and Legitimist – in his *Histoire de la littérature française sous le gouvernement de Juillet* (1854, II, p. 515 et seq.) still differs from those mentioned by Félix Martin-Doisy in his voluminous *Dictionnaire d'économie charitable* (1855–1857, IV, col. 294 & sq.) where the list of the "économistes charitables" is excessively long. In the recent literature (see for example Almodovar and Teixeira 2012), the boundaries are again different.

L'Université catholique, he closed his lectures on the history of political economy:

> It is enough for our ambition to have shown in advance the extent of their mission to the writers who would like to enter a noble and new career: we would be happy if our works ... could contribute to the emergence ... of new and Catholic Adam Smiths who could realise what we have just foreseen and indicated. (Villeneuve-Bargemont 1838, 6, p. 17)

Coux also stressed the vague boundaries of the group[44] and the embryonic state of the theories.

> But, like all things in their beginning, the Catholic school has as yet not got beyond the first rudiments of its theories; and up to this time has done little besides pointing out the fatal consequences, that, with or without reason, it attributed to the prevailing doctrines, and seeking out means to ameliorate the fate of those poor who are unable to work or to live on the fruits of their labour. (Coux 1837b, p. 176)

The school only formed slightly later,[45] but not according to Coux's hopes. While the dissemination of Catholic ideas on political economy benefited from Coux's teaching and publications, he did not have any faithful disciples. It is true, in a sense, that his action was continued by one of his students, Charles Périn, who succeeded him to the chair of political economy in Louvain in 1845. Périn started publishing a bit later, especially in reaction to the 1848 Revolution, and was quite prolific for decades. His importance can hardly be overestimated: through his many writings – some of them translated in German, Italian, and Spanish – he systematically developed a Christian approach and was one of the founders of what was to be called "social Catholicism". But social Catholicism was no longer Coux's Christian economics.

Fundamentally, Coux remained a liberal and a theorist, and could not prevent himself from thinking in terms of competition in markets – even if he was highly critical of the economic and social outcomes of competition. For him, for example, wages remained a price, determined by the supply

44 Coux also admits that certain authors sometimes included in the group do not have a specific religious attitude. "Nay, they are not all Catholics; and, if MM. de Villeneuve, Rubichon and Rainneville, profess the same faith with ourselves, MM. de Morogues, Huerne [de] Pommeuse, and many other French economists, who agree with them in all respects, and whose works have lately appeared, have no pretention to the title of orthodox believers. Their agreement is, therefore, remarkable" (Coux 1837b, p. 188).

45 For a detailed history of the post-1840 debates, Moon (1921) remains an unavoidable reference.

and demand for labour: hence his disappointing and derisory solutions to pauperism, noted above, and the blind alley in which he must have felt trapped. After Coux, any theoretical ambition to found an alternative political economy was practically abandoned. Moreover, wages, most authors insisted, were not to be considered as the price of a commodity, labour. Social Catholicism mainly focused on important but practical goals – hence the quasi-disappearance of the phrase "Christian political economy". Authors aimed, for example, at changing the legislation in favour of the working classes (limitation of child labour and the working day, improvement of working conditions, decent housing, education, insurance, charity and the role of religion, etc.), and, among other actions, at the promotion of new forms of cooperation between workers, and between capitalists and their employees (invention of new forms of guilds or corporations). In a sense, the pragmatic and policy-oriented line of Armand de Melun (1807–1877), a friend of Villeneuve-Bargemont, and after him of Albert de Mun (1841–1914) prevailed. Périn belonged to this approach.

At the turn of the twentieth century, Justin Fèvre (1829–1907), a prelate[46] who constantly fought against liberal Catholicism, but was in favour of social Catholicism, published a book with the title *Charles Périn, créateur de l'économie politique chrétienne* (1903).[47] This was of course neither fair nor exact. But the fact is that Coux was deliberately forgotten – probably because of the liberal and democratic aspects of his thought – and his theoretical ambition was no longer on the agenda. The dream of a Christian political economy was over.

Acknowledgements

This text was presented at the third International Symposium on "Population, Poverty and Welfare in the History of Economic Thought", Tokyo, Waseda University, 12 September 2011, and at the first workshop of the research programme "The conflict-ridden development of modernity: Theology and political economy", Lyon, 19 December 2013. Useful discussions with Thierry Demals, Claire Silvant, Philippe Steiner, Katsuyoshi 'Vittorio' Watarai and Anthony Waterman, and comments by two anonymous referees, are gratefully acknowledged. A special thanks also to Mrs Marie Vouters, from the Bibliothèque Universitaire Vauban of

46 He was the editor of *Revue du monde catholique.*

47 Fèvre even tried to dismiss Coux's person and integrity, writing (1903, p. 10) that Coux's papers in *L'Avenir* have some merits, but that, "having married a rich woman, he was lost to science" (see also 1903, p. 224). It is true that, in his foreword to the book (1903, p. x), he admitted that his judgment was a bit too harsh, but he nevertheless left the main text unchanged.

the Université Catholique of Lille, who kindly gave me access to the manuscript of Coux's lectures on political economy.

Disclosure statement

No potential conflict of interest was reported by the author.

References

Almodovar, A. and Teixeira, P., 2012. 'Catholic in its faith, Catholic in its manner of conceiving science': French Catholic political economy in the 1830s. *The European journal of the history of economic thought*, 19 (2), 197–225.

Baubérot, J., 1985. *Le retour des huguenots. La vitalité protestante, XIXe-XXe siècle.* Paris/Geneva: Éditions du Cerf/Labor et Fides.

Baubérot, J. and Zuber, V., 2000. *Une haine oubliée: L'Anti-protestantisme français avant le "pacte laïque", 1870–1905.* Paris: Albin Michel.

Blanqui, J.-A., 1837. *Histoire de l'économie politique en Europe, depuis les Anciens jusqu'à nos jours.* Paris: Guillaumin.

Bressolette, C., 1977. *L'abbé Maret. Le combat d'un théologien pour une démocratie chrétienne, 1830-1851.* Paris: Beauchesne.

Chateaubriand, F.-R. de, 1802. *Génie du christianisme, ou Beauté de la religion chrétienne.* Paris: Migneret.

Corcelle, F.T., 1833. *Essais d'économie politique* par M. de Coux. *Revue des deux mondes*, 2, 372–80.

Coux, C. de, 1830a. Letter to Félicité de Lamennais, 20 February. *In* Lamennais, 1930, 80–7.

Coux, C. de, 1830b. De la seule majorité possible. *L'Avenir*, 29 October and 17 November, as in *Mélanges catholiques extraits de l'Avenir.* Paris: Agence générale pour la défense de la liberté religieuse, 1831, 1, 328–33; 334–41.

Coux, C. de, 1830c. De la position des catholiques. *L'Avenir*, 23 October, as in *Mélanges catholiques extraits de l'Avenir.* Paris: Agence générale pour la défense de la liberté religieuse, 1831, 1, 307–14.

Coux, C. de, 1830–1831. Économie politique. *L'Avenir*, 29 December 1830 and 10 January 1831, as in *Mélanges catholiques extraits de l'Avenir.* Paris: Agence générale pour la défense de la liberté religieuse, 1831, 1, 96–102; 103–10.

Coux, C. de, 1831a. De l'année 1830. *L'Avenir*, 2 January, as in *Mélanges catholiques extraits de l'Avenir.* Paris: Agence générale pour la défense de la liberté religieuse, 1831, 2, 183–9.

Coux, C. de, 1831b. Le 21 janvier. *L'Avenir*, 22 January, as in *Mélanges catholiques extraits de l'Avenir.* Paris: Agence générale pour la défense de la liberté religieuse, 1831, 1, 349–51.

Coux, C. de, 1831c. De la souscription pour les Polonais. *L'Avenir*, 29 January, as in *Mélanges catholiques extraits de l'Avenir.* Paris: Agence générale pour la défense de la liberté religieuse, 1831, 2, 45–51.

Coux, C. de, 1831d. Du crédit des deux cents millions et de la vente des bois de l'État. *L'Avenir*, 15 March, as in *Mélanges catholiques extraits de l'Avenir.* Paris: Agence générale pour la défense de la liberté religieuse, 1831, 1, 391–8.

Coux, C. de, 1831e. Des associations patriotiques. *L'Avenir,* 21 March, as in *Mélanges catholiques extraits de l'Avenir.* Paris: Agence générale pour la défense de la liberté religieuse, 1831, 2, 197–203.

Coux, C. de, 1831f. Du cens électoral dans l'intérêt des classes ouvrières. *L'Avenir,* 3 April, as in *Mélanges catholiques extraits de l'Avenir.* Paris: Agence générale pour la défense de la liberté religieuse, 1831, 1, 284–9.

Coux, C. de, 1831g. La Belgique. *L'Avenir,* 17 April, as in *Mélanges catholiques extraits de l'Avenir.* Paris: Agence générale pour la défense de la liberté religieuse, 1831, 2, 130–6.

Coux, C. de, 1831h. De l'état moral de l'Europe. *L'Avenir,* 21 April, as in *Mélanges catholiques extraits de l'Avenir.* Paris: Agence générale pour la défense de la liberté religieuse, 1831, 2, 7–12.

Coux, C. de, 1831i. Des sociétés secrètes en Italie. *L'Avenir,* 23 April, as in *Mélanges catholiques extraits de l'Avenir.* Paris: Agence générale pour la défense de la liberté religieuse, 1831, 2, 30–40.

Coux, C. de, 1831j. De la Pologne et de la Russie. *L'Avenir,* 10 May, as in *Mélanges catholiques extraits de l'Avenir.* Paris: Agence générale pour la défense de la liberté religieuse, 1831, 2, 65–70.

Coux, C. de, 1831k. De la mission du général Bonnet. *L'Avenir,* 27 May, as in *Mélanges catholiques extraits de l'Avenir.* Paris: Agence générale pour la défense de la liberté religieuse, 1831, 2, 211–7.

Coux, C. de, 1831l. De l'état des pauvres en Irlande. *L'Avenir,* 25 June, as in *Mélanges catholiques extraits de l'Avenir.* Paris: Agence générale pour la défense de la liberté religieuse, 1831, 2, 117–24.

Coux, C. de, 1831m. Du projet d'une Église nationale. *L'Avenir,* 1 July, as in *Mélanges catholiques extraits de l'Avenir.* Paris: Agence générale pour la défense de la liberté religieuse, 1831, 2, 295–300.

Coux, C. de, 1831n. Troubles de Marseille. *L'Avenir,* 25 August, as in *Mélanges catholiques extraits de l'Avenir.* Paris: Agence générale pour la défense de la liberté religieuse, 1831, 1, 448–56.

Coux, C. de, 1832. *Essais d'économie politique.* Paris: Agence générale pour la défense de la liberté religieuse.

Coux, C. de, 1835. *Discours prononcé par M. le professeur de Coux le 4 décembre 1835 à l'ouverture de son cours d'économie politique à l'Université Catholique de Louvain.* Louvain: Vanlinthout and Vandenzande.

Coux, C. de, 1836a. Cours d'économie politique [syllabus]. *L'Université catholique,* I, 56–7.

Coux, C. de, 1836b. Cours d'économie sociale. *L'Université catholique,* 1, 90–7; 274–81; 522–8; and 2, 161–8; 409–16.

Coux, C. de, 1837a. Cours d'économie sociale. *L'Université catholique,* 3, 96–102; 241–6; and 4, 81–90; 246–54.

Coux, C. de, 1837b. Christian political economy. *The Dublin review,* 3, 165–98.

Coux, C. de, 1838a. Cours d'économie sociale. *L'Université catholique,* 5, 165–71; 405–12; and 6, 405–11.

Coux, C. de, 1838b. Saint-Simonism. *The Dublin review,* 4, 138–79.

Coux, C. de, 1838c. The archbishop of Cologne. *The Dublin review,* 4, 232–45.

Coux, C. de, 1838d. Belgium and Holland. *The Dublin review,* 5, 463–96.

Coux, C. de, 1839a. Trade with France. *The Dublin review,* 6, 357–95.

Coux, C. de, 1839b. Cours d'économie sociale. *L'Université catholique,* 7, 85–92; 325–31; and 8, 165–71.

Coux, C. de, 1839c. Des nouvelles théories sociales, au XIXe siècle. Le saint-simonisme. Owen. Fourier. *Revue de Bruxelles*, August, 100–18.
Coux, C. de, 1839d. Histoire du saint-simonisme. (French version of Coux 1838b). *Revue de Bruxelles*, October, 1–58.
Coux, C. de, 1840a. Cours d'économie sociale. *L'Université catholique*, 9, 10–6; 405–10; and 10, 405–12.
Coux, C. de, 1840b. Exposé des vrais principes sur l'instruction publique, par Mgr. l'évêque de Liège. *L'Université catholique*, 10, 68–73; 149–56.
Coux, C. de, 1844. De l'école politique nationale au point de vue de la France. *Le Correspondant*, 6, 24–58.
Coux, C. de, 1844–1845. *Cours d'économie politique*. Manuscript 1M22. Lille: Université Catholique, Bibliothèque Universitaire Vauban.
De Ram, P.F.X., 1840. *Quelques mots sur l'Université Catholique de Louvain*. Brussels: Vanderborght.
Dudon, P., 1911. Lettres inédites de Lamennais à de Coux. *Études*, 78–90.
Duroselle, J.-B., 1951. *Les débuts du catholicisme social en France, 1822–1870*. Paris: Presses Universitaires de France.
Encrevé, A., 1985. *Les protestants en France, de 1800 à nos jours. Histoire d'une réintégration*. Paris: Stock.
Faccarello, G., 1986. *Aux origines de l'économie politique libérale: Pierre de Boisguilbert*, Paris: Anthropos, revised edn (1999), *The foundations of Laissez-faire. The economics of Pierre de Boisguilbert*. London: Routledge.
Faccarello, G., 2010a. Bold ideas. French liberal economists and the state: Say to Leroy-Beaulieu. *The European journal of the history of economic thought*, 17 (4), 719–58.
Faccarello, G., 2010b. "She tells him to be gone." Population, poverty and welfare in France during the first nineteenth century: the heyday of a controversy. Paper prepared for the international symposium: 'Population, Poverty and Welfare in the History of Economic Thought', Tokyo: Waseda University.
Faccarello, G., 2014. From the foundation of liberal political economy to its critique: theology and economics in France in the 18th and 19th centuries. *In:* P. Oslington ed. *The Oxford handbook of Christianity and economics*. Oxford: Oxford University Press, 73–93.
Faccarello, G. and Steiner, P., 2008. Political economy and religion in early nineteenth century France. *In:* B.W. Bateman and H.S. Banzhaf eds. *Keeping faith, losing fait: religious belief and political economy. History of political economy*, 40, annual supplement, 26–61.
Falloux, F.-A. de, 1856. *Le parti catholique. Ce qu'il a été, ce qu'il est devenu*. Paris: Ambroise Bray.
Festy, O., 1919. Le Vicomte Alban de Villeneuve-Bargemont et la condition des ouvriers français aux environs de 1830. *Revue des sciences politiques*, 42, August, 78–98; October, 234–61.
Fèvre, J., 1903. *Charles Périn, créateur de l'économie politique chrétienne*. Paris: Arthur Savaète.
Gerbet, O.P., 1832. *Introduction à la philosophie de l'histoire*. Louvain: Vanlinthout and Vandenzande.
Gerbet, O.P., 1836. Discours préliminaire. *L'Université catholique*, 1, 9–53.
Lafarelle-Rebourguil, F.-F. de, 1839. *Du progrès social au profit des classes populaires non indigentes, ou Études philosophiques et économiques sur l'amélioration matérielle et morale du plus grand nombre*, Paris: Maison.
Lallier, F., 1835. D'une nouvelle école d'économie politique. *Revue européenne*, 1, 129–48.

Lamennais, H.-F. Robert de, 1830a. Introduction. *L'Avenir*, 16 October, as in *Mélanges catholiques extraits de l'Avenir*. Paris: Agence générale pour la défense de la liberté religieuse, 1831, vol. 1, 1–8.

Lamennais, H.-F. Robert de, 1830b. Des doctrines de l'Avenir. *L'Avenir*, 7 December, as in *Mélanges catholiques extraits de l'Avenir*. Paris: Agence générale pour la défense de la liberté religieuse, 1831, vol. 1, 9–17.

Lamennais, H.-F. Robert de, 1831a. De l'avenir de la société. *L'Avenir*, 28 and 29 June, as in *Mélanges catholiques extraits de l'Avenir*. Paris: Agence générale pour la défense de la liberté religieuse, 1831, vol. 1, 53–74.

Lamennais, H.-F. Robert de, 1831b. Ce que sera le catholicisme dans la société nouvelle. *L'Avenir*, 30 June, as in *Mélanges catholiques extraits de l'Avenir*. Paris: Agence générale pour la défense de la liberté religieuse, 1831, vol. 1, 75–85.

Lamennais, H.-F. Robert de, 1834. *Paroles d'un croyant 1833*. Paris: E. Renduel.

Lamennais, H.-F. Robert de, 1838. L'omnium, association du crédit général. *Revue des deux mondes*, 3, September, 576–89. [In the table of contents of the issue, this article has a different title: D'un nouveau système de crédit général].

Lamennais, H.-F. Robert de, 1930. *Le portefeuille de Lamennais. Publié et annoté par Georges Goyau*. Paris: La Renaissance du Livre.

Lamennais H.-F. Robert de, et alii, 1831. *Mélanges catholiques extraits de l'Avenir*. Paris: Agence générale pour la défense de la liberté religieuse.

Leroy-Baulieu, A., 1902. *Les doctrines de la haine. L'antisémitisme, l'antiprotestantisme, l'anticléricalisme*. Paris: Calmann-Lévy.

Louandre, C., 1847. De la production intellectuelle en France depuis quinze ans. *Revue des deux mondes*, 20, 255–86; 416–46; 671–703.

L'Université catholique. Recueil religieux, philosophique, scientifique et littéraire (1836–1855). Paris: E.J. Bailly & Cie, and Au Bureau de l'Université Catholique.

Martin-Doisy, F., 1855–1857. *Dictionnaire d'économie charitable*. Paris: J.-P. Migne.

Montalembert, C. F. de, 1863. *L'Église libre dans l'État libre*. Paris: Ch. Douniol, and Didier & Cie.

Montlosier, F.-D. de Reynaud de, 1826a. *Mémoire à consulter sur un système religieux et politique tendant à renverser la religion, la société et le trône*. Paris: Ambroise Dupont, Roret and Moutardier & Cie.

Montlosier, F.-D. de Reynaud de, 1826b. *Dénonciation aux cours royales, relativement au système religieux et politique signalé dans le "Mémoire à consulter", précédée de nouvelles observations sur ce système, et sur les apologies qu'on en a récemment publiées*. Paris: Ambroise Dupont & Cie, and Baudouin Frères.

Montlosier, F.-D. de Reynaud de, 1827. *Les jésuites, les congrégations et le parti prêtre en 1827*. Paris: Ambroise Dupont et Cie.

Moon, P.T., 1921. *The labor problem and the social Catholic movement in France. A study in the history of social politics*. New York, NY: Macmillan.

Nettement, A., 1854. *Histoire de la littérature française sous le gouvernement de juillet, 1830-1848*. Paris: Jacques Lecoffre.

Ozanam, A.-F., 1873. *Œuvres complètes de A.-F. Ozanam*, vol. X: *Lettres I*. Paris: Lecoffre.

Périn, C.H.X., 1864. Notice sur Monsieur de Coux. *Revue Catholique*, 15, February, 117–21.

Périn, C.H.X., 1865. Notice sur M. le Professeur de Coux. *Annuaire de l'Universtié Catholique de Louvain*, 365–73.

Périn, C.H.X., 1881. Le modernisme dans l'Église d'après des lettres inédites de Lamennais. *Revue Trimestrielle*, 15 October (offprint), Paris: Librairie Victor Lecoffre.

Ring, M.I., 1935. *Villeneuve-Bargemont, precursor of modern social Catholicism*. Milwaukee, WI: The Bruce Publishing Company.

Rousseau, L., 1841. *Croisade du XIXe siècle. Appel à la piété catholique à l'effet de reconstituer la science sociale sur une base chrétienne. Suivi de l'exposition critique des théories phalanstériennes.* Paris: Debécourt.
Russell, M., 1893. The early Dublin reviewers. Unpublished memoranda of authors' names [Part I]. *The Irish monthly*, 21, 78–90.
Sacquin, M., 1998. *Entre Bossuet et Maurras. L'antiprotestantisme en France de 1814 à 1870.* Paris: École Nationale des Chartes.
Tanaka, T., 2001–2002. La question sociale et la politique. Une origine philosophique de l'État social dans les années 1830 en France. *北大法学論集 (Hokkaido law review)*, 52 (4), 382–27 and 52 (6), 268–19 (Japanese numbering).
Théry, A., 1911. *Un précurseur du catholicisme social, le vicomte de Villeneuve-Bargemont.* Lille: A. Taffin-Lefort.
Thibeaud, H., 1864. Le comte de Coux. *Revue de Bretagne et de Vendée*, 5, 234–43.
Tiano, A., 1993. *Alban de Villeneuve-Bargemont (1784–1850): Le précurseur de l'Etat social ou un grand notable bien ordinaire?* Nîmes: C. Lacour.
Villeneuve-Bargemont, J.-P.-A. de, 1829. Le département du Nord sous la Restauration. Rapport du préfet de Villeneuve-Bargemont en 1828. Edited by E. Beaujot *Revue du Nord*, 25 (4), n. 100, 1939, 243–77, and 26 (1), n. 101, 1943, 21–45.
Villeneuve-Bargemont, J.-P.-A. de, 1834. *Économie politique chrétienne ou Recherche sur la nature et les causes du paupérisme en France et en Europe et sur les moyens de le soulager et de le prévenir.* Paris: Paulin.
Villeneuve-Bargemont, J.-P.-A. de, 1836. Cours sur l'histoire de l'économie politique. *L'Université catholique*, 1, 83–90; 223–9; 269–74; 356–62; 421–35; 509–22; and 2, 15–23; 85–95; 168–75; 241–9; 321–34.
Villeneuve-Bargemont, J.-P.-A. de, 1837. Cours sur l'histoire de l'économie politique. *L'Université catholique*, 3, 14–26; 165–77; 332–47; 401–16; and 4, 90–104; 161–76; 254–74; 321–39.
Villeneuve-Bargemont, J.-P.-A. de, 1838. Cours sur l'histoire de l'économie politique. *L'Université catholique*, 5, 11–37; 85–98; 245–61; 325–47; and 6, 7–17.
Villeneuve-Bargemont, J.-P.-A. de, 1839. *Histoire de l'économie politique.* Brussels: Société nationale.
Villeneuve-Bargemont, J.-P.-A. de, 1841. *Histoire de l'économie politique.* Paris: Guillaumin.
Villeneuve-Bargemont, J.-P.-A. de, 1844. Notice sur l'état actuel de l'économie politique en Espagne et sur les travaux de Don Ramon de la Sagra. *Journal des économistes*, 7, 358–80, as in *Économie politique. Recueil de monographies. Examen des questions sociales, agricoles, manufacturières et commerciales.* Bruxelles: Au Bureau du Journal des Économistes, 1844, I, 225–40.
Waterman, A., 1991. *Revolution, economics and religion. Christian political economy, 1798–1833.* Cambridge: Cambridge University Press.

Appendix 1. Syllabus of the 1832 Paris lectures on political economy

[This syllabus is to be found in Gerbet (1832), on an advertisement by the publisher, inserted between pp. 122 and 123. It shows how, at that time, Coux's system was not entirely formed.]

First part

1st Lecture. Introduction.

2nd – Of moral and material wealth.
3rd – Of Catholicism and philosophy as generators of wealth.
4th and 5th – Of legitimate and legal orders.
6th – Of property and inheritance.
7th – Of the Blessed Virgin as the type of the Christian woman.
8th – Of parties-priests ("Des Partis-Prêtres").[48]
9th – Of religious and philosophical beliefs in relation with population.

Second part

10th lecture. Of exchange.
11th – Of domestic and foreign trades.
12th – Of real value and artificial values.
13th – Of credit and public debts.
14th – Of wages, machines and religious holidays.
15th – Of taxes in their relation with national wealth.
16th – Of luxury and alms considered in the same perspective.
17th – Of Catholicism as the only possible protection against a universal bankruptcy.

Third part

18th lecture. Of the ancient era and the new era in political economy.
19th, 20th, and 21st – Of the causes of the actual disease.
22nd – Of Spain and Great Britain.
23rd, 24th, and 26th – Of Catholic regeneration, as the only permanent means of salvation for the society.
26th – Of a transitory system.

Appendix 2. Syllabus of the Malines and Louvain lectures on political economy (Coux 1836a)

[This syllabus (Coux 1836a) is in fact essentially a general presentation of Coux's lectures on social economics, which were to be published in *L'Université catholique.* The table of contents of his unpublished lectures on political economy proper is given below, in Appendix 3.]

48 The phrase "parti-prêtre" was coined by François-Dominique de Montlosier in the 1820s to refer to the propensity of the Catholic hierarchy to control everything in a state, including the political power (see for example Montlosier 1826a, 1826b, 1827). Coux used it again later in a paper on public instruction in Belgium (Coux 1840b).

Political economy is the science of the laws that govern the formation, distribution, and increase of the wealth of peoples. It was at first imperfect, and considered only one part of its vast field, because it dealt exclusively with the interests of the class of large industrialists. Wealth developed in consequence, but it was wrongly distributed and the fundamental conditions of its existence were disregarded. Thus, the wealth of some was made out of the destitution of others, and society, awoken from its dreams of prosperity by the cries of the poor, discovered that it had lost more in security than it had gained in opulence.

Science was thus obliged to find a new route, and the distribution of wealth, that is, the wage question, became the main subject of its study. As this question can only be solved through profound investigations into the initial conditions of human sociability, political economy was split into two distinct – while inseparable – parts, so that in the future, it will form a whole and be a science only in so far as it brings together, in the same teaching, social economics and this regulatory economics that was until recently treated as the whole of *political economy*. The lessons offered to the readers of *L'Université Catholique* will thus entail a course of social economics and a course of regulatory economics. The first will deal with the causes of wealth and the general laws, which govern its distribution and increase. The following propositions will be developed and proved:

1. The existence of wealth implies the pre-existence of any particular society, and the faith in a rewarding and vengeful God is the necessary condition of human sociability.
2. As this faith draws from each religion a special form, each religion generates a distinct society, a society, in which the development of wealth is limited by the nature of the religion on which it lies.
3. The philosophy of the non-believer – whatever the degree of perfection it reached – cannot create a society, nor keep to the society it takes possession of, the life it received from its primitive beliefs.
4. As social beliefs weaken, public prosperity loses its stability; and while a seeming progress can be brought by the invasion of incredulity, this progress necessarily ends with the destruction of the entire wealth.
5. The most favourable society to the development of wealth will be that which establishes the most clear-cut distinction between the spiritual and temporal powers, which ensures the greatest security of property, the greatest liberty to the individual, the greatest stability to the family, the greatest protection to the woman, the greatest welfare to the poor – a society, finally, in which men will have the greatest love for their fellow human beings and the greatest confidence in their love.

6. Each society will fulfil these various conditions to the degree allowed by its religion, and this degree will always depend on the analogies that exist between this religion and Catholicism.
7. Catholicism alone, and in an absolute way, fulfils the conditions proper to a cult of a perfect society. *Alone*, it liberates the worker by means of the miraculous intervention of charity, and the woman, the son, the citizen through the notion of duty – a notion grounded on love and by the help of which, in his family and in the society, he always strengthens the order through liberty, and liberty through order.
8. All the institutions, all the discipline of Catholicism, from the ecclesiastical celibacy to the celebrations, result on the human level in the increase of the wages and wellbeing of the poor.
9. The first cause of the prosperity of the Protestant peoples was the reduction of wages: hence the industrial and even agricultural inferiority of the Catholic nations – an inferiority that the latter will not deplore for a long time.
10. The Catholic society being the one that entails the greatest number of elements of wealth, these elements develop in their own proper form, with the help of agriculture, industry and commerce.
11. Agriculture produce raw products; industry gives them a shape, and commerce make them exchangeable. Thus, agriculture and industry create direct and real values, and commerce creates indirect and market values [valeurs vénales].
12. There is a fundamental difference between these two kinds of values. It comes mainly from the changes that the issuing of paper-money, on the one hand, and the progresses in industry on the other hand, bring to the market value [valeurs vénales] of industrial products. The permanent decrease in the prices of these products will soon deprive industry of the main part of its influence on the wealth of peoples, and agriculture will regain its own.

When this first part of our lessons will be finished, we shall give the programme of our course of regulatory economics.

Appendix 3. Table of contents of the unpublished Lectures on political economy (Coux 1844–1845)

Part I. On production, considered independently from consumption

Chapter I. On the various kind of wealth.
Chapter II. On direct value and indirect value.
Chapter III. On exchange and sale.

Chapter IV. On the sign of value and credit.
Chapter V. On the different modes of production.
Chapter VI. On the different kinds of capitals.
Chapter VII. On workers.
Chapter VIII. On general income and its distribution.

Part II. On consumption, considered independently from production

Chapter I. On productive consumptions.
Chapter II. On unproductive consumption.

Part III. On the mutual relations between production and consumption[49]

Chapter I. On the law of demand and supply in relation with the price.
Chapter II. On the law of demand and supply in relation with the distribution of the primitive and secondary incomes.
Chapter III. On population and its laws.
Chapter IV. On taxation.
Chapter V. On home trade and foreign trade.
Chapter VI. On corn trade.
Chapter VII. On industrial competition.
Chapter VIII. On colonies and emigration.
Chapter IX. On banks.
Chapter X. On public debts.
Chapter XI. On foreign exchange.
Chapter XII. On industrial companies.
Chapter XIII. On the mercantile system, the prohibitive system, and free trade.
Chapter XIV. On the progress of political economy.

Abstract

During the first decades of the nineteenth century, the emergence of "économie politique chrétienne", with the aim of founding a new school of political economy, marked the French intellectual landscape. The name of J.-P.A. de Villeneuve-Bargemont is usually cited in this context. But, before Villeneuve-Bargemont, Charles de Coux had launched this approach powerfully. The present paper first states the circumstances of Coux's writings and their specific intellectual context. His project is then

49 There are some discrepancies between this table of contents, at the beginning of Part III, and the chapters that follow. This part is unfinished.

analysed, and his critique of political economy, his fundamental idea for an alternative approach, and his description of the logic of an industrial economy are discussed. Finally, the solutions he proposed to eradicate pauperism are examined. A brief statement of the significance of his work and legacy concludes.

Religion and the sociological critique of political economy: Altruism and gift

Philippe Steiner

At the beginning of the nineteenth century, political economy was generally considered to be a discourse on the mode of organising post-revolutionary societies in such a way as to promote the wealth and happiness of the population. This was notably the case for those French social scientists and political thinkers who coined the term "industrialisme." Initially, this doctrine was embraced by Charles Dunoyer and Charles Comte, then directors of the *Censeur Européen*; and also by Benjamin Constant, Henri Saint-Simon and one of his secretaries, Auguste Comte. Among the founding fathers of this doctrine was Jean-Baptiste Say, the great French political economist of the period.

This doctrine soon prompted dissenting interpretations (Faccarello and Steiner 2008, Faccarello 2014). On the one hand, Constant added a religious element that Say and Dunoyer found unpalatable, since they both thought that religious sentiment should not be part of the foundation of a new society. On the other hand, Saint-Simon considered that it was not only wrong, but also politically dangerous to base a society solely on material interest; something more was needed, with a new form of religion, a "new Christianism" according to the title of his last book (Saint-Simon 1825). When his disciples added to this religious requirement, the idea of organization as a crucial element for industrialism the movement broke apart, and dispute between the three differing approaches became bitter.

Religious dimensions became a key point in the nineteenth-century French social theory, notably, but not exclusively, in what came to be known as sociology with Auguste Comte and then with Emile Durkheim and the Durkheimians, to name the most salient contributors of this new field. The connection between the sociological inquiry and religion gave birth to specific critiques of political economy, in which altruism and gift took place as key concepts, both of them being still important pieces of contemporary social sciences, economics included.

I would like to demonstrate in this article that there is a strong connection between the religious component of French sociology and the critique of political economy is at issue. Comte's theory of altruism is certainly a key point of his religious credo, but it is also a specific response to a matter of common concern for French social scientists, for whom the new social order, or industrial society, lacked adequate cultural foundations. Furthermore, as a critique of the political consequences of the diffusion of political economy, altruism gave birth to a larger debate: first, among British social scientists, prompted by Herbert Spencer's lengthy discussion of altruism in his *Data of Ethics*; and second, among leading French economists during the second half of the nineteenth century.

Durkheim reacted strongly to Spencer's interpretation of altruism, and thus he endorsed many points already made by Comte when the critique of political economy was at stake. Nevertheless, he modified substantially Comte's view of altruism and, with the decisive work of his nephew Marcel Mauss, the religious dimension of Comte's critique went on with the issue of gift-giving.

In the first section I consider how selfish behaviour, or egoism, became treated as a major threat endangering the creation of industrial society by those concerned about the diffusion of political economy. I then summarise the methodological critique set forth in the *Cours*, before connecting this critique to the economic content of the *Système* and the concept of altruism. In the following section, I contrast Spencer's view of altruism to that held by Comte, and then I consider the reaction of French political economists, defending the moral value bought about by their science. In the final section, I explain how the Comtean approach was re-enacted by Durkheim and then by Mauss, at the head of the "sociology of religion" section of *L'Année sociologique*, the Durkheimian journal, to give birth to the theory of gift-giving behaviour that Mauss used to critique political economy in the 1920s.

1. Comte on altruism

Following the path initiated by Saint-Simon, Saint-Simonians abandoned the idea that industrial society could be based on egoism alone. They now insisted on the moral dimension, since a stable social order requires a common moral doctrine: "An enduring society cannot exist without common moral ideas; this is as necessary on a spiritual level as a community of interests is on a temporal level. These ideas cannot be common if they do not have as their base a philosophical doctrine universally adopted in society. This doctrine is fundamental: it is the link that unites and consolidates all parties" (Saint-Simon and Comte 1821, p. 51). From this period onwards, the idea that a moral link balancing egoism, which they view as rampant, emerges as a leading principle in their writing on industrialism (Saint-Simon and Comte 1821, pp. 51–2; pp. 85–95, etc.).

The core message of the Saint-Simonian school, as exposed by Saint-Amand Bazard and Prosper Enfantin (1829), can be summed up as follows. They linked contemporary political and social instability (citing as an example the issue of the abolition of slavery) to the duality at the heart of human agency: "In two words, calculation or reasoning, science, applied to material interests, is not the sole factor motivating human action; we also act on the sympathy which fine arts arouse and favor; we are men of reason, but we are also impassioned, we are self-interested, but nonetheless we know how to devote ourselves to the most general." (Bazard and Enfantin 1829, p. 27). A commitment to the well-being of other people, and to other-oriented action, was then ascribed to religion, and the historical method finally emerged as a powerful tool explaining how religion could once more take its place in industrial society. They argued that industrial effort was made in isolation and egoism prevailed as a consequence of the slogan: *Laissez-faire, laissez-passer*. Every "industrial" sought to achieve his goal according to his own personal interest, without taking into account the collective interest. Does competition really offer a social mechanism capable of transforming self-interested behavior into a socially beneficial outcome, as the economists claimed? According to the Saint-Simonians, the answer was in the negative, as the recurrence of commercial crises plainly showed; they consequently felt the need to promote an "enthusiasm for collective life" and to spread a "love of the universal family of man" (Bazard and Enfantin 1829, p. 104). A new religion would help achieve this: "By proclaiming that religion is destined once more to reclaim its rule over societies, we are undoubtedly far from claiming that it is necessary to restore any one religious institution from the past, no more than we call for the reinstatement in societies of the ancient orders of war or of slavery. We are proclaiming a new moral condition, a new political condition; and thus also a very new religious condition; because, for us, religion, politics, morals are only different names for the same thing. This problem [...] is no less likely to be posed and solved in terms at once simple and clear; the paths of investigation to be followed, the means of demonstration to be used in this connection, are the same as those which we previously employed" (Bazard and Enfantin 1829, p. 415).

As a former secretary of Saint-Simon, Comte was following a similar path, but in his own way.

Comte gave a new twist to his own system by the end of the 1840s, according to some of his disciples who disagreed with his so-called "subjective synthesis" (Littré 1869, pp. 538–52). In the lectures that Émile Littré has attended in 1849 with some members of the Positivist Society, and then in the massive four volumes *Système de politique positive*, Comte placed great emphasis on the functioning of the human brain, and on the idea that the heart (emotions) should prevail over the brain (mind).

The importance of the brain was nothing new to Comte, since he had already considered this topic in his *Cours de philosophie positive* – in the last lecture on biology, just before the part devoted to society and social sciences. Comte relied on Franz-Joseph Gall's phrenology,[1] and his anatomical hypothesis about the location of the various functions of mind in the human brain. Contrary to the "metaphysical" approach to psychology followed by Descartes and Malebranche, and then by Antoine Destutt de Tracy and the French Idéologues, Comte emphasised the positive approach adopted by Gall. He particularly appreciated Gall's distinction between the affective and the intellectual parts of the brain, and his mapping of the various functions of the brain. However, he found Gall's work wanting and scientifically fuzzy: "In my view, to give it a scientific form one has just to acknowledge that the first category [appetency] is about the isolated individual or, at best, the family, and their successive needs, such as reproduction, education of offspring, sustenance, place to live, accommodation, etc.; whereas the second category [feelings] is more specific, requiring the existence of some forms of social relations" (Comte 1975, I, p. 868).

Comte went no further in his *Cours*; but he came back to Gall's phrenology when he developed his approach to religion and altruism. What was a plausible hypothesis in the 1820s was considered a dead end by the later 1840s, hence the negative reaction of Littré. Nevertheless, Gall's phrenology was at the root of Comte's theory of human intellectual structure summarised in the table dedicated to the "Classification of the 18 functions within the brain" which can be read as Comte's contribution to the provision of a "scientific form" for phrenology. This "cerebral table" was for him of definitive importance: he emphasised to the reader that he had

1 Phrenology, or the science of the mind, was initiated by Gall (1758–1828), a German physician, who was among the first to consider the brain as the sole source of mental activity. Comte used that term in his *Cours*, but he qualified his reference in stating firstly, that it was a science in progress and not an established one; and second, that animals should be included (Comte 1975, I, p. 851).

had to go through ten successive drafts before reaching the final version of the table (Comte 1890, I, p. 680). This was then reproduced in the *Système*, in the *Catéchisme* and in his political pamphlet (*Appel aux conservateurs*).

Comte's comments on his table stretch over 50 pages of the first volume of the *Système* (Comte 1890, pp. 680–726), which he prefaces with a eulogy to Gall's achievements. The presentation of the cerebral table opens with a statement of the great human problem, the subordination of individuality to sociality, interpreted as the "natural basis of the true general theory of affective life" (Comte 1890, p. 692). Comte then explains the structure and meaning of his table. First, there is a threefold division – a very general feature of Comte's thought – between the heart (the loving part of the human being), the mind (the thinking part) and the character (the active part). The altruism versus egoism conflict is located in the loving dimension, in which Comte distinguishes no less than ten instincts. The instincts are sorted according to the dual rule of decreasing energy and increasing social importance. For example, the first instinct, the instinct of nutrition, is the most energetic one, since nutrition is an absolute necessity, but it is less important in term of morality; the opposite applies to kindness or the love of humanity, the 10th instinct, which is morally the most important, but the least energetic.

Comte sorts these 10 instincts into three categories. Five instincts (nutrition, sex, maternal, military or destructive, and industrial or constructive) make up *interest* or pure egoism; then two intermediate tendencies (domination and approbation) are egoistic, but require social relations in order to satisfy the human drive toward *ambition*; and, finally, there come three pure altruistic instincts (attachment, veneration and kindness). Comte's next step is to locate these groups of instincts. The five instincts constitutive of interest are situated at the rear of the brain, in closer contact with stimuli coming from the body; the two intermediate tendencies occupy the upper middle part of the brain, upper because their moral dignity is superior to interested instincts, and middle because they are in-between egoism and altruism. Finally, the three altruistic instincts are in the middle of the forefront of the brain: kindness first, followed by veneration, while attachment makes the link with egoistic instincts.[2]

Some comment may be of some use at this point in order to understand the meaning attached to this classification, and its connection to the critique of political economy. First, localising basic instincts within the brain seemed at the time to be a strange approach to the social sciences – and

2 Attachment, as we shall see below, is often characterised as a form of "collective egoism", notably within the family; this explains why Comte placed this instinct in close proximity to the egoistic instincts.

this explains the negative reaction of some positivists, such as Littré, while other social scientists interested in altruism simply paid no attention to this approach. However, the approach now conforms to recent research in neurobiology, and the conception of altruism as an instinct (Pickering 2009, II, p. 345). Furthermore, it also corresponds to recent neuro-economics, where economists use imagery related to brain function to identify the regions implicated in the decision-making process[3]. Second, it is important to emphasise that Comte does not treat egoism and altruism as two radically opposed instincts. Instead, he carefully explains that egoism and altruism can blend, as is the case with the two intermediary tendencies: "between the direct interest of the isolated individual and true social feeling there exists an indirect interest, which is still individual but which brings each individual into relation with the other in order to obtain individual satisfaction" (Comte 1890, I, p. 694). Third, Comte devotes one whole volume to explaining how these altruistic instincts – attachment, veneration and kindness – are supported by social categories, particularly by the sociocratic clergy in society, and by women in the family. The important point here is that both Comte's description of the ideal functioning of industrial society and his critique of political economy were based upon his views concerning altruism.

2. From the methodological critique of political economy to altruism as a counterforce to egoism

Auguste Comte's work is not thought to form a significant contribution to political economy, although his methodological critique of political economy had some influence during the second half of the nineteenth century, when the historical school challenged the more abstract conception of political economy then gaining momentum.[4] If Comte's critique is considered to be of minor interest, then the second part of Comte's intellectual career, dominated by the development of his religion of humanity, is entirely overlooked. For example, John Stuart Mill considered Comte's

3 "Brain imaging is currently the most popular neuroscientific tool. Most brain imaging involves a comparison of people performing different tasks – an "experimental" task and a "control" task. The difference between images taken while subject is performing the two tasks provides a picture of regions of the brain that are differentially activated by the experimental task" (Colin Camerer, George Loewenstein and Drazer Prelec 2005, p. 12).

4 Comte's methodological critique was in line with those of some leading German (Karl Knies) and Irish (John Kells Ingram and Thomas Cliffe Leslie) economists associated with the historical school. Modern commentators consider this connection to be very slight (Shinoya 2005).

Cours de philosophie positive to be a significant contribution to the philosophy of science, whereas he considered his later work, dominated by the *Système de politique positive*, to be a pointless enterprise, tainted by a regulatory mania emanating from the pen of "a morally-intoxicated man" (Mill 1865, p. 336). As scientist-philosopher, Comte is therefore considered to be of limited interest to historians of economic thought;[5] and as a religious thinker, he is of no interest to them at all. Conversely, historians of the social sciences take no interest in the economic content of his social and religious thought.[6]

There are two reasons for challenging this situation. First, there is now a growing interest in the religious underpinnings of political economy, treating it as a political discourse whose scope extended far beyond the strictly economic domain. This is especially evident in France (Faccarello and Steiner 2008), given the political and social role played by the Catholic Church before and after the fall of the *Ancien Régime*; and it is also true of other countries, such as England and the United States (Bateman and Banzhaf 2008). Hence, historians of economic and social thought might treat Comte's religious views as a to key his post-theistic social theory, to use Andrew Wernick's words, and to the economic organisation that should be brought into being by the "sociocracy", a new religious elite spreading the credo of the religion of Humanity. Second, Comte's later works repay attention, since this is where altruism, a new word in the French language was established. Altruism is now a concept commonly used by economists. However, this was not Comte's intention when he coined the word in the mid-nineteenth century to counter the idea that human action had a selfish foundation, an idea that he and many other social observers saw as pervasive in an industrial society[7]. By focusing his attention on the opposition between egoism and altruism, an opposition deemed to be the "great human issue," Comte was not merely elaborating his own system of thought in terms of a so-called "subjective approach," and by developing the religion of humanity at the heart of his *Catéchisme*

5 According to Schumpeter, Comte's view of science was not of great interest, and his critique of political economy "a comedy of errors" due to an "honest ignorance" of the subject (Schumpeter 1954, p. 394, p. 418).

6 See notably Andrew Wernick's study devoted to Comte's religion of humanity (Wernick 2001), Thomas Dixon's study of the cultural history of altruism in Victorian Britain (Dixon 2008) and Mary Pickering's monumental intellectual biography of Comte (Pickering 2009, vols. II and III). French scholarship on Comte is no different on this score (Grange 2000, Karsenty 2006).

7 The origin of this new word is generally attributed to Comte; nevertheless, according to Hyppolite-Philémon Deroisin (1909, p. 139), a disciple of Comte, altruism was invented by François Andrieux, professor of literature in Ecole Polytechnique when Comte was a student (see as well Leroy 1954, p. 103).

positiviste (Comte 1852) and his *Système de politique positive* (Comte 1890). He also extended his critique to political economy, exposed in the 47th lecture of his *Cours de philosophie positive* (1830-42). In the later 1820s, having parted from Saint-Simon, Comte had no reason to take the "reform of political economy", the program that Saint-Simon had given him when they initiated their collaboration in August 1817, any further.[8] The few book reviews related to political economy or industrial activities that Comte wrote during that period show that this task did not enthuse him[9] – although they also show that his knowledge of political economy was meager, to say the least. Nevertheless, his classification of sciences, and the role that he intended to give to sociology, forced him to explain why political economy was not the science of the social realm that would organise industrial society in terms of the positivist motto: "Order and Progress." A critique of the methodological foundations of political economy thus became a central issue in the 47th lecture of his *Cours de philosophie positive.*

2.1 The methodological critique

Comte's 47th lecture is devoted to the social sciences, which he would soon label sociology rather than social physics (*Physique sociale*) because Adolphe Quételet, the Belgian astronomer, statistician and social scientist, had already used this formulation in the subtitle for his *Sur l'homme. Essais de physique sociale* (1835). As commonly found in Comte, he launched into an overview of the historical development of the social sciences before explaining what he had in mind. He briefly mentioned the approaches taken by Montesquieu and Condorcet, and then wrote "Some philosophical reflections on the nature and the topic of political economy" (Comte 1975, II, p. 92–8). His criticisms were mainly methodological:[10] first, economists were wrong to isolate their science from political science; second, since they had been educated as men of letters and lawyers, economists

8 When the young Comte became Saint-Simon's secretary, his major task was to "reform political economy" (Gouhier 1970, III, pp. 189–96).

9 In the later 1820s, he wrote two short papers, on the budget (1819) and on political economy and industry (1828), and two reviews, both published in 1828: of J.-B. Bidaut, *Du monopole qui s'établit dans les arts industriels et dans le commerce,* and of Swan, *Courtes observations sur l'état actuel du commerce et des finances de l'Europe* (Comte 1970, pp. 133–9 and pp. 171–93).

10 This is well known, so I limit myself to remind Comte's major point in this paragraph. The reader can find more detailed accounts of these methodological criticisms in previous studies: see for example Swingewood (1970), Steiner (2011, pp. 165–75).

did not have the scientific training needed to build a new science. An exception was made for Adam Smith, notably because Comte thought so highly of his *History of Astronomy* that he put that essay on the reading list that he drew up for workers in his *Catéchisme positiviste* (Comte 1852, p. 37)[11]. Third, political economy was highly metaphysical, since it supposed that economic actors were perfect calculators of their own interest. The language of science (mathematics) used by some economists – Comte had in mind Destutt de Tracy's long introduction to his *Traité d'économie politique* – appeared meaningless to him because it was tainted by metaphysical conceptions of psychology. At this point, his critique of political economy and his comments on Gall's phrenology converged. The metaphysical approach to psychology and to the functioning of the brain attributed a superiority of reason over the passions, a position deemed erroneous by Comte. The remaining unique passion was "egoism under the command of the intellect," an erroneous conception that was at the root of a misconception of human beings: "Hence, man has been portrayed, against all evidence, as an intellectual being, processing continuously, without noticing, a vast number of imperceptible calculations, without any form of spontaneity, from his most tender childhood" (Comte 1975, I, p. 856). A few pages later, targeting Helvetius's utilitarian views on ethics,[12] he rejected the idea of "egoism treated as the necessarily unique principle of ethics, it being not necessary to stress here the considerable danger of this view" (Comte 1975, p. 862). He favoured instead the Scottish school of Hume, Smith and Ferguson, notably because they took account of both egoism and sympathy (Comte 1975, pp. 862–3). Fourth, there was no progress in political economy; economists wasted their time in endless polemics over value, utility, production and the like. Fifth, and this was more political or sociological than methodological, Comte rejected the slogan of free trade on the grounds that it represented an unwarranted attempt to legitimate the lack of market regulation. Consequently, political economy was condemned for systematising the current state of (economic) anarchy. Comte finally criticised the economists' view of the machinery question, and

11 Comte was familiar with Smith's *Wealth of Nations* (Comte 1975, II, p. 93); however, by the early nineteenth century Smith's Theory of Moral Sentiments had slipped into obscurity, and Comte is not unusual for the time in showing no knowledge of its arguments. This could well explain why he did not recognize the way in which the egoism with which Smith's work was then associated led to a very partial understanding of the distinction between self-love, vanity and benevolence in *Wealth of Nations.* For a comparison between Smith and Comte on the issue of morality, see Rutten (1972, chapter 3).

12 See Helvetius's *De l'esprit* (1758) and his posthumously published book, *De l'homme* (1773).

claimed that economists could not neglect issues related to time and transition periods.

This very negative assessment of political economy left room for one enduring favourable comment: political economy paved the way for positive philosophy, since it rightly emphasised and explained the role of the division of labour. Economists were therefore praised for their explanation of the solidarity between the various interests within society (Comte 1975, II, pp. 95–6).

The main response to Comte's criticisms came from Mill in his *Logic*: he argued that the rational behavior of economic agents was a hypothesis, and not a description of actual behaviour; and also that political economy as a separate science was of use in understanding an extensive category of phenomena "in which the psychological law mainly concerned is the familiar one, that a greater gain is preferred to a smaller" (Mill 1843, II, p. 901). French economists did not react publicly to these criticisms, and it is possible to speculate that, had the *Journal des économistes* been founded earlier than December 1841, it would have swiftly answered and rebutted Comte's strictures on the method of political economy. Curious as it may now appear, a number of socialist thinkers were given the opportunity to explain their points of view in the pages of the *Journal des économistes.*[13] The situation changed when political economists felt that they had to fight not only against their arch-enemy – the protectionists – but also against socialist thinkers, who became more prominent after the fall of the constitutional monarchy in July 1848 and the launching of the second republic.[14] The open-mindedness that characterised the period during which French economists launched the *Journal des économistes* was over. It was not by chance that Gustave de Molinari (1850) wrote a review of Comte's booklet on positivism – his *Discours sur l'ensemble du positivisme* – and that Henri Baudrillart (Baudrillart 1854), professor of political economy at the Collège de France, published in the *Journal* some years later his

13 As with Pierre-Joseph Proudhon, who eventually published his *Système des contradictions économiques ou philosophie de la misère* with Guillaumin, the leading publisher of French economists Louis Blanc and Etienne Cabet were also invited to write for the *Journal des économistes* at the very beginning of the 1848 revolution.

14 One should bear in mind that during the 1848 revolution the government had abolished the few existing professorships in political economy because of their supposed connection to the monarchy, and because the new government wished to further the development of a truly republican political economy. See "Suppression de la chaire d'économie politique au Collège de France", *Journal des économistes,* April 1848: 57–67 and "Protestation de la société d'économie politique contre la suppression de l'enseignement de l'économie politique", *Journal des économistes,* May 1848: 113–28.

opening lecture, which was devoted to dismissing the idea that political economy was a science favouring individualism at the cost of solidarity.

Molinari opened his review with a harsh statement: "This is a new sect" (Molinari 1850, p. 247), meaning that Comte's views were similar to those already studied and criticised by Louis Reybaud in his *Etudes des réformateurs sociaux ou socialistes modernes.*[15] The review was mostly negative, and not intended to offer a dispassionate assessment of Comte's views. Molinari briefly mentioned the *Cours*, but moved immediately to the philosophical and religious substance of Comte's doctrine. Molinari explained that, at the scientific level, sociology was simultaneously "the science of social relations, the political economy and the political science of positivism" (Molinari 1850). This sociology seemed to him mainly confusing: property was conceived in the same way communists saw it; the process of the accumulation of capital was not clear, and Comte misunderstood the Malthusian theory of population. Coming to the religious dimension of positivism, Molinari mocked the detailed table displaying the weekly feasts of the "Abstract cult of humanity," which he reproduced in his review. Positivist ethics and the positivist philosophy of history were not well regarded because they were either trivial – to ask for more benevolence, friendship, and justice is not so very different from Christian morality – or hypothetical. Molinari was pleased to note that Comte did not hint at a statist approach to social change, and he praised Comte's philosophical mode of life; he was a distinguished mathematician, he added. Summing up, he told the reader: "positivism has nothing to offer that is superior to what we already have. This is simply a utopia, like the utopia of Saint-Simon, Fourier, Cabet, Blanc, and Proudhon" (Molinari 1850, p. 255).

Baudrillart's article dealt with a group of writers who complained of the absence of solidarity as a topic in the writings of political economists; no specific writers were named, neither Comte nor any other being mentioned. For Baudrillart solidarity was a mystery, comparable to the Christian dogma of the Fall of Man and his redemption (Baudrillart 1854, p. 322). These mysteries did not belong to the subject matter of political economy; nonetheless, economists could take the existence of solidarity into account. Accordingly, a large part of the article was devoted to showing that solidarity was not limited to fraternity, and that solidarity was at

15 The first edition was published in 1840, and the fourth in 1844. The preface to the sixth edition of 1864 contains an interesting comment on his change of mind: "I saw myself confronted with nothing but small sects that appeared to be animated by a real devotion. Benevolence was possible. I was led to see these incipient disparities as curiosities and not as dangers, a gentle madness that could be cured through appropriate healing. Later on things went awry, and the response had to change." (Reybaud 1864, I, p. ii)

the very root of political economy, if under a different name: exchange was conceived to be the basis of human solidarity, and thus economists were in fact aiding the development of solidarity in their relentless fight against the protectionists (Baudrillart 1854, p. 333). Baudrillart was also adamant in ruling out the criticism of egoism. This critique lacks precision, he wrote, because self-interest is a good thing, whereas egoism is not. Referring to the seventeenth century dispute over "pure love,"[16] he pointed out that his opponents were more rigorous than Christian theologians, since they required that people act out of a purely disinterested motive, such that egoism would play no part at all in the economic domain. This was deemed impossible even for the religious domain, according to received Catholic faith. Baudrillart's comments on Comte's critique were however mistaken since, as we shall see in the next section, Comte had a different approach to these two topics, and he openly differed from the socialists and the communists, whom he explicitly criticised (Comte 1855: part 3).

Comte's views on political economy are mostly limited to the methodological criticisms of the 47th lecture of his *Cours*, conveying the idea that in the second phase of his work he had omitted the issues that had been central at the beginning of his intellectual career. Commentators acknowledge that he did pay attention to the material dimension of an industrial society suffused with the religion of humanity, but this was deemed to be of secondary importance, and no assessment of Comte's final views on political economy are offered. This apparent lack of interest can be explained. Comte's psychological health was fragile. He had had to break off his lectures on positive philosophy in 1826–1827. In the mid-1840s, he had an emotional crisis related to his encounter in 1844 with Clotilde de Vaux, followed by her death in April 1846. This was an episode of his life to which he referred in all his writings published after 1850, and to which he attributed his own regeneration as far as his capacity for love and feeling was concerned. Furthermore, during this second phase of his career Comte took for granted his views on positive sciences and gave primacy to religion. His personal history, the religious tone of his writings, the changes that he introduced with the "subjective synthesis" that Littré

16 This famous quarrel opposed Fénelon to Bossuet, two leading religious and political thinkers during the reign of Louis XIV. Fénelon claimed that pure love was possible within the Catholic faith, while Bossuet objected to this, notably because one has to abandon religious hope. For this theological debate and its connection to interest and the birth of political economy see Pierre Force's study (Force 2003). Mill also referred to this issue when he applauded the wisdom of the men who constructed Catholic ethics and compared Comte to "extreme Calvinists requiring that all believers shall be saints, and damns them if they are not" (Mill 1865, p. 338).

regretted so much, and the statements given by authoritative thinkers such as Mill; all of this suffices to explain why commentators could neglect his economic thinking after the *Cours*.

2.2 From methodological critique to the economy of altruism

However, a cursory examination of Comte's *Système de politique positive* shows that he continued his critique of political economy through the opposition of egoism to altruism, an issue already present in the *Cours* at the juncture between biology and sociology, where Comte rejected the metaphysical view of man as a rational maximiser. Curiously enough, he was in the meantime led to praise Charles Dunoyer for his brilliant comprehensive conception of production, Dunoyer being a utilitarian economist and fierce advocate of pure laissez-faire, who might at first sight appear to have been completely at odds with Comte's own ideas.

Comte found great merit in *De la liberté du travail* (Dunoyer 1845), reading it despite his practice of "cerebral hygiene" (he had stopped reading anything written by his contemporaries). He appreciated the "constructivist" view that Dunoyer adopted in one chapter, arguing that, contrary to Say's opinion, government should be considered to be a productive institution since it was concerned with the most important productive task of all: the production of civilised and moral men. Despite Comte's complete rejection of political economy and the principle of competition, both of which he thought irrelevant to industrial society, he appreciated Dunoyer's work and went so far as to recommend it to Mill in one of his letters: "Despite the fact that he comes from the milieu of economists, Mr. Dunoyer makes great efforts to head in an altogether healthier direction, making a remarkable distinction between two sorts of arts, the one acting on things and the other on men, and energetically reproaching political economy for only having concerned itself with the former. His rehabilitation of competition and his vigorous critique of the so-called labor organizations that thrive today can have, I fear, too absolute a character, and might tend to prevent indefinitely a genuine systematization of industry. But since he insists at length on the need to bring about reform within the population before instituting it at the governmental level, I think that his influence, despite an essential flaw in his conception, could be very useful in the current context" (Mill 1899, p. 411, Comte's letter to Mill, 28 February 1845). In this letter Comte acknowledged his interest, and confidence, in the power of government to modify the moral complexion of the population. It is important to understand here that Comte's new departure was to take his critique of political economy further, while explaining and

Table 1 Transmission processes according to Comte

Forms of transmission	Disinterested	Interested
Violent	Inheritance	Conquest
Voluntary	Gift	Exchange

advocating the beneficial role of altruism to the social fabric, thanks to Dunoyer's treatment of the "production of civilized man."

The economic dimension of social life was dealt with in chapter 2 ("Sociological assessment of the human problem, or positive theory of material property") of *Système de politique positive* volume II. The material strength of society is said to follow two "economic laws": the first stating that a man can produce more than he needs for his own consumption, while the second states that products can be stored. These two laws make possible the accumulation of wealth: a surplus may exist and it can be stored because goods are durable. These production and accumulation processes require that products be appropriated since, according to his theory of mind, the industrial instinct, a sub-category of "interest", belongs to the egoistic dimension of man. Property is therefore necessary to initiate the energetic instinct of improvement, of which the industrial instinct is a sub-category. However, the issue of property rights was not important to Comte, and he did not enter into more detail on this point; instead, he emphasised the role played by a third process, that of the transmission of accumulated wealth.

He had a broad and unusual view of the transmission process (see Table 1), which can be divided into four different forms – gift, (market) exchange, inheritance and conquest – distinguishing between violent and voluntary transmissions on the one hand, disinterested and interested ones on the other (Comte 1890, II, p. 155). Inheritance and exchange are common within industrial society, but conquest and gift were matters from the past, notably the latter being common among some tribes living in Oceania who "offer wonderful examples of the power of such as institution" (Comte 1890, p. 156).[17] Positive philosophy claimed that war had no real place in industrial society, and so Comte thought there was no

17 It is likely that Comte learned from Antoine Edouard Foleÿ about the role of gift exchanges in that region. A former student at the École polytechnique, Foleÿ lived in New Zealand from 1843 to 1846, then came back to Paris where he became a member of the inner circle of the Positivist Society. Later on he published a memoir of his travel – *Quatre années en Océanie*, Paris, Hetzel, 1866 – the second volume being devoted to the mores and customs of the natives. However, there are no comments on gift-giving behaviour in that book.

reason to ascribe any importance to conquest as a mode of transmission. Gift was a completely different affair since, as a disinterested and voluntary form of transmission, Comte considered that the "oldest and noblest form of material transmission will be more helpful to industrial reorganization than anything related to the useless metaphysics of our crude economists" (Comte 1890, p. 156).

At this point, Comte came back to his positive remarks on the division of labour, which had been identified in the *Cours* as the great discovery of modern economists. He explained that voluntary transmission was instrumental in the accumulation of capital, and therefore important to the division of labour that brought "each active citizen to function essentially for others" (Comte 1890, p. 159). This collective dimension of economic activity, exemplified by the division of labour, became the central tenet of Comte's approach to altruism in industrial society.[18] He suggested that the division of labour be considered at both a given point in time, and as something that occurred through the succession of generations (Comte 1890, p. 405). Hence, the importance attributed to the law governing bequests as a gratuitous form of transmission that was as important as gift-giving in realising the idea of altruism. Comte asked why, if such solidarity objectively existed, present citizens were unable to understand what they actually did, and why they conceived their exchanges and the division of labour in terms of self-interest. This discrepancy arose from "modern anarchy" – a general term pointing to the lack of any regulatory apparatus in the economic domain, and the spread of an individualistic way of thinking – and the lack of "a systematic doctrine of pacific behaviors, so that the latter is performed without giving each participant a just feeling of social dignity" (Comte 1890, p. 161). The issue of altruism was thus bound up with the critique of political economy. Nevertheless, in the *Système* Comte did not stop at a methodological critique, but sought to explain how disinterested behavior was at work within industrial society, even in its present unsatisfactory and incomplete form. Two social institutions were thus brought centre stage: first, the family, characterised by the affective domination of women; second, the clergy of the new positive religion, performing the art of bettering humankind.

According to Comte's sociology, society is not composed of individuals, but of families.[19] Therefore, the chapter on material wealth was followed by a chapter dealing with the functioning of the family and, more specifi-

18 This is mentioned in the *Catéchisme* as well: "As material activity is becoming more and more collective, it is tending ever more towards its altruistic character" (Comte 1852, p. 59).

19 His views on family are very conservative, as Mill pointed out: "[...] his opinion on the proper constitution of the family, and in particular of the marriage institution [...] is of the most orthodox and conservative sort" (Mill 1865, p. 310).

cally, with the way in which altruism is realised within a family. The three dimensions of altruism (veneration, attachment and kindness) are successively relevant to any living person: a child develops veneration for the parents who take care of her, and particularly for the mother; wife and husband develop attachment when they marry; and finally, parents experience kindness when they care for their children (Comte 1890, pp. 185–9). All appears to be for the common good, and these successive positions within the family create a system in which there is reciprocity between the veneration of the children and the kindness of the parents, a reciprocity which overlaps from generation to generation, and which is directly at the root of the feelings linked to the transmission of wealth through the law of inheritance. Nevertheless, according to Comte the situation is more complex, since behaviours within families are impure: familial altruism is generally tainted with egoism. This is the case whenever parents have an egoistic view of their children, as the object of their pride and vanity; this is also the case when children impatiently await their inheritance. These situations give birth to what Comte calls "domestic egoism" (Comte 1890, p. 200, p. 212), a situation that he suggests can be resisted by giving fathers an absolute freedom to make bequests which, associated with the possibility of adopting a child, weakens the biological links between father and sons and, at the same time, raises the level of efficiency in the transmission of capital whenever the adopted child has abilities and capacities greater than those of biological offspring. Besides these points, the idea to which Comte constantly returns is the affective superiority of women. They should not receive any material wealth from their parents; they should be protected from industrial egoism and stay at home while the husband performs the role of breadwinner. This sheltered position and this affective superiority gave women a unique power to solve "the great human problem, the subordination of egoism to altruism" (Comte 1890, p. 204)[20] through their role in the affective education of children.

The second institution necessary to solve the "great human problem" is spiritual power, a combination of the intellectual power that the sociocratic clergy has in the political domain, and the moral power of women within the family (Comte 1890, p. 313). The connection between these two powers comes from the fact that they both participate in the education of the child: women until they are fourteen years old for the affective aspect, and then the clergy dealing with the intellectual aspect. At this point, Comte made clear the importance he attached to Dunoyer's distinc-

20 The "great human problem" is mentioned on many occasions in Comte's writings of the period, notably in the *Catéchisme* (Comte 1852, p. 50, p. 60, p. 166, p. 170, p. 207, p. 262, p. 279, etc.).

tion between industries that apply their art to things, and industries that apply their art to human beings (Dunoyer 1845, II, p. 103; III, pp. 1–6). The former are the usual industries that one can find in Say's *Traité d'économie politique* – manufacture, commerce, agriculture – while the latter are divided into those industries acting on the body of men (physical education), and those operating on affective faculties, intellectual faculties, moral habits, and on religion. For this "unnoticed discovery", Dunoyer was lauded as "a wise economist" (Comte 1890, II, p. 319), repeated some pages later (Comte 1890, pp. 408–9); a public appreciation consistent with the private one evident in the letter to Mill quoted above. Apart from that point of agreement, Comte disagreed with Dunoyer's praise of competition,[21] and did not accept this "state of anarchy" as the ultimate rule for the proper functioning of the economic order. Instead, in the following chapter, Comte explained how the sociological clergy can "aspire to the modification of human will" thanks to the scientific and moral knowledge systematized in his positive philosophy (Comte 1890, pp. 356–7). The impulse at the root of the education provided by this clergy is to "prepare everybody to live for others in order to live in others" (Comte 1890, p. 371), which are according to Comte the two faces of altruism – objective and subjective. The objective face is nothing other than the division of labour, whereas the subjective face relates to the cult of humanity, according to which the salient elements of the life of the dead are remembered by the living. The major issue with which the clergy has to deal is the anarchy that reigns in the material dimension of contemporary society: in other words, the economy has need of a regulatory power founded upon new principles. Two of them are considered at this point in particular.

First, Comte again quoted again Dunoyer very favourably, since he was one of the few economists of the time to defend the idea of a completely unrestricted freedom to make bequests in whatever way was thought best.[22] As noted above, this freedom of bequest is necessary to weaken the "domestic egoism" that spontaneously appears within the

21 Dunoyer devoted an entire chapter to the social benefits of competition (Dunoyer 1845, I, pp. 408–71).

22 Throughout the nineteenth century, French economists discussed the role and the effects of the egalitarian law of inheritance set up by the Civil Code of 1804 (Steiner 2008); most considered that this egalitarian stance, subject to a minimum portion (at least a quarter of the legacy) left to the free disposal of the owner, conformed to the principles of the majority of French people, and they did not object to it beyond arguing about the size of the residual minimum portion. Dunoyer was among those who were in favour of a complete freedom of bequest right up until the very last moments of an owner's life (Dunoyer 1845, III, pp. 471–511).

family; it is also useful in order to achieve the efficient transmission of wealth from one generation to the next (Comte 1890, p. 406), since this freedom of bequest makes it possible to go beyond the family circle when transmitting accumulated capital. Second, Comte developed his "religious theory of wages," the central principle here being gratuitousness.[23] Labour, he argued, understood as service to humanity, cannot be properly compensated by a wage; the only proper remuneration for this service is to be found in the action itself. However, there must be a wage for the goods consumed during the performance of the service and, quite probably, for the training of the person performing the service. This payment applies only to workers or proletarians, who should receive from the capitalists a minimum living wage – plus an additional sum related to their actual performance so that they might be able to own a minimum amount of property: accommodation, furniture, and the like. This would bring to an end the unsustainable situation in which "proletarians are just itinerants living temporarily in the midst of occidental society" (Comte 1855, p. 412). The other social classes do not receive any wage: the clergy is paid by gifts offered to them as evidence of veneration; women are cared by their husbands; and finally, capitalists define themselves by their possession of a share of total wealth. They are prevented from expanding their share because of the "healthy competition" existing between them, and because they wish to gain the approval of the remainder of society. If this were not enough, Comte considers the possibility of discharging inefficient and greedy capitalists (Comte 1890, II, p. 417, p. 419).

This leads to an industrial world in which altruism prevails over egoism. The latter instinct is still present, since the alimentary instinct must be satisfied; this is the task of men entering the market so that they can provide their wife and children with food, clothing, and housing. Egoism is still present among the capitalist class, but is moderated by the "healthy competition" that Comte mentioned, without actually explaining what it really meant. Beyond that, altruism rules: in the family, thanks to the affective power of women; in society, thanks to the sociocratic clergy spreading the gospel of the religion of humanity, and receiving gifts as remuneration; in industrial relations, since the wage relation shrinks; finally, altruism also rules in intergenerational relationships, since the law of inheritance and policy favouring adoption bypass "domestic egoism" and permit greater efficiency in the transmission of accumulated capital.

23 The same argument is to be found in the *Catéchisme* (Comte 1852, pp. 146–7).

These "altruistic economic ideas" outlined by Comte were, to say the least, at odds with the current development of political economy.[24] One might expect that political economists would not pay very much attention to the idiosyncratic views of the Great Priest of the Positive Church. But this was not the case. Comte's views regarding altruism were successful in the sense that the most prominent contemporary economists and social thinkers did indeed pay attention to them.

3. Herbert Spencer, French economists and altruism

I have limited my investigation here to French economists, leaving out their English contemporaries. I will however take into account Spencer's contribution, since his *Data of Ethics* was a major contribution to the debate on altruism, and because he was so widely known and his book so widely translated and spread among the French economists that it is impossible to give an assessment of Comte's views on altruism without taking into account Spencer's approach to the subject.

3.1 Spencer and the conciliation approach

Beyond the role played by the Parisian devotees of Comte's work, Spencer played a decisive role in the spreading of Comte's ideas, not the least because of his use of the word "sociology", even after he had made public his methodological and political differences with Comte[25]. This is also true for the issue of altruism, however much Spencer might have sought to conceal his intellectual debt to Comte.[26]

Spencer paid great attention to altruism, and elaborated a quite different view of the concept.[27] There are some similarities of course: Spencer put great emphasis on the family as a congenial context for altruistic

24 Mill paid scant attention to them, even if he was ready to consider Comte's views as morally desirable (Mill 1865, pp. 340–1).

25 See his "Reason for Dissenting from the Philosophy of M. Comte" (Spencer 1864) and his book: *Man versus the State* (Spencer 1882).

26 In his study of the definition and meaning of altruism in Victorian Britain, Thomas Dixon states that "Spencer was by far the most influential theorist of altruism in nineteenth century Britain" (Dixon 2008, p. 183) and that, beyond what he wrote in his *Principles of Psychology* and *The Study of Sociology*, his *Data of Ethics* was instrumental in the diffusion of the word altruism in Britain (Dixon 2008, pp. 190–4).

27 Mill limited himself to a critique of altruism which he interpreted as the leading example of Comte's extreme views on morality, even if he was most favourable to the cultivation of other-oriented behaviours: "It is as much a part of our scheme as of M. Comte's, that the direct cultivation of altruism, and the

Table 2 Towards altruism: Spencer's four stages theory

From egoism to altruism	Egoism	Altruism
Competition	"to get his share"	"no more than his due share of altruism"
Compromise	"no more than his share"	"taking care that others have their share of altruism"

behaviour (Spencer 1879, p. 221, pp. 232–4, p. 293); he mentioned the role played by the transmission process between successive generations (Spencer 1879, p. 221, p. 293); finally, he stressed the necessity of combining egoism and altruism, but in such a different way that differences are here more salient than similarities. The first modification comes from the fact that Spencer considered altruism to be a specific form of action, and not an instinct; this is clear in his definition of altruism as "all action that, in the normal course of things, benefits others, instead of benefiting self" (Spencer 1879, p. 232).[28] This definition allows him to introduce the idea of non-conscious forms of altruism, notably when parents use their bodies for the birth of children, thereby diminishing the strength of their own body (Spencer 1879, p. 233). Interpreted in terms of the means-end relations, this form of altruism would then play a substantial role in his final view of sociality, as we shall see below. Second, Spencer held an evolutionary interpretation of the growth of altruism, instead of the historical approach of Comte. At first sight, Spencer appears to follow a meta-historical approach to the rise of altruism: from unconscious to conscious altruism in the family, from familial altruism to social altruism, and then with a four stages theory of the passage from egoism to altruism (see Table 2) as a consequence of his views on the evolution of cooperation cast into the means-end distinction (Spencer 1879, pp. 161–4).

Egoism is the necessary starting point, since without a clear effort–reward relation insufficient wealth will be produced, and there will be no possibility of acting altruistically. The first stage is thus a competition between egoistic actors. Then, due to positive externalities – to use a term absent from Spencer's book – a better situation is reached when egoistic actors find a compromise, where nobody claims more than his due share

subordination of egoism to it, far beyond the point of absolute moral duty, should be one of the chief aims of education" (Mill 1865, p. 339).

28 This definition obviously matches the current definition of altruism, in which the altruist benefits from the increased welfare gained by the recipient (Hammond 1987).

of the wealth produced. With the growth of wealth and the growth of human capacity to understand feelings experienced by others, altruism intervenes and, as the number of opportunities for altruistic actions declines with the amount of wealth, competition arises over opportunities for altruistic action. The final stage is reached when altruistic actors deliberately leave open the rare opportunities for altruistic action to other (Spencer 1879, pp. 296–7).

The ultimate difference is now quite easy to grasp. According to Spencer's evolutionary view, there were various evolutionary processes that moved society from egoism to altruism. Both types of action are thus necessary to engender a wealthy industrial society, contrary to Comte's view, who thought that the real danger embedded within industrial society was the supremacy of egoism over altruism, requiring therefore a cultural change to be made by the positivist clergy, women, and the proletarians, thanks to the positive religion of humanity. Spencer's views utilitarian and economic, the most surprising being the idea of "altruistic competition" (Spencer 1879, p. 296); furthermore, his argument was based upon an economic approach – a crude cost-benefit calculation – which limited the debate over altruism versus egoism to the benefit accruing directly or indirectly to individuals. Altruism and egoism were treated as if they were behaviours *on the same continuum*, in sharp contrast to Comte, who considered altruism to be an instinct and a value *different from* egoism, and who distinguished egoistic altruism from pure altruism. As a consequence, Spencer's conception of altruism involved no critique of political economy, whereas such a critique was central to Comte's approach to altruism as a set of instincts distinct from self-interested motivations. It was not by chance that Spencer separated off altruism from the religious content that was so central to Comte's account of altruism: in so doing Spencer excluded the dualistic view held by Comte, a perspective that had been shared with Saint-Simon during their collaboration in the early 1820s.The reaction to Comte's position by contemporary French economists took a different line, since they placed their anti-statist credo to the fore, using Comte's distinctions of wife/husband and family/market to counter his criticisms and his unconventional political conceptions.

3.2 Altruism, self-interest and French economic liberalism

By the end of the nineteenth century, critique of Comte's ideas was clearly an issue for French liberal economists. In 1864, Reybaud added a long chapter on Comte and positivism, mainly devoted to the vagaries of his personal life and mental illness (Reybaud 1864, I, pp. 284–380). Clémence Royer (1891) wrote a critique of Comte's sociology in Léon Say's and

Joseph Chailley's *Dictionnaire de l'économie politique*, so harsh that the editors explained in a footnote that they did not endorse all of his views. André Liesse's entry on sociology was no less critical, claiming that the so-called science of society advocated by Comte had not produced a single positive result; the only sociological author worth reading was Spencer (Liesse 1891). During the same period, Maurice Block dealt with the issue of sociology and egoism versus altruism in a book written to update the treatment of the principles and main achievements of political economy since Adam Smith (Block 1890). His assessment of Comte's achievements was negative: sociology, Block wrote, was the fruit of Comte's imagination, and it would never reach the status of a true science (Block 1890, I, p. 51). Block's main point concerned the confusion between science and art: Comte's synthetic approach was worthless in the domain of science, where the principle of the division of labour compels scientists to specialise. The same line of argument was presented in a chapter devoted to altruism and egoism: Block categorically rejected the idea that economists were preaching an egoistic point of view; instead, they were dealing with "legitimate self-interest" or "enlightened" interest. Paul Leroy Beaulieu concurred with Block, rejecting Comte's "pretense to subordinate political economy to sociology" (Leroy-Beaulieu 1894, I, p. 64).

Paul Leroy Beaulieu (1843–1916) needs to be singled out when considering the reaction of French economists to altruism. Founder and director of *L'économiste français* (1873–1938), a weekly newspaper devoted to the diffusion of sound economic ideas among an extensive public, and professor of political economy in different institutions such as l'École libre de sciences politiques and the Collège de France, his public lectures were published in a four-volume handbook which went through six editions from 1896 to 1914. A prolific author, he wrote on issues related to the social question – notably on women as a labor force in large-scale industry (Leroy-Beaulieu 1873) – and like many French political economists of the time, he made significant efforts to spread an understanding of political economy among the middle classes (Leroy-Beaulieu 1888, 1906); in this, he was successful, since these two books also went through numerous editions. A fierce liberal and a relentless advocate of European colonization, he was a central figure of French political economy in the decades preceding World War I.

Written as a response to the introduction of political economy in French high schools, his *Précis d'économie politique* stated in its opening pages that, contrary to a common view, political economy "is not a theory of egoism, and has a place for feelings of sympathy" (Leroy-Beaulieu 1888, p. 5). A society possessing a high level of morality would have obvious economic advantages, such as greater productivity, a reduced amount of speculation, and greater fairness in the distribution of wealth. He came back to this issue in the second chapter of his book on the economic role of the state, lamenting the incomplete view of human action that economists had borrowed from Adam Smith, focusing on self-interest, or more precisely, on the pecuniary interest (Leroy-Beaulieu 1890, pp. 34–5). This is not true, he wrote, notably because with the growth of wealth, the pecuniary interest ceases to be the sole spring of action and religious beliefs; sympathy and a number of other motivations including the refinements of *sport* gave rise "to institutions in favor of the common good" (Leroy-Beaulieu 1890, p. 35). Referring to Spencer's views on altruism, he emphasised that charitable institutions resulted from the decision of individuals (Leroy-Beaulieu 1890, p. 36). And in opposition to statist thinkers, notably German philosophers (Hegel and Lorenz von Stein) and economists, the so-called "academic socialists" (Adolph Wagner and Albert Schäffle), he stressed the role of self-interested behavior in the administration in the modern state, the true setting for the development of an obnoxious form of egoism. According to his (negative) views on republican government, he explained that greedy politicians knew that they were in control for a limited period of time, and that their behavior was not "driven or moderated by self interest" (Leroy-Beaulieu 1890, p. 71). If they were ruled by a feeling of honour, then they would look for "what is great instead of what is useful" (Leroy-Beaulieu 1890), an administrative vanity that would be worse than self-interested behavior. Altruism and egoism were not to be found where one might expect them.

In the introductory chapters of his four-volume *Traité théorique et pratique d'économie politique,* Leroy-Beaulieu examined in greater depth the issue of egoism and altruism, this time taking a different approach. Based on his own experience as a settler in North Africa, he first emphasized that self-interest is a spring for action found throughout the world, and cannot be attached to a specific moment of history, as the Comtean meta-history would have us believe. Then he considered the egoism versus altruism issue. On the one hand, following a longstanding philosophical tradition (Force 2003), he made a distinction between self-interest and egoism or self-love, explaining that egoism had nothing to do with self-interest, because the former was a morbid exaggeration of the latter (Leroy-Beaulieu 1894, I, pp. 68–9). If egoism does not leave room for other feelings, notably "what is called, after Auguste Comte, altruistic feelings or altruism," this is not true of self-interest, which can be reconciled with other-oriented feelings. He then modified what he had written about Smith's works, explaining that long before Comte, altruism was a core idea of the founder of modern political economy, since "one should not forget that Adam Smith is the author of a *Theory of Moral Sentiments*" (Leroy-Beaulieu 1894, p. 71). On the other hand, altruism actually did have an important role to play within political economy. According to him, self-interest was at work whenever the production and distribution of wealth was at stake, but altruism took over in the consumption process and, more generally, within the family (Leroy-Beaulieu 1894, pp. 71–2). Additionally, the generous donations made by wealthy entrepreneurs in the United States and also in France were of the greatest benefits to their fellow citizens. As a conclusion, he endorsed Spencer's conception of conciliation: "Thus, the principles of self-interest and altruism are not exclusive; they often exist in the same soul and to a high degree, but they do not apply to the same domain. The former motivates men in their economic activities, the latter guides the spending of their income and wealth" (Leroy-Beaulieu 1894, p. 76).

Leroy-Beaulieu's distinction between self-interest in the production of wealth, and altruism or sympathy, in the consumption process within the family, led him to Comte's views on education and inheritance. Like Comte, Leroy-Beaulieu had a most traditional view of woman's role, limited to household work and the care of the children; accordingly, it was better that young women be knowledgeable in the domestic arts rather than be given a formal education (Leroy-Beaulieu 1873, pp. 146–8, pp. 448–9). However, he did not believe it necessary to prevent women entering the modern labour force and, even worse, preventing them from doing so by creating legal and statutory obstacles, since "it is no business of the state to establish virtue, wisdom and health" (Leroy-Beaulieu 1873, p. 201). Instead, citing evidence from a manufacturer, he emphasised the beneficial consequences of efforts on the part of wise and other-oriented entrepreneurs in shortening hours of work in their firms, and establishing more humane conditions for women after childbirth. These economic sacrifices are not economically inconsistent, he wrote, since through the improvement of the health and productivity of his labour force "the sacrifice made by the manufacturer was not lost: it brought him a female labor force that was healthier, more assiduous, and more dexterous" (Leroy-Beaulieu 1873, pp. 438–9). This conciliation of self-interest and altruism was again central to his views on inheritance that, together with saving, was the bedrock of the accumulation of capital. Both are sacrifices for the well-being of others (Leroy-Beaulieu 1888, pp. 57–8) and he was pleased to quote Alfred Marshall's view that inheritance could be treated as a form of saving based on "family affection" (Leroy-Beaulieu 1894, I, p. 597). Following that line of thought, he did not fail to emphasise the need for life insurance as an excellent form of saving, especially for middle-class fathers (Leroy-Beaulieu, p. 598, 1906, pp. 322–3). Conciliation was also at the centre of his views on human capital. Personal skills are definitely to be counted as part of the capital of a nation; they are as productive as any other form of capital, and thus yield revenues to the holder of that capital. Nevertheless, he added, "other considerations can and must enter into decisions concerning the use of this specific capital, so strongly related to human personality: sympathy, the interest of Humanity, the love of glory" (Leroy-Beaulieu 1894, I, p. 244).

4. Durkheim and the Comtean legacy

"When there is a society, there is altruism, because there is solidarity" wrote Durkheim in his book on the division of labour (Durkheim 1893, p. 215), acknowledging his adhesion to the Comtean principle, against the point of view endorsed by economists. Nevertheless, Durkheim proposed a new approach to altruism, stressing its collective dimension and, above all, critiquing the interpretation provided by Spencer.

4.1 De la division du travail social

"Altruism" does not appear many often in *De la Division du travail social* – about ten times. Durkheim did not oppose systematically altruism and egoism, since the latter was as well contrasted with morality, solidarity, the pressure coming from society and professional ethics. Instead, Durkheim upheld the idea according to which group egoism has the power to curb individual egoism, pointing to a Russian doll structure of egoisms: "The unique power that can moderate individual egoism is the power of the group; the unique power that can moderate the egoism of a group is the power of a larger group" (Durkheim 1893, p. 455). Egoism was thus a general characteristic of social life and had no reason to be limited to the world of market exchanges. Nevertheless, in that first period of time, Durkheim pointed toward an economic institution – the professional group – when it came to find a group able to moderate individual egoism through the creation of moral limits that would delineate what the individual is entitled to. In the same years, these ideas were as well developed in Durkheim's lectures on socialism when he stressed the necessity to find moral limitations to regulate the economic world and, consequently, the egoistic feelings that were fostered by economic activity (Durkheim 1895, p. 267).

In fact, the main thrust of his thinking was directed toward a critique of Spencer's *Data of Ethics,* the book that gave Comte's ideas its international audience. Durkheim rejected the evolutionary schema set forth by Spencer according to which altruism came last as an embellishment available in a sophisticated and wealthy society. On the contrary, claimed Durkheim, altruism, that is to say the pressure of society upon its member, came first; the individual was the product of a long evolution and individual egoism followed suit: "Thus, altruism is not appearing, as Spencer says, as a kind of enjoyable ornament of our social life, but is always its fundamental basis.

How could we do without altruism? Men cannot live together without understanding each other, without doing mutual sacrifices, without making strong and durable bonds between them" (Durkheim 1893, p. 249).

This line of thinking was re-enacted later on, after the "intellectual revolution" that Durkheim went through in the end of the 1890s, with the strong emphasis put on religion as the basis of society.

4.2 Sacrifice and the production of altruism

The key point is to understand what is the social process that produces altruism as a moral force that brings the individual to make sacrifice and thus creating these strong bonds that are at the root of solidarity. Answering this issue requires to consider Durkheim's last great book, the one he devoted to the social process at the root of religious beliefs — *The Elementary Forms of Religious Life.* Here, Durkheim examined the power that religion's negative rituals give to believers; by negative rituals, he understood those rituals that prevent to do something, or that require some abstinence (food, sex, interaction, etc.). Negative rituals produce ascetic behaviours but they should not be limited to these proscription and interdiction since through the sacrifice of some useful behaviours, the individual increases her power, the power to going beyond herself and thus to coming closer to the society as a whole, that is a cognitive and sublimation process similar to the one at the root of faith[29]. This applies as well to the society: "Society, as well, is only possible at this price [...] Society requires necessarily a series of perpetual sacrifices from the individuals; society narrows our whishes, precisely because society raises the individuals above themselves" (Durkheim 1912, p. 452). As an other oriented behaviour, altruism is as well a form of restriction, a form of ascetism that produces as well this superior power that permits the individual to go beyond her own egoistic volitions and to link herself to the collective. Durkheim reaches then his final answer to Spencer's paradox on altruistic societies according to which altruistic actors, eager to give back what they receive from their

29 Without entering too much into the detail of Durkheim's sociology of religion, it may useful to remind the reader that, contrary to Comte and to Pierre-Joseph Proudhon who claimed that religion should be based on Humanity or on Revolution, as the new transcendental basis of faith, Durkheim did not consider that society is the modern form of transcendence. Instead, he considered that the *relation* between the individual and her society was similar to the *relation* between the believer and her god. This relational homological structure is the basis of his view according to which the process that explains how the society appears as a superior entity to the individual gives a clue to our understanding of the superiority that the believer gives to her god.

altruistic fellows, would not reach any positive outcome. Instead of such zero sum (or even negative sum) interaction, they would reach altogether a superior state of society through the power they have got while performing these mutual sacrifices.

However, Durkheim's approach does not point out clearly what are the current social practices that, in the economic domain, correspond to the sacrifice that can produce this superior state of solidarity among individuals in a modern society. This issue received a most interesting answer in Marcel Mauss' works.

The religious dimension of sacrifice was at the centre of Henri Hubert and Mauss' essay where they explained that sacrifices were religious practices thanks to which human beings could communicate with their god. Obviously, they linked the practice of sacrifice with the issue of egoism and altruism, or interested and disinterested behaviours (Hubert and Mauss 1899, pp. 304–5). According to the two Durkheimian scholars, sacrifice is disinterested in the sense that some resources are offered to the god, but it is interested since the one that offers a sacrifice expects to receive something from her god. This situation is exactly the one that Mauss put in key passages of his essay on gift-giving: gifts are supposed to be generously and freely donated when they are offered under the constraint of social pressure and associated with self-interested expectations (the counter-gift) (Mauss 1925, p. 262, see as well 147). Mauss' theory of gift-giving is thus an important development of the altruism versus egoism debate.

First, Mauss connected his theory of gift-giving to the production of solidarity: his wide knowledge of past societies was mobilised to explain how bonds among human beings and human groups were built. Furthermore, he explained in some bold passages of his conclusion that the same thing was at stake with the first institutional building blocks of what we call now the Welfare State (Mauss 1925, p. 258, p. 263). Second, Mauss connected his theory to the critique of political economy, explaining that interest was a new notion, almost unknown before the end of the eighteenth century. He thus followed the point of view already advocated by Bronislav Malinowki: men in archaic societies were not driven solely by self-interested behaviour, even if such behaviour was obviously at work. The point was to make clear that the purely self-interested behaviour of the so-called "economic man" is a social construction that belongs to the future, or better, that is one *possible* future of humankind (Mauss 1925, p. 272). Finally, in a move similar to Adam Smith's theory of the rules that men follow when exchanging commodities (Smith 1776, end of chapter 4, p. 44), Mauss was bold enough to add to his critique of political economy an explanation of the rules that men follow when they enter into gift-giving behaviour: hence, the famous three obligations to give, to receive, and then to give back.

An important step was thus achieved. Leaving the opposition between altruism and egoism for studying gift-giving actual social practices, Durkheim and the Durkheimians gave a new twist to Comte's critique of political economy. They still stressed the same methodological critiques of that social science (Steiner 2011: chap. 1; 2016: chap. 1 and 2), but they left out the Comtean discourse on the religion of Humanity and showed how individuals built their societies thanks to an alternative system of exchange, deeply different from market exchange but firmly associated to it.

5. Concluding remarks

Throughout these books, directly or indirectly, Leroy-Beaulieu was responding to Comte's strictures on political economy. He disentangled self-interest from egoism, the latter being an excess of self-interest as self-love;[30] following Spencer, he explained how self-interest and altruism can be reconciled through a shorter working day and better working conditions. Finally, in line with his positive appreciation of Comte's view on the social *consensus*, that is to say interdependence (Steiner 2016, p. 64), he considered the social dimension of the economy, notably saving and inheritance, including the use of human capital and gift-giving. By the later nineteenth century, therefore, Comte's views were not without influence on methodological debates among economists, and on sociologists such as Spencer.

However, the religious dimension that had been so important to Comte was lost. Altruism as a new form of religious belief and way of life had no place at all in the perspectives of Mill, Spencer, or of Leroy-Beaulieu on the functioning of modern industrial society. Leroy-Beaulieu thought that Christian and Muslim faiths were sufficient for nurturing the moral values required for the proper functioning of the industrial order, but beyond some specific points of contact, they belonged to two separate spheres of social life.

Does that mean that the initial religious impetus, so important in Comte's definition of altruism was entirely lost? The Durkheimian school demonstrated the contrary.

Altruism as a political challenge to egoism had still a religious dimension in the last part of Durkheim's work with his emphasis on the connection between sacrifice and social solidarity. At that time, Durkheim was no

30 It is worth pointing out that in his well-known study *Le suicide* (1897), the French sociologist Émile Durkheim followed the same line when he defined egoistic suicide as a result of an *excess* of individualism – he also defined altruistic suicide as a consequence of a lack of individualism. Durkheim progressively excluded the egoism versus altruism issue (Steiner 2016, chap. 3).

longer interested in the critique of political economy that occupied a significant part of his intellectual activity in the 1890s. The issue was given a new twist with Mauss who, on the one hand, followed Malinowsky in the debate over the historicity of "economic man" (Pearson 2000), and, on the other, stressed the role of gift-giving as a political counter force to the development of the market economy in his study of the current functioning of market society.

Acknowledgements

I am grateful to Gilbert Faccarello, Thierry Demals and the anonymous referees for their very helpful comments on previous versions of this paper.

Disclosure statement

No potential conflict of interest was reported by the author.

References

Bateman, B. and Banzhaf, S., eds., 2008. *Keeping faith, losing faith: religious beliefs and political economy. History of political economy. Annual supplement.*

Baudrillart, H., 1854. De la solidarité. À propos du reproche d'individualisme adressé à l'économie politique. *Journal des économistes*, March, 321–39.

Bazard, S.-A. and Enfantin, P., 1829. *Exposition de la doctrine de Saint-Simon. Première année.* Paris: Bureau de l'Organisateur.

Block, M., 1890. *Les progrès de la science économique depuis Adam Smith. Révisions des doctrines économiques.* Paris: Guillaumin.

Camerer, C., Loewenstein, G. and Prelec, D., 2005. Neuroeconomics: how neurosciences can inform economics. *Journal of economic literature*, 43 (1), 9–64.

Comte, A., 1975 [1830–1842]. *Cours de philosophie positive.* Paris: Herman.

Comte, A., 1852 [1922]. *Catéchisme positiviste.* Paris: Librairie Garnier Frères.

Comte, A., 1890 [1851–1853]. *Système de politique positive ou Traité de sociologie instituant la religion de l'humanité.* Paris: Larousse.

Comte, A., 1855. *Appel aux conservateurs.* Paris: Chez l'Auteur.

Comte, A., 1970. *Auguste Comte. Ecrits de jeunesse.* Paris: Mouton.

Deroisin, H.-P., 1909. *Notes sur Comte par un de ses disciples.* Paris: Librairie Ancienne et Moderne.

Dixon, T., 2008. *The invention of altruism. Making moral meaning in Victorian Britain.* Oxford: Oxford University Press.

Dunoyer, C., 1845. *De la liberté du travail ou simple exposé des conditions dans lesquelles les forces humaines s'exercent avec le plus de puissance.* Paris: Guillaumin.

Durkheim, E., 1893. *De la division du travail social. Etudes sur l'organisation des sociétés supérieures.* Paris: Alcan.

Durkheim, E., 1895 [1976]. *Le socialisme : sa définition, ses débuts, la doctrine Saint-Simonienne.* Paris: Presses Universitaires de France.

Durkheim, E., 1912 [1968]. *Les formes élémentaires de la vie religieuse.* Paris: Presses Universitaires de France.

Faccarello, G., 2014. From the foundation of liberal political economy to its critique: theology and economics in France in the eighteenth and nineteenth centuries. *In*: P. Oslington, ed. *The Oxford handbook of Christianity and economics.* Oxford: Oxford University Press, 73–93.

Faccarello, G. and Steiner, P., 2008. Religion and political economy in early nineteenth-century France. *History of political economy. Annual supplement*, 40, 26–61.

Force, P., 2003. *Self-interest before Adam Smith: a genealogy of economic science.* Cambridge: Cambridge University Press.

Grange, J., 2000. *Auguste Comte, la politique et la science.* Paris: Odile Jacob.

Gouhier, H., 1970. *La jeunesse d'Auguste Comte et la formation du positivisme.* 2nd ed. Paris: Vrin.

Hammond, P., 1987. Altruism. *In*: J. Eatwell, M. Milgate, and P. Newman, eds. *The new Palgrave. A dictionary of economics.* London: MacMillan, vol. I, 85–7.

Hubert, H. and Mauss, M., 1899 [1969]. *Essai sur la nature et la fonction du sacrifice. In:* M. Mauss, *Œuvres*, Paris: Éditions de Minuit, vol. 1.

Karsenty, B., 2006. *Politique de l'esprit. Auguste Comte et la naissance de la science sociale.* Paris: Hermann.

Leroy, M., 1954. *Histoire des idées sociales en France. D'Auguste Comte à P.-J. Proudhon.* Paris: Gallimard.

Leroy-Beaulieu, P., 1873. *Le travail des femmes au 19e siècle.* Paris: Charpentier et Cie.

Leroy-Beaulieu, P., 1888. *Précis d'économie politique.* Paris: Delagrave.

Leroy-Beaulieu, P., 1890. *L'Etat moderne et ses fonctions.* Paris: Guillaumin.

Leroy-Beaulieu, P., 1894 [1906]. *Traité théorique et pratique d'économie politique.* 4th ed. Paris: Guillaumin and Alcan.

Leroy-Beaulieu, P.. 1906. *L'art de placer et de gérer sa fortune.* 10th ed. Paris: Delagrave.

Liesse, A., 1891. Sociologie. *In*: L. Say and J. Chailley, eds., *Nouveau dictionnaire d'économie politique.* Paris: Guillaumin, 889–900.

Littré, É., 1869 [2007]. *Auguste Comte et la philosophie positive.* Paris: L'Harmattan.

Mauss, M., 1925 [1980]. *Essai sur le don. Forme et raison de l'échange dans les sociétés archäiques. In* M. Mauss, ed. *Sociologie et anthropologie.* Paris: Presses Universitaires de France.

Mill, J.S., 1843 [1974]. *A system of logic, ratiocinative and inductive. The collected works of John Stuart Mill*, vol. VII. Toronto: Toronto University Press.

Mill, J.S., 1865 [1974]. *Auguste Comte and positivism. In: The collected works of John Stuart Mill*, vol. X. Toronto: Toronto University Press, 261–368.

Mill, J.S., 1899. *Lettres inédites de John Stuart Mill à Auguste Comte.* Paris: Alcan.

Molinari, Gd., 1850. Le positivisme ou doctrine sociale de M. Auguste Comte. *Journal des économistes*, October, 247–55.

Pearson, H., 2000. Homo œconomicus goes native, 1859-1945. The rise and fall of the economic man. *History of political economy*, 32 (4), 933–89.

Pickering, M., 2009. *Auguste Comte. An intellectual biography.* vols. II and III, Cambridge: Cambridge University Press.

Reybaud, L., 1864. *Études sur les réformateurs sociaux ou socialistes modernes.* 6th ed. Paris: Guillaumin.

Royer, C., 1891. Positivisme. *In*: L. Say and J. Chailley, eds., *Nouveau dictionnaire d'économie politique.* Paris: Guillaumin, vol. 2, 529–40.

Rutten, C., 1972. *Essai sur la morale d'Auguste Comte.* Paris: Les belles lettres.

Saint-Simon, H., 1825 [1966]. *Le nouveau Christianisme. In*: *Œuvres de Saint-Simon*, vol. III, Paris: Anthropos.

Saint-Simon, H. and Comte, A., 1821 [1966]. *Du système industriel. In: Œuvres de Saint-Simon*, vol. III, Paris: Anthropos.
Schumpeter, J., 1954. *History of economic analysis.* London: Macmillan.
Shionoya, Y., 2005. *The German historical school: the historical and ethical approach to economics.* London: Routledge.
Smith, A., 1776 [1976]. *An inquiry into the nature and causes of the wealth of nations.* Oxford: Oxford University Press.
Spencer, H., 1879 [1900]. *The data of ethics.* New York: Collier.
Steiner, P., 2008. L'héritage au 19e siècle en France : loi, intérêt de sentiment et intérêts économiques. *Revue économique*, 59 (1), 73–95.
Steiner, P., 2011. *Durkheim and the birth of economic sociology.* Princeton: Princeton University Press.
Steiner, P., 2016. *Donner... Une histoire de l'altruisme.* Paris: Presses Universitaires de France.
Swingewood, A., 1970. Comte, Marx and political economy. *The sociological review*, 18 (3), 335–49.
Wernick, A., 2001. *Auguste Comte and the religion of humanity.* Cambridge: Cambridge University Press.

Abstract

This article shows that there is a strong connection between the religious component of French sociology and the critique of political economy. In the first section, I consider how selfish behaviour, or egoism, became treated as a major threat endangering the creation of industrial society by those concerned about the diffusion of political economy. I then summarise the methodological critique set forth in the *Cours*, before connecting this critique to the economic content of the *Système* and the concept of altruism. In the following section, Spencer's view of altruism is contrasted to that held by Comte, and then I consider the reaction of French political economists, defending the moral value bought about by their science. In the final section, I explain how the Comtean approach was re-enacted by Durkheim and then by Mauss, at the head of the "sociology of religion" section of *L'Année sociologique*, the Durkheimian journal, to give birth to the theory of gift-giving behaviour that Mauss used to critique political economy in the 1920s.

Henry Sidgwick, moral order, and utilitarianism

Keith Tribe

> I wonder what he [Sidgwick] would have thought of us; and I wonder what we think of him. And then his conscience – incredible. There is no doubt about his moral goodness (John Maynard Keynes, Letter to B. W. Swithinbank, 27 March 1906, in Harrod (1951, p. 117)).

> Sidgwick rather startled one by sudden and unexpected combinations and arch inversions of commonplace. His skill in using his stammer was often noticed. His hearers watched and waited for the coming thought which then exploded the more effectually. Sidgwick not only conceded but eagerly promoted contributions of talk from his companions. He would wait with slightly parted lips for an answer to some inquiry, showing a keen interest which encouraged your expectation that you were about to say a good thing, and sometimes, let us hope, helped to realise the expectation (Leslie Stephen 1901, p. 13).

In his biographical essay on Alfred Marshall, Maynard Keynes wrote that

> Marshall's Cambridge career came just at the date which will, I think, be regarded by the historians of opinion as the critical moment at which Christian dogma fell away from the serious philosophical world of England, or at any rate of Cambridge (Keynes 1972, p. 168).[1]

Keynes is usually taken here as referring to a general decline in Christian belief in the later nineteenth century: the idea that the rise of a critical and scientific mentality had contributed to the kind of doubt and agnosticism symbolised by the personal predicament of Charles Darwin; that

[1] Simon Cook points out (2009, pp. 87–8) that Keynes' account here of later nineteenth-century Cambridge is to some extent contaminated by his reliance on Marshall's reminiscences, as mediated by Mary Paley Marshall. Coase's work on Marshall's biography (1990) demonstrates that Alfred Marshall was not that reliable about aspects of his own early biography.

from mid-century a "crisis of faith" emerged, engendered by the rise of a modern scientific sensibility which superseded faith of any kind.[2] In Cambridge and Oxford movements for educational reform intersect with this chronology, since as institutions their prime function had long been the training of clergy. From mid-century, the challenge represented by new secular institutions – the University of London,[3] Owens College Manchester and then, somewhat later, the new provincial colleges – implied that in Oxford and Cambridge, the institutional and theological Anglican orthodoxies upon which their colleges were based had to be dismantled if a modern curriculum and a new educational function could develop.

By the second half of the nineteenth century, German universities were widely acknowledged as the model institutions of teaching and learning in the natural sciences and humanities. As state institutions, their professors being state employees in much the same way that schoolteachers were, German universities embodied a constitutional settlement[4] that gave them the vocational function of training clergy, while not themselves being theological institutions; in fact, German universities were essentially vocational bodies, their prime task being to train the priests, lawyers and physicians that the state required. By contrast, the two English universities[5] mainly existed to train clergy for the Anglican ministry; teaching in law and of medicine was provided by the Inns of Court and teaching hospitals, and for much of the nineteenth century, Oxford and Cambridge played a

2 Likewise, Mark Bevir (2011) makes a "crisis of faith" during the last third of the nineteenth century a major explanatory axis for the "rise of British socialism"; he provides, however, no account of what this "crisis" involved, nor, if it existed, why it might explain the development of new forms of urban association. See my critique (2014).

3 The University of London opened in 1828 as an institution with no religious tests, open to both genders and teaching a modern curriculum; King's College was the Anglican response, opening in 1831. Subsequently, the University of London was formed as an examining body in 1836 with two constituent colleges, University College London and King's College. Reforms in the 1850s permitted its BA and BSc examinations to be sat externally, laying the foundation for the emergence of a number of provincial colleges which by the turn of the century had mostly become universities, and which were later referred to as the "redbrick" universities.

4 This confessional constitutional settlement is elaborated by Ian Hunter (2015) in the context of his demonstration that the association of "secularisation" with modernity is a function of the emergence of modern politics.

5 And not the four Scottish universities, which performed a vocational function rather similar to the Continental model, including faculties of law and of medicine, especially in the case of Edinburgh.

minor role in the development of the arts and sciences in England.[6] Until the 1850s,[7] admission to the University of Oxford required that students swear their allegiance to the Thirty-Nine Articles[8]; by contrast, no student could formally graduate from the University of Cambridge without doing so. College Fellows had to profess adherence to the Articles, while the character of the colleges as religious institutions was emphasised by the requirement that fellows be male and unmarried – the requirement that led Marshall to become founding Principal of University College Bristol on his marriage to Mary Paley in 1877.

While in part the response in Oxford to the emergence of competing university institutions was associated in mid-century with an Anglo-Catholic renewal, Cambridge has come to be associated with a general falling away from Anglicanism – a falling-away which went in the direction not of dissent, but agnosticism. As is endlessly repeated about Henry Sidgwick, Knightbridge Professor of Moral Philosophy from 1883, Keynes is reported as remarking that "He [Sidgwick] never did anything but wonder whether Christianity was true and prove that it wasn't and hope that it was".[9] The general conclusion drawn from this is that "progressive Cambridge", which included Sidgwick, Marshall and Neville Keynes, was by the last third of the century disenchanted, the secularisation of the role of the university being

6 There is no record that during Adam Smith's spell at Balliol College Oxford 1740–1746 (from the age of 17 to 23) he did anything beyond private reading; this would remain the most profitable occupation for the greater part of resident students and scholars until the later nineteenth century, at both Oxford and Cambridge.

7 The Oxford University Act of 1854 abolished the requirement to swear allegiance to the Thirty-Nine Articles on matriculation, and the Cambridge University Act of 1856 removed religious tests for all degrees apart from Divinity, while maintaining restrictions on college fellowships and membership of Senate (Winstanley 1947, p. 37).

8 An Anglican catechism appended to the *Book of Common Prayer* – see below.

9 Cited by Stefan Collini in his *Oxford Dictionary of National Biography* entry on Sidgwick, referring to Roy Harrod (1951, p. 116), and not p. 135 as given by Collini. This is an extract from the letter to B. W. Swithinbank, written 27 March 1906, in which Maynard Keynes describes his responses to *Henry Sidgwick, A Memoir* (which JMK refers to as "Sidgwick's Life"), in a passage preceding the comment in the epigraph to this essay. Bart Schultz (2004, p. 4) cites this, suggesting that it is part of a general "Bloomsbury view", but he fails to record the passage immediately following. Further, Schultz's endnote 6 on p. 727 gives as his source for this letter the Keynes Papers, King's College, discouraging any reader from looking further, when in fact the relevant passages have been in print since 1951.

doubled by that of its leading teachers.[10] And with the decline of Christian faith went the emergence of a new science of economics that, by the 1930s, had completed its emancipation from the Moral Sciences and their ethical foundations. So the story goes.

However, if we go back to Keynes' remarks on "Marshall's Cambridge" and read further, rather a different story begins to develop. The passage immediately following that previously quoted above runs as follows:

> In 1863 Henry Sidgwick, aged twenty-four, had subscribed to the Thirty-Nine Articles as a condition of tenure of his Fellowship, and was occupied in reading Deuteronomy in Hebrew and preparing lectures on the Acts of the Apostles. Mill, the greatest intellectual influence on the youth of the age, had written nothing which clearly indicated any divergence from received religious opinions up to his *Examination of Hamilton* in 1865. At about this time Leslie Stephen was an Anglican clergyman, James Ward a non-conformist minister, Alfred Marshall a candidate for holy orders, W. K. Clifford a High Churchman. In 1869 Sidgwick resigned his Trinity Fellowship, "to free myself from dogmatic obligations." A little later none of these could have been called Christians. Nevertheless, Marshall, like Sidgwick, was as far as possible from adopting an "anti-religious" attitude. He sympathised with Christian morals and Christian ideals and Christian incentives. There is nothing in his writings depreciating religion in any form; few of his pupils could have spoken definitely about his religious opinions. At the end of his life he said, "Religion seems to me an attitude", and that, though he had given up Theology, he believed more and more in Religion (Keynes 1972, pp. 168–9).

And Maynard Keynes then proceeds to sketch in the "great change-over of the later sixties" as an "intellectual change, not the ethical or emotional change which belongs to a later generation…" (Keynes 1972, p. 169). Writing here in the mid-1920s, Keynes seems here to be looking back to his own position in 1906, distinguishing between the new ethics (associated with G. E. Moore), and a broader intellectual change that had been brought about from the 1860s to the 1890s. Marshall shifted from Metaphysics to Ethics, but

> It would be true, I suppose, to say that Marshall never departed explicitly from the Utilitarian ideas which dominated the generation of economists which preceded him (Keynes 1972, p. 170).

[10] Simon Cook identifies Leslie Stephen as a key element in the creation of this story – see (2009 p. 94): "In … his later *Dictionary of National Biography* entries on both Coleridge and Maurice, and his book *The English Utilitarians,* Stephen established the framework that Keynes later used to recount Marshall's crisis of faith. Such a framework passed over not only Maurice, but also more generally the liberal Anglicanism of the Broad Church movement and, in doing so, reduced the diversity of a generations' struggles with religious faith to a simple binary choice between orthodox Evangelicism and agnostic unbelief."

So how exactly does this admixture of utilitarianism and ethics relate to a general move from Anglicanism to a Christian agnosticism?

Part of our problem here is that the Anglican focus of religious controversy in Oxford and Cambridge has come to obscure the fact that, as Simon Cook implies,[11] Anglicanism was but one thread among many in the varieties of Christian belief during the nineteenth century, as it had been since the seventeenth century. Overlooking this elementary point makes it seem as though expression of a lack of belief in the Thirty-Nine Articles amounts to a falling away from Christianity. While Dissenters were by definition a minority, they were a very significant minority by virtue of being Dissenters: they thought enough about religion to decide that the Anglican version of Protestantism was a botched theological compromise, and so took a positive interest in theological argument. It is quite probable then that Dissenters were numerically either equal to, or more numerous than, those Anglicans sufficiently interested in theological controversy to articulate a view about their faith. Most "Anglicans" were uninterested in matters religious or theological. That was (is) the whole point of an "Anglican faith".

In England, the Reformation had initially taken the form of the monarch appropriating control of the Church in a kind of logical extension of the idea of the Divine Right of Kings, realised de facto in the dissolution of the monasteries as a power play that was more property scam than theological revolution. *The Book of Common Prayer* was devised initially as a new script for church services in 1549, underwent several revisions and reached its final form in the wake of the Civil War in 1662, with however a "Declaration" by King Charles I affixed to it which rather negated the whole point of the Civil War.[12] In the process, the *Book of Common Prayer* became transformed into the central text of Anglican liturgy, appended to which were the articles which spelled out the tenets of an Anglican faith that was reformed, insofar as it did away with those inventions of the

[11] See the quote in fn. 10.

[12] "His Majesty's Declaration" states in its second paragraph "That the Articles of the Church of England (which have been allowed an authorized heretofore, and which our Clergy generally have subscribed unto) do contain the true Doctrine of the Church of England agreeable to God's Word: which we do therefore ratify and confirm, requiring all our loving Subjects to continue in the uniform Profession thereof, and prohibiting the least difference from the said Articles; which to that end We command to be new printed, and this Our Declaration to be published therewith" (*The Book of Common Prayer* 2004, p. 608).

Roman Church that were unsupported by biblical authority,[13] but which simply substituted the English monarch for the Pope as the head of the Church. Biblical authority was established in Article VI: "Holy Scripture containeth all things necessary to salvation: so that whatsoever is not read therein, nor may be proved thereby, is not to be required of any man, that it should be believed as an article of the Faith, or be thought requisite or necessary to salvation".

While this is an expression of the principle common to Protestantism, and most nineteenth-century Protestants would have found only limited difficulty in assenting to many of the Thirty-Nine articles, there were several articles at which one or more of the various Protestant tendencies would baulk: the presumption that God was a Trinity, that Jesus was as the Son of God an incarnation of God who rose again from the dead (Articles II, III, IV, V); the doctrine of original sin (Art. IX) and the linked idea that men and women lacked free will (X); that faith, and not works, was the foundation of justification (Art. XI); of predestination (Art. XVII); and the authority of the Church to "decree rites and ceremonies" (Art. XX). Unitarians did not believe in the doctrine of the Holy Trinity, maintained that Jesus was inspired by God but was not God Himself, they rejected the doctrines of original sin and predestination, hence saw the Christian faith as one open to all, and maintained that the Bible was written by humans and so subject to error. Unitarianism was for example linked in the early part of the century with social reform – this was Harriet Martineau's family background and the version of Christianity that David Ricardo adopted when he converted from Judaism; later in the century, when a Unitarian church existed, Stanley Jevons was a Unitarian, while Philip Wicksteed was a Unitarian minister. Alternatively, some Christians rejected the idea that the scriptures revealed the divinity of God and that they were the source of religious knowledge, but believed that observation of the natural world would yield sufficient proof of the existence of a single creator, God having created both the universe and the human capacity of reason. Others believed simply that a Being existed who was the cause of all things, which was perfectly compatible with the idea that Jesus Christ was an exemplary preacher. And there were also Methodists of different colours, Baptists, some Evangelicals, Quakers, Presbyterians, all of whom were lumped together as "Dissenters" and who, furthermore, bore collective

[13] Article XXII. Of Purgatory: "The Romish doctrine concerning Purgatory, Pardons, Worshipping, and Adoration, as well of Images as of Reliques, and also invocation of Saints, is a fond thing vainly invented, and grounded upon no warranty of Scripture, but rather repugnant to the Word of God" (*Book of Common Prayer* 2004, p. 620).

responsibility for the greater part of what was "progressive" about nineteenth-century English, Scottish and Welsh society. To detach oneself from an Anglican faith did not necessarily imply a detachment from Christian faith. More importantly, a turn away from an Anglican faith was not symptomatic of the "advance of secularism"; for as Ian Hunter has convincingly demonstrated, the linkage of "secularisation" to modernity and the rise of "reason" is a *trompe de l'oeuil* created by a philosophical history that sought to place itself in the vanguard of Reason (Hunter 2015). As Hunter also emphasises, the historical "advance of Reason" and the associated "displacement of Faith" that is the axis upon which this philosophical history turns actually never happened.

The second problem we have for our understanding of the way in which utilitarianism, ethics, Christian faith and agnosticism formed the context in which "new sciences" emerged in the later nineteenth century is that even the most recent commentary treats theology and science as entirely separate domains. Piers Hale's attempt to link Malthusian populationist arguments to Darwin's version of evolution, of that to Herbert Spencer's social Darwinism, and thence to emergent socialist debate of the 1880s, ignores theology almost entirely while at the same time presenting a caricature of early nineteenth-century ethical argument. Charles Darwin experienced a struggle with his Anglican faith every bit as significant as Henry Sidgwick, while Malthusian arguments about population were designed as a quasi-empirical vindication of a theodicy that saw the existence of inequality as a necessary part of God's will. Where Adam Smith had argued that Providence had placed in men and women the vanity which was the root of the endless striving that resulted in the wealth of nations, Malthus proposed that Providence had placed evil in the world so that men and women had to struggle in order to become moral persons.[14] While the populationist mechanics of Malthusian theodicy had a major, if entirely unwarranted,[15] impact upon arguments about social progress, Hale reduces the impetus for social reform in the 1830s to a caricature of Philosophic Radicalism in which Benthamism and Malthusianism converge

14 For the argument about Malthus, see my (2015) work, posted on my academia.edu page.

15 As a way of understanding demographic change in nineteenth-century industrial societies, the positive and preventive checks proposed by Malthus (arising from the intersection of a potential for geometric expansion of the population with the constraint of arithmetic increase of food resources) have little empirical explanatory value. Malthus' populationist arguments were only apparently "empirical", and should properly be understood as a Trojan Horse for a theological anthropology (see Cremaschi 2014, ch. 3).

(2014, pp. 45, 69). For the time being however, the need for a more ramified understanding of the social, political, theological and ethical context in which utilitarianian argument came to the fore can be here put to one side, for as we shall see there is a more immediate context for Sidgwick's ethics that we first need to deal with: the Cambridge Moral Sciences Tripos.

Henry Sidgwick had entered Trinity College in the autumn of 1855 at the age of 17, and graduated in 1859 with firsts in both the Classics and the Mathematics Triposes, coming top of the list of classicists and 33rd among the mathematicians. In his second year at Trinity, he was invited to become a member of The Apostles, discovering the "life of thought - thought exercised upon the central problems of human life" (Sidgwick 1906, p. 35). However, since he had no independent means, he accepted a college lectureship in classics in 1859, also giving private tuition for the first two years to supplement his college income. During the vacations at this time he read philosophy, primarily studying J. S. Mill, although he later reported that this rather discouraged him from the idea that one might find in the study of philosophy "the fundamental questions as to the nature of man and his relation to God and the universe" (1906, p. 36). For several years, Sidgwick divided his interests between philosophy and theology; but "...under Mill's influence I was also strongly led as a matter of duty to study political economy thoroughly, and give no little thought to practical questions, social and political" (1906, p. 36). Prompted in 1862 by his reading of Renan's *Études d'histoire religieuse,* Sidgwick determined to study Hebrew and Arabic to understand Christianity as a "historical religion". This study was continued until about 1865, not least because there were two chairs for Arabic in Cambridge, and only one for Moral Philosophy. However, by the mid-1860s, he began to realise that it would take too much of his time to develop the specialist knowledge of Arabic that candidacy for a chair in the subject would require, while also diverting him from the "central problems which constituted my deepest interest" (1906, p. 37). He proceeds to list these as follows:

> Was Jesus incarnate God, miraculously brought into the world as a man? Were his utterances of divine authority? Did he actually rise from the grave with a human body glorified, and therewith ascend into heaven? Or if the answers to these questions could not strictly be affirmative in the ordinary sense of the term, what element of truth, vital for mankind, could be disengaged from the husk of legend, or symbolised by the legend, supposing the truth itself capable of being established by human reasoning? (1906, pp. 37–8).

These questions summarise issues that culminated in his resignation of his College Fellowship in 1869, a move that he did not however conceive as a secession from the Church of England, let alone Christianity.[16]

The sequence of events associated with his resignation is important for an understanding of the issues involved. Sidgwick had written to his mother in early June 1869 stating that he had just resigned the Assistant Tutorship he had held since 1859, and that he also intended to resign from the College Fellowship to which he had been elected in the same year, remarking that the College might be prepared to re-appoint him to a College Lectureship in Moral Sciences, which was in fact then confirmed in mid-June. The Lectureship was a new post; hitherto all teaching in the colleges had been done by the Assistant Tutors, but they had become increasingly overburdened by the increase in demand for tuition in all subjects. In the later 1860s colleges had begun to appoint College Lecturers, and eventually these superseded the tutors as the prime teaching appointment.[17] And so Sidgwick's move from an Assistant Tutorship in Classics to a College Lecturer in Moral Sciences was part of a general change in the organisation of teaching – St. John's College had appointed Alfred Marshall to an equivalent post in 1868. As for the symbolic renunciation of the Fellowship, this too lacks quite the significance often attributed to it. Parliamentary efforts to abolish religious tests went back to the 1830s, and several bills had been introduced into the House of Commons in the course of the 1860s that sought to end the linkage of college fellowships to the Church; that this had not already happened by 1869 had more to do with the resistance of the House of Lords than anything else, and this was broadly recognised (Winstaley 1947, pp. 43–89). After much wrangling during 1870, an act removing all religious tests from Fellows went on the

[16] See on this Medema (2008, pp. 197–8) for a succinct account of this period.

[17] It should also be made clear at this point that, until the end of the century at least, systematic teaching was done in college, mostly in the form of classes and exercises – see the description of teaching in the Moral Sciences in *The Student's Guide to the University of Cambridge* (1893, pp. 71–2). Following his appointment as Knightbridge Professor, Whewell began a systematic course of lectures in April 1839, something of an innovation for the time (Palfrey 2002, p. 162ff.). Reforms in 1848 then made it necessary for candidates for an ordinary degree (Poll Men) to gain a certificate attesting to their attendance at one course of professorial lectures, and these students consequently predominated among those attending professorial lectures. Far from Professorial (university) lectures being the central element of teaching, from the point of view of Honours students, they were the least significant. This was certainly the case when in the 1870s Neville Keynes was studying the Moral Sciences: Henry Fawcett, Professor of Political Economy, lectured almost exclusively to poll men (Deane 2001, p. 23, fn. 29).

Statute Book in June 1871. Sidgwick's move thus anticipated a change that had been under discussion for many years, and which was finally completed two years later. Rather than regarding Sidgwick's resignation and appointment being a principled and singular move, his contemporaries would have seen it more as pushing at an open door.

Making this point is not intended as any diminution of Sidgwick's convictions, but to clarify the misleading character of the slant given to them by Leslie Stephen's later description of the situation at this time:

> He [Sidgwick] and his friends were convinced of the need of a social reconstruction guided by scientific methods and of a religious reform founded upon an examination of the evidence for historical Christianity conducted "with strict scientific impartiality." His striking remarks upon Tennyson's "In Memoriam" explain his feeling. He could never read the lines beginning "If e'er when faith had fallen asleep" (in the 124th poem) without tears. "In Memoriam" had impressed upon him "the ineffaceable and ineradicable conviction that humanity will not and cannot acquiesce in a godless world." He could not find rest in agnosticism, and, though accepting the methods of modern science, revolted against its atheistic tendencies (1901, p. 4).

Stephens is here quoting Sidgwick from a letter he sent to Tennyson's son, included in *Alfred Lord Tennyson. A Memoir* and written in the mid-1890s,[18] placing the emphasis upon a conflict of "science" and "religion". But Sidgwick had emphasised that it was the "defence of 'honest doubt', the reconciliation of knowledge and faith in the introductory poem" that appealed most strongly to him then. And describing the way in which he was moved to tears, he wrote:

> These lines I can never read without tears. I feel in them the indestructible and inalienable minimum of faith which humanity cannot give up because it is necessary for life; and which I know that I, at least so far as the man in me is deeper than the methodical thinker, cannot give up (Sidgwick and Sidgwick 1906, p. 541).

The problem then is that Sidgwick's "crisis of faith" has been assimilated to a narrative of secularisation created by intellectuals themselves sceptical of religious faith of any kind; which was certainly not Sidgwick's own position.

After further summary of the autobiographical fragment, Stephen's obituary then turns to remarks passed on to him by John Venn, who had returned to Cambridge in 1862 to lecture in moral science, finding only Rev. J. B. Mayor representing the Tripos. Together with Sidgwick and others, Stephens writes, they formed a discussion circle which came to be known as the Grote Society, dining once a term with John Grote,

[18] From *Alfred Lord Tennyson. A Memoir by his son* Vol. I, Macmillan, London 1897, pp. 300–4, reprinted in (Sidgwick and Sidgwick 1906, pp. 538–42).

Knightbridge[19] Professor of Moral Philosophy, in his Trumpington vicarage,[20] which brings us to John Grote, the Moral Sciences Tripos, and Sidgwick's role as eventual successor of Grote, and author of *Methods of Ethics.*

As Simon Cook has noted, as originally devised by Whewell in 1848, the Moral Sciences Tripos was an attempt to

> subordinate the relations of the various moral sciences to his [Whewell's] version of Anglican authority. But his attempt to use the new tripos as a vehicle for integrating law, history, and political economy with Christian moral philosophy proved too ambitious...[21]

The original scheme included five subjects: moral philosophy, political economy, modern history, general jurisprudence and the Laws of England. By the later 1850s, student numbers were dwindling; Grote, appointed Knightbridge Professor from 1855, first of all presented a comprehensive set of lectures, rather than the annual dozen of Whewell; then in 1860, he was successful in reorganising the Tripos with a Moral Sciences Board to administer the degree, exchanging the Laws of England for Mental Philosophy and adding Logic. Then, in 1867, the Moral Sciences Board recommended that History and General Jurisprudence should be excluded, and that Political Philosophy, previously treated as part of History, should be grouped with Moral Philosophy in the Tripos. The Moral Sciences thus became four subjects: Moral and Political Philosophy, Mental Philosophy, Logic, and Political Economy. This remained the basic structure until Marshall established the Economics Tripos in 1903, upon which the subject was excluded from the Moral Sciences Tripos, which in turn morphed into a Philosophy Tripos which in turn excluded logic, political theory, and psychology. Sidgwick's tenure of the Knightbridge

[19] On its foundation in 1683, the Knightbridge chair was for "Moral Theology and Casuistical Divinity". On resurrecting the chair, Whewell renamed it as a chair in "Moral Theology and Casuistry". In 1857, Grote had sought to change the title to "Moral Philosophy", but was vetoed by the Vice Chancellor.

[20] Grote had been given a college living in 1847 as Vicar of Trumpington, then a small village to the SW of Cambridge. The importance of John Grote to the Moral Sciences Tripos in particular, and to later nineteenth-century philosophy in general, has been recently emphasised by John R. Gibbins (2007).

[21] Simon Cook (2009, pp. 60–1). See pp. 95ff. for an invaluable account of the rise of the Broad Church movement and its ramifications: "...Mansel's 'defense of orthodoxy' (to quote Keynes) was not a defense of religious belief against some infidel creed of unbelief. Rather, it was a defense of an earlier nineteenth-century orthodoxy founded on the Atonement against the rising tide of incarnationalist theology and Coleridgean philosophy within the Church of England" (p. 99).

chair, from 1883 to 1900, thus coincided with the period when the Moral Sciences Tripos bore a close resemblance to the PPE degree, founded in Oxford in 1920: uniting moral philosophy, logic, political theory, economics and psychology.

When in the early 1860s Sidgwick had turned his attention to questions of philosophy and theology, he was a leading member of the Grote Society – indeed, one of those attending later recollected that the Society amounted to an extended conversation between Grote and Sidgwick.[22] The importance of Grote to Sidgwick was also recalled by another who had attended Grote Society meetings, writing to Mayor, who had married Grote's ward and niece Alexandrina Jessie Grote in 1863:

> You asked me about the Grote Society, and I have rather wandered from it – Am I not right in saying that Professor Grote, like Henry Sidgwick, was rather ethical than metaphysical? Tell me; you will know. I have his Treatise on the Moral Ideals (which you edited, and were so kind as to send me) before me, and it seems to me that that, though the word "ideal" has real metaphysical affinities, yet that these are not pressed by him in the way of building up an abstract system. There seems to me a likeness between Grote and Sidgwick in this, and I believe they were more on the same plane than any other two of us five – I can remember no one else as belonging to the society during the years between 1863 and September 1864, when I went to Clifton and was absent from Cambridge for a year – when I came back in September 1865, I know that others joined it, e.g. Alfred Marshall and Henry Jackson: but I have less remembrance of what kind of line they took, or how soon it was that Marshall determined himself into Political Economy – then Maurice became the head of the Society, and we found him, as everybody did, very charming, but not exactly a philosopher in the sense that Grote was… I am afraid that these remembrances are rather about the persons than about the society – but Professor Grote was an admirable person for getting men together; he was so sympathetic, without being at all vague.[23]

Mayor later recalled that the Grote Society had originated in 1861, when he was College Lecturer in Moral Sciences at St. Johns and he had consulted with Grote in order to co-ordinate his lectures with him. Grote had suggested it would be a good thing to have a periodic meeting for discussion amongst those with an interest in philosophy, and the first meeting took place in Mayor's rooms, when Grote read an introductory paper. The next meeting was in Grote's own rooms in Trinity, after which Mayor "fell into the habit of going to dine with him at Trumpington", with discussion afterwards that "took the form of papers exchanged between G. and S".[24]

---

[22] Implied by Mayor in his letter to Eleanor Sidgwick, 28 April 1904 Queensgate House, Kingston Hill (Trinity College Library Add Ms. C 1104/68).

[23] J. R. Mozley to J. B. Mayor, 21 April 1904 [Holly Bank, Headingley, Leeds] Trinity College Library Add. Ms. c. 104/66.

[24] Letter of J. B. Mayor to Eleanor Sidgwick, 28 April 1904 (see fn. 22).

As Simon Cook has suggested, Grote sought "to fashion a philosophy conducive to both theology and science," and he was hostile to "Positivism", "which mistook phenomena for the whole of reality" (Cook 2009, p. 103). But he was comfortable with "phenomenalism", the study of material facts:

> Grote could even agree with Mill that there may be a phenomenalist science of human nature, according to which actions are determined by circumstances and character, and character is itself determined largely by circumstances. Nevertheless, Grote insisted, "Before we can *act* ... we must know what we *want*," and so while it is all very well to know what circumstances will produce this and that character, this is not the same thing as knowing what kind of character we want to produce from any particular regime of education (op cit, p. 104).

On his early death in 1866, Grote left behind some occasional essays and the first part of a treatise on these issues, from which Simon Cook is quoting above (Grote 1865). However, when John Stuart Mill had in the autumn and early winter of 1861 published a critique of utilitarianism in *Fraser's Magazine*,[25] Grote had begun to draft a response, assembling a mass of notes that were then edited by Mayor and published posthumously in 1870 as *An Examination of the Utilitarian Philosophy*. Moreover, with the encouragement of a number of Oxford philosophers, Mayor later put together a second part for *Exploratio Philosophica*, in the preface acknowledging the assistance of Sidgwick in reading the proofs (J. B. Mayor, "Preface" to Grote 1900, p. xii). This should remind us that the period in which Grote had originally drafted his critique of Mill on utilitarianism coincided with that period in the Grote Society when Sidgwick and Grote were reported as being so closely engaged in discussion. Even without here embarking upon any detailed examination, there are clear filiations between Grote's critique of utilitarianism[26] and Sidgwick's own *Methods of Ethics* of 1874. And if we are prepared to allow this possibility, then our approach to Sidgwick is no longer in terms of a supposed "crisis of faith" of the early 1870s, but in the very different context of argument about moral action and moral order in the early 1860s: Grote's extended evaluation of Mill's philosophy and of the manner in which the study of society and ideals for its betterment might be reconciled with a belief in a Christian God. What seems likely to emerge from this is a Sidgwick who looks very much less like the Sidgwick being written about today,[27] is actually

[25] Republished in book form as *Utilitarianism* in 1863.

[26] It is more than probable that the clarity of the 1870 *Examination* owes more than a little to Mayor's editing, since the text has a narrative coherence absent in much of Grote's other writings.

[27] Most recently in Katarzyna de Lazari-Radek, Peter Singer (2014); and Roger Crisp (2015).

less original as a moral philosopher than such writings might suggest, but whose location in the Moral Sciences Tripos made the composition of his *Principles of Political Economy* not an aberration, but a logical development of his ideas.[28]

It is notable that Collini dismisses *Principles of Political Economy* as an essentially Millian, conservative work, suggesting that it should be viewed as an attempt to "fend off the twin challenges to the status of traditional political economy posed by the late nineteenth-century enthusiasm for socialism and sociology".[29] Collini's arguments are here adapted from Leslie Stephen, who did however recognise the significance of Sidgwick's book:

> Meanwhile, whatever the true answer, the effect of his elaborate scrutiny into the fundamental conceptions of Ethics gave, as I think from my own experience and that of others, the most important of all modern contributions towards a clear realisation of the conditions of approaching the problems involved.
>
> A similar tendency marks his Political Economy. His early interest in social problems had led him to the subject. His love of all intellectual activities took him far into some technical discussions, upon bimetallism for example, which have little bearing upon ethics. But his main point is closely connected with the problem of what Bentham called "self-regarding conduct." He had been again greatly influenced by Mill. He adopts old methods, but endeavours to restate the results so as to meet later criticisms. The "classical economists" had insisted upon the supreme importance of self-interest and had deduced the laissez faire doctrine. Sidgwick by a careful and acute investigation of their arguments, tries to recognise the true place of the "self-interest" principle, and to get rid of the excessive absolutism of his predecessors. He refutes in particular, the "wage fund" theory, which had been used as an argument against the possibility of social improvement. The old rigid system is thus broken down, and free play is left for hopes of social regeneration (Stephen 1901, p. 15).

Stephen here identifies a filiation between *Methods of Ethics* and the *Principles of Political Economy* that has since become obscured, on the one hand by modern moral philosophers uninterested in the contemporary context of Sidgwick's ethics, and on the other by intellectual historians unfamiliar with the terrain of political economy in the 1870s and 1880s. As for the

[28] Much the same goes for John Stuart Mill. Moreover, the contrast between Oxford and Cambridge, between T. H. Green and Henry Sidgwick, also needs recalibrating. Roger Backhouse has likewise pointed to the neglect of Sidgwick's political economy, and his appropriation by modern moral philosophers (2006, p. 41, fn. 17).

[29] ODNB, but summarising his outline in Stefan Collini, Donald Winch and John Burrow (1983, p. 283), where he also suggests that *Principles* was "Mill modified in the light of Jevons's marginalist theory of value." That it is possible to effect this modification to Mill suggests that the standard view of Mill is mistaken.

latter, properly appreciating how Marshall's economics emerges in this context requires that we understand John Stuart Mill rather better than we do: his "utilitarianism", his "ethics", as well as his political economy – for this was the basis upon which Jevons, Marshall, Ashley, Cannan, Wicksteed and many other contemporaries all built.

A sense of what is at stake here can be gained from an early passage in Grote's critique of Mill:

> The difficulty of utilitarianism in regard of its claims exclusively to determine action, arises not so much from the supposition of the *unattainableness* of happiness, which is what Mr Mill in the main sets himself to controvert .... as from the difficult of determining, after we have passed the narrow limits of food and raiment, of health, peace, and competence, what, for different people, it consists in, and of comparing the supposed happiness of one person with that of another. ...Have we a clear enough view of it to be able to balance and calculate the different ingredients of it, the different pleasures, as Bentham did ... so that our reason may be able to determine the desirableness of actions in *this* way to the exclusion of others? (Grote 1870, pp. 32–3).

The problematic path from a utilitarian conception of right action for an individual to the "greatest happiness of the greatest number" is also something that Grote highlights. While for Mill actions are right insofar as they tend to promote happiness, he points out that

> It is the individual who feels and acts; it is he who seeks for the *summum bonum*: it is his *summum bonum* or ideal welfare which is sought for: it is he also who, as a matter of fact, desires that which is pleasant, that namely which is pleasant to *him*. This, as an idea or notion, is not the same as the abstractly, or as the generally, desirable. We cannot practically speak about happiness without considering *whose* happiness it is we mean (Grote 1870, p. 85).

This was later thematised by Sidgwick in *Methods of Ethics* as the distributional problem: given that there could be in effect no intersubjective comparison of "happiness", how could we move from the level of the rightness of individual action to the welfare of the society as a whole? In this way, therefore, one of the central issues of a welfare economics emerging in the 1930s was prefigured by Grote's arguments from the 1860s.

As Backhouse and Nishizawa have pointed out, up until Mill political economists equated "wealth" with "welfare", the potential difference between measurable wealth and the utility which an individual derived from it being reflected in arguments around the relationship of value in use and value in exchange. The development with Jevons of a subjective account of utilitarianism broke with this tradition, but highlighted the problem of how individual utilities might be summed or compared

(Backhouse and Nishizawa 2010, p. 204)[30] Sidgwick's *Principles of Political Economy*, while broadly Millian in construction, built upon this; instead of contrasting wealth and utility, he identified the divergence between wealth as measured by prices, and wealth in terms of the utility created by the goods and services at the disposal of the individual. It was the nature of these latter utilities that he addressed; the relation of their "ethical value" to their money value.

Sidgwick's *Principles of Political Economy* has a main text of nearly 600 pages; small revisions added to, and subtracted from, a basic structure laid down in 1883 and thereafter left unchanged.[31] Books I and II comprise the "Science of Political Economy, "as it is ordinarily conceived in England" (1883, p. 28), hence a conventional account of the trinity production, distribution and exchange. Book III, "The Art of Political Economy" "deals with a special department of governmental interference, designed to improve either the social production of wealth or its distribution…".[32] Stated in this way, the resemblance to Mill's Principles evident in the design of Sidgwick's Books One and Two is not continued into Book III. Book IV of Mill's Principles had dealt with the "progress of society", considering the augmentation of production and population, the tendency of profits to fall to a minimum, and in its final chapter "The Probable Futurity of the Labouring Classes". Mill's own treatment of taxation comes in Book V, "On the Influence of Government", where the treatment of equality recognises the differential impact of a given tax, but does not conceive tax itself as an instrument of social policy in the achievement of equity. Sidgwick's treatment of government activity and its economic consequences has moved beyond Mill in a fashion that his treatment of production and distribution has not.

Even so, Sidgwick's treatment of wealth in Book I, Ch. III has detached itself from Mill, confirming the influence of Jevons whom he had acknowledged in the "Preface", writing that Jevons' "leading ideas have been continually in my thoughts".[33] Sidgwick notes that the difficulties of

[30] It should also be pointed out that Jevons' original presentation of his "Mathematical Theory" was in a paper read before a meeting of the British Association in Cambridge in 1862, and so quite probably originates, like Grote's own work, as a response to Mill's *Fraser's Magazine* series of the previous year.

[31] Henry Sidgwick, *The Principles of Political Economy*, Macmillan, London 1883; second edition 1887; third edition, prepared by John Neville Keynes, 1901. References here are to the first edition unless indicated otherwise.

[32] Sidgwick (1901b, p. 33) – see here fn. 1 for Sidgwick's explanation of the revision of his original phrasing concerning the "Art of Political Economy".

[33] Sidgwick (1883, p. v). There are 44 direct references to the work of Jevons in the first edition.

comparing wealth over time or across space founder on the lack of a common measure of value, and earlier writers had responded by resorting to discussion of the respective utilities of commodities. But as he points out, this implies a relationship between purchased and unpurchased utilities; and given the various difficulties arising, Mill had resorted to the Ricardian solution, that utility should be treated as the sole standard: a man is rich or poor according to the necessaries and luxuries he can command; and if he can get two sacks instead of one, he gets double the quantity of riches, double the quantity of utility. Sidgwick objects:

> But surely any man who got two sacks of corn where he had only counted on one would willingly exchange a great part of the second for things which he would not take in exchange for an equal part of the first: if such an exchange is out of the question, though he might find a use for the second sack it will certainly not be as useful as the first.[34]

And he goes on:

> In fact, as Jevons has admirably explained, the variations in the relative market values of different articles express and correspond to variations in the comparative estimates formed by people in general, not of the total utilities of the amounts purchased of such articles, but of their final utilities... (1883, pp. 74–5).

Following on from this idea, Sidgwick then raises the point that a given commodity is "more useful when bought by the poor, because the poor have fewer luxuries and therefore get more enjoyment out of what they have" (1883, p. 76). This raises the awkward point that, if we measure wealth simply by its utility, then the amount of wealth in a given country will be altered by the way in which it is distributed among the population.

There is an associated distributional problem running through *Methods of Ethics*. Sidgwick drew a distinction between egoistic hedonism – the proposition that "the reasonable ultimate end of each individual's action [is] his own greatest happiness: i.e. a life so arranged that the excess in it of pleasurable over painful consciousness shall be the greatest possible" (1874, p. 109); and universalistic hedonism – the proposition that "the conduct which, under any given circumstances, is externally or objectively right, is that which will produce the greatest amount of happiness to all whose interests are affected....the conduct which will produce 'the

[34] Sidgwick (1901b, p. 81). In the first edition, the same point was made, but with respect to a harvest that was twice as big; the additional amount therefore not having the same utility as the amount equivalent to the previous year (p. 74). The clarifying passage regarding the two sacks of corn was later inserted immediately preceding this passage, which was retained.

greatest possible happiness to the greatest possible number'" (1874, p. 381). As we have seen, this is a problem that Grote had pointed to in Mill: the lack of a mechanism linking individual choices relating to personal welfare to the welfare of the society as a whole, that there appeared to be no certainty that any kind of ethical conduct could in fact secure the "greatest happiness of the greatest number" beyond a simple aggregation of individual actions. Sidgwick did acknowledge Grote's identification of this problem,[35] but he never satisfactorily resolved it in the closing pages of his book. Instead, he concluded that it was impossible to "construct an absolute code of Utilitarian Morality unless we can shew that there is some final perfect form of society, towards which the process of human history is tending". And he went on:

> Now in the present rudimentary condition of sociology it does not appear to me that we have sufficient data for deducing the best rules of mutual behaviour for human communities, as they are to exist at some future period (1874, p. 438).

Hence from the utilitarian point of view he thought it inadvisable to dispense "with the morality of instinct and tradition. I think that for the present ... the Utilitarian method must start with the existing social order, and the existing morality as part of that order..." (loc cit).

This basic pragmatism is also in evidence in Book III of the *Principles*, where he argues that if the wealth of a country depends on its distribution among its inhabitants, then government policy with respect to taxation and tariffs can increase or diminish the wealth of a country. And so while the arguments of the *Methods of Ethics* presumed the existence of "natural liberty", its consequences led to an affirmation of the role of government that went far beyond the prevailing orthodoxy in Britain, that government should interfere as little as possible with the existing distribution of wealth, and that any such intervention would tend to impair aggregate production more than it could improve utility through better distribution (1883, p. 400).

While recognising that there is a "large element of truth" in the idea that self-interest creates and keeps "in true economic order the vast and complex fabric of social industry" (1883, p. 402), Sidgwick maintains that it is more relevant for a practical politician to have a clear view of the qualifications to this argument; his chapter therefore directs itself to these qualifications and exceptions. His general supposition is that, even in a society composed primarily of "economic men" the system of natural liberty would in particular respects have "no tendency to realise the beneficent

[35] Sidgwick (1874, p. 403, fn. 1) referring to Grote's *Examination.*

results claimed for it" (p. 403). He first examines the distributional implications over succeeding generations of such choices, and then turns to the fact that any one individual will be able, through free exchange, to gain proper compensation for services rendered to society.

> ... there are some utilities which, from their nature, are practically incapable of being appropriated by those who produce them or who would otherwise be willing to purchase them. For instance, it may easily happen that the benefits of a well-placed lighthouse must be largely enjoyed by ships on which no toll could be conveniently imposed. So, again, if it is economically advantageous to a nation to keep up forests, on account of their beneficial effects in moderating and equalising rainfall, the advantage is one which private enterprise has no tendency to provide; since no one could appropriate and sell improvements in climate (pp. 406–7).

This observation is then linked to inequalities in distribution and their relation to investment; specifically, that the distribution of skills and the remuneration linked to this could lead it to be profitable for the community to provide cheap technical education, even if private enterprise could not do so. This leads into a general discussion of the ways in which a divergence of private and public interest might arise, and the prospect that this divergence could be ameliorated by the action of government – by direct engagement through the provision of education, or through legislation.

He then proceeds to elaborate "The Relations of Government to Industry", where "industry" means human economic activity in general, and the form of intervention relates to legislation: the enforcement of contracts, the creation of a body of rules and regulations governing food standards, the regulation of child labour and provision of education, or the securing of intellectual property. This is followed by a chapter that details the works that government might actively promote – roads, canals, railways, postal services, currency and the financial system, immigration and colonisation. There then follows a chapter on free trade and protection, a general chapter on distributive justice, and then one devoted to the economic arguments for government interference, picking up on the earlier argument concerning the impact of distribution on the measurement of wealth. Having first discussed the impact of various conceptions of socialism and communism, Sidgwick considers the likely effect of minimum wage legislation and, by extension, poor relief and the case for government provision for the sick and infirm, together with the possibility of compulsory health insurance (1883, p. 536). By contrast, Mill's review in Book V of *Principles*, "On the Influence of Government" is more conventionally economic, built around discussion of forms of taxation and a conception of the "ordinary functions of government" (Chs. VIII and IX) focussed on the legal framework for personal property and commercial undertakings. The social and political agenda of the 1880s was very different to that of the late 1840s.

Two years after Sidgwick's Principles first appeared, he gave the Presidential Address to Section F of the British Association, meeting that year in Aberdeen. He took as his point of departure an account of Adam Smith's "system of natural liberty", carefully distinguishing Smith's nuanced appraisal of self-interest from more dogmatic accounts of laissez-faire, and identifying the importance of the Physiocrats, contrasting the latter's advocacy of a limitation in the functions of government with Rousseau's advocacy of a change in the structure of government.[36] In the course of his address, he described the role of political economy as follows:

> There will probably always be considerable disagreement in details among competent persons as to the propriety of Governmental interference in particular cases; but, apart from questions on which economic considerations must yield to political, moral, or social reasons of greater importance, it is an anachronism not to recognise fully and frankly the existence of cases in which the industrial intervention is desirable, even with a view to the most economic production of wealth. Hence, I conceive, the present business of economic theory in this department is to give a systematic and carefully-reasoned exposition of these cases, which, until the constitution of human nature and society are fundamentally altered, must always be regarded as exceptions to a general rule of non-interference (Sidgwick 1962, p. 77–8).

His address continues to survey this issue as represented by historical economists (citing Roscher, Hildebrand, Knies, and Schönberg's handbook), and also by European sociology (Comte, Spencer and Schäffle). Far from this being the kind of rearguard defence of an essentially Millian perspective that Collini suggests, Sidgwick here sketches out a conception of the relationship of state and society that is entirely congruent with that of Alfred Marshall and, after him, Pigou.

In May 1900, Sidgwick delivered an address to the Oxford Philosophical Society, aware that he was terminally ill with cancer. He died just over three months later. He returned to T. H. Green's *Prolegomena to Ethics*, discussing its metaphysical aspects, having published a review of its ethical doctrine in 1884. For Green, argued Sidgwick, thinking activity is the source of a system of notions that constitute the world, but this thinking activity cannot "think itself":

[36] Sidgwick (1962, p. 77). Sidgwick's appreciation of Smith's system of natural liberty was more or less unique in Britain for the time; in *Methods of Ethics*, he describes Adam Smith as "one of the most penetrating and ingenious of English moralists"; not then a common view of Adam Smith (1874, p. 431).

> It is because there is a Divine consciousness realising or reproducing itself in man, that the true good of man is argued to be not pleasure, but Virtue or Perfection, and Perfection is held to consist in the realisation of capabilities already realised in the Divine Existence: briefly put, man's true good is development in the direction of becoming liker to God (1901a, p. 26).

However, Sidgwick continues, he does not see how this conception can be maintained if God is also conceived as having no character apart from being self-given in "unifying the manifold of nature: for this unification is surely equally effected in the lives of sinners and in the lives of saints, as both are equally capable of being scientifically known" (1901a, pp. 26–7). There is a gulf between Green's metaphysics and his ethics. Nonetheless,

> The conception, indeed, of the world as a systematic whole, having unity and order through the complex relations of the parts, as well as infinite plurality and diversity; and the conception of the progress of knowledge and unity in what first presents itself as an almost chaotic diversity – these are conceptions of the highest value.

Despite this value, a Divine Mind then becomes a "hypostasised logical element" in Green's approach: there is a lack of a logical necessity for a spiritual principle.

> Green answers that the existence of the relations involves "the unity of the manifold, the existence of the many in one... But," he says, "a plurality of things cannot of themselves unite in one relation, nor can a single thing of itself bring itself into a multitude of relations... there must" - therefore - "be something other than the manifold things themselves which combines them" (Sidgwick 1901a, p. 27).

Sidgwick concluded that this argument was unthinkable; and it was his final word on the matter.

All the same, we might recognise something else in these lines: Alfred Marshall's motto for *Industry and Trade*: "The many in the one, the one in the many". This implies a kind of religious faith that, as we have grown used to supposing, Alfred Marshall had left far behind him, in the later 1860s when he too distanced himself from a strictly Anglican faith. As with Sidgwick, doubt in the tenets of an Anglican faith does not necessarily involve an agnosticism, and certainly not an atheism; although we should recognise that for individuals experiencing the self-doubt that such scepticism brought with it, it might well do so. The shift away from an Anglican faith made by Marshall, Sidgwick and many of their Cambridge colleagues in the later 1860s was not eased by the embrace of any replacement or substitute. And this state of positive scepticism is evident in the closing passage of the first edition of the *The Methods of Ethics*, removed from later editions:

> Hence the whole system of our beliefs must fail, without a hypothesis unverifiable by experience reconciling the Individual with the Universal Reason, without a belief, in some form or other, that the moral order which we see imperfectly realized in this actual world is yet actually perfect. If we reject this belief, we may perhaps still find in this non-moral universe an adequate object for the Speculative Reason, capable of being in some sense ultimately understood. But the Cosmos of Duty is thus really reduced to a chaos: and the prolonged effort of the human intellect to frame a perfect ideal of rational conduct is seen to have been foredoomed to inevitable failure.[37]

If we read this in the context of an understanding of *Methods of Ethics* as an attempt to determine rules for right conduct, for making the right choices, then we can see how the way in which Sidgwick's rehearsal of the paradoxes of any rational choice converges upon the kind of arguments developed in the 1930s by Hicks and Robbins, who did however maintain that in arriving at rules for right conduct it was necessary to reject the "utilitarian heritage". Instead, they simply transposed this heritage into a different language that made it seem that they had invented a new way of dealing with issues already familiar some seventy years before.

But there is also a second reading we can draw from the way that Sidgwick concluded the 1874 edition of his *Methods of Ethics*: that what he sought to do was reconcile a modern theory of right conduct with a Christian faith in a God that was the fount of Reason. That he failed in this is the real dilemma with which he wrestled: that he found himself unable to reconcile his Christian faith with a terrestrial reason. But this only highlights the fact that to conceive of the achievement of this reason as perfection is in any case misconceived – this only opens up the gap that the neoclassical economists of the 1930s sought to fill. Rather, Sidgwick was on stronger ground elsewhere, where he conceded the fallibility of human reason, its incapacity to encompass the world, moral or empirical; and such a perspective was after all consistent with Christian faith. And so we should read Sidgwick's struggle with faith not as a sign of the advance of a secular reason, but as a (personal) struggle with the limits of reason and their relationship to faith. While he experienced this as a personal struggle, it was not just a personal problem, but one related to a sense of the modern world as increasingly fragmented, disenchanted, a sense that was shared with many of his contemporaries. His real faith in science was demonstrated by his relentless efforts to submit claims regarding communication with the spiritual world to empirical proof. But faith in science amounts to a faith in transience, the expectation that what is now known will in time be superseded; while a faith in God involves a sense of eternity that is denied by faith in science.

[37] (1874, p. 473). Cf. 7th edition of 1907 (1981, p. 509).

Acknowledgements

I would like to thank Jonathan Smith, Archivist and Modern Manuscript Cataloguer, Trinity College Library, Cambridge for his help with details of Sidgwick's relationship to the College in the later 1860s, and with material relating to the Moral Sciences Tripos; and Simon J. Cook, Chris Stray, John Winckler and two anonymous referees for helpful comments and suggestions in revising the original draft.

References

Anon., 1893. *The student's guide to the University of Cambridge.* 5th ed. Cambridge: Cambridge.

Anon., 2004. *The book of common prayer.* Cambridge: Cambridge University Press.

Backhouse, R., 2006. Sidgwick, Marshall, and the Cambridge School of Economics. *History of political economy*, 38, 15–44.

Backhouse, R.E. and Nishizawa, T., 2010. Introduction. *In*: Backhouse and Nishizawa, eds. *No wealth but life. Welfare economics and the welfare state in Britain, 1880–1940.* Cambridge: Cambridge University Press, 1–24.

Bevir, M., 2011. *The making of British socialism.* Princeton, NJ: Princeton University Press.

Coase, R.H., 1990. Alfred Marshall's family and ancestry. *In*: Rita McWilliams-Tullberg, ed. *Alfred Marshall in retrospect.* Aldershot: Edward Elgar, 9–27.

Collini, S., Donald, W., and John, B., 1983. *That noble science of politics. A study in nineteenth-century intellectual history.* Cambridge: Cambridge University Press.

Cook, S.J., 2009. *The intellectual foundations of Alfred Marshall's economic science. A rounded globe of knowledge.* Cambridge: Cambridge University Press.

Cremaschi, S., 2014. *Utilitarianism and Malthus' virtue ethics: respectable, virtuous and happy.* Abingdon: Routledge.

Crisp, R., 2015. *The cosmos of duty. Henry Sidgwick's methods of ethics.* Oxford: Oxford University Press.

Deane, P., 2001. *The life and times of J. Neville Keynes. A beacon in the tempest.* Cheltenham: Edward Elgar.

Gibbins, J.R., 2007. *John Grote, Cambridge University and the development of Victorian thought.* Exeter: Imprint Academic.

Grote, J., 1865. *Exploratio philosophica. Rough notes on modern intellectual science. Part I.* Cambridge: Deighton, Bell, and Co.

Grote, J., 1870. *An examination of the utilitarian philosophy*, J.B. Mayor, ed. Cambridge: Deighton, Bell, and Co.

Grote, J., 1900. *Exploratio philosophica. Rough notes on modern intellectual science. Part II.* Cambridge: Cambridge University Press.

Hale, P.J., 2014. *Political descent. Malthus, mutualism, and the politics of evolution in Victorian England.* Chicago, IL: Chicago University Press.

Harrod, R., 1951. *The life of John Maynard Keynes.* London: Macmillan.

Hunter, I., 2015. Secularization: the birth of a modern combat concept. *Modern intellectual history*, 12, 1–32.

Keynes, J.M., 1972. Alfred Marshall. *In*: *The collected writings of John Maynard Keynes.* Vol. X: *Essays in biography.* London: Macmillan, 161–231.

Lazari-Radek, K.D. and Singer, P., 2014. *The point of view of the universe. Sidgwick and contemporary ethics.* Oxford: Oxford University Press.

Medema, S.G., 2008. 'Losing my religion': Sidgwick, theism, and the struggle for utilitarian ethics in economic analysis. *History of political economy*, 40, 189–211.
Palfrey, D., 2002. The moral sciences tripos at Cambridge University, 1848–1860. Thesis (PhD). University of Cambridge.
Schultz, B., 2004. *Henry Sidgwick: eye of the universe. An intellectual biography.* Cambridge: Cambridge University Press.
Sidgwick, A. and Sidgwick, E.M., eds., 1906. *Henry Sidgwick. A memoir.* London: Macmillan.
Sidgwick, H., 1874. *The methods of ethics.* London: Macmillan.
Sidgwick, H., 1883. *The principles of political economy.* London: Macmillan.
Sidgwick, H., 1901a. The philosophy of T. H. Green. *Mind n.s.*, 10, 18–29.
Sidgwick, H., 1901b. *The principles of political economy.* 3rd ed. London: Macmillan.
Sidgwick, H., 1906. Autobiographical fragment. *In:* A. Sidgwick and E.M. Sidgwick, eds. *Henry Sidgwick. A memoir.* London: Macmillan, 33–8.
Sidgwick, H., 1962/1885. The scope and method of economic science. *In*: R.L. Smyth, ed. *Essays in economic method.* London: Gerald Duckworth, 73–97.
Sidgwick, H., 1981/1907. *The methods of ethics.* Indianapolis: Hackett Publishing.
Stephen, L., 1901. Henry Sidgwick. *Mind*, 10 (37), 1–17.
Tribe, K., 2014. Socialist historiography. *History of European ideas*, 40, 734–40.
Tribe, K., 2015. Demographic change and social structure, paper given at the workshop "Economies and societies in uncertain times". Université de Cergy-Pontoise.
Winstanley, D.A., 1947. *Later Victorian Cambridge.* Cambridge: Cambridge University Press.

Abstract

Henry Sidgwick is today remembered as a later nineteenth-century moral philosopher who struggled with his Christian faith, having difficulty reconciling this with an emergent modern and secular philosophy. In this paper, it is suggested that the only accurate part of this statement relates to the century in which Henry Sidgwick lived. It is argued that modern readers lack sensitivity to questions of faith and religiosity that were commonplace in the later nineteenth century, and that to have doubts in an Anglican faith did not necessarily imply any weakening of Christian faith. Furthermore, a misreading of Sidgwick as a moral philosopher in the modern sense neglects Sidgwick's central role in a Moral Sciences Tripos that included logic and political economy. Only after Marshall extracted political economy and political science from the Moral Sciences Tripos in 1903 did that Tripos become the foundation for a new Philosophy Tripos, and it is an error to read that later configuration back into the Tripos that Sidgwick led from 1883 to 1900.

Pigou on philosophy and religion

Daniela Donnini Macciò

'And, when to our friend who never speaks of it,
and whom we do not ask to speak, God stands evident and real,
are we so confident that he is deluded and we are not the blind?'
(A.C. Pigou, 1908a, p. 63, emphasis in the original)

1. Introduction

The vibrant dialogue between economists and philosophers on the blurred boundaries between welfare economics and moral philosophy has led to important developments in ethics, normative economics, and political philosophy. It is therefore not surprising to find substantial evidence of ethical awareness in one of the founding fathers of the so-called 'old' welfare economics. The essays discussed in this article, *Robert Browning as a Religious Teacher* (*RB*, 1901a) and the writings collected in *The Problem of Theism and Other Essays* (*PT*, 1908a), reveal Pigou's search for a moral philosophy which, discarding religion as logically untenable, preserved its ethical plea and substantiated a commitment to good. This quest produced significant resonances in his economic theories.[1]

Pigou shared this moral quest with many late Victorian intellectuals. In Keynes's words, 'the decade of the 1860 was the critical moment at which Christian dogma fell away from the serious philosophical world of England or, at any rate, of Cambridge' (Keynes 1972, p. 168). It was another step in the secularisation of the western world, a process defined by Charles Taylor as 'a move from a society where belief in God was unchallenged, and

A previous version of this article was presented to the workshop *The conflict-ridden development of modernity: theology and political economy*, 17–18 December 2014, Lyon, France.

1 Very few studies have been devoted to Pigou's philosophy: McLure (2011); McLure and Knight (2012).

indeed unproblematic, to one in which it is understood to be one option among others' (Taylor 2007, p. 3). An ethical void had to be filled, and the biographies of many late Victorians testify to the unrest, and even agony, of this quest. Sidgwick, who struggled in vain to find scientific evidence for Christian dogmas, was torn between his religious needs and his philosophical principles for most of his adult life (Medema 2008, p. 9). Pigou, apparently, was not caught in the 'storm and stress' (Sidgwick 1898, p. 33) of the religious crises suffered by Sidgwick and Marshall; however, he also lived a tension, not assuaged by religious faith, between his moral sensibility and an acute awareness of the pervasiveness of evil on earth.

Most historians of economic thought consider Pigou as 'an extension' of Sidgwick (O'Donnell 1979, p. 589; Medema 2008, 2009, p. 60).[2] Central elements of Pigou's economics, such as the notion of external effect and the welfare criteria, derived from Sidgwick's *Principles of Political Economy* (1883); and the philosophical structure of Pigou's economic thinking, like Sidgwick's, may be defined utilitarian in view of its focus on welfare maximisation. However, some commentators have argued that Pigou's acceptance of utilitarianism was not unconditional (Arrow et al. 2002, p. 6); others have remarked that he was 'at best, an eclectic utilitarian' (Aslanbeigui and Oakes 2015, p. 64). According to Koslowski and Shionoya (1993), Pigou was not a utilitarian at all; and, in an essay that uncovers the influence of a comprehensively defined 'idealism' on the making of the British welfare state, José Harris has hinted at Pigou's attempt to 'smuggle certain idealist preconceptions into neo-classical political economy through the medium of welfare economics' (Harris 1992, p. 141).[3] What is certain is that Pigou's philosophical background reveals a plurality of inspirations deserving recognition. In particular, considering that in *Wealth and Welfare* (*WW* 1912) Pigou quoted G. E. Moore's *Principia Ethica*

2 Aslanbeigui and Oakes (2015, p. 63) indicate some differences between Pigou and Sidgwick.

3 For 'idealist' it is not here intended a complete adhesion to the principles of philosophical idealism, as put forward, for instance, by T. H. Green; rather, Harris has signalled the recurrence, in British social thought between 1870 and 1940, of some idealist themes and arguments, such as the organic view of society, with a focus on its moral personality; the emphasis on the material elevation of humanity as a means to its spiritual progress, considered as the true end of social action; and the 'search for a modernist reformulation of (or ethical substitute for) traditional Christianity' (Harris 1992, p.135). On the impact of idealism on British social and political thought see also Boucher and Vincent (2000) and Offer (2006).

(*PE*, 1903), and equated welfare with Moore's idea of the good, it is essential to consider the impact of the philosopher on him.[4]

Pigou's first accomplishments were in the fields of literature and philosophy. His poem *Alfred the Great* won the Chancellor's Gold Medal for English Verse in 1899; and in 1900 the above-mentioned *RB* won the Burney Prize, awarded to essays on a 'moral or metaphysical subject, on the existence, nature, and attributes of God, or on the truth or evidence of Christian religion' (Cambridge University 1901, p. 613).[5] This work introduces the main themes that Pigou elaborated on in his subsequent philosophical writings, namely, the proof of God's existence and the meaning of good and evil.[6] In the same years Pigou, building on Marshall's economics, was also lying the groundwork for *WW*, later enlarged and reworked as *The Economics of Welfare* (*EW* 1920) (Tribe 2011). Pigou's intellectual development is difficult to pin down because, in the years between 1900 and 1912, he moved back and forth between the economic and the philosophic discourses. To demonstrate that Pigou the philosopher somehow matched Pigou the economist is the goal of this article.

The building blocks of Pigou's welfare economics are the following: (i) the notion of economic welfare, measured by the national dividend; (ii) the acceptance of a utilitarian/welfaristic social welfare function, implying interpersonal comparability; (iii) the study of distributional

4 Regrettably, no personal recollections of Pigou's inmost convictions and beliefs have survived, as his personal papers were for the most part destroyed after his death. Arthur Cecil Pigou (1877–1959) was born in a prosperous family of Huguenot descent. In 1896, he got a scholarship to King's College, Cambridge, to study History and Modern Language and, after a First in History, he moved on to the Moral Sciences Tripos to study ethics, political philosophy, and advanced political economy. He was mentored by Alfred Marshall, becoming his successor as professor of Political Economy in 1908. Pigou's remarkably rapid academic career was crucial for the preservation of both the newly established Economic Tripos and the Marshallian orthodoxy in Cambridge (Aslanbeigui and Oakes 2015).

5 Pigou submitted the essay to King's College for a prize fellowship, but failed. He succeeded in his second attempt with a thesis on *The Causes and Effects of Change in the Relative Values of Agricultural Produce in the United Kingdom during the last Fifty Years*, winner of the Cobden Prize in 1902. On both dissertations, see Mc Lure (2011).

6 The first reference to the 'problem' of the good from an economic viewpoint appeared in *The Principles and Methods of Industrial Peace* (1905b). Here, Pigou, anticipating a similar hesitation in *WW* and *EW* with regard to the relationship between economic and non-economic welfare (see Section 6), briefly drew attention to the ethical aspects of the labour market, and then chose not to confront them: 'The inquiry, indeed, is an ethical one, but it can, for the most part, be conducted without reference to those fundamental controversies in which the science of the "good" is involved' (Pigou 1905b, p. 3).

conflicts of interest; (iv) the possibility of market failures, due to malfunctions in the allocation process; and (v) the advocacy of governmental intervention to correct economic disturbances. It is possible to show that each of the above elements has a philosophical counterpart in the ethical texts. In the case of (i), Pigou himself pointed to the equivalence between the philosophical concept of good and that of welfare, whose economic constituents are the focus of *WW* and *EW*. In other instances, the resonances are discernible through textual analysis. It will be argued that interpersonal utility comparisons (ii) and distributive issues implying conflict of interest (iii) have a parallel in the comparability, and possible antagonism, between the good of different individuals. Pigou's analysis of market failures (iv) arguably reflects his philosophical pessimism, which was the horizon of his ethical perspective. Finally, an ethical warranty for public interferences with individual interest to foster economic welfare (v) is implicit in Pigou's rejection of determinism.

The first section of this article deals with the focal points of Pigou's philosophical reflection as appearing in the essay on Browning. A methodological overview of *PT* (Section 2) is followed by an account of Pigou's assessment of Christian theism (Section 3), and by two related sections dealing, respectively, with Pigou's analysis of the nature of the good (Section 4), and with his discussion of interpersonal comparability of good (Section 5). Section 6 illustrates how these themes were taken up in *WW*, describes Ralph Hawtrey's Moorean criticism to Pigou's notion of welfare, and highlights the similarities between Pigou's and Moore's philosophical approaches. The concluding section sums up the main features of Pigou's economic philosophy.

2. A refutation of philosophical optimism

Pigou appraised twice Browning's poetry[7], the first time in *RB*, the second time in connection with George Meredith's.[8] To Pigou, who highly valued the poets' power of perception and philosophical insight,[9] Browning's

7 Robert Browning (1812–1889) was one of the most celebrated and popular Victorian poets and playwrights. Among his works, *Dramatis Personae* (1864), and *The Ring and The Book* (1868–1869).

8 Pigou 1905a and *PT*. George Meredith (1828–1909) was an English poet and novelist, influenced by German Romanticism and idealism. In his writings (among the most popular, *The Egoist*, 1879; *Diana of the Crossways*, 1885) he postulated the elevation of the individual to a higher spiritual condition.

9 See Pigou's essay on Nietzsche (Pigou 1908c and *PT*): 'the spirit of wonder and reverence that prompts the greatest poetry is also the impulse of philosophy. The difference between them is not in attitude, but in method, the one following the hard road of systematisation, the other flying to the same goal with wings of intuition. ... Positive construction in ethics is insight and little else. Here the poet and the philosopher meet' (*PT*: pp. 109–10).

poems revealed a distinct, although not coherent, philosophical system. Its central themes were love – God's love to man, man's love to God and other human beings – and a peculiar sort of religious optimism. As to the first element, Browning envisaged an ideal form of love derived from the direct perception of God by the individual – an experience inspiring actions for the common good. As to optimism, the poet's faith in a loving and omnipotent God was coupled with the belief that evil was ultimately an illusion, and that only good was real. In Pigou's words, 'defect ensures completion; hope is the promise of supply; evil will perish; and good will triumph' (*RB*: p. 7). Browning's theory of salvation involved a rejection of the doctrine of eternal punishment, for God would eventually save all, good and evil alike – the only difference was that for the righteous the process would be much quicker, so that 'the result of a man's choosing evil is the postponement of his day of blessedness' (*RB*: p. 107). In any case, as Pigou pointed out, for Browning God's design 'marches steadily on towards its consummation, sublimely regardless of all human efforts' (*RB*: p. 105). Moreover, as God's design was too vast for human comprehension, moral life was guided by the 'voice of conscience', the direct knowledge of one's duty. The categorical imperative of ethics was for Browning only a 'form', whose content everyone had to discover for him/herself. Pigou was not prepared to accept the uncomfortable implications for morality of this conclusion. Against Browning's dangerous moral relativism, Pigou believed in the objectivity of moral value, in tune with Moore (*RB*: p. 128). Pigou, in particular, did not accept Browning's denial of the reality of evil. Besides being contrary to human experience, this view was morally dangerous and logically inconsistent with any ethical theory.

However, Pigou agreed with Browning's critical assessment of psychological hedonism: the individual was not 'an inert mass, chained … to the irresistible power of imagined pain and pleasure' (*RB*: p. 103). Like Browning, Pigou rejected moral determinism – the idea that every human decision or action is the inevitable and necessary consequence of antecedent conditions – and pointed to a 'limited' but 'efficient' freedom of the will, as suggested by common sense (*RB*: p. 103; also in *PT*: pp. 65–9; p. 79). Pigou also approved of Browning's views on social reform. For the poet, one should not try to revolutionise society – an enterprise reserved for individuals of exceptional qualities – but to 'strive for a slow and gradual bettering of the conditions of human life … without any admixture of subversive experiments'. This meant that it was a duty 'to alleviate the bodily sufferings of the multitude; for, though is very true that there are other things than the satisfaction of animal wants, yet if a man is starved, it is impossible to feed his soul' (*RB*: p. 130). Pigou clearly approved of this aspect of Browning's thought, matching the Cambridge tradition of Sidgwick and

Marshall. Pigou dealt with a related issue – charity – in a later essay. Unoriginally, he stated that 'wise charity' should aim at improving 'both character and material conditions' of the indigent (Pigou 1901b, p. 237). 'Indiscriminate' or 'misdirected' charity, either by the state or private individuals, crushed the spirit of independence among the poor, and encouraged opportunistic and dissolute behaviour on their part. Pigou confirmed this view in *WW*, *EW* and in *Employers and Economic Chivalry* (1923a).[10]

As documented by Boyd Hilton (1988, p. 336), Browning's religious optimism, combined with an emphasis on 'enthusiasm' and sentimentality, was a distinctive feature of a specific current of though in mid-Victorian culture, also expressed in the works of Charles Dickens, George Meredith, and Charles Swinburne. The strictures of the earlier 'age of atonement' and the theology of the Cross were replaced by trust in the alliance between God and humanity and in a future of continuous moral and economic progress. In *RB* as well as in the later essay on Browning and Meredith (Pigou 1905a; and *PT*: pp. 125–39), Pigou condemned the belief that good would eventually and certainly triumph over evil, either because personality survived after death, as in Browning, or because humanity, struggling toward perfection, would ultimately win over evil, as in Meredith. Although the latter did not indulge in the belief that evil is unreal, the goodness of Meredith's utopic world was contradicted by the plain fact of physical extinction: 'unless death is done away, evil will not be overcome and disappear' (*PT*: p. 138). In insisting on the reality of evil, and on the necessity of a firm moral perspective to tackle it, Pigou displayed a sombre view of human destiny, which would resurface in his analysis of the economic evils of society. At the same time, the vindication of free will provided a ray of hope, substantiating public action to contrast them.

3. Pigou's essays on ethics and theology: an overview

Pigou's inquiry into the good continued in a series of articles published in *The International Journal of Ethics*: 'The Ethics of the Gospels' (1907b), 'Some Points of Ethical Controversy' (1907c), and 'The Ethics of Nietzsche' (1908c). Together with the already mentioned 'The Optimism of Browning and Meredith', published in 1905 in *The Independent Review*, and three original essays – 'The General Nature of Reality', 'The Problem of Theism', and 'Free Will' – they make up *The Problem of Theism and Other Essays* (*PT*, 1908a. 'Some Points of Ethical Controversy' was included in *PT* with the title 'The Problem of Good'). Pigou defined the book as tentative

10 Aslanbeigui and Oakes have stressed Pigou's 'intellectual circumspection and conservatism' (2015, p. 100).

and amateurish. However, the fact that Pigou collected and republished these articles just a few months after their first appearance suggests that they were part of a unitary project, and that he ascribed more than a marginal significance to them. *PT* was Pigou's last overtly philosophical work; later, he channelled his ethical concerns in his economic theories.

For Pigou, economics was a positive science (Pigou 1908b, p. 13; *EW*: 5) which needed an ethical foundation 'to pass judgment on questions of the relative goodness-in-themselves of various states of conscious life'. To put it differently, economic and ethics were mutually dependent as social reform, as indicated above, required both. This did not necessarily involve a division of labour: 'may I add that it is an urgent need for the economist that he be also a student of Ethics?' (Pigou 1908b, p. 14). Pigou's view of economics made him a true disciple of Marshall (Cook 2009, p. 291), as an ethical impulse was the core of Marshall's work and characterised the economic tradition he founded.[11] However, Marshall limited somewhat the implications of that impulse, since his priority was to establish a Cambridge economic orthodoxy by reinforcing the independent scientific status of the discipline and make it foremost among the social sciences (Kadish 1989; Kadish and Tribe 1993). Eventually, Robbins' epistemological revolution cleared British economic science of the remnants of its previous ethical foundations (Robbins 1932).

In the introduction to *PT*, Pigou credited Sidgwick for the 'general philosophical standpoint' of his research. However, throughout the book, he refused to adhere consistently and unquestioningly to any specific philosophic approach, and Sidgwick's, T. H. Green's, and Moore's arguments received fundamental criticism. This attitude corresponds to what Aslanbeigui and Oakes have called Pigou's 'methodological pragmatism' in economic theory (2015, p. 100; 2013). For Pigou, 'each particular case must be considered on its own merit in all the details of its concrete circumstances. High-sounding generalizations ... are irrelevant fireworks' (Pigou 1935, pp. 27–8; 1929, p. 4).

G. E. Moore exerted an influence here, arguably. He warned in *PE* that 'to search for unity and system at the expense of truth, is not, I take it, the proper business of philosophy, however universally it may have been the practice of philosophers' (*PE*: pp. 222–3). Moore's ethics aimed to establish the correct method of tackling discrete moral problems, rather than attempting to solve them by a settled doctrine. To Pigou, clear and

11 See A. Robinson's quote in Marcuzzo et al. (2008, p. 578): 'Pigou, the complete Marshallian, always regarded economics as a subject one studied not for itself, but for the benefit it might bring. And this was the prevalent outlook of virtually the whole of the Cambridge staff of the period'.

rigorous case-by-case analysis was fundamental in economics, as it had been to Moore in ethics[12]. Though Moore's inspiration was not explicitly recognised by Pigou, in the introduction to *PT* he acknowledged the help of J.M. Keynes and Bertrand Russell, two Cambridge Apostles who were then very close to Moore.[13] The point to note is that both Pigou's philosophical essays and *PE* had the same focus: the good. The following four sections examine the features of Pigou's reflection on the good in relation to his economic theory.[14]

4. The value of religious experience

The starting point of Pigou's *PT* was a metaphysical investigation to ascertain whether, behind the world of phenomena, there existed an independent reality, separate from the observer's mind. He concluded that a hidden level of reality existed, with the dimensions of space and time belonging to it (*PT*: pp. 1–17; *RB*: p. 11). In rejecting both materialist and idealist explanations of the fundamental reality, Pigou wondered whether the theological argument that the ultimate independent reality was God was sustained by evidence. This is the subject of the second chapter of Pigou's book.

The belief in the existence of a benevolent spiritual Being – powerful enough 'to make good prevail over evil in the long run' (*PT*: p. 22) – was Pigou's definition of Christian theism. He discussed two claims advanced to support it: the argument from design, which infers the existence of a supreme Creator from the seeming adaptation of means to ends in nature; and the argument based on religious experience. He refuted the first by denying that finality prevails in nature and by arguing that, even when a purpose was apparent, it did not prove God's existence for a harmonious

12 This view was also reflected in Pigou's claim that to draw a clear-cut distinction between the cases in which state action and *laissez-faire* were respectively appropriate was 'unreal and misleading' (Pigou 1935, p. 110).

13 Moore's influence on Pigou was not conveyed by personal acquaintance in the Apostles Society, one of the main philosophical incubators of Cambridge intellectuals. Pigou, in fact, 'managed to slip through the net' of the Society (Skidelsky 1983, p. 118).

14 According to Austin Robinson, Pigou 'applied to economic material the method of the philosopher, clarifying the issues, dissecting them and analysing them, trying to see how different assumptions regarding the material might modify conclusions—the analytical method applied with great precision to an essentially qualitative argument ... While Pigou, as his working life continued, gradually acquired the habits of mathematical economics, he was not by instinct and training a mathematical economist. His thinking remained primarily that of a philosopher trained in analysis' (Robinson 1968).

effect could be the result of uncoordinated, conflicting forces. Interestingly, whereas T. Chalmers (1833), R. Whately (1833), and F. Bastiat (1850) had considered the functioning of the market economy as evidence for the argument from design (Waterman 1991), Pigou used the same example to undermine that thesis.[15]

Pigou showed a far greater interest in the argument for God's existence based on religious experience. Thanks to his studies on Browning, Pigou knew that for the believer 'the existence of God, like the existence of self, is incapable of proof simply because of its absolute self-evidence' (*RB*: p. 15). Though Pigou could not share this belief, he was fascinated by the forms of the individual's inner perceptions of God, and by their effects on character and behaviour. He declared to appreciate 'liberal Christianity', amounting to undogmatic beliefs characterised by 'the very slight emphasis which is laid upon theology as contrasted with religion' (*PT*: p. 42). Drawing most of his examples from William James' *Varieties of Religious Experience* (1902)[16], he emphasised both the diversity of religious feelings and the similarities between them – the existence of 'a common language of the soul' – as expressed in works of poetry and literature or reported by ordinary people. Yet, these subjective sensations resisted criticism and logical analysis, hence they could not be discussed on purely rational terms. This presented a formidable challenge to 'scientific theology'.[17] Religious experience afforded only a 'slight *prima facie* probability to Christian Theism' (*PT*: p. 61). In fact, it did not provide sufficient evidence for the existence of an omnipotent spiritual entity; it proved the existence of *both* good and evil, but said nothing about their respective strength. Pigou, therefore, concluded that Christian theism remained unproven. Nevertheless, Pigou, like Mill (1874) and Sidgwick (1897, p. 584), acknowledged that religion had a significant value for its encouragement to morality and self-improvement. Accordingly, as in the quote in epigraph, religion deserved the utmost respect and attention from the scientist. Indeed, like

15 'Unity in the cause cannot rightly be inferred from coherence in the effect. The measure of harmony in the economic world – the many-motived machine of industry working not otherwise than it might do under the guidance of a single hand – shows us that, so long as both act constantly, the operation of a single force is indistinguishable from that of a complex of conflicting forces' (*PT*: p. 37).

16 In relation to Pigou's views, it appears significant James' definition of 'healthy minded' religious persons as individuals having a deep feeling of 'the goodness of life' (James 1902, p. 79) and the endorsement of liberal Christianity against 'old hell-fire theology' (James 1902, p. 91).

17 In Pigou's definition, the discipline aiming to determine 'for what, if any, theistic inference the many records of religious experience can afford a solid basis'. (*PT*: p. 50).

Mill (Carr 1962), Pigou was reluctant to embrace complete scepticism, and his assessment of religion seems inspired by a longing for the comfort and inspiration of faith, to which he was attracted though he could not persuade himself to believe.

Pigou's quest for the good continued in another chapter of *PT*, dealing with the moral content of the New Testament. To Pigou, the ethical message of Christ appeared incomplete and obfuscated by its theological content. Pigou pointed to the fact that, for Jesus, goodness and badness belonged not to actions but to states of consciousness, and intrinsic goodness consisted in love more than in virtuous deeds. This view, emphasising intentions over consequences, led Pigou to draw attention to a gap between utilitarian and Christian ethics.[18] For Jesus, love consisted in complete devotion, without purpose of reward or self-aggrandisement, and love was both an end in itself and a means to the good. The object of love, 'Jesus tells us, is God and Man, and furthermore, not Man merely, but every man, for every man is our neighbour' (*PT*: p. 107).[19] Christ's life demonstrated that for him happiness, like love, was good in itself, as he cared for other people's happiness and tried to mitigate their sufferings. That love should be universal, though, seemed questionable to Pigou, 'for all men are not alike'.[20] Unfortunately, 'we are without guidance as to the way in which our love were best distributed' (*PT*: p. 108). In conclusion, Pigou did not find a complete ethical doctrine in the Gospels, but he acknowledged their 'unrivalled clearness of moral perception, unrewarding of formulas and unfettered by tradition, that throws into bright light broad tracts on the sphere of good' (*PT*: p. 108).[21]

18 Sidgwick's intellectual crisis originated from a similar awareness: Sidgwick 1866, p. 23; Schneewind 1977, pp. 45–7; Medema 2008, p. 14.

19 Sidgwick too remarked that 'the cardinal doctrine of Jesus of Nazareth' was altruism (quoted in Medema 2008, p. 21).

20 This statement by Pigou supports the allegation of 'analytic hierarchicalism' moved by Peart and Levy to post-classical economics in general and to Pigou in particular (Peart and Levy 2005; 2008). For reason of space, however, this point will not be discussed here.

21 In another chapter of *PT* Pigou tackled intrinsic goodness in relation to Nietzsche's theorization of the Superman in *Thus Spoke Zarathustra*. This subject cannot receive full treatment here. In extreme synthesis, for Pigou Nietzsche had not specified the exact qualities pertaining to the Superman, but had only advanced some vague and often inconsistent indications on this issue. The conclusion of Pigou's research, once again, was negative; neither the Gospels, nor Nietzsche's philosophy, nor Browning's poetical world could stand the consistency requirements of Pigou's philosophical analysis, but all were still significant to him: in particular, both the Superman and 'the glowing faith of Him that died on Calvary', before whom 'the cool transparencies of thought' must bow in respect (*PT*: p. 64), provided a much needed inspiration to humanity.

Pigou's views on religion can be compared to Sidgwick's and Moore's. Sidgwick admitted the impossibility to prove God's existence, but was unable to accept the idea of a godless universe and maintained his belief in the existence of a supreme creator. In 'The Value of Religion' (1901), Moore too refused to profess atheism, by arguing that, if there was no proof of the existence of God, there was no evidence of the contrary either. Nevertheless, against Sidgwick, Moore believed that faith in God was not the necessary foundation of morality.[22] Therefore, to Moore, the value of religious research appeared limited.[23]

For Sidgwick, religious faith expressed itself as love for one's fellow human beings, and inspired public-spirited action. Moore, on the contrary, eschewed theistic arguments in dealing with the good. Pigou took an intermediate stance. He acknowledged the importance of religion as a source of moral inspiration, but he was not disposed to stretch his intellectual convictions to accommodate religious beliefs unsupported by evidence. Though his awareness of the inescapable reality of evil could not be mitigated by religious faith, he retained a keen interest in the subjective aspects of religious feelings and in their effect on the individual's mental states and actions.

5. A goodness function

The impossibility of validating Christian theism left Pigou's ethical quest still unanswered. His search for the meaning and content of the good thus proceeded in the third chapter of *PT*, 'The problem of good', whose subject takes on a special importance in view of its successive elaboration in his welfare economics. Like Moore's *PE*, the chapter contains a critical review of competing ethical doctrines. To Pigou, the main areas of disagreement concerned (i) the method of ethical inquiry; (ii) the qualities

22 In a passage somehow anticipating his focus in *PE* on aesthetic enjoyment and personal affections as the highest intrinsic goods, Moore pointed to two psychological attitudes that had made religion promote morality in ancient times, but were not relevant any more. The first was the intrinsic value of 'contemplation' of what was considered to be the most perfect and truly good. He argued, however, that there were now plenty of these ideal objects in literature and art. The second was the need to believe that some good things existed; and these things, too, could be found without calling God into play.

23 'It surely might be better to give up the search for a God whose existence is and remains indemonstrable, and to divert the feeling which the religious wish to spend on him, towards those of our kind, who though perhaps less good than we can imagine God to be, are worthy of all the affections that we can feel, and whose help and sympathy are much more certainly real. We might perhaps with advantage worship the real creature a little more, and his hypothetical creator a good deal less' (Moore 1901, p. 98).

making up the goodness of an individual; and (iii) the way in which the good of a person is related to the good of other individuals. As for the first issue, Pigou rejected the method which sought to determine *a priori* what things were good – this approach, expounded by T.H. Green, was 'mischievous and idle' (*PT*: p. 82). Pigou embraced intuitionism instead. Just as in Moore's *PE*, Pigou's quest was for the intrinsic (as distinct from the instrumental) good[24], and, as he was like Moore a believer in the intuitive grasp of ethical truths, he assumed that direct perception was the only way to ascertain if a thing was good. In borrowing the example about the qualities 'good' and 'yellow' from Moore's *PE*, Pigou wrote that we perceive some things to be good and some bad, 'just as we perceive that some are yellow and other red' (*PT*: p. 82).

As to the second point of controversy, Pigou claimed that the only things of which it was possible to assess the intrinsic goodness were states of consciousness.[25] Basing his claim on ordinary experience, Pigou advanced the view that the goodness of any given mental state depended not on one, but on several variables: pleasure, love, good will, the kind of ideals one pursued, one's attitude towards the external world, and enthusiasm in pursuing one's aims (*PT*: p. 86). Though he did not write it down as such, Pigou clearly conceived the relation between the goodness of a state and these factors as a mathematical function, $G = F\ (p;\ l;\ gw; i; a; e)$, where p is for pleasure, l for love, gw for good will, i is for ideals, a for attitude, and e for enthusiasm. He aimed to ascertain, first, whether the function's value was always directly correlated to any of those variables; second, whether the sign of any of them determined the function's sign, independently of the others; and, finally, he wondered what it could be said about the nature of the goodness' function if the above questions were answered in the negative.

For Pigou, the goodness of a state was not always directly correlated to the quantity of pleasure it contained, as in the case of pleasure deriving

24 As a testimony of the importance Moore ascribed to the distinction between intrinsic and instrumental good, see Ralph Hawtrey's unpublished *Right Policy*: 'When I went up to Trinity, Cambridge, as an undergraduate, I had the good fortune to come under the influence of G E. Moore, who had just been elected a Fellow, and it is from him that I owe the view that the Good is a matter of direct judgment and is not to be explained away in terms of anything else, a view which I have found to be an unfailing clarifier of ethical thinking ... Moore was especially insistent on distinguishing ends from means, for only what is good as an end, good in itself, is an object of direct judgment' (Hawtrey n.d., p. 1).

25 In this respect, he followed Sidgwick rather than Moore, for whom goodness belonged not only to conscious states but also to 'organic unities', complex states of consciousness and objects. As shown below, this point resurfaces in *WW*: 'welfare includes states of consciousness only, and not material things or conditions' (*WW*: p. 3).

from evil doing. Furthermore, Pigou claimed that a great devotion to one's ideals did not contribute to goodness if what was enthusiastically pursued was evil. In a similar way, a greater intensity of love added to the goodness of a state only if the object of love was a worthy one (this was a favourite argument of Moore's: see e.g. *PE*: Ch. VI). As to the first question concerning the function, then, Pigou concluded that it was impossible to say that an addition to any of the variables led to a greater goodness of the state. As for the second question, namely the existence of a variable whose sign always determined the sign of the goodness function, Pigou answered again in the negative; in particular, he denied that pleasure was an essential component of goodness. Perhaps, he wrote, good will may be essential, but he was doubtful. As for the third question, Pigou was once again sceptical about the possibility to reach any general conclusion about the nature of the function. He thus introduced virtue as another element likely to affect goodness, and he stated that, *ceteris paribus*, there was a positive correlation between virtue and happiness, on the one hand, and goodness, on the other. In conclusion, he argued that it was safe to say that a good state of consciousness was one in which happiness corresponded to virtue (*PT*: p. 89), though he did not elaborate on this point.

Apparently, Pigou was uncertain about the originality of his goodness function. He wrote Keynes asking whether the representation of the goodness of a conscious state as function of several variables had ever been advanced before, confessing to be 'rather behind in things lately written on Ethics', and also to have 'very likely forgotten things read' on the subject.[26] In particular, he asked Keynes if the idea of a function featured in 'Moore's book' (presumably *PE*). The letter is undated, unfortunately, and the goodness function does not feature in Pigou's later writings, even if it is implicit in the first chapter of *WW*.[27] However, the document indicates that Pigou believed that his idea was relevant, and that, if not derived directly from Moore's philosophy, it was at least in line with it. It was not, actually, since a goodness function encompassing several variables clashed with Moore's notion of good as simple and indefinable.[28] Regrettably,

26 Pigou's letter is among Keynes's Papers in the Modern Archive of King's College Library, Cambridge.

27 'Every conscious state is a complex of many elements, and includes not only satisfactions but also cognitions, emotions, and desires' (*WW*: p. 5).

28 'Good, then, if we mean by it that quality which we assert to belong to a thing, when we say that the thing is good, is incapable of any definition, in the most important sense of that word. The most important sense of "definition" is that in which a definition states what are the parts which invariably compose a certain whole; and in this sense "good" has no definition because it is simple and has no parts' (*PE*: §10).

Keynes's answer is also unknown. Pigou's goodness function, so similar to the utility function, is significant as an attempt to create an analytic tool bridging philosophy and economics.

6. The relational aspects of good: interpersonal comparability and competition

The third point of ethical controversy tackled by Pigou concerns two related issues, which are significant both in ethics and in economic theory. These are (i) the comparability of the good of different individuals, and (ii) the possible conflict between the good of different individuals. Anticipating his stance in favour of interpersonal comparisons of utility in *WW* and *EW*, Pigou declared that it was possible, and indeed necessary, to assess and to compare the effects of given actions on the good of different individuals, despite the fact that they were separate centres of consciousness (*PT*: p. 90). Many decades later, in a belated reply to Robbins' criticism of interpersonal comparisons of utility (Robbins 1932), Pigou took a stance later vindicated by Sen (1970, 1998). With words that closely resemble those used in *PT*, Pigou argued for the fundamental role of interpersonal comparisons in any form of knowledge aiming to have an impact on practice:

> 'Nobody can prove that anybody besides himself exists, but, nevertheless, everybody is quite sure of it. We do not, in short, start from a *tabula rasa*, binding ourselves to hold every opinion which the natural man entertains to be guilty until it is proved innocent. The burden is the other way. To deny this is to wreck, not merely Welfare Economics, but the whole apparatus of practical thought. On the basis of analogy, observation, and intercourse, personal comparisons *can*, as I think, properly be made'. (Pigou 1951, p. 292, emphasis in the original)

As to the second issue (conflicts among the good of distinct individuals), Pigou maintained that the most authoritative philosophers of his time had dealt with it unsatisfactorily. T. H. Green's definition of the good, for instance, ruled out competition on the grounds that, since man is a social animal, the good of one individual included that of others. Pigou's pessimism led him to point out that the reverse was true: more often, A's good may increase only at B's expense. For Sidgwick, this issue was particularly important, leading to a dualism of practical reason. He in fact acknowledged two moral imperatives: according to the first, one ought to pursue his/her own good regardless of that of others, but, according to the second, one ought to pursue the general good regardless of his/her own good. This amounts to saying that each individual is to be considered as an end in him/herself, and therefore his/her good cannot be sacrificed to anything or anyone else; but there is also a duty to pursue the general good, irrespective of consequences. As Pigou observed, unless the individual's good and other individuals' good dictated the same course of action, this involved a contradiction. How to reconcile one's duty with the pursuit of one's happiness? Sidgwick's solution was to assume the existence of an afterlife where the ultimate harmony of virtue and happiness was finally reached. However, though spending much time on spiritualist research, Sidgwick failed to find any evidence of immortality.

The need to reconcile Sidgwick's two moral imperatives was not for Pigou a sufficient reason for accepting the idea of either God or life after death. The same conclusion was reached in *PE*, where Moore claimed that there was an insoluble contradiction between the claims that both an individual's happiness, and that everybody's happiness, should be *the sole good*, even if the same conduct would secure both (*PE*: p. 99). For Pigou, however, Moore's criticism of Sidgwick was not to the point, as the formulations of the issue in Moore and Sidgwick were not equivalent: to say 'I ought to pursue A's happiness' (Sidgwick) is not equivalent to say 'A's happiness is the sole good' (Moore). Pigou did not embark on a defence of Sidgwick, however, because he was disposed to admit that the good of different individuals can compete. He rejected both of Sidgwick's two moral imperatives, and, consequently, there was no necessity to postulate a life after death.[29]

The view that it was possible, and indeed crucial, to compare the good of different individuals was reflected in Pigou's acceptance of interpersonal comparisons of utility. The philosophical problem of the possible conflicts among different individuals' good underlies the distributive issues that play a prominent part in Pigou's economics. In a different form, it is also implicit in the analysis of negative externalities put forward in *WW* and *EW*: social interest and private interest may diverge. In *The Unity of Political and Economic Science* (1906), Pigou defined the maximum satisfaction principle as adopted in both economics and politics 'a fallacy'. It amounted to the belief that economic freedom maximised 'economic good', and that 'pure democracy' led to the greatest 'legislative good' (Pigou 1906, p. 379); but these outcomes were not warranted. Moreover, the argument that each individual is the best judge of his/her own interest rested on the erroneous assumption that one

29 'I do not perceive that I ought to pursue my own good regardless of others' good, and I do not regard any man as an end in himself ... Possibly every man is an end in the sense that he has "claims to possess the good which cannot be altogether cancelled by any amount of good possessed by other people" [McTaggart 1906, p. 17]. But, if this be true – which I do not myself believe, and which, given that states of consciousness are the only things ultimately good or bad, cannot as a matter of fact be the case – merely asserts that fairness as between people is one element among good things. It does not imply propositions about A and B, which can, under any circumstance, become inconsistent with one another' (*PT*: p. 92).

is always the best judge of what he/she *ought* to want. 'Even … if it were true that freedom of each did conduce to a maximum satisfaction of the desires of all, it would not follow that it conduced to their maximum good or true satisfaction. This conclusion is obviously applicable to both economics and politics' (Pigou 1906, p. 380). Ralph Hawtrey (1926) replicated this argument, albeit more forcefully, as will be shown in the next section. Granted that the free market mechanism could not counteract the negative effects of certain types of self-interested behaviour on the economy as a whole, *WW* and *EW* explained how governments could 'control the play of economic forces in such wise as to promote the economic welfare, and through that, the total welfare, of their citizens as a whole' (*EW*: p. 113).

7. The good and *Wealth and Welfare*

As Shionoya (2005, p. 7) has observed, the concept of the good is an 'interface' between the two worlds of economics and moral philosophy. Pigou explicitly recognised this aspect. His research into the meaning and content of the good, in fact, closely parallels his inquiry into economic welfare. *WW* opens with a quote from Moore's *PE*: 'If I am asked, "what is good?" my answer is that good is good, and that is the end of the matter' (*PE*: p. 6). For Pigou, welfare (in general terms) was synonymous with the philosophical good. He declared that 'welfare means the same thing as good. It, too, cannot be defined, in the sense of being analysed in its parts. At the same time, we can say, and indeed it is the chief task of ethics to say, whether, and in what way, particular things belong to welfare'. Pigou advanced two propositions in this regard. The first is that welfare is non-materialistic, as it includes states of consciousness only, 'and not material things or conditions'. The second states that welfare 'can be brought under the category of greater and less' (*WW*: p. 3). The starting point of *WW* was thus a reflection on the general notion of good/welfare. At this point, there arises the question of the disciplinary boundaries of economics: he contends that economics deals with economic welfare, defined as the part of welfare 'arising in connection with the earning and spending of the national dividend', which is just a part of general welfare. Such a distinction followed, arguably, from the necessity to delimit the realm of economics.[30] Unfortunately, Pigou's discussion of the relationship between general and economic welfare was not free from hesitations.[31] Pigou acknowledged that this relationship was complex, and often uncertain; changes in economic welfare, in particular, seldom produced an equivalent change in general

30 On the relationship between economic and social welfare in Pigou and Pareto see McLure (2014).

31 Steedman (2011, p. 26) noticed a similar ambivalence in Marshall.

welfare. This effect depended in large extent on non-economic conditions prevailing in a given society, especially on its political and religious settings (*WW*: p. 12). In some cases, economic and non-economic welfare could be negatively correlated. This aspect is dealt with more extensively in *EW*. Here, to explain the possibility of conflicts between economic welfare and welfare in general, Pigou drew a contrast between two human types. The first was the intrinsically good person, 'attuned to the beautiful in nature and in art ... simple and sincere, whose passions are controlled and sympathies developed', whose disposition directly contributed to non-economic welfare. The second was the instrumentally good individual, who was necessary 'to perform complicated industrial operations' advancing material welfare (*EW*: 13). It was up to society to decide which of the two human types should be promoted, granted that the development of the latter, to the detriment of the former, necessarily implied the sacrifice of non-economic welfare to economic welfare. Pigou mentioned contemporary Germany as a nation that had made a deliberate choice in favour of the second type, though he stressed that it was not the only one. Quoting G. L. Dickinson's *Letters from John Chinaman* (1901)[32], a book that asserted the moral superiority of Eastern civilisation over Western (particularly British) materialism, Pigou argued that it was indeed possible that 'the effort devoted to the production of people which are good instruments may involve a failure to produce people who are good men' (*EW*: 14; see also Pigou 1923b, p. 81).

Pigou did not develop this line of argument, so reminiscent of the chapter on the stationary state of Mill's *Principles* (1848). Remaining on safe ground, he concluded that, even with the above provisos, it was probable that the effects of a change in economic welfare on general welfare would be 'equivalent in direction, though not in magnitude'. Therefore, 'conclusions about the effect of an economic cause upon economic welfare will hold good also of the effect on total welfare' (*WW*: p. 11), and this is why the study of economic welfare, which had the crucial advantage of being measurable by money, was not a futile endeavour[33]. On the contrary,

32 Goldsworthy Lowes Dickinson (1862–1932) was an exponent of Cambridge Idealism and an Apostle. He taught Analytical and Deductive Politics at Cambridge from 1896 to 1920, and collaborated with Marshall on the establishment of the Economic Tripos. In *John Chinaman* Dickinson compared eastern and western societies, and pointed to the former, supportive and stable, as morally superior to the latter, dominated by the 'cash nexus' and individualism.

33 'The failure of economic welfare to serve as an index of total welfare is no evidence that the study of it will fail to afford this latter info: for, though a whole may consist of many varying parts, so that a change in one part never measures the change in the whole, yet the change in the part may always *affect* the change in the whole by its full amount. If this is the case, the importance of economic study is fully established' (*WW*: p. 9).

it was of great relevance as it 'concerned chiefly to lay bare such parts of knowledge as may serve directly or indirectly, to help forward the betterment of social life' (*WW*: p. 4). Pigou showed that, *ceteris paribus*, economic welfare was increased by: (i) an increment in the national dividend; (ii) an increase of the absolute share of the national dividend accruing to the poor; and (iii) a diminution in the variability of the national dividend, especially in the share of income received by the lower classes. As to the first factor, addressed in part II of *WW*, Pigou argued that the national dividend decreased when the marginal net products of resources in different uses were unequal, as in the case of externalities deriving from the divergence between marginal net social product and marginal net private product. Whenever this divergence occurred, there was a sub-optimal resource allocation, and welfare maximisation required state intervention through taxes or subsidies. As to the second cause, tackled in part III of *WW*, Pigou dealt with redistribution from the relatively rich to the relatively poor through both 'interferences with the natural cause of wages' and taxation. In part IV, Pigou discussed the causes and effects of fluctuations in the labourers' income, with both philanthropic and state action called for to counteract the negative effects of variability in the job market. A substantial part of Pigou's analysis was also devoted to the possible inconsistencies between the three above mentioned causes influencing the national dividend.

It is to be stressed that Pigou did not define economic welfare in terms of utility, and drew a distinction between the consumer's *desire* for a product, which determines his/her preferences, and the *satisfaction* that he/she actually obtains from it (*WW*: p. 11). In this regard, it is interesting to mention Ralph Hawtrey's criticism to Pigou's concept of welfare, as it came from Moorean quarters and led to an even bolder stance in favour of the ethical character of economics (for Hawtrey's indebtedness to Moore see Donnini Macciò 2013a). In *The Economic Problem* (1926), Hawtrey criticised Pigou because, with his notion of welfare as 'aggregate of satisfactions', he had assumed 'a disposition to prefer the greatest good, just as the hedonist assumed a disposition to prefer the greater pleasure'. That was an improvement on the hedonist perspective to Hawtrey, but it was still a questionable presupposition (a similar argument in M.G. O'Donnell 1979, p. 590). For Hawtrey, in fact, consumers' preferences have often little to do with the 'true' goodness of the things they choose. This claim had been acknowledged by Pigou (see end of Section 5 above); however, Hawtrey advanced it more forcefully, and used it to undermine Pigou's notion of welfare: 'The aggregate of satisfactions is not an aggregate of welfare at all. It includes good satisfactions which are welfare and bad satisfactions which are the reverse' (Hawtrey 1926, p. 215). For Hawtrey, good was 'something inherent in a human experience, not a mere measure of the individual preferences' (*Right Policy*: 3). Hawtrey's definition of welfare could hardly be more reminiscent of *PE*:

> Welfare is an ethical term; it comprises those things in human life, or perhaps we should say, those experiences, which are good in themselves, and which therefore ought to be chosen as ends of action, economic or other. It must not be regarded as confined to material well-being or subject to any similar limitations. It is co-extensive with the simple concept 'good' as applied not to means, but to ends. (Hawtrey 1926, p. 185)

Welfare, so defined, could not be assessed by 'the measuring rod of money' as Pigou had done. Not only was economics the 'handmaid' of ethics, but the Hawtreyan economist was entitled to ascertain whether, and to what extent, any particular kind of satisfaction was good. Hawtrey thus emphasised the 'ethical value' of a product, which depended on the experience it afforded to the consumer: 'to the extent that this experience is good, the product has ethical value' (Hawtrey 1926, p. 185).

Even with these differences, Hawtrey's and Pigou's accounts of intrinsic value were similar. Both economists concerned themselves with states of consciousness, not with material conditions or actions, and they did not identify the good with utility. Like Moore, Pigou cherished a plurality of values of which pleasure was not the principal one (McLure 2014). Granted that for Moore the conscious states that were good in the highest degree were those of personal affections and aesthetic enjoyment – they were 'the rational end of human action and the sole criterion of social progress' (*PE*: p. 113) – most commentators, including Skidelsky (1988) and Baldwin (1990), have characterised Moore's ideal as devoid of any social dimension[34]. Admittedly, values like justice, equality, or freedom hardly feature in *PE*, and they are never considered as *ends in themselves* (or 'intrinsic goods'), but only as *possible means* to the good. As a consequence, the influence of Moore on Cambridge social sciences has been underestimated (Donnini Macciò 2013a, 2013b, 2016a). Yet, closer analysis reveals that *PE* features a more articulate set of values. Moore referred to the love of what is evil or ugly, as expressed by cruelty and lust, as a 'great intrinsic evil'; the hatred of what is good or beautiful, as in the case of malice, envy, and contempt, as well as the consciousness of pain, also were intrinsic evils. He also defined A class of 'mixed goods', including courage, 'resolute defiance', and compassion, which contained 'something positively evil or

34 J. M. Keynes's statement that, compared to the unworldliness of *PE*, 'the New Testament is a handbook for politicians' has supported this interpretation (Keynes 1972 [1938], p. 444).

ugly', but which were 'nevertheless great positive goods on the whole' (*PE*: p. 216). In Moore's ethical system, as in Pigou's, the acknowledgment of evil was essential.[35] Pigou certainly appreciated both Moore's refutation of egoism as 'absolute contradiction' (*PE*: p. 99), and the philosopher's rejection of utility maximisation (*PE*: § 58–61), which amounted to an indirect endorsement of social reform. In particular, Moore acknowledged that, since pain was a great intrinsic evil, it was a duty to prevent and reduce it (*PE*: § 127). This was also Pigou's view with reference to the economic evils of society. A further instance of Moore's influence lies in Pigou's interest in the mental state of religious love – an instance of Moore's states of consciousness – from the ethical standpoint. Moore conceived of the good as an indefinable, unanalysable, and degreed property, and in *WW* Pigou ascribed all these qualities to welfare. Yet, from Moore's point of view, Pigou committed a 'naturalistic fallacy', namely, he attempted to explain the good in terms of some other natural property.[36] In *EW* the equation between good and welfare was eventually dropped, but the description of welfare as a degreed property consisting in states of consciousness was retained.

Pigou's ethical essays throw new light on the philosophical foundations of his economic theories. *WW* and *EW* were the culmination of a comprehensive research on the good, which began with the study on Browning's poetry, continued with those on ethics and religion, and ended with two treatises on social and economic reform. If the ethical urge is not immediately evident to the reader of Pigou's major economic writings, this is due to their deliberately restrained, and often convoluted, literary style. A strong ethical impulse was nevertheless the driving force of Pigou's economic analysis, an impulse echoing in the religious undertones of the closing sentences of *WW*:

> The misery and squalor that surrounds us, the injurious luxury of some wealthy families, the terrible uncertainty overshadowing many families of the poor – these are evils too plain to be ignored. Whether the life of man ends with his physical death, or is destined to pass unscathed through that gateway, the good and the evil that he experiences here are real; and to promote the one and restrain the other is a compelling duty. (*WW*: p. 488)

35 'Pity for the undeserved sufferings of others, endurance of pain to ourselves, and a defiant hatred of evil dispositions in ourselves or in others, seem to be undoubtedly admirable in themselves; and if so, there are admirable things, which must be lost, if there were no cognition of evil' (*PE*: p. 217).

36 'No difficulty need be found in my saying that "pleasure is good" and yet not meaning that "pleasure" is the same thing as "good", that pleasure *means* good, and that good *means* pleasure' (*PE*: § 12).

8. Concluding remarks

This paper has contended that taking into account Pigou's philosophical writings leads to a better understanding of his economics. According to Terence Hutchison, Pigou's *EW*, though displaying 'wealth of analysis and great range of political conclusions', was an 'amalgam of Benthamite concepts, Comteist social enthusiasm, Marshallian moral uplift, and G. E. Moore's definitions' (Hutchison 1953, p. 289). Pigou's normative position was murky indeed, but this depended mainly on his reluctance to trespass on openly ethical territory in the economic texts. There were good reasons for such a hesitation. On the one hand, Pigou could not fail to embody his master's ideal of the warm-hearted, but cool-headed, social scientist (Marshall 1925, p. 174); Marshall had built the Economic Tripos on the separation of economics from the moral sciences, and Pigou's position at Cambridge required that he carefully guarded that demarcation. Nevertheless, far from being casual or episodic, Pigou's reflections on ethics were not extraneous to either Cambridge economics or the Edwardian social reform movement. Recalling Harris' point mentioned in the introduction (Harris 1992), it is arguable that Pigou was somewhat influenced by the 'idealist' (*latu sensu*) climate permeating contemporary British social thought. Cook (2009) and Raffaelli (2012) have advanced a case for the influence of idealism on Marshall; and it may well be that Pigou assimilated through his mentor some idealist tenets, such as the individual's obligations to others. However, the influence of Moore's 'ideal utilitarianism' seems prevalent in Pigou (Rashdall 1907). It was a consequentialist ethical theory, valuing actions not in terms of the happiness or pleasure they produced, as in classical utilitarianism, but in terms of the goodness of the states of affairs they brought into being. Pigou's ethical sensibility was at odds with the Benthamite perspective, especially with psychological hedonism, which he defined 'an untenable and exploded doctrine'. Significantly, Moore's *Principia Ethica* was the most popular criticism of hedonistic utilitarianism in Cambridge at the beginning of the twentieth century. Both Moore and Pigou were ethical intuitionists, rejected naturalistic definitions of ethical values, were extremely careful in distinguishing between intrinsic and instrumental value, and emphasised intrinsic goodness.[37] The similarities between their

37 *PE*: p. 18 ss., p. 94 ss., p. 146, p. 164, p. 171 ss., p. 194; Pigou 1906, p. 372; 1907a, p. 280; 1908a, p. 80; p. 105, p. 130, p. 117; 1908b, p. 9; 1912, p. 9, p. 59; 1920, p. 14; 1923b, pp. 80–1. See also the essay on Nietzsche (Pigou 1908c and *PT*: p. 111 ss.), whose stated intent was to dispel the most common misinterpretations of the philosopher's theories. Pigou believed that, by applying the end-means distinction to Nietzsche's seemingly contradictory, and even immoral, or anti-moral, statements, it was possible to unearth their true meaning, discovering that they were much less controversial than generally maintained.

philosophical approaches corroborate Hugh Dalton's claim that his teacher Pigou 'accepted' Moore's philosophy (Dalton 1953, pp. 54–5; Collard 2011, p. 18)[38], and suggest that Moore's *PE* had a wider impact on Cambridge economics than generally acknowledged.

Recalling the importance of the distinction ends-means, it is significant that Pigou considered the study of religious experience as intrinsically valuable, whereas economic science was instrumentally good for the betterment of society. 'If I desired knowledge of man apart from the fruits of knowledge, I should seek it in the history of religious enthusiasm, of passion, of martyrdom, and of love; I should not seek it in the market-place' (Pigou 1908b, p. 11, also in *EW*: 4). Pigou's metaphor of economics as worthy of pursuit for its being 'fruit-bearing', rather than 'light-bearing' (*EW*: 3), reveals that his approach to economics was eminently practical. This is why, in his inaugural lecture and in *EW*, Pigou chastised the excess of abstraction in economic theory, and distinguished between 'pure economics', dealing with 'the commercial doings of a community of angels', and 'realistic economics', concerned with 'the world known in experience' (Pigou 1908b, p. 15; *EW*: p. 6). Pigou shared with Moore the belief that our ordinary view of the world is largely correct; an emphasis on the value of experience is evident in Pigou's 'fundamental postulate' that 'unless they are proved to be guilty, the data of consciousness are innocent of fraud' (*PT*: p. 9, p. 79). This view belongs in the tradition of Thomas Reid's refutation of scepticism and endorsement of common sense – a tradition revived by Moore (1925).

Pigou's refutation of philosophical optimism (*RB* and *PT*: pp. 125–39) coupled with an acknowledgment of the inescapable reality of evil, not sorted out by an afterlife or by other forms of future palingenesis. This philosophical standpoint oriented his professional concern towards the economic evils of society, in particular unemployment and poverty. Economic analysis should be instrumental in overcoming destitution, inequality, and insecurity, granted that bettering the condition of human life was the economist's task. As the acknowledgment of free will provided a philosophical answer to evil, so state intervention was meant to reduce the

38 Interestingly, Hugh Dalton, a contemporary Cambridge economist and politician, mentioned Pigou to reject the allegations of 'unworldliness' against *PE*: 'to accept Moore's good never meant to disinterest oneself from doing good. Otherwise, such men as Pigou and Lowes Dickinson would never have accepted him. ... As a practical politician, when I see happy, healthy, well-dressed, well-fed people in my constituency, where a few years ago there was a quite different picture, I am proud and glad, especially in the knowledge that I have helped to make this change. And I judge that not a bad state of mind. ... Generally, it *is* good to see that one has *done* good'. (Dalton 1953, pp. 54–5).

impact of market failures and business fluctuations on economic welfare. According to Medema, the belief that a qualified state intervention could correct market imperfections – the 'hallmark of Cambridge welfare tradition' from Sidgwick to Pigou – was the equivalent of Sidgwick's philosophical optimism (Medema 2008, p. 27). Sidgwick acknowledged that optimism had no rational basis, but he maintained that it was 'an indispensable creed … for progressive humanity as a whole', and that Christian faith substantiated it (Sidgwick 1898, p. 508). Though Pigou followed Sidgwick as far as public action was concerned, in his case this optimistic underpinning was absent altogether.

Pigou's ethical essays conjure up a subtle psychological image of their author, whose 'elusive' personality still baffles his biographers (McLure and Knight 2012; Aslanbeigui and Oakes 2015). Pigou's rigorous work ethic and frugal lifestyle, his humanitarian and moderate approach to social issues, and the aversion to violence which inspired his conscientious objection and charitable service as ambulance driver in WWI[39], are consistent with his ethical stance. The unselfish commitment to one's ideals, which he often emphasised as a fundamental moral obligation, was another trait of Pigou's life and career. He acknowledged that the difficulties involved in promoting good and restraining evil were indeed formidable, but they should not deter. He recommended moderation and perseverance, as in his beloved mountaineering experiences, where 'neither by the timidity that waits at a distance, nor by the wild rush of undisciplined ardour is the summit of great mountains attained' (*WW*: p. 488).

Acknowledgements

I wish to thank Gilbert Faccarello, Keith Tribe and all participants in the workshop *The conflict-ridden development of modernity: theology and political economy*, 17–18 December 2014, Lyon, France for their helpful comments. I am also grateful to the referees and editors of this journal for their valuable suggestions and generous work in revising the submitted article. Pigou's letter to Keynes discussed in Section 4 is a copyright of the Master and Fellows of King's College, Cambridge. Ralph Hawtrey's unpublished *Right Policy* is quoted with the permission of the Master and Fellows of Churchill College, Cambridge.

Disclosure statement

No potential conflict of interest was reported by the author.

39 For Moore's influence on pacifism at Cambridge see Donnini Maccio' (2016b).

References

Arrow, K., Sen, A.K., and Suzumura, K., 2002. *Handbook o f social choice and welfare*, vol. I, New York: Elsevier.

Aslanbeigui, N. and Oakes, G., 2013. Introduction: reclaiming a forgotten master. *In:* A.C. Pigou, *Economics of welfare*. Basingstoke: Palgrave Macmillan, ix–xv.

Aslanbeigui, N. and Oakes, G., 2015. *A.C. Pigou*. Basingstoke: Palgrave Macmillan.

Baldwin, T., 1990. *G. E. Moore*. London: Routledge.

Bastiat, F., 1850. *Harmonies économiques*. Paris: Guillaumin.

Boucher, D. and Vincent, A., 2000. *British idealism and political theory*. Edinburgh: Edinburgh University Press.

Cambridge University, 1901. *Cambridge University calendar for the year 1901–1902*. Cambridge: Deighton Bell.

Carr, R., 1962. The religious thought of J.S. Mill: a study in reluctant scepticism. *Journal of the history of ideas*, 4 (23), 475–95.

Chalmers, T., 1833. *The Bridgewater treatises on the power, wisdom and goodness of god, as manifested in the adaptation of external nature to the moral and intellectual constitution of man*. London: Henry Bohn.

Collard, A.D., 2011. *Generations of economists*. London: Routledge.

Cook, S., 2009. *The intellectual foundations of Alfred Marshall's economic science. A rounded globe of knowledge*. Cambridge: Cambridge University Press.

Dalton, H., 1953. *Call back yesterday. Memoirs 1887–1931*. London: F. Muller Ltd.

Dickinson, G.L., 1901. *Letters from John Chinaman*. London: Brimley Johnson.

Donnini Macciò, D., 2013a. G. E. Moore's Philosophy and Cambridge Economics: Ralph Hawtrey on ethics and methodology. *European journal of the history of economic thought*, 2 (2), 163–97. Available from: http://www.tandfonline.com/doi/full/10.1080/09672567.2013.792371.

Donnini Macciò, D., 2013b. On economics and philosophy: G. E. Moore's imprint on the Cambridge Apostles from *Principia Ethica* to *My Early Beliefs*. PhD Dissertation. University of Macerata (Italy).

Donnini Macciò, D., 2016a. The Apostles' justice: Cambridge reflections on economic inequality from Moore's *Principia Ethica* to Keynes's *General Theory* (1903–1936), *Cambridge journal of economics*, 4 (3), 701–26.

Donnini Macciò, D., 2016b. Ethics, economics, and power in the Cambridge Apostles' internationalism between the two World Wars. *European journal of international relations, 22* (3), 696–721.

Harris, J., 1992. Political thought and the Welfare State 1870–1940: an intellectual framework for British social policy, *Past and present*, 135 (May 1992), 116–41.

Hawtrey, R., 1926. *The economic problem*. London: Longmans & Co.

Hawtrey, R., n.d. Right policy: the place of value judgments in politics. *The papers of Ralph Hawtrey*, Churchill College Archives. HTRY/12/1. Typescript.

Hilton, B., 1988. *The age of atonement. The influence of evangelicalism on social and economic thought, 1795–1865*. Oxford: Clarendon Press.

Hutchison, T.W., 1953. *A review of economic doctrines 1870–1929*. Oxford: Clarendon Press.

James, W., 1902. *The varieties of religious experience. A study in human nature*. London: Longmans and Green.

Kadish, A., 1989. *Historians, economists and economic theory*. London: Routledge.

Kadish, A. and Tribe, K., eds., 1993. *The market for political economy: the advent of economics in British university culture*. London: Routledge.

Keynes, J.M., 1972. [1938]. My early beliefs. *The collected writings of J. M. Keynes. Essays in biography*. X, London: Cambridge University Press: Macmillan and Cambridge.
Koslowski, P. and Shionoya, Y., 1993. *The good and the economical. Ethical choices in economics and management.* Berlin: Springer-Verlag.
Marcuzzo, M. C., Naldi, N., Rosselli, A., and Sanfilippo, E., 2008. Cambridge as a *Place* in economics. *History of political economy*, 40 (4), 569–93.
Marshall, A., 1925. The present position of economics. *In:* A.C., Pigou, ed. *Memorials of Alfred Marshall.* London: Macmillan, 152–74.
McLure, M., 2011. Assessment of A. C. Pigou's fellowship theses, The University of Western Australia, Economics Discussion Paper 10.22.
McLure, M., 2014. Pareto, Pigou and third-party consumption: divergent approaches to welfare theory with implications for the study of public finance. *In:* G. Faccarello and R. Sturn, eds. *Studies in the history of public economics.* London: Routledge, 99–120.
McLure, M. and Knight, K., 2012. *The elusive Arthur Pigou.* Business School, University of Western Australia. Economics Discussion Paper 12.05
McTaggart, J.E., 1906. *Some dogmas of religion.* London: Arnold.
Medema, S., 2008. Losing my religion: Sidgwick, Theism and the struggle for utilitarian ethics in economic analysis. *History of political economy*, 40 (5), 189–211.
Medema, S., 2009. *The hesitant hand. Taming self-interest in the history of economic ideas.* Princeton: Princeton University Press.
Mill, J.S., 1848. *Principles of political economy with some of their applications to social philosophy.* London: Longmans.
Mill, J.S., 1874. *Three essays on religion. Nature, the utility of religion, and Theism.* London: Longmans.
Moore, G.E., 1901. The value of religion. *International journal of ethics*, 12 (1), 81–98.
Moore, G.E., 1903. *Principia Ethica.* Cambridge: Cambridge University Press.
Moore, G.E., 1925. A defence of common sense. *In:* J.H. Muirhead, ed. *Contemporary British philosophy.* 2nd series. London: Allen & Unwin, 192–233.
O'Donnell, M.G., 1979. Pigou: an extension of Sidgwickian thought. *History of political economy*, 11 (4), 588–605.
Offer, J., 2006. *An intellectual history of British social policy. Idealism versus non-idealism.* Bristol: The Policy Press.
Peart, S.J. and Levy, D.M., 2005. *The "Vanity of the Philosopher": from equality to hierarchy in post-classical economics.* Ann Arbor: University of Michigan Press.
Peart, S.J. and Levy, D.M., eds., 2008. *The street porter and the philosopher. Conversations on analytical egalitarianism.* Ann Arbor: University of Michigan Press.
Pigou, A.C., 1901a. *Robert Browning as a religious teacher.* London: J.C. Clay and Sons.
Pigou, A.C., 1901b. Some aspects of the problem of charity. *In*: *The heart of the Empire.* London: T. Fisher Unwin, 236–61.
Pigou, A.C., 1905a. The optimism of Browning and Meredith. *The independent review*, 6 (May–Aug.), 92–104.
Pigou, A.C., 1905b. *Principles and methods of industrial peace.* London: Macmillan.
Pigou, A.C. 1906. The unity of political and economic science. *The economic journal*, *16* (63), 372–80.
Pigou, A.C., 1907a. Social improvement in the light of modern biology. *The economic journal*, *17* (1), 358–69.
Pigou, A.C., 1907b. The ethics of the gospels. *International journal of ethics*, 17, 275–90.
Pigou, A.C., 1907c. Some points of ethical controversy. *International journal of ethics*, 18, 99–107.
Pigou, A.C., 1908a. *The problem of theism and other essays.* London: Macmillan.

Pigou, A.C., 1908b. *Economic science in relation to practice: an inaugural lecture given at Cambridge 30th October, 1908.* London: Macmillan.
Pigou, A.C., 1908c. The ethics of Nietzsche. *International journal of ethics*, 18, 343–55.
Pigou, A.C., 1912. *Wealth and welfare.* London: Macmillan.
Pigou, A.C., 1920. *The economics of welfare.* London: Macmillan.
Pigou, A.C., 1923a. Employers and economic chivalry. *In:* A.C. Pigou. *Essays in applied economics*, II, London: P.S. King and Sons, 12–23.
Pigou, A.C., 1923b. Eugenics and some wage problems. *In:* A.C. Pigou. *Essays in applied economics*, VIII, London: P.S. King and Sons, 80–91.
Pigou, A.C., 1929. *The function of economic analysis.* London: Milford.
Pigou, A.C., 1935. *Economics in practice: six lectures on current issues.* London: Macmillan.
Pigou, A.C., 1951. Some aspects of welfare economics. *American economic review*, XLI, (3), 287–302.
Raffaelli, T., 2012. On Marshall's presumed idealism: a note on the intellectual foundations of Alfred Marshall's economic science. A rounded globe of knowledge by Simon Cook. *The European journal of the history of economic thought*, 19 (1), 99–108.
Rashdall, H., 1907. *The theory of good and evil.* Oxford: Clarendon Press.
Robbins, L., 1932. *An essay on the nature and significance of economic science.* London: Macmillan.
Robinson, A., 1968. Pigou, Arthur Cecil. *International encyclopaedia of the social sciences.* 1968. *Encyclopedia.com.* (September 6, 2016). http://www.encyclopedia.com/doc/1G2-3045000942.html
Sen, A.K., 1970. *Collective choice and social welfare.* S. Francisco: Holden-Day.
Sen, A.K., 1998. The possibility of social choice. *American economic review*, 89 (3), 349–78.
Shionoya, Y., 2005. *Economics and morality: the philosophy of the welfare state.* Cheltenham: Elgar.
Sidgwick, H., 1866. Ecce Homo. *Westminster review*, July 1866, 58–88. Reprinted in *Miscellaneous essays and addresses*, 1904. London: Macmillan.
Sidgwick, H., 1883. *The principles of political economy.* 2nd ed. London: Macmillan.
Sidgwick, H., 1897. *The elements of politics.* London: Macmillan.
Sidgwick, H., 1898. *Henry Sidgwick. A memoir.* London: Macmillan.
Skidelsky, R., 1988. Keynes's political legacy. *In:* O. F. Hamouda and J. N. Smithin, eds. *Keynes and public policy after fifty years.* Vol. I. *Economics and politics.* Aldershot: Elgar, 3–28.
Skidelsky, R., 1983. *John Maynard Keynes. Hopes betrayed 1883–1920.* London: Macmillan.
Steedman, I., 2011. Economic theory and happiness. *In*: Atherton, Graham and Steedman, eds. *The practices of happiness: poltical economy, religion and wellbeing.* London: Routledge, 23–41.
Taylor, C., 2007. *A secular age.* Cambridge, MA: Harvard University Press.
Tribe, K., 2011. *Welfare economics in the shade of new liberalism. Part I: the making of Pigou's wealth and welfare.* Institute of Economic Research, Hitotsubashi University. Available from: http://www.ier.hit-u.ac.jp/extra/symp110313/Tribe.pdf
Waterman, A.M.C., 1991. *Revolution, economics and religion. Christian political economy 1798–1833.* Cambridge: Cambridge University Press.
Whately, R., 1833. *Introductory lectures on political economy delivered in Oxford.* Oxford: J.W. Parker and Sons.

Abstract

This article discusses a group of essays on ethical issues written by Pigou between 1900 and 1908. It is argued that they contain the foundations of his economic philosophy. Pigou's research on the meaning and content of the good merged into his definition of welfare, and his interest in religion as a subjective experience resurfaced in the subjective framework of his economics. A methodological pragmatism informed his economics as well as his ethics; moreover, the endorsement of interpersonal comparisons of the good in the ethical texts was consistent with Pigou's adoption of utility comparisons in welfare economics. Pigou's philosophical pessimism was reflected in his analysis of the economic evils of society, eventually leading to his advocacy of governmental intervention to foster economic welfare. The article contends that Pigou's philosophy derived not only from Sidgwick, as commonly believed, but also from G.E. Moore's *Principia Ethica.*

Keynes and Christian socialism: Religion and the economic problem

David Andrews

1. Introduction

From his undergraduate period onward, John Maynard Keynes' writings are filled with religious references, but in his posthumously published memoir *My Early Beliefs* (1949) reflecting on the views he shared with his friends in the Apostles before the First World War, he described his early hostility toward religion. He recalled that he had regarded Christians as "the enemy" because "they appeared as the representatives of tradition, convention and hocus pocus" (9: 446).[1] During that early period, he wrote, he had considered his own system of beliefs to be unequivocally free of religious taint, "as entirely rational and scientific in character ... nothing more than the application of logic and rational analysis to the material presented as sense data" (9: 438).

The reasons for Keynes' early hostility toward Christianity are not hard to discern. There was a long tradition in Great Britain, with which Keynes' family had been associated, of disagreement and separation from the established Anglican Church, going back to the sixteenth century, including Unitarians, Puritans and Quakers, among a number of dissenting and nonconforming groups. Turmoil within the church intensified in the middle of the nineteenth century with the catholic revival known as the Oxford Movement, along with a series of highly influential challenges to the historical accuracy of the biblical narrative. David Strauss's *Life of Jesus* (1835) pointed to the mythological character of the supernatural events depicted in the Bible. Charles Darwin's *On the Origin of Species* (1859)

1 References to passages in Keynes' writings are designated by the volume number and the page number in *The Collected Writings of John Maynard Keynes* (1971–1989) in which the relevant text appears.

challenged the creation story. Orthodox clerical members of the Church of England sanctioned historical criticism in the *Essays and Reviews* (1860). In 1862, Bishop John William Colenso published his *The Pentateuch and the Book of Joshua Critically Examined*, in which he attacked the literal accuracy of the story presented in the first books of the Bible. In his *Examinations of Sir William Hamilton's Philosophy* (1865), John Stuart Mill attacked the philosophical defense of orthodox belief put forth by H. L. Mansel in his Bampton Lectures of 1858.

Despite these challenges, the Church of England retained a great deal of power and influence in the life of the country. In the late nineteenth century, therefore, reformers at the University of Cambridge directed their energies against such Church-inspired religious constraints as the requirement that Fellows affirm the Thirty-Nine Articles of Religion. At the beginning of the twentieth century, the young Keynes and his friends viewed themselves as the leaders of the next wave of reform, the pernicious influence of the Church appearing to them as the primary obstacle to be overcome.

The later Keynes took a very different view. First, he came to see his own early beliefs as constituting a "religion," as "some sort of relation of neo-Platonism," despite his very different perspective during those early years: "I have called this faith a religion ... But we should have been very angry at the time with such a suggestion" (9: 438). In 1938, he reaffirmed his commitment to his early religion: "It seems to me looking back, that this religion of ours was a very good one to grow up under. It remains nearer the truth than any other that I know, with less irrelevant extraneous matter and nothing to be ashamed of ... It is still my religion under the surface" (10: 442).

Moreover, Keynes came to see another force as the central problem of modern society, namely, the greedy, selfish and materialistic attitude expressed in the philosophy of Jeremy Bentham, "the Benthamite calculus, based on an over-valuation of the economic criterion": "I do now regard that as the worm which has been gnawing at the insides of modern civilization and is responsible for its present moral decay" (9: 445–6).

From this perspective, Keynes came to view religion and tradition in a positive light, because they stood in opposition to the selfish and materialistic tendency. In his 1930 *The Economic Possibilities for our Grandchildren* (1930), he predicted that that economic progress would allow humanity to escape from Benthamism, leaving people "free ... to return to some of the most sure and certain principles of religion and traditional virtue" (9: 371).

In this essay, I first consider Keynes' later, broader understanding of religion; next I provide an account of Keynes' own religion in terms of that definition. Finally, I argue that Keynes' later beliefs reflect those of early generations of "Apostles," members of the famous secret society to which Keynes belonged.

2. A broad definition of religion

There is no evidence that he ever believed in any sort of deity, but religion, for Keynes did not require the affirmation of dogmas or belief in God or gods. These were not necessarily inconsistent with religion, but they were not necessary for it either. In *A Short View of Russia* (1925), in which he described Leninism as a kind of religion, he divided believers into two categories, "high and low": on the one hand were the "mystical sleep-walkers" and on the other, the "practical idealists." He explained as follows: "There are two distinct sublimations of materialistic egotism—one in which the ego is merged in the nameless mystic union, another in which it is merged in the pursuit of an ideal life for the whole community of men" (9: 254). The first category includes those who participate in religion through a certain kind of individual mental experience relating to the divine, for example, in prayer, thanks or celebration. The second category includes those who do not accept current conditions and work to create a better world for everyone. Without providing examples, Keynes pointed out that some great religious leaders belonged to both groups.

The second group makes for an unusual definition of religion, as Keynes pointed out, giving rise to some conclusions that may be surprising. For example, Keynes pointed out that on this view Leon Trotsky was "amongst the most religious" people in the world despite his explicit condemnation of religion in terms that Keynes quoted at length. But Trotsky's condemnation only referred to religion in the first of Keynes' senses. Keynes justified calling him religious by citing other writings demonstrating that Trotsky was deeply committed in the second sense, because Trotsky anticipated, in Trotsky's words quoted by Keynes, "a society which will have thrown off the pinching and stultifying worry about one's daily bread … in which the liberated egotism of man—a mighty force!—will be directed wholly towards the understanding, the transformation, and the betterment of the Universe." Keynes also cited a similar passage from Trotsky's *Literature and Revolution* pointing to the same eventuality:

> The Revolution itself is not yet the Kingdom of Freedom. On the contrary, it is developing the features of 'necessity' to the greatest degree … Revolutionary literature cannot but be imbued with a spirit of social hatred, which is a creative historic factor in the epoch of proletarian dictatorship. But under Socialism solidarity will be the

> basis of society. Literature and Art will be tuned to a different key. All the emotions which we revolutionaries, at the present time, feel apprehensive of naming—so much have they been worn thin by hypocrites and vulgarians—such as disinterested friendship, love for one's neighbor, sympathy, will be the mighty ringing chords of Socialist poetry (Keynes 9: 255).

That is, even though Trotsky explicitly rejected what he considered to be religion, he looked to a higher ideal for humanity than that which was dominant in the existing society and in this Keynes saw true religion, above that of the professed believer who could not see any higher mode of human existence than that which currently existed. Socialism, in this sense, was, for Keynes, an inherently religious enterprise.

3. Keynes' religion in the first sense

The religion Keynes described as his own in *My Early Beliefs*, following the philosophy of G.E. Moore, was a religion in the first sense, involving individuals in states of "nameless mystic union," as can be seen in Keynes' belief that what was most important for human life was to experience "good states of mind" consisting of "timeless, passionate states of contemplation and communion" (10: 436). Moore thought this to be a self-evident matter of common sense from which there was no dissent: "Indeed, once the meaning of the question is clearly understood, the answer to it, in its main outlines, appears to be so obvious, that it runs the risk of seeming to be a platitude" (Moore 1903: 188).

Moore's ideas about good states of mind depend on his distinction between ends, which are pursued for their own sakes, and means, which are pursued in order to achieve ends. Linguistic complications arise for two reasons. First, there are intermediate ends, that is, goals that appear to be ends, but are really means toward the achievement of some further end. Second, in ordinary language, 'good' is frequently applied to means, to indicate that those means are effective for the achievement of the ends to which they are directed. The goodness that was of interest to Moore, goodness in its ethical sense, is the goodness of ends in themselves, pure ends that do not serve as intermediate ends directed toward any other purpose.

The most important pure end, according to Moore, is love, broadly understood, not in an abstract sense, but the actual mental and physical experience of loving and being loved. He took this to be a matter of common sense, about which there was universal agreement. If someone disputed that love as an experienced state of consciousness is good, Moore could only conclude that either there was some misunderstanding or that the person was being intentionally contrary. Another important pure end for Moore was the creation and appreciation of beauty. Again, it was the actual physical and mental experience that Moore thought good, not the idea of beauty in the abstract. Moore believed the goodness of such experience to be a matter of common sense to anyone who gave it any thought:

> By far the most valuable things, which we know or can imagine, are certain states of consciousness, which may be roughly described as the pleasures of human intercourse and the enjoyment of beautiful objects. No one, probably, who has asked himself the question, has ever doubted that personal affection and the appreciation of what is beautiful in Art or Nature, are good in themselves, nor, if we consider strictly what things are worth having purely for their own sakes, does it appear probable that any one will think anything else has nearly so great a value as the things which are included under these two heads (Moore 1903: 188).

Moore's analysis of these led him to add truth to the list of things that are intrinsically good. Again, not truth in an abstract sense but the activity of pursuing and contemplating truth. He believed that thoughtful, educated, and informed people were essentially agreed on this point (Moore 1903: 199).

At least in his youth, Keynes accepted the same three objects as good in themselves, the sources of good states of mind: "The appropriate subjects of passionate contemplation and communion were a beloved person, beauty and truth, and one's prime objects in life were love, the creation and enjoyment of aesthetic experience and the pursuit of knowledge. Of these love came a long way first" (10: 436–7).[2]

4. Keynes' religion in the second sense

While the "passionate states of contemplation and communion" qualify as religious in the first sense described above, Keynes was also religious in the second sense, in that he was a practical idealist seeking "an ideal life for the whole community of men." According to Moore's moral philosophy, duty requires that one act in such a way as to maximise goodness construed in the manner described above, as a property of states of mind: "the

2 The emphasis on experiences of love, beauty, and truth is not to deny that states of mind other than these can be good, but only that these are the best and most important states of mind. In *My Early Beliefs*, Keynes suggested that Moore's understanding of pure ends and good states of mind was overly narrow and that other things could be added to the list (10: 444). Ralph Hawtrey, a contemporary of Keynes', also influenced by Moore, included a whole range of good states of mind (1944: 194).

assertion 'I am morally bound to perform this action' is identical with the assertion 'This action will produce the greatest possible amount of good in the Universe'" (Moore 1903: 147). Or, again,

> By far the most valuable things, which we know or can imagine, are certain states of consciousness, which may roughly be described as the pleasures of human intercourse and the enjoyment of beautiful objects ... it is only for the sake of these things – in order that as much of them as possible may at some time exist – that anyone can be justified in performing any public or private duty ... they ... form the rational and ultimate end of human action and the sole criterion of social progress (Moore 1903: 188–9).

Keynes saw two related obstacles to the maximisation of goodness in the universe. On the one hand, the problem of supplying the material needs of people simply to maintain their physical existence in the world, what Keynes called the economic problem, was an enormous obstacle to the experience of good states of mind. Keynes considered material comfort, along with physical calm and intellectual freedom, to be a precondition for the experience of good states of mind. This is not to say that one might not experience good states of mind without these conditions, but rather that their absence substantially hinders such experience. Poverty and hunger are generally not good states of mind. A difficulty arises, however, because the acquisition of material comfort is or can be an uncertain and time-consuming process that does not typically produce good states of mind directly. Creating the conditions for good states of mind therefore requires activity that does not produce them, that may even produce bad states of mind. The solution of the economic problem, the creation of a situation in which scarcity could be replaced with abundance, in which people would no longer have to devote the primary share of their attention to activities enabling them to procure their material needs, would therefore allow more people a much greater opportunity to experience good states of mind than they could have in a world in which the economic problem was not resolved.

On the other hand, this difficulty is exacerbated by the fact that the struggle to acquire the means of physical subsistence produces the greedy, selfish behaviour, described above as Benthamism, that seriously detracts from good states of mind, because it serves as an obstacle to love, the creation and appreciation of beauty, and the pursuit of truth. The dominant role in human history of the necessity of coping with the economic problem, with the struggle for material survival, leads to the pervasiveness of self-interested behaviour. Keynes perceived deleterious consequences:

> At any rate it seems clearer every day that the moral problem of our age is concerned with the love of money, with the habitual appeal to the money motive in nine-tenths of the activities of life, with the universal striving after individual economic security

> as the prime object of endeavor, with social approbation of money as the measure of constructive success, and with the social appeal to the hoarding instinct as the foundation of the necessary provision for the family and the future (9: 268–9).

It was in this connection that Keynes had a limited degree of sympathy for Leninism. His criticisms of the Soviet government can hardly be overstated, but despite these criticisms, Keynes found an element of Leninism that he could embrace, that "may ... contribute something to the true religion of the future, if there be any true religion." Specifically, Keynes wrote: "*Leninism is absolutely, defiantly non-supernatural, and its emotional and ethical essence centers about the individual's and the community's attitude toward the love of money*" (Keynes 9: 259, emphasis in original).

Keynes recognised that Leninism's attitude toward the love of money was not original. Jesus objected to the love of money and at several points Keynes likened Leninism to Christianity. He suggested, for example, that the Archbishop of Canterbury, the leader of the Church of England, would deserve to be called a Bolshevik "if he seriously pursues the Gospel precepts" (Keynes 9: 253). In this, Keynes was sympathetic to Christian ideals despite his youthful antipathy for the actually existing Church. The supernatural character of Christianity, apparent in such crucial aspects as the miracles and the resurrection, was among its least attractive elements for Keynes and the expression of what he perceived to be similar ideals in a non-supernatural form had a strong appeal for him.

What Keynes found to be new in the Soviet experiment was the attempt to carry this ideal out in practice for a community as a whole. The goal of Leninism, as Keynes saw it, was to build a world in which this ethical principle could be realised, to "construct a framework of society in which pecuniary motives as influencing action shall have a changed relative importance" (9: 259–60). This was to be accomplished not by legal exclusion of money-making, but by restructuring the pattern of incentives in order to make a career based on it impractical. Keynes illustrated this by comparison with the United Kingdom of his own day, in which a young person might, without discredit, choose a life devoted to public service or a life devoted to private business. The intention was that in the future in Russia, on the contrary, this choice would not arise: "the career of money-making, as such, will simply not occur to a respectable young man as a possible opening, any more than the career of a gentleman burglar or acquiring skill in forgery and embezzlement" (9: 260).[3]

3 Keynes objected to the violent means with which the Soviets sought to achieve this outcome. Highlighting their brutality, he likened the Russian communists to "the early Christians led by Attila . . . using the equipment of the Holy Inquisition and the Jesuit missions to enforce the literal economics of the New Testament" (9: 257).

Like Trotsky, however, Keynes was religious in the second sense because he too anticipated a society free from what Trotsky called, in the passage cited above, "the pinching and stultifying worry about one's daily bread." In *The Economic Possibilities for our Grandchildren,* that is, Keynes predicted that the economic problem would be solved. With ongoing improvements in productivity, developing the technical capacity for solving the problem was largely a matter of time, or so he thought. The crucial consequence of the solution of the economic problem would be to demonstrate that the economic problem is not the basic problem of human life, despite its overwhelming importance in the history of humanity. The true problem of human life, according to Keynes, is how to live one's life in a satisfactory manner: "Thus for the first time since his creation man will be faced with his real, his permanent problem—how to use his freedom from pressing economic cares, how to occupy the leisure which science and compound interest will have won for him, to live wisely and agreeably and well" (9: 328).[4]

With the solution of the economic problem, the approval and encouragement given to the Benthamic tendency toward selfish materialism could be abandoned:

> When the accumulation of wealth is no longer of high social importance, there will be great changes in the code of morals. We shall be able to rid ourselves of many of the pseudo-moral principles which have hag-ridden us for two hundred years, by which we have exalted some of the most distasteful of human qualities into the position of the highest virtues. We shall be able to afford to dare to assess the money-motive at its true value. The love of money as a possession—as distinguished from the love of money as a means to the enjoyments and realities of life—will be recognized for what it is, a somewhat disgusting morbidity, one of those semi-criminal, semi-pathological propensities which one hands over with a shudder to the specialists in mental disease. All kinds of social customs and economic practices, affecting the distribution of wealth and of economic rewards and penalties, which we now maintain at all costs, however distasteful and unjust they may be in themselves, because they are tremendously useful in promoting the accumulation of capital, we shall then be free, at last, to discard (9: 329).

Once these materialistic customs and practices have been abandoned, humanity would be free "to return to some of the most sure and certain principles of religion and traditional virtue—that avarice is a vice, that the exaction of usury is a misdemeanor, and the love of money is detestable, that those walk most truly in the paths of virtue and sane wisdom who take the least thought for the morrow. We shall once more value ends above means and prefer the good to the useful." Keynes concludes the passage

4 The idea of living a "good life" has a long history, from the ancient Greeks through the present day. Similar ideas were not uncommon in Keynes' own time, for example, in Max Weber's 1905 *Protestant Ethic and the Spirit of Capitalism.*

with a reference to the words of Jesus according to the King James Bible: "We shall honor those who can teach us how to pluck the hour and the day virtuously and well, the delightful people who are capable of taking direct enjoyment in things, the lilies of the field who toil not, neither do they spin" (9: 330–1 referring to Matthew 6: 28).

5. Religion, business and progress

Keynes was committed to the idea that this better future state for humanity would eventually come into existence, but there is some ambivalence in his views about how it would come to pass. In *The Economic Possibilities for our Grandchildren*, Keynes claimed that the solution of the economic problem would come about in the normal course of economic progress, but that it would be necessary to wait for this to happen. He indicated a willingness to accept the otherwise objectionable consequences of market-oriented economic life because this was the price that had to be paid for the technological improvement that would allow the masses the opportunity to cultivate their higher moral and intellectual capacities.

Yet Keynes made this concession with some irony: "The time for this is not yet. For at least another hundred years we must pretend to ourselves and to everyone that fair is foul and foul is fair; for foul is useful and fair is not. Avarice and usury and precaution must be our gods for a little longer still. For only they can lead us out of the tunnel of economic necessity into daylight" (9: 331). In claiming that it is necessary to "pretend" that "fair is foul and foul is fair," Keynes called attention to the fact that fair is not foul and foul is not fair, not pretending at all, directly undermining the apparent sense of his own statement.

In *A Short View of Russia*, written five years before *The Economic Possibilities for our Grandchildren*, he took a more complex view. There Keynes expressed reservations about whether the cost of waiting for a state of abundance to be achieved for the inclusion of moral considerations in economic life was worth the expected benefits. He acknowledged the economic advantages of cultivation of greed but wondered if the moral price this exacted were too high, asking "whether the material advantages of keeping business and religion in different compartments [of the soul] are sufficient to balance the moral disadvantages" (9: 268).

Keynes identified three different attitudes toward the relationship between business and religion. First, the "Protestant and Puritan" could easily keep business and religion separate because he distinguished sharply between that which is worldly and that which concerns God: "the first activity pertained to earth and the second to heaven, which was elsewhere." Keynes displayed no sympathy for this position. It implied contentment with the existing social organisation without any concern for moral improvement on earth, either now or in the future. Moral goodness was to follow death and be realised in a supernatural realm. Although his family was historically connected to Protestant dissenters, his religion was consistently nonsupernatural and therefore always excluded any notion of heaven beyond the natural world.

Second, Keynes described the view he would take in *The Economic Possibilities for our Grandchildren*, the "believer in progress," who was willing to keep religion and business separate for the sake of the progress that would result from the absence of moral or religious constraints on business, because that progress would eventually allow for a moral world in the future: "The believer in progress could separate [business and religion] comfortably because he regarded the first as the means to the establishment of heaven upon earth hereafter." But in 1925, he used language that distanced himself from this view: "We used to believe that modern capitalism was capable, not merely of maintaining the existing standards of life, but of leading us gradually into an economic paradise where we should be comparatively free from economic cares ... Now we doubt whether the business man is leading us to a destination far better than our present place" (9: 268). That he "used to" believe in progress suggests that when he wrote this he no longer believed in it. His voice retains an element of uncertainty, but his skepticism toward the belief in progress, expressed explicitly in the word "doubt," is evident.

The third attitude toward the relationship between business and religion was different from both of the first two in that it challenged the separation of religion and business immediately. Keynes did not give it a representative name: "But there is a third state of mind, in which we do not fully believe either in a heaven which is elsewhere or in progress as a sure means towards a heaven upon earth hereafter; and if heaven is not elsewhere and not hereafter, it must be here and now or not at all" (9: 268). This is the view of the socialist, not only of the Russian type, who is unsatisfied with the current social order but is unwilling to rely on economic progress and technical advance, and who therefore works to make the ideal state a reality in the present.

Having expressed no interest in the first alternative and casting doubt on the second, Keynes' language suggests that his sympathy here, if not his unqualified support, is with the third alternative. He did "not fully believe" in the first two possibilities. This tentative support for the third alternative would become solid if it were to become clear that the second alternative were not to be fulfilled. Keynes concluded: "If there is no moral objective in economic progress, then it follows that we must not sacrifice, even for a day, moral to material advantage; in other words, that we may no longer keep business and religion in separate compartments of the soul" (9: 268).

6. The Apostles and religion in the first sense[5]

Keynes' understanding of what constitutes religion, the particulars of his own religion in both senses, and his ambivalence over the source of progress toward the rejection of materialism are all reflected in the history of the Cambridge Conversazione Society, popularly known as the Apostles, the secret society that had a profound impact on Keynes' life.[6] The dominant figure in the Apostles throughout the nineteenth century and into the twentieth was Frederick Denison Maurice, an adherent of the Platonic-Christian philosophy of Samuel Taylor Coleridge that was highly influential at Cambridge:

> No one talks of a 'Cambridge theology.' There is such a thing, nevertheless:–at least there is a theology, perfectly distinct and characteristic of the age, formed by Cambridge men, and born with the impress of Cambridge studies, though not elaborated on the spot. Coleridge taught at Highgate; but he poetised and learned at Jesus College half a century before: and the men through whom chiefly his Platonic gospel has passed into the hearts of our generation, Julius Hare and Frederick Maurice, acknowledged the same *alma mater* (Martineau 1866: 334–5).

There are obvious differences between the philosophy of Plato and the counsels of Jesus, but both emphasised that what was good involved the elevation of moral concerns over material concerns, as, for example, in Plato's *Apology* and Jesus' Sermon on the Mount. It was this call for a turn from the material to the spiritual that shaped Coleridge's and Maurice's philosophy.

Keynes' religion, in the sense drawn from Moore of the pursuit of good states of mind, reflects the Apostolic tradition to which Keynes was heir. Moore did not invent or discover the objectivity of goodness. From his early childhood he was immersed in Christianity. At Cambridge he became closely acquainted with Plato. When Moore was an undergraduate, Sidgwick was the dominant personality in Cambridge philosophy. At the end of the nineteenth century and beginning of the twentieth, the Apostles of Sidgwick's circle were ascendant within the University of Cambridge and shaped the intellectual atmosphere in which Moore and Keynes were educated. Henry Montagu Butler was Master of Trinity College, James Ward was Professor of Mental Philosophy and Logic, Richard Claverhouse Jebb was Regius Professor of Greek and F. W. Maitland was Downing Professor of English Law.

5 This section and the following one draw on Andrews (2010).
6 See Andrews (2010).

Henry Jackson, who taught Plato to Moore, would soon become Regius Professor of Greek. Other Apostles contributed to Moore's education by engaging in extended discussions with him, including Bertrand Russell, John M.E. McTaggart, and Goldsworthy Lowes Dickinson. Many of these people disagreed about the details; McTaggart was Hegelian, for example, and Ward was Kantian, but, even as the distinctively Christian elements of their beliefs faded away, they all believed that goodness was objective, they all admired Plato greatly, and they all rejected moral skepticism.

The belief that only states of mind could have the property of goodness was not original with Moore, but came from Sidgwick, evidently as the result of his attempt to synthesise Mill's utilitarianism with Maurice's Christianity. Maurice held that what was highest and best was the state of being in a right relationship with God, a spiritual or mental state: "I believe wickedness, impenitence, and unbelief, to be the worst tortures to which men can be subjected; that as the possession of righteousness, love, truth, constitute eternal blessedness, these constitute eternal damnation and misery" (Maurice 1854: 25). Mill, on the other hand, used the language of utilitarianism, but claimed that some mental or spiritual pleasures were higher than others, and that the highest were spiritual rather than material. Sidgwick's description of that which can be good as a state of "desirable consciousness" (Sidgwick 1907: 398), the source of Moore's "states of consciousness" and Keynes' "states of mind" is sufficiently broad to allow it to include the ideals of both Maurice and Mill. In each case, what is truly good is a very specific sort of human experience with a strong emotional, intellectual or spiritual component.

7. The Apostles and religion in the second sense

Maurice, an ordained priest in the Church of England, developed Coleridge's philosophy into a demand for radical social change, through what has become known as the Theology of the Incarnation. Maurice held that, as the result of the incarnation and of the sacrifice of Jesus on the cross—of God in human form—all people without exception are, within the sight of God, redeemed, regardless of whether they understand themselves to be redeemed or wish to be redeemed. This implies that God's Kingdom on earth has already begun. Thus, the task of humanity is to reform the world in a manner appropriate to that fact, that is, to make the actually existing world worthy of what it already is, the home of God's blessed people rather than a home for greedy, selfish materialists: "The Kingdom of Heaven is to me the great practical existing reality which is to renew the earth and make it a habitation for blessed spirits instead of demons. To preach the Gospel of that Kingdom, the fact that it is among us and is not to be set up at all, is my calling and business ... if ever I do any good work, and earn any of the hatred, which the godly in Christ Jesus receive, and have a right to, it must be in the way I have indicated, by proclaiming society and humanity to be divine realities, as they stand, not as they may become" (Maurice 1884, 2: 137–8).

For Maurice, then, the world is not as it may appear to be. The world as it appears today, dominated by greedy materialism and the institutions and behaviours to which it gives rise, is not its true reality. The problem is to make the world conform to its true reality: "Competition is put forth as the law of the universe. That is a lie. The time is come for us to declare that it is a lie by work and deed" (Maurice 1884, 2: 32).

Keynes' definition of religion in the second sense—including those who, like Trotsky, appealed to higher principles in opposition to selfish materialism—echoes Maurice's defense of the religiosity of Shelley, the author of *The Necessity of Atheism.* According to Maurice: "Shelley's professed atheism ... is more truly religious than the essential atheism of such men, for Shelley was, in spirit and habit of feeling, the most strongly opposed of all men to that philosophy, if philosophy it may be called, which spends itself among physical causes, and can find satisfaction in mere phenomena. He uniformly referred, for the reason and the truth of things, to invisible principles within us or without, of which natural appearances are merely the clothing and the shadow" (quote in Allen 1978: 8).

Like Keynes, Maurice believed that the growth of selfish materialism was a core problem in modern society: "Our English theology, popular as well as systematic, has been gradually reconstructing itself on the commercial or material bases ... this commercial theology ... is ... helping to destroy our commercial as well as our personal morality" (Maurice 1884, 2: 460). In words that Keynes would echo in *The Economic Possibilities for our Grandchildren,* Maurice claimed that greed was an illness, referring to "the slow disease of money-getting and money worship" (Maurice 1884, 2: 517).

For Maurice, the problem of remaking the world was not one of seizing power or imposing appropriate institutions. He understood all institutions to be constructed on a basis of the underlying human relationships. Thus, he understood the problem of morality in human relationships is necessarily prior to and more important than the institutions built on that basis:

> The reorganizers of society and the conservators of society are at war because they start out from the same vicious premises; because they tacitly assume land, goods, money, labor, some subjects of possession, to be the basis of society, and therefore wish to begin by changing or maintaining the conditions of that possession; whereas, the true radical reform and radical conservation must go much deeper and say: "Human relations not only should lie, but do lie beneath all of these" (Maurice 1884, 2: 114).

The problem, then, is to change people, to change their morals and the way they interact. This in turn should lead people to make the needed changes in institutions.

Maurice did not treat these simply as intellectual issues, but also as practical problems to be solved. Maurice believed that the needed change involved the cultivation of the higher, truly human, faculties of the intellect and emotions. The key to this moral and spiritual transformation, he believed, was education and persuasion. Since wealthy men had access to education, he put a great deal of emphasis on providing access to education for women and working class men. Maurice was a central figure in the founding of Queen's College, London, as an educational institution for women, and was later associated with the founding of Girton and Newnham Colleges, women's colleges at Cambridge. He was also a founder and the first principal of the Working Men's College.

Maurice understood that the major obstacles to such cultivation, for a great part of the population, was not just their lack of access to education, but also their lack of leisure, for which economic security is a prerequisite: it is not possible for workers to be educated when exhausted from long hours of hard physical labour. The Christian Socialist movement, of which Maurice was a founder, was intended to help improve the economic condition of the working class on the basis of Christian values of cooperation and solidarity rather than through selfishness and competition.

The early Apostles hoped to persuade the upper and middle classes to take up the moral transformation that Coleridge had urged. Maurice served as editor of the *Literary Chronicle* and, with his fellow Apostle John Sterling, he owned the *Athenaeum* for a brief period. (Keynes later chaired the Board of Directors of the successor journal to the *Athenaeum*, the *Athenaeum and Nation*, later the *Nation and New Statesman*.) These journals had served as important outlets for the early Apostles' perspective:

> The *Literary Chronicle* and *Athenaeum* thus strongly emphasized the need for social reform, but the goal desired by Maurice and Sterling was essentially a spiritual change, one to be achieved through education. Sterling perhaps best expressed their common belief at this time: 'A change of institutions is necessary; and this change cannot take place without an alteration in the mind of the country. To this reform of thought and feeling, it is not likely that England will arrive, until she has been taught by much sorrow, been disciplined into wisdom by suffering, and learnt to listen to the voices of the teachers, of such men as [William] Wordsworth and Coleridge' (Allen 1978: 80).

Sterling's own case illustrates the issues involved. He shifted from an initial concern with the need for change in institutions to a position emphasising the need for moral change. A letter of 1830 from the Apostle Joseph

Williams Blakesley to the Apostle Alfred Tennyson described the evolution of Sterling's thought:

> Sterling ... saw the abuses of the present system of things, which is upheld by the strong hand of power and custom, and he attacked them accordingly. For this conduct he was dubbed a radical. He soon saw that the reforms proposed by that party were totally inadequate to the end which they proposed: that if carried to their fullest effect they would only remove the symptoms and not the cause of evil, that this cause was the selfish spirit which pervades the whole frame of society at present, and that to counterbalance the effects the cause of them must be removed. The end he at first probably thought, with [Percy Bysshe] Shelley, might be effected by lopping off those institutions in which that selfish spirit exhibits itself, without any more effort. He afterwards saw, with Wordsworth, that this was not the true method, but that we must implant another principle with which selfishness cannot co-exist, and trust that this plant as it grows up will absorb the nourishment of the weed, in which case those wickednesses and miseries, which are only the forms in which the latter develops itself, will of their own accord die away, as soon as their principle of vegetation is withered and dried up (cited in Brookfield 1906: 286–7).

Sterling first believed that the fundamental problem was the result of corrupt institutions and that a change of institutions would therefore solve the problem. Later he came to believe that the change that was necessary was a change of heart. His desire to bring change remained unaltered, but his beliefs about the nature of the problem and therefore his understanding of the appropriate solution did not. In order to improve the condition of society, the challenge was to "implant another principle with which selfishness cannot co-exist." The principle the early Apostles looked to was a religious principle, broadly conceived, emphasising the cultivation of higher human capacities, including such things as love, appreciation of beauty and the pursuit of truth.

Maurice's influence on the Apostles was still very strong in the 1850s and '60s and continued to the end of the nineteenth century and into the twentieth. Nevertheless, as Peter Allen has argued, there appears to have been a significant shift in the perspective of the Apostles of the second half of the nineteenth century, as a result of the influence of John Stuart Mill, who, although not an Apostle, had a powerful influence on influential Apostles, most notably Henry Sidgwick.

Although Mill began as a follower of Jeremy Bentham, he later came under the influence of Coleridge, largely through Maurice.[7] To Mill, Bentham represented the culmination of the Enlightenment philosophy of

7 "Few persons have exercised more influence over my thoughts and character than Coleridge has; . . . I consider him the most systematic thinker of our time, without excepting even Bentham, whose edifice is as well bound together, but is constructed on so much simpler a plan, and covers so much less ground. On the whole, there is more food for thought—and the best kind of thought—in Coleridge than in all other contemporary writers" (Mill 12: 102).

the eighteenth century, favouring empiricism, reason and institutional reform against the shackles of scholasticism, superstition and tradition. Through Coleridge, Mill came to appreciate the reaction against the Enlightenment and the eighteenth century. Mill attempted to synthesise what he saw as the partial truths of the eighteenth and nineteenth centuries, of the Enlightenment and Romanticism, of Bentham and Coleridge.[8]

Like Maurice, the later Mill foresaw a radical transformation of society, a "moral revolution," but following the St. Simonians, a French social and political movement of the first half of the nineteenth century, Mill came to see progress as a series of stages that would follow as the result of the natural course of technological development.[9] He saw the unsatisfactory characteristics of his own society as "disagreeable symptoms" of a stage of development, of "one of the phases of industrial progress" (Mill 1963, 3: 754). Progress would come about as the result of rational institutional reform, but major changes would be driven by economic progress. With appropriate steps to limit population and to reduce income inequality, economic development could lead, in a relatively short time, to a society in which advanced technology would provide people with the leisure required to cultivate the higher mental pleasures. Thus, "the trampling, crushing, elbowing, and treading on each other's heels, which form the existing type of social life" (Mill 1963, 3: 754) was just the price that had to be paid to get to a better point in the future. Economic progress would lead to a situation in which this form of social life would be replaced by something more civilized, in which it would be possible for a "much larger body of persons than at present, not only exempt from the coarser toils, but with sufficient leisure, both physical and mental, from mechanical details, to cultivate freely the graces of life and afford examples of them to the classes less favourably circumstanced for their growth" (Mill 1963, 3: 755).

The Apostles of the second half of the nineteenth century, led by Sidgwick, were deeply influenced by Mill's view of progress. In earlier periods, there had been utilitarians among the Apostles, such as Charles Buller, but the general tendency was to side with the Coleridgeans. By the 1860s,

8 A recent biographer, Nicholas Capaldi, has pointed out how uneven Mill's synthesis of Bentham and Coleridge really was: "Mill identified Jeremy Bentham and Samuel Taylor Coleridge as 'the two great seminal minds of England in their age.' Mill clearly intended . . . to present himself as the positive synthesis of these two perspectives, the best of the Enlightenment and the best of the Romantic movement. What is remarkable . . . is how little of the Enlightenment Project actually remains to be praised" (Capaldi 2004: 140).

9 St. Simonianism also eventually took a religious direction, first in St. Simon's own "new Christianity" and then in Auguste Comte's "religion of humanity."

however, Mill's view became dominant among the Apostles. As opposed to Maurice and his followers, the Apostles came to believe that economic progress combined with institutional reform based on reason would bring about moral progress. In an autobiographical fragment, Sidgwick described how he, in the early 1860s and "with others of my generation," under the influence "primarily of Mill, but partly of Comte seen through Mill's spectacles," came to share an "ideal": "What we aimed at from a social point of view was a complete revision of human relations, political, moral, and economic, in the light of science directed by comprehensive and impartial sympathy; and an unsparing reform of whatever, in the judgment of science, was pronounced to be not conducive to the general happiness" (Sidgwick and Sidgwick 1906: 39–40).

Mill's influence can be seen in Sidgwick's language of general happiness, but also in the emphasis on institutional reform. Social changes would be the means to the end of an increase in general happiness. This faith in the continuing reform of human life based on the application of reason leads to a view of continuing moral progress as people are liberated from the nonrational constraints of ignorance and tradition. In a sense, this change inspired by Mill represents a return to the position that changing institutions would produce better people rather than the converse.

Thus, the Apostles preceding Keynes shared his commitment to the pursuit of a better world in the future, one in which universal economic security would enable all people to abandon selfish, greedy materialism and to cultivate higher human capacities. Keynes' apparent ambivalence over the process by which the future abundance providing universal economic security would be achieved is also reflected in the history of the Apostles. Would abundance come more or less inevitably as the result of technical advances resulting from the normal course of economic progress or would people first have to undergo a much more difficult process of moral conversion? The position Keynes took in *The Economic Possibilities for our Grandchildren*, as the "believer in progress" for whom improved circumstances would produce improved people, resembles that of the late nineteenth-century Apostles under the influence of Mill and Sidgwick. Keynes' third position, according to which heaven "must be here and now," corresponds closely to the view of moral progress advocated by the early Apostles, reflecting Maurice's Theology of the Incarnation according to which the Kingdom of Heaven on earth has begun and "is ... the great practical existing reality."

8. Conclusion

The belief that, as the result of technological improvements in productivity, economic progress would allow people universally to enjoy economic security was very influential in the nineteenth century, endorsed by thinkers as diverse as J. S. Mill and Karl Marx. Universal economic security was seen by both as an opportunity for more leisure, with less time lost to work that was not intrinsically rewarding. Marx and Mill both assumed that this leisure would allow people to develop themselves, physically and mentally in a manner that was consciously and freely chosen. They differed over how this would transition would be achieved. Mill held that it would occur in the natural progress of society. Marx thought it would take purposive human action to bring about the transition.

Keynes' writings addressed in this essay must be understood in this context. In *The Economic Possibilities for our Grandchildren*, he adopts the view of the Mill, the believer in progress who would wait for the transition to come about without active intervention. In *A Short View of Russia*, however, he makes a case for the socialist, who demanded the transition be made immediately through purposive action, because the existing order did not seem to be leading society into a period of abundance.

Although Keynes displays ambivalence about the manner in which progress toward a better society would proceed, he shared Maurice's view that the better world to come is the true world, the current state of affairs an aberration. The love of money as a possession should be seen, today and always, as a mental illness. Dominating social life, greed and selfishness have been viewed as positive qualities, but this is, in fact, merely a pernicious error.

In 1944, after another decade of depression and several years of war, Keynes expressed the Maurician viewpoint again, in his letter to Friedrich Hayek on the publication of his *The Road to Serfdom* (1944), a letter in which Keynes invokes religious imagery to argue that the key problem is not in politics or institutions but rather in the morality of the human beings who composed the institutions:

> I should say that what we want is not no planning, or even less planning, indeed I should say that we almost certainly want more. But the planning should take place in a community in which as many people as possible, both leaders and followers, wholly share your own moral position. Moderate planning will be safe if those carrying it out are rightly oriented in their own minds and hearts to the moral issue. This is in fact already true of some of them. But the curse is that there is also an important section who could almost be said to want planning not in order to enjoy its fruits but because morally they hold ideas exactly the opposite of yours, and wish to serve not God but the devil.... No, what we need is the restoration of right moral thinking—a return to proper moral values in our social philosophy.... Dangerous acts can be done safely in a community which thinks and feels rightly, which would be the way to hell if they were executed by those who think and feel wrongly (27: 387–8).

In the letter, Keynes is no longer willing to wait, but argues for actively building a better world through some degree of economic planning. He argues that before such planning can be carried out safely, it is necessary that we have a return to "right moral thinking." The problem, one he thought could be overcome, was that some people in policy-making roles were greedily pursuing their own interests rather than serving the interests of society as a whole. Keynes calls for moral change, the return of explicitly religious values, according to which avarice would no longer receive social approbation.

This question has become particularly relevant today. At the same time that neoliberal policies increase inequality and reduce economic security, feeding social unrest, it becomes increasingly clear that the solution of the economic problem worldwide is not fundamentally a technical problem of production. Mill's smooth and peaceful transition does not appear to be taking place, yet compelling moral, political and economic reasons oppose the use of the force Marx believed necessary. Keynes offers a third alternative, a moral socialism, without violence, a socialism protective of individuality and freedom.

Acknowledgements

An earlier version of this paper was presented at the workshop: "The conflict-ridden development of modernity: Theology and political economy," at the University of Lyon, December 2014. The author is grateful for comments by participants in the workshop, especially Jean-Pierre Potier and Gilbert Faccarello. He also acknowledges the helpful suggestions of two anonymous referees.

References

Allen, P., 1978. *The Cambridge Apostles: the early years.* Cambridge: Cambridge University Press.

Andrews, D., 2010. *Keynes and the British humanist tradition: the moral purpose of the market.* London: Routledge.

Brookfield, F.M., 1906. *The Cambridge "Apostles".* London: Sir Isaac Pitman and Sons.

Capaldi, N., 2004. *John Stuart Mill: a biography.* Cambridge: Cambridge University Press.

Hawtrey, R.G., 1944. *Economic destiny.* London: Longmans, Green.

Keynes, J.M., 1971–1989. *The collected writings of John Maynard Keynes.* Various volumes. London: Macmillan.

Martineau, J., 1866. *Essays, philosophical and theological.* London: Trübner.

Maurice, F.D., 1854. *The word 'Eternal' and the punishment of the wicked.* New York: C.S. Francis.

Maurice, F.D., 1884. *The life of Frederick Denison Maurice, chiefly told in his own letters.* New York: Charles Scribner's Sons.

Mill, J.S., 1963–1991. *Collected works.* Toronto: University of Toronto Press.
Moore, G.E., 1903. *Principia ethica.* Cambridge: Cambridge University Press.
Sidgwick, H., 1907. *The methods of ethics.* London: Macmillan.
Sidgwick, A. and Sidgwick, E.M., 1906. *Henry Sidgwick: a memoir.* London: Macmillan.

Abstract

Keynes rejected religion in his youth but embraced it later in his life. This essay addresses Keynes' peculiar definition of religion, his description of his "religion," and the sources of his religion. Keynes characterised religion as not only a personal experience of communion, but also as the pursuit of a better world for all people, although he showed some ambivalence about how this better world might come about, ultimately adopting a position similar to that of the nineteenth-century Christian Socialist Movement, to which he was connected through the Cambridge Apostles.

Index

Note:
Page numbers in *italic* type refer to figures
Page numbers in **bold** type refer to tables
Page numbers followed by 'n' refer to notes

abolition 56
abstinence 277
abstraction 125, 128, 133–6, 152
abundance 69, 70, 73, 339
academic socialists 274
accumulation 265, 275
action: collective 2; creative 72; daily 134; decentralised 120; individual 300; inspiring 311; other-oriented 254, 271, 277; public-spirited 317; right 297
activists, Catholic 208, 211
adâlat 54
administration 68, 193, 201; state 194, 274
adoption 267
affection 275, 325
affective superiority 267
afterlife 321
agency 254
agents, economic 261
agnosticism 162, 172n5, 283, 285
agreement 56
agriculture 231, 232, 249
a kâm 51
alliance 80; divine 70, 71
allocation 27
alms 78
altruism 12, 316n19
âmal 57
Anabaptists 169
analysis 128
analytic hierarchicalism 316n20
analytical method 314n14
anarchy 225, 260, 266, 268
Andrews, D. 10, 334–53
Anglicanism 287, 334
animal appetites 130, 131
annuities 91n8, 92, 96
anti-Semitism 207
anti-thesis (Hobbesian) 32, 39
anticipation 41
appetite 74
Aquinas, T. 36, 88
Arabic 290
arbitrariness 54
Aristotle 31; Ibn Rushd commentary 46n1
army 233
arrogance 217
art 273, 338
artifices 120
asceticism 67, 75, 78, 277; worldly 79
association 56, 58; divine 226; international 201
associationist psychology 120n2
asymmetries 27, 30, 32; starting positions 37–8
atheism 163, 166, 172, 181, 317
Athenaeum 347

attachment 256, 256n2, 267
Aufklärer 164
Augustinian tradition 35
authority: biblical 288; monarchical 85
autonomy 29, 80
avarice *see* greed
L'Avenir 208, 210n14
Averroes 46–61
aynân 51

badness 316
bankruptcy 228
bargaining power 57
Baudrillart, H. 261–3
Bauer, C. 65–83
beauty 338
bees 130n14, 191
behaviour 5; ascetic 277; best 300; guide 133–6; moral 133; normal 225; optimal 124; pacific 266; rational 261; reforming 236; self-regarding 296; virtuous 170, 225–6, *see also* conduct
Being 314
Belgium 209, 212
beliefs 165, 167, 181, 336; collective 187, 188, 195; declining 283, 286; religious 227; social 189, 248; as wealth 223
believers 73, 78, 336, 337, 343
Belsham, T. 165
benefit, mutual 27, 29–33
benevolence 172
Bentham, J. 335
Benthamism 339
bequests 266, 268–9
betterment 336
bias 143–7, 145; retrospective 25
biblical narrative 334
Biéler, A. 66n5
biology 267
blame 217
Block, M. 273
blood 191, 192
Blumenberg, H. 4
bodily suffering 311
body 191, 192; social 191
Boisguilbert, P. de 6
bon prix 139
bondage 231
bonds: human 278; social 186, 187
Book of Common Prayer, The 287
books 151
borrower 57, 88, 100; profits of 92, 104; well-informed 104
brain 255, 256; imaging 257n3
Broad Church movement 293n21
Broedersen, N. 95
brother 104n34
brotherliness 180
Browning, R. 310–11
business 342–3; life 133

calling 73
calm 339
Calvin, J. 8
Calvinism 178
Cambridge Conversazione Society 344
Cambridge theology 344
capacities 195, 198
capital 57, 58; accumulating 275; increasing 177; market 228; money as 92; national 275; using 112
capitalism 66n5; constrained 343; development 77, 78
capitalists 269
career 340
carentia pecuniae 90
case analysis 313, 314
cases 61
casino 228
casuistry 53, 87, 92
Catholic activists 208, 211
Catholic ideas 240
Catholic institutions 233
Catholic society 227, 236, 249
Catholic worship 206
Catholicism: consequences 215; and economic development 216; liberal 205, 238; social 209, 240; useful 237; values 234
cause 126; efficient 128; explanatory 188; final 127, 128, 130, 147, 148, 154, 173
celibacy 233, 234
cerebral table 255–6
chance 48
change 348; social 185, 197
chaos 303
character 256, 295

charity 70, 75, 79, 105, 112; abundant 233; neighbourly 92, 234; wise 312
children 71, 229, 267
choices 41; individual 2; modifying 153; rational 21
Christian moralists 9
Christian theism 314
Christianism 252
Christianity 162; declining 283, 286; historical 291; liberal 315; new 185, 197, 199–200; regenerating 196
Church: Moravian 102; power 207, 335
Church of England 335
Church of Utrecht 94
circulation 191–2, 198
circumstances 140, 295
citizens 234
clergy 196; sociological 268; training 284; wages 269
co-property 150
coercion 29–33, 31, 39
coins 90
Coleridge, S.T. 344, 347, 348–9
collaboration, divine 72
comfort 316, 339
commerce 96, 249
commercial theology 346
commodity 106, 111, 224, 240
common sense 337, 338
communion 198, 199, 337
communism 301
community 336
comparison 320
compassion 325
compensation 109; fair 91
competences 195
competition 139, 227, 271; consequences 254; free 143; healthy 269; international 229, 234, 235; interpersonal 320; market 240
complementarity 81
complexity 135
compromise 271
concepts 3–4, 6–7, 18, 19
conciliation 270, 275
conditions, exchange 31, 39, 40
conduct 133–6, *135*; self-regarding 296; virtuous 170, 225–6, *see also* behaviour
Conférences de philosophie catholique 211
confidence 54, 229
confiscation 230, 231
conquest 265
conscience 99, 131, 311
consciousness 318, 322, 325, 338, 345
consent 38, 55; mutual 61, 106
consequences 120, 316; collective 136; material 218; public 136
consequentialism 327
constraints 120
constructivism 264
consumer theory 6
consumers 87, 93, 191, 324
consumption 76, 275
contemplation 317n22, 337
contentment 74
contract: free 30; incomplete 33, 41; terms 21
contradiction 326
controversy 170, 171, 287
conversions 169
conviction 170
cooperation 120n2, 195, 198; worker 240
corporations 240
corporatist community 22–3
corporeal property 51
Le Correur, J. 91–3
corruption 348
costs, reducing 231
countryside 109
courage 325
craftsmanship 39
creation 67, 69; divine 71; shared 79; social 71
creative action 72
creator 174, 175, 288; proof 308, 314, 315, 317, *see also* God
credit 59, 109, 228
credit market 112
Cremaschi, S. 160–84
crisis: economic 238; faith-based 284, 284n2, 292, 308
critique 10, 11
cruelty 325
cultivators 140
cupidity 224–7
currency 191
customs 341

daily actions 134
damage 89, 109
damnum emergens 89
Darwin, C. 283, 289, 334–5
Data of Ethics (Spencer) 270, 276
De Roover, R. 24, 47
dearths 174
death 321, 343
defiance 325
definitions, ideal 22
delay 51, 52, 53
delegation 58
demand and supply 222, 233
démocratie chrétienne 205, 214
demographic change 289n15
dependence 57
dependency, human 81
depravity 163
description 52
design 134; argument from 314, 315; divine 311
desire 324
despotism 123n4, 124; legal 122, 123, 147–54
destiny 218
destitution 217
determinism 311
development: social 151; stages 349
devotion 316
dhimma 51
Dickinson, G.L. 323
Die Legitimität der Neuzeit (Blumenberg) 4
dignity 266
disapproval 28
disciplinary development 1
discipline 78, 79, 201
disenchantment 3n4
dishonesty 227, 229
dishonour 111
disinterest 132
disorder 111
dissent 334
dissenters 287, 288, 343
distress 217
distribution 20, 22, 28; choice of 40; income 222, 233; of profits 75; responsible 76; wealth 222, 248, 299, 300
distributive standards 39
diversity 303, 315
doctrine 199, 205, 313
dogma 218, 283, 336; declining 307
dogmatism 77
donations 275
doubt 181, 218, 283, 292, 343
drama, universal 134
Dublin Review, The 213
Dunoyer, C. 264, 268
Durkheim, E. 201
duties 132, 132n16, 141; knowledge of 311; moral 133, 144
duty 249

economic agenda 23
economic agents 261
economic coercion 29–33
economic crises 238
economic development 216
economic history 1
economic man 278
economic planning 352
economic problem 60, 339, 341, 342, 352
economic security 347, 350, 351, 352
economic theories 6–8, 217, 219, 239, 240
economics, social 219, 220
L'économiste français 273
economists 148
education 164, 267; community 301; moral 268; women's 275, 347
educational networks 198
effect, external 307
efficiency 28, 40, 41; allocation 27
egalitarianism 70
Ege, R. 46–64
egoism 120n2, 253, **271**; collective 256n2; counterforce 257–75; domestic 267; group 276; individual 276; materialistic 336
egoistic feelings 276
emotions 347
empirics 36
employment terms 31
end 127, 128; determined 154
end-means distinction 327, 337
enemies 91n9, 334
energy 256
England 216, 217, 288, 335

enigma 214–16
enjoyment 299, 325; direct 342; refusing 79
enrichment 70, 74, 225; collective 81
enterprise 193
enthusiasm 312, 318
entrepreneurs 195, 224, 229; charitable 275
equilibrium 23, 26, 31; better 32; social 39
equity 79
L'Ère Nouvelle 214
eternity 304
ethics 47, 61, 286, 287, 296
evidence 308, 315
evil 84, 312; causes 176; defining 163–4; explaining 170, 172, 180; illusory 311; inescapable 328; intrinsic 325, 326; justified 179; moral 173; natural 173; necessary 289; partial 176; short-run 174; social 176, 179
evolution 272, 276
excess 75, 227
exchange 263, 265; agency-sensitive 18, 20, 29, 32, 39; coerced 31; conditions 31, 39, 40; contested 21, 31, 33, 41; contractual 38; encompassing embedment of 30; free 21, 301; voluntary 22
exclusive corporations 138
exhaustion 229, 347
expediency 132, 136
experience 128, 325
externalities, negative 321
extinction 312

Faccarello, G. 1–15, 204–51
factory 195, 198; system 231, 232
facts 60, 134, 136
failure 228
fairness 22, 170
faith 73, 165; crisis of 284, 284n2, 292, 308; displacing 289
faithfulness 71n7
Fall 225, 226
falsehood 167
families 111, 221, 270; functioning 266–7
family affection 275
famine 217, 222
farmers 144
farming 109
feelings 272; egoistic 276
festivals 233, 234, 235
feudal-military society 185, 196
finality 314
flows 198
Foleÿ, A.E. 265n17
foreigners 105, 107, 234
formalism 48
fragility 71n7
France 84–115, 185–201, 204–41, 270–6
fraternal communion 198
fraternity 79, 199, 201
free market 118, 322; society 233
freedom 85, 153, 171; economic 321; intellectual 339; religious 166–7; uncontrolled 109; using 341, *see also* liberty
French Revolution 185, 204
Friedman, D. 26, 28, 39, 40
friendship 105
frugality 152
fruiting 71

Gall, F.-J. 255, 256
Gallicans 207
gaming 228
garden, cultivating 68
generosity 92; divine 70, 80
Germany 284, 323
ghâ'ib 52
gharar 48, 52, 57, 59
gifts 78; divine 75
give 278
God 65, 336; communication with 278; devotion to 69; earthly 201; evidence for 126; image of 69; intentions 127–8; as law-giver 176; and liberty 208–10; loving 311; place of 68; proof 308, 314, 315, 317; as reality 314; rewarding 227; vengeful 227; will of 133, *see also* creator
godlessness 292
golden age 200
good 308n6, 309, 312; commitment to 307; common 67; comparing 320–2; competing 320–2; creating 339; defining 163, 319n28, 322–3, 326; explaining 326; individual 310,

320–2; instrumental 318n24; intrinsic 318, 318n24, 327; life 341n4; maximising 338, 339; for the other 53, 60; person 323; problem of 317–20; pursuing 320; will 319
goodness 316, 343; function 317–20
goods 57; idolising 75; luxury 75n10; managing 67; material 222; sharing 80; storing 265
Gossen, H.H. 6
government 123; dangerous 190, 190n3; excluding 195; expenditure 193; intervention 300, 301, 302, 329; moral power 264; productive 264; role of 152, 300; Soviet 340
grâce efficace 84
gratitude 92
gratuitousness 269
Great Britain 334–5
greed 74, 137–8, 229, 237, 335, 339; cultivating 342; as illness 346
Green, T.H. 302, 303
Grote, J. 292–3, 293n20, 297
Grote Society 292, 294
group power 276
growth 74
guilds 240

habit 152
ḥāḍir 52, 54
Halévy, E. 118–19
happiness: comparing 297; earthly 200, 236; general 350; material 237; maximising 176–8, 299; of others 321; poor people 221, 299; promoting 179, 297; temporal 216; and virtue 319
harm 120
harmony 74, 80, 124, 315n15; with God 69; natural 118
Harrison, P. 3
hatred 336
healing 71n7
heart 192, 255, 256; changing 348
heaven 343, 345
hedonism 299, 324, 327; psychological 311
heretics 85
heterogeneity 17
hierarchicalism, analytic 316n20
hierarchy 70
Hinduism 162–3
historians 258
hoarding 340
Hobbes, T., anti-thesis 32, 39
holidays 102, 103
Holland 87, 94–7
Holy Scriptures 98, 99
honour 274
hope 179, 235, 312
hornets 191
Hubert, H. 278
human affairs 134
human communion 79
human nature 69, 99n24, 225, 226
human role 68
human types 323
humanism 201
humanity: creating 81; united 199
Hume, D. 128
hunger 229, 230
Hunter, I. 289
husbandman 140
hygiene, cerebral 264

Ibn Rushd 7, 46–61
ideal definitions 22
ideal life 338
ideal state 343
idealism 308, 308n3, 327; practical 336, 338
ideals 319; Christian 340
ideas 77, 140; Catholic 240; common 200; general 189; moral 200, 223, 253–4; positive 196; as wealth 223
identity, natural 119
ideology 5
idleness 71, 88, 92
idol 197
idolatry 169
ignorance 48, 52, 55, 164, 350
illness 351
immediacy 51, 55
immortality 321
impartiality 121
imperative, moral 320
impersonalisation 180
impressions, moral 167, 168
improvement 230, 265; earthly 343; moral 177, 179

incarnation 345
incentives 340
income: distribution 222, 233; fair 22; lower class 324, *see also* wages
incompleteness 33
India 162, 163
individualism 262
individualistic thinking 266
industrial religion 12
industrial society 205, 222, 227–30, 272; foundations 253
industrialism 220–30
industrialisme 252
industrialists 248
industry 249, 268, 301
inequality 349; necessary 289
infinity 236
influences 16–17
information 33; available 53; perfect 53; quality 52
infrastructure 140
inheritance 265, 267, 275; egalitarian law 268n22
inspiration, moral 317
instability 254
instinct 130, 136n22, 152, 256, 257
institutions: Catholic 233; changing 346–7; common 189; corrupt 348; productive 264
intellect 347
intellectual being 260
intentions 316
interdependence 60, 79
interest(s) 5, 7, 8, 50, 55; collective 254; community of 200; congruent 143–7; defining 131; disguised 56; enlightened 125, 132–3, 136, 141–3, 154; eternal 226; fusion of 120, 133; general 119, 122, 139; identity of 121, 136–47; long-run 144; material 218, 252; merchant 122, 137; opposing 122, 144, 145; partial 144; pecuniary 274; permanent 144; private 118, 119, 124, 136, 254; public 118, 124, 133, 137–41, 137n23, 301; renouncing 79; temporal 227, 236; true 131; understanding 152, 321–2; unenlightened 132, 146
interventionism 36
intuitionism 318, 327
invention, human 189
investment 76, 78, 228, 301
invisibility 52, 55n11
invisible hand 85, 128
iqâla 56
Islamic economic thought 48n7
itinerants 269

jâhiliyya 52
jâ'iz 47
Jansenism 8
Jaucourt, L. de 105
jâza 47
Jesuits 107
Jesus Christ 290, 316, 344, 345
Jevons, S. 298–9
job 72; changing 73
Journal des économistes 261
judgement 127
jus gentium 37, 37n11
justice 6; normative theory 178; respecting 225; strict 111

Keynes, J.M. 10, 283, 286, 307, 319–20
kindness 256, 267
kingdom 345
kings 206, 287
knowledge 38; circulating 142; empirical 35; immediate 145; limits to 180; practical 134; problems 33; promoting 140; rational 165; sacred 187; scope of 175; sensational 149n33; sentimentalist 127, 148; spreading 154; systems 16, 17; theories 148; useful 180

La Porte, J.-B.-B. de 109
labour 57, 58, 59; as commodity 224, 240; division of 79, 266, 268, 276; market 25; national 234, 235; productive 191; rewarding 269; supply 229, 232, 233, *see also* work
labourers *see* workers
laesio enormis 27
Laforest, P. de 105–6
laissez-faire 254, 296, 302
Lallier, F. 211, 212
Lammenais, H.-F.R. de 208, 211–12
land 143, 231
Langenstein, H. von 23n3

Langholm, O. 29–30
language 260
latitude 37
law: civil 100; discovering 129; distribution of 222; divine 34, 36, 36n10, 219; economic 265; egalitarian 268n22; expedient 136; general 134; goal of 148; legitimising 188; modern natural 87, 99; moral 181; natural 38, 99, 109, 124, 129, 176; positive 36; providential 133; psychological 261; rational choice account 176; Roman 88; scientific 187–8; teaching 153
lawfulness 7
laziness 69
learning mechanism 23
lectures 291n17; Catholic 211
legend 290
legislation 301; class 240
legislator 120, 140, 144
leisure 341, 347, 349, 351
lenders 57, 228
lending 5
Leninism 5n8, 336, 340
Leroy-Beaulieu, P. 273–5, 279
Lessius, L. 89, 89n6
liability 51, 59
liberalism 118, 205, 272–6
liberté: animale 124, 136n22, 149, 153; *d'intelligence* 124, 126, 136n22, 149
liberty: and God 208–10; natural 300, 302; and order 249, *see also* freedom
lie 346
Liesse, A. 273
lieutenant 68n6, 71
life: conduct 5; insurance 275; spiritual 70
Lindsay, J. 166n3
Lindsey, T. 166n3
liquidity, lost 90
Literary Chronicle 347
living conditions 311, 328, 343
loan 50
logic 334
loss 89, 90; genuine 109
Louis XIV, King of France 206
love 248, 249; abstract 234; brotherly 198; Christian 316; divine 127; as end 337; ideal 311; intense 319; neighbourly 225; pure 263; universal 180, 254, 316
loving 256, 337
lucrum cessans 89, 90
lust 225, 325
luxury 75n10, 233, 233n40, 237, 299

Macciò, D.D. 10, 307–33
machinery question 260–1
machines 129, 228, 229, 233
majhala 48, 59
makruh 48
Malthus, T. 174–7, 217, 220, 289
management 194; moral 195
manufactories 232
manufacturers 140, 144
manufacturing 231
market(s): anarchism 40n15; autonomous 24; capital 228; competitive 240; failures 40; foreign 232; free 118, 233, 322; instrumental 39; limits of 39; logic 180; perfect 39; struggle 227
marriage 221, 267
Marshall, A. 303, 313
Marx, K. 4, 351
masses 234
material conditions 325
material transmission **265**, 266
materialism 3n5, 148–9, 323, 335; selfish 341, 346
Maurice, F.D. 344–7
Mauss, M. 278
maximum satisfaction principle 321
Mayor, J.B. 292, 294
measure 75
mechanisation 228
mechanisms, perfect 32, 32n8, 33
mediation 188
medieval thought 22
mental experience 336, 338
mental pleasures 349
mental states 318, 325, 337, 338n2, 345
Menuet, M., and Orain, A. 84–117
mercantile policies 139
merchant credit 86
merchants 88, 92, 98; interests 122; poor 105
merit 80
Merton thesis 3

metaphysics 175, 255, 260, 286, 314
methodological critique 259–64, 278
methodological pragmatism 313
methodology 48
Middle Ages 47
Mignot, E. 99, 100, 110
Mill, J. 165, 171–4, 177
Mill, J.S. 3, 290, 295, 297, 348–9
mind 125, 130–3, 255, 256; divine 303; good states of 337; perfectibility of 147–54; states of 318, 325, 337, 338n2, 345
miracles 170
miser 145
misery 131, 176, 326
missionaries 163
moderation 75, 131, 329
modernity 2n1, 5; defining 2; foundations 35
mohatara 56
Molina, L. de 37
Molinari, G. de 261, 262
monarchy 85, 288
money 180, 325; absent 90; as blood 192; as commodity 111; fertility of 93; good 191; loving 341, 351; motive 339–40; noxious 191; present 90; and priests 217; as tool 98; trading 95; using 88, 104
monopolies 137, 138, 139
Montalembert, C.F. de 208, 210n11
Montesquieu, C.-L. de Secondat de 103
Montesquieu/Herrenschwand approach 231–2
Moore, G.E. 308–14, 317–18, 325, 327, 337–9
moral constraint 177
moral determinism 311
moral dilemma 216–17
moral disapproval 28
moral doctrine 253–4
moral evaluation 178
moral ideas 200, 223, 253–4
moral imperative 320
moral impressions 167, 168
moral improvement 177, 179
moral judgement 127
moral modification 264
moral obligations 132, 167
moral relativism 311
moral value 311
morality 9, 77; applied 194, 195; by-product 133; corrupted 93; earthly 196; economic benefits 273; encouraging 315; foundations 99, 317; industrial 195, 199; natural 162–5, 168–71, 181; Pauline 198, 200; philanthropic 197, 201; of production 195; revealed 162–5; utilitarian 300
Moravian Church 102
mother 267
motives 119n1, 124, 125–41, *135*
mountaineering 329
Muhammad, Prophet 49
mukhâṭara 55
multiplying 221
muqtasid 48n6
Musso, P. 11, 185–203
mystery 262
mystic union 337
mystical enthusiasm 86
mystics 7

nâjiz 51
nameless mystic union 337
narrative, biblical 334
nasî'a 52, 53
nation 195
national dividend 308, 324
national wealth 223, 226
naturalism, providential 126–30
naturalistic fallacy 326
nature 147, 338; state of 226
navigation 204
necessaries 299
necessitarianism 173, 178
necessity 336
needs 230; material 339; reducing 233; worker 233
neighbourhood 234
neighbours, love towards 198
neo-liberal governmentality 40n15
neoliberalism 352
neshekh 50n8
networks 198
neurobiology 257
Nietzsche, F. 316n21
nominalism 35
non-believers 168, 248

normative considerations 17
norms 23

obligation, moral 132, 167
oblivion 18
observation 128, 133, 135n21, 288, 314
omnipotence 177
opinions 168
opponents 168
opportunity cost 89, 112
Opstraët, J. 95
optimism 178–9, 181, 310–12, 328, 329
Orain, A., and Menuet, M. 84–117
order: benevolent 126, 147, 149; designed 149; harmonious 122; ideal 149; legal 227; legitimate 227; and liberty 249; maintaining 152n36; moral 60n12, 304; natural 118, 122, 129n13, 147, 149; perceiving 134; perfect 69; providential 125; societal 148, 187; stable 253–4
original sin 7, 69, 288
other 61
ought 48
overpopulation 220, 221
Owen, R. 178
owner 88
Ozanam, A.-F. 211

pacifism 198
pain 69, 163–4
Paine, T. 190n3
pantheism 201
paradise 198, 200, 343
parents 267
partiality 135, 137–41
partnership 56–9
pass through 47
passions 124, 131, 136, 137–41; controlling 177, 323; moderating 151
Pasteur, L. 3n5
Paul, Saint 198
pauperism 204, 205, 217, 227–30; eradicating 230–7; mass 238
peace 228
perception 133, 149, 318
perceptual errors 151
perfectibility 125, 176; mental 147–54
perfection 303
performance 269
Périn, C. 215, 240
periodicals 209
persecution 85
perseverance 329
persuasion 168
pessimism 235, 237, 310, 320
Petty, W. 5
phenomenalism 295
philanthropy 198–9, 201, 234
philosophers 133, 134
philosophical studies 152
philosophical system 187
philosophical trials 171, 172
philosophy 234, 235; positive 261
phrenology 255, 255n1, 260
physical realm 130
physics, social 259
physiocrats 302
piety 77
Pigou, A.C. 10
pity 326n35
planning 351
Plato 344
pleasure 163–4, 318, 345, 349
poena convetnionalis 89
poetry 310–11, 310n9
policy 195, 297
political economy 154; defining 142
political interventionism 36
political religion 5
political theology 19
Political Theology (Schmitt) 4
politicians 274
poor people 80, 87, 91, 97, 98n23, 112; enjoyment 299; happiness 221; ignorance 164; improving 198, 230, 311; labour value 224
Popper, K. 35
population: growth 139, 175–7, 220, 221; principle 175–7, 220–2
populationist arguments 289
positivism 259, 261, 262, 295
possession 72, 341, 351
Potron, M. 6
poverty 76, 78, 328; debating 204; defining 106; reducing 179; relative 230; and wealth 176, 205
power: bargaining 57; Church 207, 335; evil 172; government 264; group 276;

imbalance 57; intellectual 267; moral 267; spiritual 207, 267
powerlessness 93, 237
practice, unenlightened 135
practitioners 133, 134, 137–41, 143–7
pragmatism 300
predestination 178, 288
preferences 324, 325
prejudice 54, 136–47
present 90
pressure, social 278
pretending 342
prevention 277
price 53, 138, 139, 222, 223, 297; just 7; labour 240; market 112; natural 139
principles 195; divine 199; industrial 197; instinctive 130; invisible 346
private sphere 12
problems: economic 60, 339, 341, 342; fundamental 39; great 256; modern 346; practical 347; solved 21, 28, 39; true 341; understanding 348; unsolved 29, 41
procreation 221
producers 88, 93, 98, 190; and scientists 195
production 76; celebrating 199; costs 228; as goal 197; increasing 224, 231; limited 174; mechanised 228; morality of 195; science of 194; superfluous 232; technology of 342, 349–51; wealth 265
productive activity 98
productive capacities 79
productive institutions 264
productivity 68, 342, 349–51
professional group 276
professions 72, 140
profit 50, 71; borrower 92; lost 89; maximising 227, 228; search for 78; stopping 89, 90; usury as 98; and wages 224
progress 17, 18, 154, 200, 289; continuous 312; economic 342–4, 349, 350; industrial 349
promise 54
proof 304, 308
property 150, 265; private 230; rights 40, 265
prosecution 167
prosperity 65, 70, 74, 81; measuring 223; national 146, 226; public 225, 248; and religion 216
protectionism 234, 235, 263
Protestant nations 216
Protestantism 206, 288, 342; public opinion 206–7
proto-economics 24
providence 6, 143, 174
providential naturalism 126–33
prudence 164
psychology 255, 260
public opinion 228
public service 340
public sphere 2
punishment 173; divine 221; eternal 311
Puritanism 77, 342
purpose 314

qirâ 57
qualities, inherent 17
quality 229
quantity 75
Quran 49, 50

racism 207
radical movement 152n36
radicals 165, 166, 348
rationalised world 180
rationalism 38
rationality 2, 5, 261
Rawls, J. 6
realism, moral 127
reality: hidden 314; true 346
reason 88, 99, 109, 151, 304; advancing 289; fallible 304; individual 133; limits of 304; role of 127, 130, 182
reasoning 254
receive 278
reciprocity 32, 33, 267
reform 165, 289, 335, 347; institutional 350; social 311, 313, 326
reformation 287
refuge 104n34
regeneration 296
regret 56
regulation 266; social 154
relationality 60
relations 75

relationship: human 346; interpersonal 234; social 186, 218, 225
relatives 104
relativism 311
religion: discarding 307; historical 290; and science 291; value 315
religious experience 314–17
religious movements 84
religious opinions 166
religious purpose 179–80
religious tests 285, 285n7, 291
remuneration 112
rentes constituées 92, 96
repayment 89, 91
resources 174
resources growth 175
responsibility 65, 75, 181
restriction 277
revelation 226
revolution 261n14, 336–7, 349; French 185, 204; imminent 218; intellectual 277; social 236, 236n41
reward 226, 227, 316
ribâ 50, 55
rich people 80, 91, 98n23; borrowing from 105
rights: contract 21; divine 287; fundamental 208; property 40, 265
rigorists 109
risk 52, 228
rituals, negative 277
roads 140
Roman Law tradition 30
Royer, C. 272–3
Ruellou, T. 9, 118–59
ruin 111
rules: created 28; enforceable 39; trade 96

sacrifice 218, 225–6, 275, 277–9, 345
saḥîḥ 5
Saint-Simon, H. 252
Saint-Simonism 213, 249, 253
saints 169
Salamanca School 37n12
sale 49–56
salvation 86, 311
sanctification 80
satisfaction 321, 324
saving 152, 190, 191, 194, 275
Say, J.-B. 252
scarcity 174, 339
scepticism 316; limited 175, 179, 181; positive 303
Schmitt, C. 4, 19
Schneewind, J.B. 34
scholastic duality 17
Scholastic thought 7
Scholastic tradition 90–100
schools of thought 239
science 2n3, 168; abstract 135; and art 273; autonomous 193; conflict with religion 291; of industry 191; natural 19; new 1, 289; positive 313; secular 182; social 189, 220n31, 259; of society 189; useless 223
scientific system 187
scientification 2
scientists 195, 196, 197
Scottish Enlightenment 127
Scotus, J.D. 35
scriptures 288
scruples 104
secularisation 2–5, 2n2, 285, 289, 292, 307; theorem 4
security 347, 350, 351
self-improvement 315
self-interest 130, 141, 225, 227, 272–5, 279; benefits 85, 263; conceptual history 7; and egoism 274; enlightened 138; future 278; legitimate 273; limits to 300; as motive 118, 119; promoting 132
self-interest principle 296
self-love 125, 130, 131, 138n24, 237, 274, 279
selfishness 6, 119n1, 131, 225, 253, 335, 339; avoiding 197; material 341, 346
sellers 122
sensationalism 148, 149n33
sentimentality 311
settler 274
sharika (partnership) 57, 58
sharikat al-abdân 58
sharikat al- inân 58
sharikat al-mufâwa a 58
sharikat al-wujûh 59
Sidgwick, H. 9, 317, 321, 344
similarities 4

sin 6, 69; original 7, 69, 288; struggle against 84
skills 134, 275; abstraction 152; communion of 199
slavery 224
sleep-walkers 336
Smith, A. 260, 285n6, 302
sobriety 75
sociability 219, 226, 237, 248
social classes 123, 133n18, 134, 146; inferior 152; poorest class 198; predestined 178; wages 269; working class 236, 237, 240
social construction 278
social contract 189
social Darwinism 289
social improvement 296
social policy 297
social product 324
social reform 311, 313, 326
social regeneration 296
social relationship 186, 218, 225
social sciences 220n31, 259
social stratification 22
socialism 301
socialist thinkers 261, 274
sociality 256
society: advancing 68; as body 70, 79, 192; Catholic 227, 236, 249; enduring 253–4; flows in 191–2; fundamental basis 276; ideal 257; industrial 205, 222, 227–30; models of 191–2; perfect 249, 300; political 148; science of 189; steering 153; transactional 227; unitary 227; well-being of 222
sociocracy 258
sociological critique 252–80
sociology 12, 189, 259, 262, 270, 273
soil 150, 151
solidarity 262, 263, 276, 279
Sombart, W. 22
sovereignty 19n2
Soviet experiment 340
Spain 216
speculation 228
Spencer, H. 253, 270–2, 276
spending 75, 275; public 194
spiritual life 70
spiritual pleasures 345
spiritual power 207
spiritualism 3n5
stammer 283
standards, required 46
state: administering 194, 274; concepts 19; diminishing 201; future 167; theory 4, 19
Steiner, P. 12, 252–82
Stephen, L. 286n10, 291
Sterling, J. 347–8
stewardship 65–81
stock exchange 228
storm 31, 32
Strauss, D. 334
struggle 339
Sturn, R. 16–45
subjective approach 258
subjective synthesis 255
subsidies 324
success 78, 80
suffering 164, 230; reducing 176, 311, 316
summum bonum 297
Sumner, J.B. 163
super-society 200
superiority 267
superman 316n21
supernature 200, 340
superstition, replacing 187
supply and demand 222, 233
Supreme Being 129–30, 172, 173
surplus 265
survival 57, 339, 341
suspicion 123n4
symbolism 198
sympathy 120n2, 254, 274, 275, 276
synthesis 128
system 129, 173, 195, 197, 313

tastes 230
taxation 192, 193, 230–1, 297, 300, 324
tears 292
technological improvement 342, 349–51
teleology 126, 143
text 288
theft 88
theodicy 9, 154, 289
theology 126, 146; commercial 346; scientific 315

theory, general 61
thinkers 17
thinking activity 302
Thirty-Nine Articles 285, 286, 287, 288, 335
time 54, 55n11; preferences 90n7, 112n44
titles, extrinsic 50n9, 87, 89, 93, 98, 112
top-down position 140–1
trade 93, 95; free 122, 142, 148, 260; harming 109–10; international 143; restricting 138; rules 96
tradition 335, 350; blind 200
Traité théorique et pratique d'économie politique (Leroy-Beaulieu) 274
transaction: costs 40; non-cash 53
transactional society 227
transcendence 277n29
traverse 47
trials 171, 172
Tribe, K. 9, 283–306
Trotsky, L. 336
trusts 67
truth 26, 128, 191, 313; contemplating 338; proving 216; speculative 168

ugliness 325
Ultramontanes 207
unbelief 236
unbelievers 167
uncertainty 55, 57
understanding, mutual 277
unemployment 229, 231, 328
Unigenitus (1713) 85
union 337
Unitarians 166, 288
unitary societies 227
United Kingdom (UK) 340
unity 303, 313
L'Univers 213
L'Université catholique 209, 209n10, 212–13, 247–9
university 284n3; Catholic 209, 212; English 284, 284–5; German 284; secular 284; state 284
University of Oxford 285
unrest 352
usury 7, 8, 11n14, 50, 88n5; defining 106; liberal view 86, 87, 97–100, 112; masking 95
utilitarian heritage 304
utilitarianism 9, 119n1, 142; critique 295, 297; eclectic 308; hedonistic 327; ideal 327; limits of 198–9; rise of 286, 287, 290
utility 297, 299; interpersonal comparisons 320; maximisation 326
utopia 262

value: creating 72, 81; ethical 297, 325; exchangeable 223, 297; instrumental 327; intrinsic 139, 325, 327; measuring 299; money 297; moral 311; utility 223, 297
values 3; market 249; nurturing 279; plural 325
vanity 289
veneration 256, 267
Viaixnes, D.T. de 93–7
vice 176, 341
Victorian culture 312
view, dominant 10
virtue 170, 173, 223, 303; defining 223n33; and happiness 319; human 39
virtue-ethical perspective 39
visibility 52
vitiation 51
vocation 72, 73, 80
vocational training 284
volenti non fit injuria 25, 30

wage fund theory 296
wages 139, 269; clergy 269; family subsistence 37; high 233; increasing 231, 232, 249; insufficient 222; minimum living 269; pressure 229; as price 240; and profits 224; question 224, 227, 236, 248; reducing 228, 229, 249; secret 30–1; sufficient 233, *see also* income
waiting 342, 351
wants 295
war 225, 265
wasf 52
weakness, human 81
wealth: accumulating 265; causes 197, 248; circulating 193; collective 223; conceptualising 106, 222–3; development 248; distribution 222, 248, 299, 300; imperishable 226;

increasing 74; latent 227, 227n35; measurable 297; national 223, 226; and poverty 176, 205; producing 219, 222, 265, 271, 275; pursuit of 142, 225; relative 230; sharing 70, 71; social 223; societal 75; thirst for 77; transmission **265**, 266, 267, 271
Weber, M. 179–80
welfare: economics 10, 297; ideal 297; individual 300; material 218; personal 300; state 278
well-being 325; societal 222, 254
will: divine 33, 142, 153; free 311, 312, 328; mixed 31; modifying 268
wisdom, divine 128, 221
wolves 225
women 229, 266, 267, 269, 275; education of 275, 347
words, last 215
work 8, 59; as commodity 224; cooperative 195; major 199; and morality 201; and poverty 222; universal 198; value of 199, *see also* labour
workers 57; blaming 217; deskilling 229; desperate 230; education 347; health 275; security 229; wages 324; women 275
working class 236, 237, 240
working community 195
working conditions 229, 240, 275
workshop 195, 198, 199
world, explaining 188
worry 341

zero sum interaction 278

For Product Safety Concerns and Information please contact our EU representative GPSR@taylorandfrancis.com Taylor & Francis Verlag GmbH, Kaufingerstraße 24, 80331 München, Germany